Lecture Notes in Computer Science 11762

More information about this series at http://www.springer.com/series/7409

Pascal Hitzler · Sabrina Kirrane ·
Olaf Hartig · Victor de Boer ·
Maria-Esther Vidal · Maria Maleshkova ·
Stefan Schlobach · Karl Hammar ·
Nelia Lasierra · Steffen Stadtmüller ·
Katja Hose · Ruben Verborgh (Eds.)

The Semantic Web: ESWC 2019 Satellite Events

ESWC 2019 Satellite Events
Portorož, Slovenia, June 2–6, 2019
Revised Selected Papers

 Springer

Editors
Pascal Hitzler
Kansas State University
Manhattan, KS, USA

Olaf Hartig ⓘ
Linköping University
Linköping, Sweden

Maria-Esther Vidal ⓘ
Leibniz Information Centre
for Science and Technology
University Library (TIB)
Hannover, Germany

Stefan Schlobach ⓘ
Vrije Universiteit Amsterdam
Amsterdam, The Netherlands

Nelia Lasierra
F. Hoffmann-La Roche AG
Basel, Switzerland

Katja Hose ⓘ
Aalborg University
Aalborg, Denmark

Sabrina Kirrane ⓘ
Vienna University
of Economics and Business
Vienna, Austria

Victor de Boer ⓘ
Vrije Universiteit Amsterdam
Amsterdam, The Netherlands

Maria Maleshkova ⓘ
University of Bonn
Bonn, Germany

Karl Hammar ⓘ
Jönköping University
Jönköping, Sweden

Steffen Stadtmüller
Robert Bosch GmbH
Stuttgart, Germany

Ruben Verborgh ⓘ
IMEC
Ghent University
Ghent, Belgium

ISSN 0302-9743   ISSN 1611-3349   (electronic)
Lecture Notes in Computer Science
ISBN 978-3-030-32326-4   ISBN 978-3-030-32327-1   (eBook)
https://doi.org/10.1007/978-3-030-32327-1

LNCS Sublibrary: SL3 – Information Systems and Applications, incl. Internet/Web, and HCI

This Springer imprint is published by the registered company Springer Nature Switzerland AG
The registered company address is: Gewerbestrasse 11, 6330 Cham, Switzerland

Preface

The 16th edition of ESWC took place in Portoroz (Slovenia), during June 2–6, 2019. The program included three keynotes by Peter Haase (metaphacts, Germany), Diana Maynard (University of Sheffield, UK), and Daniele Quercia (King's College London and Nokia Bell Labs, UK). The main scientific program of the conference comprised 39 papers: 26 research papers, eight resource papers, and five in-use papers, selected out of 134 reviewed submissions, which corresponds to an acceptance rate of 28% for the research papers submitted, 31% for the resource papers, and 33% for the in-use papers. The proceedings were published by Springer as LNCS volume 11762.

This volume includes accepted contributions from the posters and demos track, the PhD Symposium, the industry track, and a selection of the best workshops papers. During the poster and demo session, researchers had the chance to present their latest results in the form of face-to-face presentations. In total, 20 demos and 18 posters were included in this session. In addition, five students took part in the PhD Symposium, and three contributions were presented as part of the industry track.

Three workshops and seven tutorials were held as satellite events of the conference. The three workshops were:

- Workshop on Deep Learning for Knowledge Graphs – DL4KG
- Workshop on Large-Scale RDF Analytics – LASCAR
- Knowledge Graph Building – KGB

The seven tutorials were:

- SANSA's Leap of Faith: Scalable RDF and Heterogeneous Data Lakes
- Semantic Data Enrichment for Data Scientists
- Build a Question-Answering System Overnight
- Practical and Scalable Pattern-Based Ontology Engineering with Reasonable Ontology Templates
- Querying Linked Data with Comunica
- Continuous Analytics on Linked Data Streams
- Generating and Querying (Virtual) Knowledge Graphs from Heterogeneous Data Sources

The workshop organizers were asked to nominate the best papers from their respective workshops. The authors of these papers were invited to submit improved or extended versions of the papers, taking into account reviewer feedback and discussions at the workshop. Two of the three best-of-workshop papers are included in this volume; the third has been published via CEUR-WS[1].

As general chair, poster and demo chairs, PhD symposium chairs, industry track chairs, and workshop chairs, we would like to thank everybody who was involved in

---

[1] http://ceur-ws.org/Vol-2377/paper_7.pdf

the organization of ESWC 2019. Special thanks go to the track and workshop Program Committees who contributed to making ESWC and its satellite events a real success. We would also like to thank the Organizing Committee and especially the local organizers and the program chairs for supporting the day-to-day operation and execution of the workshops.

August 2019

Pascal Hitzler
Sabrina Kirrane
Olaf Hartig
Victor de Boer
Maria-Esther Vidal
Maria Maleshkova
Stefan Schlobach
Karl Hammar
Nelia Lasierra
Steffen Stadtmüller
Katja Hose
Ruben Verborgh

Organization

General Chair

Pascal Hitzler   Kansas State University, USA

Research Track Program Chairs

Miriam Fernandez   The Open University, UK
Krzysztof Janowicz   University of California, Santa Barbara, USA

Resource Track Program Chairs

Amrapali Zaveri   Maastricht University, The Netherlands
Alasdair J. G. Gray   Heriot-Watt University, UK

In-Use Track Program Chairs

Vanessa Lopez   IBM Research, Ireland
Armin Haller   The Australian National University, Australia

Industry Track Program Chairs

Nelia Lasierra   F. Hoffmann-La Roche AG, Switzerland
Steffen Stadtmüller   Robert Bosch GmbH, Germany

Poster and Demo Chairs

Sabrina Kirrane   Vienna University of Economics and Business, Austria
Olaf Hartig   Linköping University, Sweden

PhD Symposium Chairs

Victor de Boer   Vrije Universiteit Amsterdam, The Netherlands
Maria-Esther Vidal   TIB Leibniz Information Centre For Science and
                                    Technology, Germany, and Universidad Simon
                                    Bolivar, Venezuela

Workshops and Tutorials Chairs

Maria Maleshkova   University of Bonn, Germany
Stefan Schlobach   Vrije Universiteit Amsterdam, The Netherlands

Challenge Chairs

Katja Hose   Aalborg University, Denmark
Ruben Verborgh   Ghent University – imec, Belgium

Sponsoring Chairs

Laura Hollink   Centrum Wiskunde & Informatica, The Netherlands
Anna Tordai   Elsevier, The Netherlands

EU Project Networking Chairs

Ioanna Lytra   University of Bonn, Germany
Laura Koesten   University of Southampton, UK

Publicity and Web Presence Chairs

Agnieszka Ławrynowicz   Poznań University of Technology, Poland
Jedrzej Potoniec   Poznań University of Technology, Poland

Semantic Technologies Coordinator

Blake Regalia   University of California, Santa Barbara, USA

Proceedings Chair

Karl Hammar   Jönköping University, Sweden

Local Organizers

Stefano Borgo   ISTC-CNR, Italy
Marija Komatar   PITEA d.o.o., Slovenia

Program Committees

Poster and Demo Papers Program Committee

Maribel Acosta   Karlsruhe Institute of Technology, Germany
Nitish Aggarwal   Roku Inc., USA
Asan Agibetov   Medical University of Vienna, Austria
Henning Agt-Rickauer   Hasso-Plattner-Institut, Germany
Céline Alec   Université de Caen-Normandie, France
Grigoris Antoniou   University of Huddersfield, UK
Luigi Asprino   University of Bologna and STLab (ISTC-CNR), Italy
Payam Barnaghi   University of Surrey, UK
Pierpaolo Basile   University of Bari, Italy
Davide Buscaldi   LIPN, Université Paris 13, Sorbonne Paris Cité, France

Miguel Ceriani	Sapienza University of Rome, Italy
Michelle Cheatham	Wright State University, USA
Diego Collarana	Fraunhofer IAIS, Germany
Ernesto William De Luca	Georg-Eckert-Institute – Leibniz-Institute for International Textbook Research, Germany
Mauro Dragoni	Fondazione Bruno Kessler - FBK-IRST, Italy
Anca Dumitrache	Vrije Universiteit Amsterdam, The Netherlands
Daniel Faria	Instituto Gulbenkian de Ciência, Portugal
Catherine Faron Zucker	Université Nice Sophia Antipolis, France
Agata Filipowska	Poznan University of Economics, Poland
George H. L. Fletcher	Eindhoven University of Technology, The Netherlands
Flavius Frasincar	Erasmus University Rotterdam, The Netherlands
Daniel Garijo	Information Sciences Institute, University of Southern California, USA
Anna Lisa Gentile	IBM Research, USA
Rafael S Gonçalves	Stanford University, USA
Giovanna Guerrini	University of Genoa, Italy
Peter Haase	Metaphacts GmbH, Germany
Karl Hammar	Jönköping University, Sweden
Olaf Hartig	Linköping University, Sweden
Jörn Hees	TU Kaiserslautern and DFKI, Germany
Benjamin Heitmann	RWTH Aachen University, Database and Information Systems Group (i5), Germany
Sven Hertling	University of Mannheim, Germany
Daniel Hienert	GESIS - Leibniz Institute for the Social Sciences, Germany
Pascal Hitzler	Kansas State University, USA
Tomas Horvath	Eötvös Loránd University, Hungary
Takahiro Kawamura	Japan Science and Technology Agency, Japan
Sabrina Kirrane	Vienna University of Economics and Business, Austria
Laura Koesten	University of Southampton, USA
Kouji Kozaki	Osaka Electro-Communication University, Japan
Ismini Lourentzou	University of Illinois at Urbana - Champaign, USA
Aditya Mogadala	Saarland University, Germany
Stefano Montanelli	University of Milan, Italy
Varish Mulwad	GE Global Research, USA
Vit Novacek	Insight, National University of Ireland Galway, Ireland
Fabrizio Orlandi	Trinity College Dublin, Ireland
Francesco Osborne	The Open University, UK
Heiko Paulheim	University of Mannheim, Germany
Rafael Peñaloza	University of Milano-Bicocca, Italy
Antonella Poggi	Sapienza University of Rome, Italy
Jedrzej Potoniec	Poznan University of Technology, Poland
María Poveda-Villalón	Universidad Politécnica de Madrid, Spain
Freddy Priyatna	Universidad Politécnica de Madrid, Spain
Gustavo Publio	AKSW/KILT, Universität Leipzig, Germany

Martin Rezk	Google, USA
Martin Riedl	University of Stuttgart, Germany
Giuseppe Rizzo	LINKS Foundation, Italy
Mariano Rodríguez Muro	Google, USA
Alessandro Russo	STLab, ISTC-CNR, Italy
Idafen Santana-Pérez	Universidad Politécnica de Madrid, Spain
Ralf Schenkel	Trier University, Germany
Michael Schmidt	Amazon, USA
Barış Sertkaya	Frankfurt University of Applied Sciences, Germany
Pavel Shvaiko	Informatica Trentina, Italy
Kuldeep Singh	Nuance Automotive, Germany
Hala Skaf-Molli	University of Nantes - LS2N, France
Jennifer Sleeman	University of Maryland Baltimore County, USA
Timo Stegemann	University of Duisburg-Essen, Germany
Simon Steyskal	Siemens AG, Austria
Ilaria Tiddi	Vrije Universiteit Amsterdam, The Netherlands
Tabea Tietz	FIZ Karlsruhe, Germany
Raphaël Troncy	EURECOM, France
Ricardo Usbeck	Paderborn University, Germany
Marieke van Erp	KNAW Humanities Cluster, The Netherlands
Maria Esther Vidal	Universidad Simon Bolivar, Venezuela
Serena Villata	CNRS - Laboratoire d'Informatique, Signaux et Systèmes de Sophia-Antipolis, France
Kewen Wang	Griffith University, Australia
Krzysztof Wecel	Poznan University of Economics, Poland
Ondřej Zamazal	University of Economics, Prague, Czech Republic

Poster and Demo Papers Additional Reviewers

Francesco De Fino
Gaetano Rossiello

PhD Symposium Program Committee

Philippe Cudre-Mauroux	University of Fribourg, Switzerland
Claudia d'Amato	University of Bari, Italy
Victor de Boer	Vrije Universiteit Amsterdam, The Netherlands
John Domingue	The Open University, UK
Paul Groth	University of Amsterdam, The Netherlands
Karl Hammar	Jönköping University, Sweden
Sabrina Kirrane	Vienna University of Economics and Business - WU Wien, Austria
Manolis Koubarakis	National and Kapodistrian University of Athens, Greece
Maria Maleshkova	University of Bonn, Germany

Andrea Giovanni Nuzzolese	University of Bologna, Italy
Heiko Paulheim	University of Mannheim, Germany
Hala Skaf-Molli	University of Nantes - LS2N, France
Steffen Staab	Institut WeST, University Koblenz-Landau, Germany, and WAIS, University of Southampton, UK
Rudi Studer	Karlsruhe Institute of Technology, Germany
Frank Van Harmelen	Vrije Universiteit Amsterdam, The Netherlands
Maria-Esther Vidal	Universidad Simon Bolivar, Venezuela
Amrapali Zaveri	Maastricht University, The Netherlands

Industry Track Program Committee

José María García	University of Seville, Spain
Georgios Georgiadis	Qamcom Research and Technology AB, Sweden
Peter Haase	Metaphacts GmbH, Germany
Karl Hammar	Jönköping University, Sweden
Daniel Herzig	Metaphacts GmbH, Germany
Martin Junghans	SAP Labs LLC, USA
Adam Kozak	F. Hoffmann-La Roche AG, Switzerland
Elias Kärle	STI-Innsbruck, Austria
Nelia Lasierra	F. Hoffmann-La Roche AG, Switzerland
Nolan Nichols	Genentech, Inc., USA
Dominik Riemer	FZI Research Center for Information Technologies, Germany
Steffen Stadtmueller	Robert Bosch GmbH, Germany
Andreas Thalhammer	F. Hoffmann-La Roche AG, Switzerland
Anees Ul Mehdi	Robert Bosch GmbH, Germany
Andreas Wagner	Schaeffler AG, Switzerland

Contents

PhD Symposium

Industry Track

Best-of-Workshop Papers

Poster and Demo Papers

Semantic Export Module for Close Range Photogrammetry

Mohamed Ben Ellefi$^{(\boxtimes)}$ ⓘ and Pierre Drap$^{(\boxtimes)}$ ⓘ

Aix Marseille University, CNRS, Université De Toulon, LIS UMR 7020,
13397 Marseille, France
{mohamed.ben-ellefi,pierre.drap}@univ-amu.fr

Abstract. With the progress of 2D/3D visualization systems, models
and software that effectively integrate graphical content with domain-
specific knowledge become the adopted solution to allow the interroga-
tion, understanding, interpretation and manipulation of visualized information. This paper introduces a software module that extends our data-
lifting toolbox to automatic export of photogrammetry information from
the Agisoft software (photogrammetric processing of digital images and
3D spatial data generation) into a semantic knowledge base representation.

Keywords: Semantic Web · Ontology · 3D · Photogrammetry

1 Introduction

With the progress of 3D technologies, photogrammetry techniques become the
adopted solution for representing science-driven data by turning photos from
small finds, to entire landscapes, into accurate 3D models.

This paper proposes a module that explicitly couples the photogrammetry process to a semantic knowledge base modeled by our photogrammetry-
oriented ontology, Arpenteur[1]. This coupling is represented in form of an export
module for Agisoft[2] to transform the spatial 3D data into a knowledge base
modeled by the Arpenteur ontology. This exportation is particularly useful in
the pipeline process within our photogrammetry-driven toolbox Arpenteur[3] for
semantic data-lifting: from image gathering to 3D/VR modeling coupled with
the knowledge representation by Arpenteur ontology.

This module is based on Semantic Web technologies where ontologies provide
us with the theoretic and axiomatic basis of the underlying knowledge bases.
In this context, different approaches have been proposed to permit semantic
representation and modeling of synthetic 3D content, a state of the art review
is detailed in [7].

---

[1] http://arpenteur.org/ontology/Arpenteur.owl.
[2] https://www.agisoft.com/.
[3] http://www.arpenteur.org/.

© Springer Nature Switzerland AG 2019
P. Hitzler et al. (Eds.): ESWC 2019 Satellite Events, LNCS 11762, pp. 3–7, 2019.
https://doi.org/10.1007/978-3-030-32327-1_1

The paper is organized as follows: Sect. 2 presents our solution for mapping Agisoft python API to the Arpenteur ontology concepts detailing the adopted photogrammetry configuration. Section 3 depicts a use case scenario of exporting and exploiting the *Xlendi* shipwreck. Finally, Sect. 4 concludes and presents future work plans.

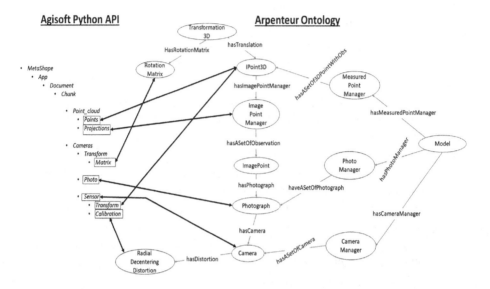

Fig. 1. Mapping Agisoft Metashape python API to the Arpenteur ontology

2   Agisoft to Arpenteur Concepts Mappings

The mapping between the two softwares is limited to the generic concept of photogrammetric model as defined in Kraus [8]: photographs, camera, internal and external orientation, 3D points and their observations done onto the photographs. For example feature description and dense cloud are not supported by this mapping.

These two photogrammetry software manipulate similar concepts but of course the translation of digital data from one to the other will have to support some adjustments. For example, the concept of *Photograph* in the Arpenteur is similar to *Camera* in Agisoft.

In Arpenteur, a *Photograph* is the image produced by a camera (film-based or digital) and the *Camera* is the object that produces the *Photograph*. This *Camera* in Agisoft is translated by the concept of *Sensor*. It should be noted that the concept of *Sensor* in Agisoft is more complex and will not be fully used, for example it supports the notion of *Plane* which refers to multi-sensor camera rig approach. This feature is not used in Arpenteur. The Arpenteur *Camera*

Radial Decentring Distortion is so mapped with the Agisoft *Sensor Calibration* which manages standard internal orientation and lens distortion. 3D points and their 2D projection on images are present of course in both softwares even if they are not modeled in the same way. Hence, an ontology mapping will allow the exchange of information between these two softwares. Figure 1 recapitulates the mapping pattern used for linking Agisoft python API to the Arpenteur photogrammetry concepts.

Radial Distortion Configuration

Since both approaches are based on a standard description of close photogrammetry, it is relatively easy to establish a direct mapping of concepts between Arpenteur and Agisoft. The only remarkably different point is how to describe radial distortion.

Distortion is a physical phenomenon that sometime may greatly impact an image's geometry without impairing quality nor reducing the information present in the image. Applying the projective pinhole camera model is often not possible without taking into account the distortion caused by the camera lens. So, most photogrammetry software models distortion using the well known polynomial approach proposed by Brown in the 1970s [4]. However, although we have the equations to compensate the distortion, how to compute the inverse function in order to apply such a distortion is not obvious. And this is a crucial technical point, currently most photogrammetric software use the same equations to manage distortion, but some use the mathematical model to apply distortion and other to compensate it and this is exactly the case of the Arpenteur vs Agisoft configuration. To solve this problem of inverse radial distortion, which is not obvious in the context of polynomial approach, some software use an iterative solution [1]. In our case this is not possible: we need to express the polynomial coefficient for Agisoft using the known coefficient used in Arpenteur.

A solution is proposed in [5] and is implemented in this paper. Here are the formula for the four first coefficients b_n for Agisoft computed from the four coefficients $-k_n$ used in Arpenteur:

$$b_1 = -k_1; \qquad b_2 = 3k_1^2 - k_2; \qquad b_3 = -12k_1^3 + 8k_1k_2 - k_3;$$
$$b_4 = 55k_1^4 - 55k_1^2k_2 + 5k_2^2 + 10k_1k_3 - k_4;$$

3   Xlendi Shipwreck Use Case

We consider the Phoenician shipwreck of *Xlendi* (Malta) as a use case scenario, where data was gathered by modern photogrammetry techniques presented in a previous work [6] in the framework of the GROPLAN project[4]. Successive dives

---

[4] http://www.groplan.eu.

on the *Xlendi* wreck have resulted in several temporal datasets corresponding to seven surveys dates.

An *Xlendi* artifacts dataset describing the typological and the morphological description of artifacts was published as Linked Open Data presented in previous work [3]. While *Xlendi* artifacts dataset was introduced manually by archaeologists, the photogrammetric description (camera settings, interior and exterior orientation parameters, extracted and matched 2D/3D points) was automatically exported from the Agisoft software to an ontology file containing the TBox + ABox description. This paper introduces the used exportation module, which is in form of a python script that can be called directly from the Agisoft Metashape sophtware. The script is made available as open source on GitHub[5].

In the context of *Xlendi* shipwreck LOD data publishing, we stored the different datasets in an Apache Jena Apache TDB[6] which is embedded in a Fuseki[7] server. Seven SPARQL GUI user interfaces are made accessible online via our 2D/3D Web tools, allowing to query *Xlendi* datasets that correspond to the seven survey dates. Listing 1.1 depicts an example of a SPARQL query retrieving the position and the orientation settings of an Xlendi photograph, i.e. the "John_Stills_CC-309"[8] photograph from the 2018-09-21 dataset[9].

Listing 1.1. An example of a SPARQL query to retrieve the position (x,y,z) and the orientation matrix of "John_Stills_CC-309" photograph to be performed on Xlendi 2018-09-21 dataset.

```
PREFIX
arp:<http://www.arpenteur.org/ontology/Arpenteur.owl#>

SELECT distinct ?x ?y ?z ?m00 ?m01 ?m02 ?m10 ?m11 ?m12
WHERE {
?photo a arp:Photograph ;
        arp:hasName ?photoName;
        arp:hasTransformation3D ?transformation.
Filter contains (str(?photoName), 'John_Stills_CC−309').

?transformation arp:hasTranslation ?translation;
                arp:hasRotationMatrix ?matrix.

?translation arp:hasX ?x; arp:hasY ?y; arp:hasZ ?z.
?matrix arp:has_m00 ?m00; arp:has_m01 ?m01;
        arp:has_m02 ?m02; arp:has_m10 ?m10;
        arp:has_m11 ?m11; arp:has_m12 ?m12;}
```

---

[5] https://github.com/benellefi/ExportAgisoftOWL.

[6] https://jena.apache.org/documentation/tdb/index.html.

[7] https://jena.apache.org/documentation/fuseki2/.

[8] http://www.lsis.org/groplan/survey/20180921/20180921_John_Stills_CC-309.jpg.

[9] http://www.arpenteur.org/ontology/temporal/20180921.html.

The lifted *Xlendi* datasets are published in a 2D/3D Web representation coupled with the knowledge base datasets in user-friendly web tools available online[10] for querying and semantic consumption of the data, as detailed in [2].

4   Conclusions

In this paper, we introduced a module (python script) for automatic export of the photogrammetry description into a knowledge base dataset modeled by the Arpenteur ontology. This module extends the Agisoft software used in our photogrammetry process. The automatic export is handled by mapping the Arpenteur ontology to the tool's API. A real data wreck scenario *Xlendi* was presented in which the photogrammetry process was automatically exported by this new module.

In parallel with the photogrammetry description, we are currently working on the implementation of an ontology-based virtual reality representation to provide a panoramic view (2D/3D/VR) of the data coupled to the semantics knowledge.

References

1. Alvarez, L., Gómez, L., Sendra, J.R.: An algebraic approach to lens distortion by line rectification. J. Math. Imaging Vis. **35**(1), 36–50 (2009)
2. Ben Ellefi, M., et al.: Ontology-based web tools for retrieving photogrammetric cultural heritage models. In: Underwater 3D Recording & Modeling. ISPRS, Limassol, Cyprus (2019)
3. Ben Ellefi, M., Nawaf, M., Sourisseau, J.C., Gambin, T., Castro, F., Drap, P.: Clustering over the cultural heritage linked open dataset: Xlendi Shipwreck. In: Proceedings of the Third International Workshop on Semantic Web for Cultural Heritage co-located with the 15th Extended Semantic Web Conference, SW4CH@ESWC 2018. LNCS, Heraklion, Crete, Greece, vol. 8, pp. 1–10 (2018)
4. Duane, C.B.: Close-range camera calibration. Photogram. Eng. **37**(8), 855–866 (1971)
5. Drap, P., Lefevre, J.: An exact formula for calculating inverse radial lens distortions. Sensors **16**(6), 807 (2016)
6. Drap, P., et al.: Underwater photogrammetry and object modeling: a case study of Xlendi Wreck in Malta. Sensors **15**(12), 30351–30384 (2015)
7. Flotyński, J., Walczak, K.: Ontology-based representation and modelling of synthetic 3D content: a state-of-the-art review. In: Computer Graphics Forum, vol. 36, pp. 329–353 (2017)
8. Kraus, K., Jansa, J., Kager, H.: Photogrammetry, vol. 1&2. Ferd. Dummler's, Verlag Bonn (1997)

---

[10] https://www.lsis.org/groplan/svg/xlendi/xlendi.html.

Mining Scholarly Publications
for Scientific Knowledge Graph
Construction

Davide Buscaldi[1], Danilo Dessì[2(✉)], Enrico Motta[3], Francesco Osborne[3],
and Diego Reforgiato Recupero[2]

[1] Paris, France
davide.buscaldi@lipn.univ-paris13.fr
[2] Cagliari, Italy
{danilo_dessi,diego.reforgiato}@unica.it
[3] Milton Keynes, UK
{enrico.motta,francesco.osborne}@open.ac.uk

Abstract. In this paper, we present a preliminary approach that uses
a set of NLP and Deep Learning methods for extracting entities and
relationships from research publications and then integrates them in a
Knowledge Graph. More specifically, we (i) tackle the challenge of knowledge extraction by employing several state-of-the-art Natural Language
Processing and Text Mining tools, (ii) describe an approach for integrating entities and relationships generated by these tools, and (iii) analyse
an automatically generated Knowledge Graph including $10,425$ entities
and $25,655$ relationships in the field of Semantic Web.

1 Introduction

Knowledge graphs (KG) are large networks of entities and relationships, usually
expressed as RDF triples, relevant to a specific domain or an organization [4].
Many of state-of-the-art projects such as DBPedia, Google Knowledge Graph,
BabelNet, and YAGO build KGs by harvesting entities and relations from textual
resources, such as Wikipedia pages.

Scientific Knowledge Graphs (SKGs) focus on the scholarly domain and typically contains metadata describing research publications such as authors, venues,
organizations, research topics, and citations. Good examples are Open Academic
Graph[1], Scholarlydata.org [7], and OpenCitations [8]. Their main limitation is
that they typically represent the content of the papers as unstructured text (title,
abstract, sometimes the full text). Therefore, a significant challenge in this field
regards the generation of SKGs that contain also a explicit representation of the
knowledge presented in the publications [2], and potentially describes entities
such as approaches, application, formats, and so on. Most of the relevant information for populating such a KG could be derived from the text of research publications. However, integrating this information in a coherent knowledge graph
is still an open challenge.

---

[1] https://www.openacademic.ai/oag/.

© Springer Nature Switzerland AG 2019
P. Hitzler et al. (Eds.): ESWC 2019 Satellite Events, LNCS 11762, pp. 8–12, 2019.
https://doi.org/10.1007/978-3-030-32327-1_2

In this paper, we present a preliminary approach that uses a set of NLP techniques for extracting entities and relationships from research publications and then integrate them in a KG. More specifically, we (i) tackle the challenge of knowledge extraction by employing several state-of-the-art Natural Language Processing and Text Mining tools, (ii) describe an approach for integrating entities and relationships generated by these tools, and (iii) analyse an automatically generated Knowledge Graph including $10,425$ entities and $25,655$ relationships in the field of Semantic Web.

2   The Proposed Approach

We collect a dataset composed by $12,007$ abstracts of scientific publications about the Semantic Web domain. It was retrieved by selecting all publications from Microsoft Academic Graph dataset which contains the string "Semantic Web" in the "field of science" heading. For extracting entities and relations, we exploited the following resources:

- An extractor framework designed by [5] which provides Deep Learning based tools for detecting entities and relations from scientific literature. It detects six types of entities (*Task, Method, Metric, Material, Other-Scientific-Term, and Generic*) and seven types of relations (*Compare, Part-of, Conjunction, Evaluate-for, Feature-of, Used-for, Hyponym-Of*).
- OpenIE [1], provided with Stanford Core NLP[2]. It detects general entities and relations among them, using verbs as predicates.
- The CSO Classifier [9], a tool for automatically tagging research papers with a set of research topics draw from the Computer Science Ontology (CSO)[3] [10]. CSO is a comprehensive ontology of research areas in the field of Computer Science, which was automatically generated from a dataset of 16 million research publications.

In order to generate the graph, we need to integrate all triples extracted from the abstracts. First we had to clean entities by removing punctuation, stopwords, merging singular and plural forms, splitting entities containing compound expressions, and handling acronyms.

For the entity merging task we exploit two data structures. The first one, labelled $W2LE$, maps each word to a list of entities that share the last token (e.g. *medical ontology, biomedical ontology, pervasive agent ontology*, and so on.). With $W2LE$ we avoided comparing those entities that syntactically could not refer to the same entity (e.g. the entities *ontology generation* and *ontology adoption* were not compared). The second one, labelled $E2E$, maps each original entity to the entity that will represent it in the KG.

Given an entity e and the list of its tokens $\{t_0, ..., t_n\}$, we chose t_n. If t_n was not present in $W2LE$, a new entry key t_n was added to $W2LE$ and its value

---

[2] https://stanfordnlp.github.io/CoreNLP/.
[3] http://cso.kmi.open.ac.uk.

is a list with e as its unique element. If t_n was in $W2LE$, then we compute the Levenshtein string similarity[4] between the entity e and all other entities $e'_0, ..., e'_m \in W2LE[t_n]$. If the resulting score met a given threshold t_L (set to 0.9 in the prototype), the entity e was mapped as e'_i in $E2E$. Otherwise e was mapped to itself in $E2E$. At the end, the entity e was added to $W2LE[t_n]$. Finally, the map $E2E$ was used to select the entities for the graph. For each entry key e_x, if its corresponding entity $e_y = E2E[e_x]$ was not in the graph, a new entity with label e_y was added.

In order to merge similar relations and reduce their number, we clustered all verbs labels. To do so we exploited WordNet [6] and a set of Word2Vec word embeddings trained on 9 million research papers from Microsoft Academic Graph[5]. In details, given the set of all verbs $V = \{v_0, ..., v_n\}$, we built a distance matrix M considering as a distance between two verbs v_i and v_j the $1-$ Wu-Palmer[6] similarity between their synsets. Then, we apply a hierarchical clustering algorithm, cutting the dendrogram where the number of clusters had the highest value of overall silhouette-width [3]. Subsequently, clusters were refined as follows. Given a cluster c, we assigned each verb $v_{i_c} \in c$ with the word embedding w_i in the Word2Vec model, and computed the centroid ce of the cluster as the average of word embeddings of its elements. Then, we ordered verbs in ascending order by the distance from ce. All verbs with a distance over a threshold t were discarded. All the other verbs were mapped on the verb nearest to ce.

3   The Knowledge Graph

In this section, we report our preliminary results about the KG produced from $12,007$ papers about the Semantic Web (using $t_L = 0.9$).

The resulting KG contains $10,425$ entities and $25,655$ relationships. It includes both verb-based relations (from OpenEI) and default relations (from the Extractor Framework). Verbs are usually more informative, but also harder

Table 1. Contribution of Extractor Framework and CSO to the KG entities.

Tools entities contribution	Count	Percentage
CSO	1,034	9.92%
Extractor Framework	8,668	83.15%
Exclusive CSO	117	1.12%
Exclusive Extractor Framework	7,751	74.35%
Entities where both tools contribute	917	8.8%
Derived Entities	1,640	15.73%

---

[4] https://pypi.org/project/python-Levenshtein/.
[5] Avaliable at http://tiny.cc/w0u43y.
[6] http://www.nltk.org/howto/wordnet.html.

to extract. The Extractor Framework is more flexible and it is able to extract a large number of relationships, but these are usually less specific. For example, the relationship (*ontology, Used-for, domain knowledge*) does not specify which action is performed by the entity *ontology*, while the relationship (*ontology, capture, domain knowledge*) does. Using both systems allows us obtaining a good balance between coverage and specificity.

Table 1 reports statistics about entities. To weight the actual contribution of each tool, we counted the number of entities that were extracted by each tool. With the label *Exclusive* we indicate the percentage of entities identified only by a specific tool. The row *Derived Entities* refers to the additional entities that were obtained by merging or splitting the original entities extracted by the tools.

Most entities come from the Extractor Framework tool, which contributes to the 83.15% of all entities, and exclusively contributes to 74.35% of them. The CSO Classifier contributes to 9.92% of them, but only a minority are exclusive. This was expected, since CSO contains fairly established research topics. Conversely, the Extractor Framework is able to identify many entities that appear in very few research papers. On average, each entity was extracted 3.69 times by one of the tools (Table 2).

Table 2. Contribution of Extractor Framework and OpenIE to the KG relations.

Tools relations contribution	Count	Percentage
Extractor Framework	23,624	92.09%
OpenIE	3,116	12.15%
Exclusive Extractor Framework	22,539	87.85%
Exclusive OpenIE	2,031	7.92%
Contribution of both tools	1,085	4.23%

Similarly to entities, the Extractor Framework produced also the majority of the relationships with a coverage of 92.09%. However, the 12.15% of relationships extracted by OpenIE are usually more informative since they are mapped to specific verbs. On average, each relationship was extracted 1.32 times.

References

1. Angeli, G., Premkumar, M.J.J., Manning, C.D.: Leveraging linguistic structure for open domain information extraction. In: Proceedings of the 53rd Annual Meeting of the ACL and the 7th IJCNLP, vol. 1, pp. 344–354 (2015)
2. Auer, S., Kovtun, V., Prinz, M., Kasprzik, A., Stocker, M., Vidal, M.E.: Towards a knowledge graph for science. In: Proceedings of the 8th International Conference on Web Intelligence, Mining and Semantics, p. 1. ACM (2018)

3. Dessì, D., Reforgiato Recupero, D., Fenu, G., Consoli, S.: A recommender system of medical reports leveraging cognitive computing and frame semantics. In: Tsihrintzis, G.A., Sotiropoulos, D.N., Jain, L.C. (eds.) Machine Learning Paradigms. ISRL, vol. 149, pp. 7–30. Springer, Cham (2019). https://doi.org/10.1007/978-3-319-94030-4_2

4. Ehrlinger, L., Wöß, W.: Towards a definition of knowledge graphs. In: SEMANTiCS (Posters, Demos, SuCCESS), vol. 48 (2016)

5. Luan, Y., He, L., Ostendorf, M., Hajishirzi, H.: Multi-task identification of entities, relations, and coreference for scientific knowledge graph construction. In: Proceedings of the EMNLP 2018 Conference, pp. 3219–3232 (2018)

6. Miller, G.A.: WordNet: a lexical database for English. Commun. ACM **38**(11), 39–41 (1995)

7. Nuzzolese, A.G., Gentile, A.L., Presutti, V., Gangemi, A.: Conference linked data: the ScholarlyData project. In: Groth, P., et al. (eds.) ISWC 2016. LNCS, vol. 9982, pp. 150–158. Springer, Cham (2016). https://doi.org/10.1007/978-3-319-46547-0_16

8. Peroni, S., Shotton, D., Vitali, F.: One year of the OpenCitations corpus. In: d'Amato, C., et al. (eds.) ISWC 2017. LNCS, vol. 10588, pp. 184–192. Springer, Cham (2017). https://doi.org/10.1007/978-3-319-68204-4_19

9. Salatino, A.A., Thanapalasingam, T., Mannocci, A., Osborne, F., Motta, E.: Classifying research papers with the computer science ontology. In: ISWC (P&D/Industry/BlueSky). CEUR Workshop Proceedings, vol. 2180 (2018)

10. Salatino, A.A., Thanapalasingam, T., Mannocci, A., Osborne, F., Motta, E.: The computer science ontology: a large-scale taxonomy of research areas. In: Vrandečić, D., et al. (eds.) ISWC 2018. LNCS, vol. 11137, pp. 187–205. Springer, Cham (2018). https://doi.org/10.1007/978-3-030-00668-6_12

Republishing OpenStreetMap's Roads as Linked Routable Tiles

Pieter Colpaert$^{(\boxtimes)}$ ⓘ, Ben Abelshausen ⓘ,
Julián Andrés Rojas Meléndez ⓘ, Harm Delva ⓘ,
and Ruben Verborgh ⓘ

IDLab, Department of Electronics and Information Systems,
Ghent University – imec, Ghent, Belgium
`pieter.colpaert@ugent.be`

Abstract. Route planning providers manually integrate different geo-spatial datasets before offering a Web service to developers, thus creating a closed world view. In contrast, combining open datasets at runtime can provide more information for user-specific route planning needs. For example, an extra dataset of bike sharing availabilities may provide more relevant information to the occasional cyclist. A strategy for automating the adoption of open geo-spatial datasets is needed to allow an ecosystem of route planners able to answer more specific and complex queries. This raises new challenges such as (i) how open geo-spatial datasets should be published on the Web to raise interoperability, and (ii) how route planners can discover and integrate relevant data for a certain query on the fly. We republished OpenStreetMap's road network as "Routable Tiles" to facilitate its integration into open route planners. To achieve this, we use a Linked Data strategy and follow an approach similar to vector tiles. In a demo, we show how client-side code can automatically discover tiles and perform a shortest path algorithm. We provide four contributions: (i) we launched an open geo-spatial dataset that is available for everyone to reuse at no cost, (ii) we published a Linked Data version of the OpenStreetMap ontology, (iii) we introduced a hypermedia specification for vector tiles that extends the Hydra ontology, and (iv) we released the mapping scripts, demo and routing scripts as open source software.

Keywords: Smart cities · Open data · Linked open data · Route planning · Journey planning · Mobility as a service

1 Introduction

When setting up a Web-based journey planner that takes into account individual user needs, developers are confronted with the daunting prospect of integrating heterogeneous datasets. Industry players provide an alternative solution to these complexities, by providing services on top of their datasets that are centralized in one location. They

---

Online version of the paper can be found at http://pieter.pm/demo-paper-routable-tiles/.

© Springer Nature Switzerland AG 2019
P. Hitzler et al. (Eds.): ESWC 2019 Satellite Events, LNCS 11762, pp. 13–17, 2019.
https://doi.org/10.1007/978-3-030-32327-1_3

are able to provide a solution for the $\sim 80\%$ of the world-wide needs and build a business around that. When trying to cater to the remaining 20%, industrial route planners are quickly confronted with diminishing returns of integrating more datasets. Take for example use cases of (i) people owning a foldable bike and the ability to take their bike on public transport, (ii) companies trying to find an optimal delivery route for their delivery service where some vehicles cannot pass through low emission zones, (iii) routes based on the real-time state of traffic control systems and probability to hit a green light, or (iv) people with special constraints or disabilities. For each of these four use cases, extra datasets are needed to calculate these end-user specific routing graphs. Such datasets are published by different organizations that often publish them openly, thanks to strategic goals or legal mandates. Every route planner will somehow need to compile their own sources over which they can execute their own route planning algorithm.

In this paper, we aim to automate data adoption in route planners. As a first step, we introduce Routable Tiles. This is a hypermedia specification for geospatial road networks. In this specification, we republished all the roads in OpenStreetMap. In the next section we will see that the ideas behind Routable Tiles itself is not novel. The contribution of this paper lies in applying the geospatial indexing idea from the database world to Web APIs, introducing an ontology for describing geospatial hypermedia controls, and launching this world-wide dataset as a resource to the Semantic Web community.

2 Related Work

2.1 Geospatial Data on the Web

Spatial Data on the Web [1] is a W3C and OGC collaboration to create a list of best practices for spatial data on the Web. It takes a strong position in favor of HTTP URIs to identify resources. The rationale is that Linked Data principles such as the use of HTTP URIs as global identifiers, raises the interoperability of geo-spatial datasets by providing a common set of semantics that can be reused by data publishers.

Slippy maps are maps often included in web-pages on which you can pan around. In order to reduce server load, the client is preconfigured with a URL template of the web-server containing image tiles. When the map is loaded, the client can calculate all URLs necessary. Vector tiles reuse this idea to, instead of raster images, publish the raw data behind the tiles. The client can then render the maps on the client-side. This gives clear benefits over raster images: (i) the styling of the maps can be done by UI developers that can use CSS and scripts to style the road elements, (ii) vector tiles can be smaller in size as vectors are typically much smaller than a rendered bitmap, and (iii) it allows for all elements on the map to become interactive. Existing implementations include the Mapbox vector tiles and Open Map Tiles. Each have their own specificities and schemas (see https://docs.mapbox.com/vector-tiles/mapbox-streets-v8/ and https://openmaptiles.org/schema/) with a strong focus on rendering maps.

Valhalla by Mapzen and now hosted by the Linux Foundation is the first project that implements the idea of vector tiles for route planners in an open-source project.

The technology proposes a tiling specification for storing routing information on disk. Tiling the data makes sure the server can be selective about the data that needs to be loaded into memory in order to execute an individual request. This tiling specification in Valhalla is however not used as an exchange format – although offline routing is an upcoming feature – and interoperability with other datasets is not a focus.

Linked Geo Data [2] is an initiative that maps OpenStreetMap data to Linked Data. It releases data dumps, subject pages and a SPARQL endpoint. Furthermore, it has their own mappings from the OpenStreetMap data model to a Linked Geo Data ontology.

2.2   Open Data Publishing

Open Data can be published in various interfaces. In order to be able to query these interfaces, Comunica [3] was built. It is a Linked Data user agent that can run federated queries over several heterogeneous Web APIs, such as data dumps, SPARQL endpoints, Linked Data documents and Triple Pattern Fragments [4]. This engine has been developed to make it easy to plug in specific types of functionality as separate modules. Such modules can be added or removed depending on the configuration. As such, by looking for affordances in Web APIs, more intelligent user agents can be created. Preconditions for an engine like Comunica to work with a dataset is: supporting a Linked Data representation and allowing cross origin resource sharing headers in the HTTP responses. The better the data is split in fragments, the better the caching will be able to provide a faster user-perceived performance.

For public transport systems, instead of publishing a dump of time schedules or a full fletched route planner, Linked Connections [5] proposes a publishing mechanism that gives clients access to the data in time fragments. It uses departure-arrival pairs from a station to another (a connection), and orders these connections by departure time. It then fragments this dataset in documents that can be published over HTTP. Links in the responses ensure a client can always find more information to take into account.

3   Implementation

Routable Tiles is a JSON-LD specification for which the working draft can be found at https://openplanner.team/specs/2018-11-routable-tiles.html. It has three main aspects: (i) it introduces a hypermedia specification reusing Hydra Collections for describing a tile server, (ii) a way to describe OpenStreetMap's nodes, ways and relations; and (iii) it introduces a mapping of the OpenStreetMap basic terms to an RDFS vocabulary.

The Linked Geo Data vocabulary has been unavailable since 2018 and not updated since 2015. Therefore we introduced our own vocabulary, that nonetheless takes a different approach. Instead of mapping everything, we decided to map only the bare minimum needed specifically for the use case or route planing. Therefore, we keep the ontology as close as possible to the actual OSM data model. We added links to the appropriate Linked Geo Data classes (ontology has yet to be published, awaiting a third party implementation).

We define 3 main classes: osm:Way, osm:Relation and osm:Node. The osm: members property describes the members of the relation and the osm:role their function in the relation. osm:restriction is used to model turn restrictions. The property osm: nodes is used to link to an rdf:List of osm:Node items. In one page, multiple lists can be described. If a Way crosses a tile, the other tile also mentioned the border Node in one of its rdf:Lists. The property osm:members is used to link to an rdf:List of osm:Member items.

The mapping scripts and server interface can be found at https://github.com/ openplannerteam/routeable-tiles. Every tile in OpenStreetMap on zoom level 14 is on the fly made available as JSON-LD. Special attention was given to the HTTP server to include a server-side cache and to compress the HTTP response with gzip. Furthermore, it sets both an etag header and a cache-control max-age header for client-side cache control. Finally, it also allows webpages on other domains to request its data by setting the appropriate Cross Origin Resource Sharing headers.

For the URIs of Ways and Nodes, we decided to reuse the subject pages provided by the OpenStreetMap project itself. We hope that at some point, OpenStreetMap decides to support a Linked Data representation on these URIs. For example: open-streetmap.org/node/366934331 and openstreetmap.org/way/242536619.

4   Demonstrator

A server instance is set up publishing data for the entire world. Entry points into the hypermedia API can be found through tiles.openplanner.team/planet/14/{x}/{y}/(e.g., with x 8411 and y 5485). A live demonstrator using this data can be found at https:// openplannerteam.github.io/leaflet-routable-tiles/. The demonstrator shows a map of all roads (in Portorož by default) in the viewport. The map is drawn on the client-side based on the JSON-LD documents fragmented in tiles. When clicking 2 locations on the map, the same JSON-LD documents are used to perform a Dijkstra shortest path algorithm.

5   Conclusion and Future Work

This demo introduced a tiling mechanism for publishing road networks in Linked Data. Compared to a SPARQL endpoint approach or server answering any individual route planning request, the server costs in our approach are indisputably lower. Thanks to the hypermedia controls, the full dataset can be automatically discovered, and HTTP caching can be leveraged. Furthermore, developers of route planning application are given more flexibility as they are now in full control of the algorithm. Just like vector tiles styling, they can tailor the routing algorithm to their end-user needs in the browser. This also opens the door to use cases where multiple sources are queried at once.

Nevertheless, it still remains an open question if applying this kind of Linked Data model/HTTP URIs to the roads related data is the optimal approach. For example, when another source wants to do a statement about a part of a road, chances are low it is already available as a separate osm:Way instance, and thus the source data would have to be altered to split the original entity into two.

There might be a need in the future to support a binary format in order to reduce size. Therefore, we will benchmark the difference in size and performance between Valhalla tiles (protobuf) and Routable Tiles (JSON-LD + gzip). By doing this, we should also look at other optimizations, such as applying summaries over different zoom levels. In order to achieve better adoption of the hypermedia controls, an actor will be added to the Linked Data query agent called Comunica [3]. This way, we will help to solve geo-spatial queries over any data source by downloading only the right tiles even beyond road networks.

References

1. Tandy, J., Barnaghi, P., van den Brink, L.: Spatial Data on the Web Best Practices. W3C (2017). https://www.w3.org/TR/sdw-bp/
2. Stadler, C., Lehmann, J., Höffner, K., Auer, S.: LinkedGeoData: a core for a web of spatial open data. Semantic Web J. **3**, 333–354 (2012)
3. Taelman, R., Van Herwegen, J., Vander Sande, M., Verborgh, R.: Comunica: a modular SPARQL query engine for the web. In: Vrandečić, D., et al. (eds.) ISWC 2018. LNCS, vol. 11137, pp. 239–255. Springer, Cham (2018). https://doi.org/10.1007/978-3-030-00668-6_15
4. Verborgh, R., et al.: Triple pattern fragments: a low-cost knowledge graph interface for the web. J. Web Semantics **37–38**, 184–206 (2016)
5. Colpaert, P., Llaves, A., Verborgh, R., Corcho, O., Mannens, E., Van de Walle, R.: Intermodal public transit routing using Linked Connections. In: Proceedings of the 14th International Semantic Web Conference: Posters and Demos (2015)

MantisTable: A Tool for Creating Semantic Annotations on Tabular Data

Marco Cremaschi[1(✉)] , Anisa Rula[1,2] , Alessandra Siano[1],
and Flavio De Paoli[1]

[1] University of Milan - Bicocca, Viale Sarca 336, Milan, Italy
{marco.cremaschi,anisa.rula,flavio.depaoli}@unimib.it,
a.siano2@campus.unimib.it
[2] University of Bonn, Bonn, Germany
rula@cs.uni-bonn.de

Abstract. This paper describes MantisTable, an open source Semantic Table Interpretation tool, which automatically annotates tables using a Knowledge Graph. MantisTable provides a graphical interface allowing users to analyse the results of the semantic table interpretation process and validate the final annotations. The tool also provides a guided mode for viewing and editing annotations by users. Thanks to MantisTable features, it is possible to create semantic annotations and favour the publication and exchange of tabular data.

Keywords: Semantic Web · Ontology · Linked Data · Knowledge Graph · Semantic Table Interpretation · Semantic annotations

1 Introduction and Motivation

A vast amount of structured data represented in tables that contain relevant information are available on the Web. Despite the huge corpus of such tables on different topics, they set limitations on artificial intelligent tasks such as semantic search and query answering. Some approaches started to propose [2,5,6] extraction, annotation and transformation of tabular data into machine-readable formats. The problem of semantically annotating tables, also known as *Semantic Table Interpretation (STI)*, presents different challenges as demonstrated by the Semantic Web Challenge on Tabular Data to Knowledge Graph Matching[1] whose aim is benchmarking systems dealing with the semantic annotation tables.

STI takes a *well-formed and normalised* relational table (i.e. a table with headers and simple values, thus excluding nested and figure-like tables), and a Knowledge Graph (KG) which describes real-world entities in the domain of interest (i.e. a set of concepts, datatypes, predicates, entities, and the relations among them) in input, and returns, a semantically annotated table in output. This process comprises different steps to semantically annotate tables such as

---

[1] https://www.cs.ox.ac.uk/isg/challenges/sem-tab/.

© Springer Nature Switzerland AG 2019
P. Hitzler et al. (Eds.): ESWC 2019 Satellite Events, LNCS 11762, pp. 18–23, 2019.
https://doi.org/10.1007/978-3-030-32327-1_4

semantic classification of columns, which classify a column either in literal or named entity. These steps are usually performed manually or semi-automatically which require more users involvement who are often not familiar with semantic modelling. They need support to understand and explore the footprint of annotation steps.

Although previous efforts partially tackled the STI problem in the past [6], there is still no full support by single tools. DataGraft[2], a cloud-based service that provides an interface to transform tabular data into RDF triples, performs semantic annotations manually. TableMiner+ is a tool that supports only Web tables for which the user must provide a URL. Moreover, a few approaches that state to provide fully automatic tools, their code is not available or accessible, and in most cases it cannot be executed for imprecise information on the configuration settings. Only a few are open source and, to the best of our knowledge, none of them fully support users with the comprehensive STI steps through an interactive interface.

On one hand, it is worth noticing that the task of annotating semantics of tables is more complicated than the annotation of textual documents, due to the lack of a context, usually deductible in the case of text documents. On the other hand, the development of tools in this domain is characterised by a certain complexity because of several elements of the table simultaneously considered. In this paper, we propose *MantisTable*[3], a web interface and an open source Semantic Table Interpretation tool that automatically annotates, manages and makes accessible to humans and machines the semantic of tables. This tool is independent of any particular context. Additional built-in guidance functionalities help to avoid common pitfalls and create correct annotations. The current implementation of MantisTable is released as open source under the Apache 2.0 License. Although an STI contains several steps, as will be explained in the next section, the key feature of our tool is the involvement of all the STI steps that run fully automatically.

2 Overview of MantisTable

The *MantisTable* tool implements STI steps through five phases:

Data Preparation aims to clean and uniform data inside the table. Transformations applied to tables are as follows: remove HTML tags and stop words, turn text into lowercase, solve acronyms and abbreviations, and normalise measurements units. The latter is performed by applying regular expressions, as described in [3].

Column Analysis whose tasks are the *semantic classification* that assigns types to columns that are named entity (NE-column) or literal column (L-column), and the *detection of the subject column* (S-column). The first step of Column Analysis phase is to identify good L-column candidates. To accomplish this task, we consider 16 regular expressions that identify several Regextypes

---

[2] https://datagraft.io/.
[3] http://mantistable.disco.unimib.it.

(e.g., geo coordinate, address, hex color code, URL). If the number of occurrences of the most frequent Regextype in a column exceeds a given threshold, that column is annotated as L-column, otherwise, it is annotated as NE-column. The second step deals with the *subject column detection* that takes into account the identified NE-columns. We can define the S-column as the main column of the table based on different statistic features (e.g. the percentage of cells with unique content and distance from the first NE-column).

Concept and Datatype Annotation deals with mappings between columns headers and semantic elements (concepts or datatypes) in a KG. In the first step of Concept Annotation, we perform the entity-linking by searching the KG with the content of a cell, to get a set of candidate entities. We use the DICE similarity measure between the content of the cell and the candidate entities to disambiguate the content of the cell. In the second step of Concept Annotation, the abstract and all concepts for each winning entity are retrieved from DBpedia[4]. For each extracted concept, we count the occurrences in the abstract. For the Datatype Annotation, the results of the Column Analysis are taken into consideration. To associate a Datatype to each column, a Regextype is applied on the content of each column.

Predicate Annotation, whose task is to find relations, in the form of predicates, between the main column and the other columns to set the overall meaning of the table. MantisTable considers the winning concept of the S-column as the subject of the relationship, and the remaining columns as objects. Further, the entities identified as subjects and objects are further searched in the KG. In order to identify the correct predicate, we compare the content of the column and the candidate predicates.

Entity Linking deals with mappings between the content of cells and entities in the KG. The annotations obtained in the previous steps are used to create a query for the disambiguation of the cell contents. If more than one entity is returned for a cell, the one with a smaller edit distance (i.e., Wagner-Fischer distance) is taken.

3   Application Interface

MantisTable is a web application developed with NodeJs[5] and the Meteor framework[6]. The source code is released through a Git repository[7]. In order to scale and therefore improve efficiency, MantisTable has been installed in a Docker container to achieve parallelisation at the application level and facilitate the deployment on servers. The management of resources is performed by a load balancer (i.e., HAproxy[8]). The five phases of the STI have been modularly implemented allowing an easy replacement or extension by other developers.

---

[4] For the demo we use DBpedia as one of the largest KG which covers different topics. Other KGs can be used.

[5] https://nodejs.org/.

[6] https://www.meteor.com/.

[7] https://bitbucket.org/disco_unimib/mantistable-tool/.

[8] https://www.haproxy.org/.

MantisTable Loading and Storing. Tables are imported and stored in a MongoDB database. In MantisTable, a list of loaded tables is displayed on the main page. For each table, a series of metadata is provided, such as name, date of loading, date of last modification, which tasks have already been performed and which are being executed thus making the user aware of the status of the annotation process. Finally, users can download the annotated tables at the end of the annotation process. Through the interface it is possible to add and load new tables (in JSON format), delete all tables of the Gold Standard (T2Dv2[9] and Limaye200 [1]) and process all tables in batch. It is also possible to update or delete every single table.

MantisTable Execution. After selecting a table, it is possible to manage the execution of the five phases described in Sect. 2. The user can either run all steps together or run them step-by-step to supervise the execution (Fig. 1 - info mode).

Fig. 1. MantisTable interface overview: Visualization Mode (1. left side bar, 2. console), Info Mode (3. right side bar), Edit Mode (4. edit form)

MantisTable Exploration. It is possible to navigate all the executed steps by clicking on each phase and analyse the results in the visualization mode (Fig. 1 - 1. left side bar). For all phases, additional information about the execution is shown in the console located under the table (Fig. 1 - 2. console). By clicking on a header or body cell, information about the current phase is reported in the info mode (Fig. 1 - 3. right sidebar).

Figure 1 shows the table after the *Column Analysis*. Different colours are used to immediately distinguish the different columns types: S-column, NE-columns, and L-columns. The L-column headers show representative icons of the Regex-type that has been assigned to them. By clicking the header cells contextualised

---

[9] http://webdatacommons.org/webtables/goldstandardV2.html.

information is displayed, e.g. features for the identification of S-column are displayed for NE-columns, and the distribution of candidate regular expressions are shown for L-column.

After the *Concept and Datatype Annotation* phase, clicking on a header cell opens the right sidebar to display the selected concepts (for NE-columns) and datatypes (for L-column). Clicking on a body cell, two tabs are opened to display the candidate entities (with the similarity scores computed to select the winning one), and candidate concepts associated with the entities (with score). To enhance the awareness of the user, the abstract from DBpedia related to the winning concept is also reported. With the same approach, the user can browse the predicate annotations by first selecting that phase on the left, and then view the annotation relating to the relationship between the S-column and the columns on the right sidebar.

MantisTable Editing. Even if MantisTable implements a fully automated annotation process, it is important to allow users to understand what has been achieved and give them the opportunity to modify and enhance the results. The former has been achieved with the exploration features sketched above, the latter has been accomplished by providing a widget to edit the annotations (Fig. 1 - 4. edit mode). The annotation validation and editing require that the user has previous knowledge about the structure of the KG. Therefore, to support the user we integrate ABSTAT[10] [4], a Resource Description Format (RDF) data set profiling tool. It takes a dataset and the relative ontology (in OWL format) in input, and produces a summary and some statistics about the dataset. In addition, ABSTAT provides access to summaries via APIs that allow to easily extract information about the KG such as the frequency of a particular concept in the KG or the frequency of a particular type of pattern. In essence, ABSTAT provides information on how concepts and properties are used within DBpedia, thus supporting the user to make better choices.

Acknowledgments. This research has been supported in part by EU H2020 projects EW-Shopp - Grant n. 732590. Special thanks to Roberto Avogadro, David Chieregato, Carlo Mattioli and Blerina Spahiu for their support during the development of the project.

References

1. Limaye, G., Sarawagi, S., Chakrabarti, S.: Annotating and searching web tables using entities, types and relationships. VLDB **3**, 1338–1347 (2010)
2. Pham, M., Alse, S., Knoblock, C.A., Szekely, P.: Semantic labeling: a domain-independent approach. In: Groth, P., et al. (eds.) ISWC 2016. LNCS, vol. 9981, pp. 446–462. Springer, Cham (2016). https://doi.org/10.1007/978-3-319-46523-4_27
3. Ritze, D., Lehmberg, O., Bizer, C.: Matching HTML tables to DBpedia. In: Proceedings of the 5th International Conference on Web Intelligence, Mining and Semantics, pp. 10:1–10:6 (2015)

---

[10] http://backend.abstat.disco.unimib.it.

4. Spahiu, B., Porrini, R., Palmonari, M., Rula, A., Maurino, A.: ABSTAT: ontology-driven linked data summaries with pattern minimalization. In: Sack, H., Rizzo, G., Steinmetz, N., Mladenić, D., Auer, S., Lange, C. (eds.) ESWC 2016. LNCS, vol. 9989, pp. 381–395. Springer, Cham (2016). https://doi.org/10.1007/978-3-319-47602-5_51

5. Venetis, P., et al.: Recovering semantics of tables on the web. Proc. VLDB Endow. **4**(9), 528–538 (2011)

6. Zhang, Z.: Effective and efficient semantic table interpretation using TableMiner+. Semant. Web **8**(6), 921–957 (2017)

Clustering Pipelines of Large RDF POI Data

Rajjat Dadwal[1], Damien Graux[1(✉)], Gezim Sejdiu[2], Hajira Jabeen[2], and Jens Lehmann[1,2]

[1] Fraunhofer Institute for Intelligent Analysis and Information Systems, Sankt Augustin, Germany
{rajjat.dadwal,damien.graux}@iais.fraunhofer.de
[2] Smart Data Analytics, University of Bonn, Bonn, Germany
{sejdiu,jabeen,jens.lehmann}@cs.uni-bonn.de

Abstract. Among the various domains using large RDF graphs, applications often rely on geographical information which is often represented via Points Of Interests. In particular, one challenge is to extract patterns from POI sets to discover Areas Of Interest (AOIs). To tackle this challenge, a typical method is to aggregate various points according to specific distances (e.g. geographical) via clustering algorithms. In this study, we present a flexible architecture to design pipelines able to aggregate POIs from contextual to geographical dimensions in a single run. This solution allows any kind of clustering algorithm combinations to compute AOIs and is built on top of a Semantic Web stack which allows multiple-source querying and filtering through SPARQL.

1 Introduction

Various organizations like DBpedia [3], Wikidata [7] etc. are constantly working for gathering information from different sources and storing it in structured form, e.g. RDF[1]. RDF data allow to model various domains and this characteristic helps to solve problems in different areas i.e., from the medical domain to the geographical domain. In this study, we are focusing on Points Of Interests (POIs). POIs are generally characterized by their geospatial coordinates along with their thematic/contextual attributes. A common POI use-case is to find hot zones according to specific topics: i.e. discovering Areas of Interest (AOIs) as a result of aggregation of POIs. With the assistance of AOIs, one can identify other similar areas in the same or a different city, recognize the distinguishing characteristics of this area, and determine potential types of users (or customers) that would be interested in that area.

In this paper, we propose a flexible architecture to design clustering pipelines for POI semantic datasets at once. Indeed, using large and detailed RDF vocabularies allow richer POI descriptions. For example, one POI related to a restaurant

R. Dadwal—This research was supported by the European project SLIPO (number 731581).

[1] https://www.w3.org/TR/rdf11-primer/.

P. Hitzler et al. (Eds.): ESWC 2019 Satellite Events, LNCS 11762, pp. 24–27, 2019.
https://doi.org/10.1007/978-3-030-32327-1_5

might be described by its latitude, longitude, food specialty, reviews, address, phone number etc. which could represent up to 50 distinct triples[2] leading then to billions of RDF records overall. As a consequence, we require scalability and build our solution on top of the distributed semantic stack SANSA [4] which benefits from Apache Spark [8]. The proposed architecture then enables any kind of clustering algorithm combinations on POI RDF data.

2   Architecture Overview

In order to process RDF (containing POIs) datasets in an efficient and scalable way, we first have to adopt a convenient processing framework. SANSA [4] is a data-flow engine for distributed computing of large-scale RDF datasets. It provides APIs for faster reading, querying, inferencing and apply analytics at scale. It uses Apache Spark [8] as an underlying engine. SANSA contains features which are utilized for processing RDF data with thematic and spatial information.

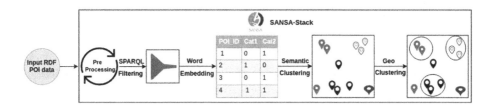

Fig. 1. A Semantic-Geo clustering flow.

Our proposed approach contains up to five main components (which could be enabled/disabled if necessary) namely: data pre-processing, SPARQL filtering, word embedding, semantic clustering and geo-clustering. In particular, in Fig. 1, we present an example of Semantic-Geospatial clustering pipeline. Indeed, we consider two types of clustering algorithms: the semantic-based ones and the geo-based ones.

In semantic based clustering algorithms (which do not consider POI locations but rather aim at grouping POIs according to shared labels), there is a need to transform the POIs categorical values to numerical vectors to find the distance between them. So far, we can select any word embedding technique among the three available ones namely one-hot encoding, Word2Vec and Multi-Dimensional Scaling. All the above mentioned methods converts categorical variables into a form that could be provided to semantic clustering algorithms to form groups of non-location-based similarities. For example, all restaurants are in one cluster whereas all the ATMs in another one. On the other hand, the geo-clustering methods help to group the spatially closed coordinates with in each semantic cluster.

---

[2] See e.g. the SLIPO ontology: https://github.com/SLIPO-EU/poi-data-model/.

Fig. 2. Visualizations (on a map) of the Semantic-Geo clustering pipeline steps. (Color figure online)

More generically, our architecture and implementation allow users to design any kind of clustering combinations they would like. Actually, the solution is flexible enough to pipe together more than two clustering "blocks" and even to add additional RDF datasets into the process after several clustering rounds. In addition, we directly embedded the state-of-the-art clustering algorithms into the SANSA Machine Learning layer[3] so that these pipelines are prone to be built out of the box.

3   Achieved Results

To illustrate the feasibility of our approach and demonstrate the potential of the RDF POI clustering library we developed in SANSA, we present –as an example– in this section the implementation results of the specific architecture presented in Fig. 1 i.e. a Semantic-Geo clustering pipeline.

In order to test the process and validate the approach, we used an RDF POI dataset which follows the ontology described in [1] containing around 18 000 triples which represent information on 623 POIs (i.e. around 28 triples per POI). We then chose Word2Vec [6] as embedding for the K-means [5] semantic-clustering algorithm, before running DBSCAN [2] as geo-clustering method. In details, we gave the following parameters to the algorithms: 8 clusters within 5 iterations for K-means and $\epsilon = 0.002$ with at least 2 points per cluster for DBSCAN. The complete process took around 20 s using a 8 GB-memory laptop running a single-node SANSA & Spark stack.

---

[3] https://github.com/SANSA-Stack/SANSA-ML.

We present the results obtained at the various steps in Fig. 2 on a map, the figure presents a zoom over a particular Austrian region. The figure is twofold, we first display (left side) the only result of the K-means where POIs are pinned on a map and where each color corresponds to a specific cluster. As expected, the semantic clusters are distributed over the entire country since POIs of a color are sharing common "sense" with regards to the categories in the ontology. As a consequence, the geographical step of aggregation allows then to break those country-spread clusters into pieces and obtain (right side of Fig. 2) relevant AOIs. In particular, four AOIs are visible: an orange one in the corner, a large red one which also embeds a green one and a little magenta.

4 Conclusion

In this article, we presented a solution to extract AOIs from big POI data while considering several dimensions at the same time. The architecture is embedded inside a state-of-the-art Semantic Web stack (i.e. SANSA [4]) and then benefits from the advantages of it. For instance, it allows source aggregation or datasets filtering via SPARQL to only focus on some interesting regions, e.g., a specific country can be selected. Moreover, even if we restricted our description in this study to a Semantic-Geo clustering pipeline, our architecture allows any kind of clustering combinations. Finally, the above-presented pipeline is also openly available from a demonstrating notebook[4] on the SANSA repository.

References

1. Athanasiou, S., et al.: Big POI data integration with linked data technologies. In: 22nd International Conference on Extending Database Technology, Lisbon, pp. 477–488 (2019)
2. Ester, M., Kriegel, H.P., Sander, J., Xu, X., et al.: A density-based algorithm for discovering clusters in large spatial databases with noise. KDD **96**(34), 226–231 (1996)
3. Lehmann, J., et al.: DBpedia-a large-scale, multilingual knowledge base extracted from Wikipedia. Semant. Web **6**(2), 167–195 (2015)
4. Lehmann, J., et al.: Distributed semantic analytics using the SANSA stack. In: d'Amato, C., et al. (eds.) ISWC 2017. LNCS, vol. 10588, pp. 147–155. Springer, Cham (2017). https://doi.org/10.1007/978-3-319-68204-4_15
5. MacQueen, J.: Some methods for classification and analysis of multivariate observations. In: 5th Berkeley Symposium on Mathematical Statistics and Probability, pp. 281–297 (1967)
6. Mikolov, T., Sutskever, I., Chen, K., Corrado, G.S., Dean, J.: Distributed representations of words and phrases and their compositionality. In: Advances in Neural Information Processing Systems, pp. 3111–3119 (2013)
7. Vrandečić, D., Krötzsch, M.: Wikidata: a free collaborative knowledge base (2014)
8. Zaharia, M., et al.: Resilient distributed datasets: a fault-tolerant abstraction for in-memory cluster computing. In: Proceedings of the 9th USENIX Conference on Networked Systems Design and Implementation, p. 2. USENIX Association (2012)

---

[4] https://github.com/SANSA-Stack/SANSA-Notebooks.

Demonstration of a Stream Reasoning Platform on Low-End Devices to Enable Personalized Real-Time Cycling Feedback

Mathias De Brouwer$^{(\boxtimes)}$ ⓘ, Femke Ongenae ⓘ, and Filip De Turck ⓘ

Department of Information Technology, IDLab, Ghent University – imec,
iGent Tower, Technologiepark-Zwijnaarde 126, 9052 Ghent, Belgium
mrdbrouw.DeBrouwer@UGent.be

Abstract. During amateur cycling training, analyzing sensor data in real-time would allow riders to receive immediate feedback on how they are performing, and adapt their training accordingly. In this paper, a solution with Semantic Web technologies is presented that gives such real-time personalized feedback, by integrating the data streams with domain knowledge, rider profiles & other context data. This solution consists of a stream reasoning engine running on a low-end Raspberry Pi device, and a tablet app showing feedback based on the continuous query results. To demonstrate this in a static environment, a virtual training app is presented, allowing a user to simulate an amateur cycling training.

Keywords: Stream reasoning · Low-end devices · Real-time feedback · Personalization · Cycling

1 Introduction

In recent years, the importance of using data in sports has significantly increased, both on a professional and amateur level. In cycling, riders can be equipped with various sensors, e.g., heart rate monitors, GPS sensors, speed sensors etc. Analyzing the data measured by these sensors in real-time allows a rider to receive immediate feedback on how he/she is performing. Especially during training, this would allow a rider to adapt his/her training in real-time according to a prescribed training plan. Personalization of this feedback is required to maximize its value. For example, the physiological profile of a rider includes the boundaries between the different heart rate training zones in cycling, which are an important aspect of real-time training feedback. These rider profiles, potentially complemented with other context data such as route information, should be integrated with domain knowledge and the sensor data streams.

In amateur cycling, resources are limited compared to professional cycling. Existing real-time sports analytics solutions used by amateur cyclists, such as Strava[1] and TrainingPeaks[2], only focus on post-processing the sensor data,

---

[1] https://www.strava.com.
[2] https://www.trainingpeaks.com.

© Springer Nature Switzerland AG 2019
P. Hitzler et al. (Eds.): ESWC 2019 Satellite Events, LNCS 11762, pp. 28–32, 2019.
https://doi.org/10.1007/978-3-030-32327-1_6

sensor platform   stream reasoning server   feedback visualization app

data streams   feedback
                                                 (query results)

Fig. 1. Architecture of the real-time training feedback platform

and do not focus on giving real-time personalized feedback. Moreover, they do not allow to integrate with various heterogeneous sensors and background data sources, e.g., domain knowledge and rider profiles [3]. By using Semantic Web technologies, this can be made possible: sensor & background data can be semantically enriched using ontologies, and stream reasoning techniques can be applied that combine semantic reasoners with stream processing techniques to consolidate & analyze the sensor data streams & available background knowledge [4]. By running these techniques on an inexpensive low-end device, e.g., a Raspberry Pi, mobile phone or tablet, such a solution can also be adopted by amateur cyclists.

In this paper, a solution is presented that gives personalized real-time cycling feedback to amateurs during training, by continuously evaluating queries on a stream reasoning engine running on a Raspberry Pi. By using Semantic Web technologies, this solution enables the real-time integration and processing of heterogeneous sensor data streams and background knowledge & context data on a low-end device. As a demonstrator of the solution, a virtual cycling training app is presented. It is virtual as it allows a user to simulate an amateur cycling training from within a static environment.

2   Platform Architecture

The architecture of the training feedback platform, which is designed to give individual feedback to a rider, is visualized in Fig. 1. It consists of three main components, which should all be mounted on the rider's bike: the sensors, the Raspberry Pi running the stream reasoning server, and a mobile phone or tablet with a feedback visualization app. Various heterogeneous sensor devices can be plugged in into the platform and communicate with the stream reasoning server over wireless technologies, by using an existing IoT platform designed in previous research [2]. The stream reasoning server [3] consists of a running instance of the C-SPARQL RDF stream processing engine [1]. A cycling ontology has been designed to model domain knowledge, rider profiles, other context data and sensor observations. This data is hosted on the stream reasoning server, and used by the C-SPARQL engine as input data. Depending on the desired feedback, different continuous queries can be registered to the engine, which publish their results on a WebSocket. A feedback visualization app can listen over Wi-Fi to this WebSocket, to visualize the query results as real-time training feedback for the rider. This can help the rider to instantly react to his/her performance.

```
SELECT ?uuid ?firstName ?lastName ?time ?tzName
FROM STREAM <http://idlab.ugent.be/cycling/stream> [RANGE 5s STEP 1s]
FROM <http://localhost:8177/cycling-riders.rdf>
FROM <http://localhost:8177/cycling-sensors.rdf>
WHERE {
  ?o sosa:hasResult ?ov . ?o sosa:resultTime ?time .
  ?ov rdf:type cycling-sosa:HeartRateObservationValue .
  ?ov schema:value ?heartRate .
  { SELECT ?sensor (MAX(f:timestamp(?x, sosa:madeBySensor, ?sensor)) AS ?ts)
    WHERE { ?x sosa:madeBySensor ?sensor . ?x sosa:hasResult ?xv .
            ?xv rdf:type cycling-sosa:HeartRateObservationValue . }
    GROUP BY ?sensor }
  ?sensor sosa:isHostedBy ?device . ?device cycling-sosa:UUID ?uuid .
  ?athlete cycling-profile:monitoredBy ?device .
  ?athlete schema:givenName ?firstName. ?athlete schema:familyName ?lastName.

  FILTER ( f:timestamp (?o, sosa:madeBySensor, ?sensor) = ?ts )

  ?athlete cycling-profile:hasThreshold ?thLB , ?thUB .
  ?thLB cycling-profile:isLowerBoundOf ?tzAthlete .
  ?thUB cycling-profile:isUpperBoundOf ?tzAthlete .
  ?thLB schema:value ?thValueLB . ?thUB schema:value ?thValueUB .
  ?tzAthlete rdf:type ?tz . ?tz rdfs:label ?tzName .

  FILTER ( ?heartRate > ?thValueLB ) FILTER ( ?heartRate <= ?thValueUB )
}
```

Listing 1. getTrainingZone C-SPARQL query (prefixes are omitted)

3   Use Case and Demonstrator: Virtual Training App

A virtual cycling training app, which is an adapted version of the visualization app in Fig. 1, has been implemented for an Android tablet as a demonstrator of the proposed solution. The goal of the designed application is to let the demo user execute a cycling training. Due to portability and complexity issues, bringing a bike with a static bike system, e.g., Tacx, is unfeasible. Therefore, the cycling part is simulated by the user using the tablet's touch screen.

The architecture of the demo set-up consists of the Raspberry Pi and the tablet app of Fig. 1. The sensors are replaced by virtual sensors in the app generating data based on the simulated cycling. On the Raspberry Pi, a C-SPARQL server is running. Two continuous queries are registered: getQuantityObservationValue to retrieve quantity sensor observations [3], and getTrainingZone, to retrieve the heart rate training zone corresponding to the rider's heart rate (Listing 1). Both queries are executed every 1 s on a window of 5 s. The C-SPARQL input data consists of the cycling ontology, the rider profile, the sensors' context data & the sensor data streams.

The tablet application consists of three different chronological parts, which can be categorized as pre-training, during training, and post-training.[3]

---

[3] The online demo page, including a video of the full demo process, is available at https://IBCNServices.github.io/cyclists-monitoring. The demo data (ontology, context data & queries) is also available at https://github.com/IBCNServices/cyclists-monitoring/tree/master/virtual-training-app-demo.

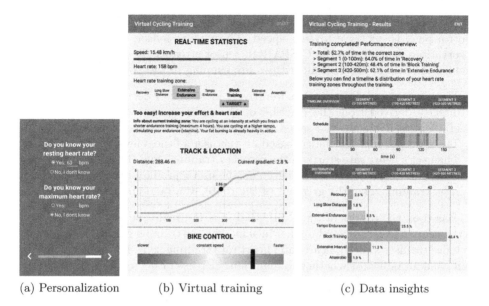

(a) Personalization (b) Virtual training (c) Data insights

Fig. 2. Screenshots of the virtual cycling training app, chronologically with respect to the user executing the demo

Personalization (Pre-training). The first part of the app consists of a set of profile-related questions, which allow to construct the user's profile based on the answers and semantically represent it in the cycling ontology. In specific, the user's name, gender, birth date, fitness level, and resting and maximum heart rate (if known) are retrieved. An example of one of the app screens asking this data is shown in Fig. 2a. Using expertise rules of thumb and the Karvonen formula, the user's personalized heart rate training zone boundaries can be determined from this data [3,5]. This enables to personalize training zone feedback for amateur cyclists, who cannot let their physiological profile be determined in expert lab tests, like in professional cycling.

Virtual Training. The second part of the app consists of the virtual training. The simulated use case involves the demo user being a rider (virtually) equipped with a heart rate monitor, riding on a bike (virtually) equipped with a speed sensor. The rider will execute a training on a specific track, where each track segment has a target heart rate training zone. The goal of the training is to ride in the target training zone as much as possible.

A screenshot of the real-time interface is presented in Fig. 2b. This part consists of two panes: the upper pane (above the separator) consists of the real-time feedback and track & location data, while the lower pane contains the bike control UI. During a real-life training, the app will only consist of the upper pane; the control pane is only added to let the user control his/her speed.

As soon as the user starts the training, the user can use the slider in the control pane to increase his/her speed. The virtual sensors will start sending observations every 1 s to the C-SPARQL sensor streams. To generate these virtual sensor values, different algorithms are running in the app:

- The user's speed, initially 0, is iteratively increased or decreased with a value directly derived from the position of the slider in the control pane. If the gradient is non-zero, the speed is corrected with a factor depending on it. The speed is upper bounded based on the user's fitness level & the gradient.
- The user's heart rate starts in the recovery training zone. The next heart rate value is iteratively calculated based on the user's profile, speed, current heart rate, training zone, the gradient of the route, & a random factor.

Based on the results of the C-SPARQL queries, real-time feedback is shown to the user, in order to help him/her in achieving the training goals. The feedback includes the user's speed, heart rate, heart rate training zone, information on this zone, and an indicator whether to maintain, increase or decrease speed & effort. To allow for quick visual feedback during the cycling, a color is given to each training zone. The user can see a graphical representation of the track, as well as his/her location on it, to ensure he/she knows the current gradient of the route and the currently targeted training zone. The latter is also visually indicated.

Data Insights (Post-training). Using the data collected by the real-time processing, various data insights can be generated after the user has completed the full training. In particular, it is interesting to see how well the user has followed the prescribed training plan in terms of heart rate training zones. Therefore, the final part of the app shows a timeline and distribution of the user's training zones throughout the training. Both an overview and a dissection per segment are visualized. A screenshot of this part is shown in Fig. 2c. Other insights could be generated using the data, e.g., by relating speed & heart rate over time.

Acknowledgements. F. Ongenae is funded by a UGent BOF postdoc grant. Part of this research was funded by the FWO SBO S004017N IDEAL-IoT and the imec.icon CONAMO, funded by imec, VLAIO, Rombit, Energy Lab & VRT.

References

1. Barbieri, D.F., et al.: C-SPARQL: a continuous query language for RDF data streams. Int. J. Semantic Comput. **4**(1), 3–25 (2010)
2. Daneels, G., et al.: Real-time data dissemination and analytics platform for challenging IoT environments. In: GIIS 2017, pp. 23–30. IEEE (2017)
3. De Brouwer, M., et al.: Personalized real-time monitoring of amateur cyclists on low-end devices. In: WWW2018, pp. 1833–1840. ACM Press (2018)
4. Dell'Aglio, D., et al.: Stream reasoning: a survey and outlook. Data Science (Preprint), pp. 1–25 (2017)
5. Kent, M.: Oxford Dictionary of Sports Science and Medicine, vol. 10. Oxford University Press, Oxford (2006)

The Function Hub: An Implementation-Independent Read/Write Function Description Repository

Ben De Meester$^{(\boxtimes)}$ ⓘ, Lander Noterman, Ruben Verborgh ⓘ, and Anastasia Dimou ⓘ

Department of Electronics and Information Systems,
Ghent University – imec – IDLab, Technologiepark-Zwijnaarde 122,
9052 Ghent, Belgium
{ben.demeester,lander.noterman,ruben.verborgh,anastasia.dimou}@ugent.be

Abstract. Functions are essential building blocks of any (computer) information system. However, development efforts to implement these functions are fragmented: a function has multiple implementations, each within a specific development context. Manual effort is needed handling various search interfaces and access methods to find the desired function, its metadata (if any), and associated implementations. This laborious process inhibits discovery, and thus reuse. Uniform, implementation-independent access is needed. We demo the Function Hub, available online at https://fno.io/hub: a Web application using a semantic interoperable model to map function descriptions to (multiple) implementations. The Function Hub allows editing and discovering function description metadata, and add information about alternative implementations. This way, the Function Hub enables users to discover relevant functions independently of their implementation, and to link to original published implementations.

Keywords: Function · Linked Data · Repository

1 Introduction

Functions are processes that perform a specific task by associating one or more inputs to an output. However, the development, maintenance, and support efforts of *implementing* these functions are fragmented [1], across different *development contexts* (i.e., a combination of programming language, programming paradigm, architecture, etc.). It is unfeasible to consolidate these efforts by limiting all developers to the same development context [7]. On the one hand, implementations are tuned to meet different requirements, and, on the other hand, there might be prior investment [1]. The same function can thus have multiple implementations, each within a specific development context. For example, a function

ⓒ Springer Nature Switzerland AG 2019
P. Hitzler et al. (Eds.): ESWC 2019 Satellite Events, LNCS 11762, pp. 33–37, 2019.
https://doi.org/10.1007/978-3-030-32327-1_7

to normalize dates may have implementations available as JavaScript source code on GitHub, as part of a Java software package on Maven, and within a REST Web API.

As such, the exploration of function implementations is fragmented across different search engines. To find the desired implementation, users need a combination of, among others, general search engines, online code repositories, and package managers. To know how to invoke an implementation, additional effort is typically needed, e.g., going through the implementation's documentation. Such manual effort involves handling different search interfaces and access methods.

This laborious process inhibits discovery and reuse. Existing implementations are not found because they are built in a different development context. Hence, the same functions are (sometimes unnecessarily) re-implemented, and the fragmentation of development efforts increases. Uniform, implementation-independent access is needed to improve the discovery process.

In this demo paper, we present the Function Hub, which is available online at https://fno.io/hub. The Function Hub enables editing and exploring function description metadata, and linking them to implementations across development contexts. Users can look for a function, optionally using advanced filtering on input and output types. The result is a list of links to existing implementations in various repositories and across development contexts, and machine-readable descriptions of how to invoke them. Access is uniform and descriptions are linked, with the potential to improve implementation reuse. Using a common semantic model, the Function Hub allows interoperability of the function description metadata, and allows agents to unambiguously infer how to use the implementation.

2   The Function Hub

We now discuss several aspects of the Function Hub: the Function Ontology as semantic model to describe the metadata, the characteristics of the Function Hub application, and the read and write interfaces.

Function Ontology. We use the Function Ontology (FnO) [3,4] to represent implementation-independent function description metadata in RDF, and link this metadata to existing and new implementations of varying development contexts. FnO distinguishes between the (*abstract*) function and the (*concrete*) implementation, similarly observed by Garijo et al. for workflows [5].

Functions, implementations, and the mappings between them are described separately. *Functions* are represented as a transformation of input data into output data. By providing an abstract description of a function, instead of a new (declarative) programming language to specify all imperative steps, existing implementations can be linked, they do not need to be re-coded in a new language. By describing the *mappings* separately, the same function can be linked to multiple *implementations*. For example: a date normalization function is linked to a Maven package, a JavaScript snippet, and a REST Web API.

Web Application. The Function Hub allows editing and exploring all relevant metadata with respect to functions, implementations, and mappings. All metadata is stored and published as Linked Data, exhibiting following advantages [6]: (i) linking resources is a native feature of Linked Data; (ii) interoperability is achieved by design, using standardized HTTP operations and formats; and (iii) already available (Web) resources can be linked, for instance, by referring to existing implementations in package managers using their published URI.

The Function Hub is a Web application, responsible for managing and publishing the function descriptions and their implementation mappings. A (public) SPARQL endpoint of the data store is provided (https://fno.io/hub/data/sparql), together with developer-friendly (JSON) APIs (https://fno.io/hub/api), and a user interface (https://fno.io/hub). Its user interface is two-fold, enabling to read and write function description metadata.

Read Interface. The Function Hub's user interface helps users explore (i.e., browse and search) function descriptions without needing to execute any queries on the public querying endpoint. When *browsing*, users can navigate the different function descriptions, and their implementation mappings, making it easy to discover the available implementations of a function, and what type of parameters are used. For every function, the Function Hub shows the name, description, parameters, outputs, and a list of implementations. The declarative mappings unambiguously describe how to invoke the found implementation. Each resource is a link that can be resolved in the browser for more information.

When *searching*, users can perform *common keyword search* over function names and descriptions, and *advanced search* which allows filtering on specific semantic constraints for parameters and outputs, e.g., by parameter or return type (Fig. 1). This allows more detailed search, returning more accurate results. The results are displayed as a list of functions, which can be further inspected via the browse functionality.

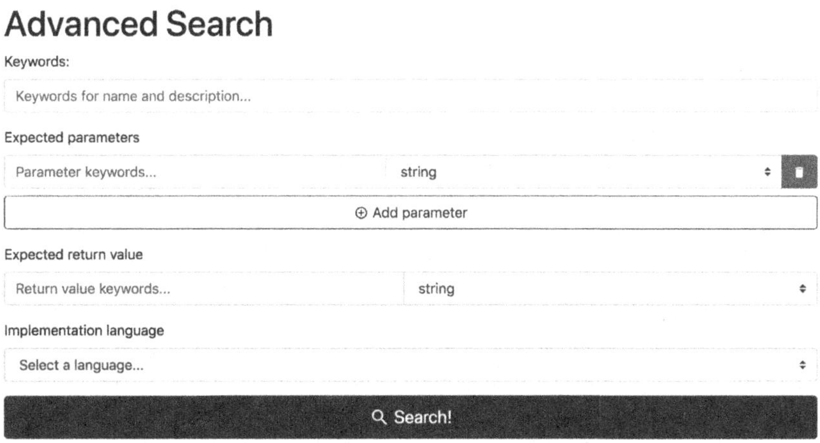

Fig. 1. Detailed, unambiguous search of functions (across implementations).

Add a function

Name

| left-pad |

Description

| Left padding a string. |

Expected parameters

| ☑ Required? | The string to be padded. | | string | ⇕ | ▪ |
| ☑ Required? | The amount of characters the output should have. | | int | ⇕ | ▪ |
| ⊕ Add parameter |

Expected return value

| ☑ Required? | The output of the left pad operation. | | string | ⇕ |

Implementation Type

| JavaScript Function | ⇕ | ▪ Remove implementation |

Implementation name

| LeftPadImplementationJavaScript | ⇕ |

URL to JavaScript file

| http://localhost:4000/implementations/js/leftpad.js |

Position of parameter *The string to be padded. (http://www.w3.org/2001/XMLSchema#string)* 1 ⇕

Position of parameter *The amount of characters the output should have. (http://www.w3.org/2001/XMLSchema#int)* 2 ⇕

| Add function and implementation to hub |

Fig. 2. Editing a function description metadata, and adding/editing links to implementations.

Write Interface. The editing environment supports creating new and editing existing function descriptions (Fig. 2). More specifically, all metadata of the function and its associated resources (inputs, outputs, problems) can be edited, and mappings with implementations can be added. Updates are directly reflected in the queryable dataset.

3   Conclusion

This demo shows how abstract function descriptions, with mappings to concrete implementations as Linked Data resources on the Web, are made available by the Function Hub. A uniform search interface is provided, usable across development contexts with more advanced search operators.

The Function Hub is interoperable and scalable. W3C recommendations are used whenever possible to improve *interoperability* with other systems, whether it be for the format (RDF, JSON) or the query interface (SPARQL). The Function Hub provides merely links to implementations: the amount of stored data is limited to metadata, leading to better *scalability* with respect to the amount of available descriptions, and allows for federated querying.

The Function Hub can be used as a development context-independent search engine that returns sufficient metadata to manually integrate an implementation of a requested function. The Function Hub can, thus, already be used in existing software projects, and its usage can be compared to typical search. However, the detailed mapping description also allows for automatic invocation of these found implementations. This future work is being pursued by implementing Function Handlers for different development contexts[1], further specified in [4].

The Function Hub's data is currently manually curated. To scale up, automatic metadata extraction approaches can be used. We can use existing frameworks to automatically generate meaningful function descriptions, based on data of package managers, such as npm [8], and based on programming code source files in Java code [2]. Further, additional non-functional metadata can also be taken into account to, e.g., represent a notion of expected quality (similar to showing the amount of stars and forks within a GitHub repository). Once this metadata is ingested, the Function Hub represents – and allows to search for – the contents of these software packages in a uniform, development context-independent way.

Acknowledgements. The described research activities were funded by Ghent University, imec, Flanders Innovation & Entrepreneurship (VLAIO), and the European Union. Ruben Verborgh is a postdoctoral fellow of the Research Foundation – Flanders (FWO).

References

1. Atkinson, M., Gesing, S., Montagnat, J., Taylor, I.: Scientific workflows: past, present and future. Future Gener. Comput. Syst. **75**, 216–227 (2017)
2. Atzeni, M., Atzori, M.: CodeOntology: RDF-ization of source code. In: d'Amato, C., et al. (eds.) ISWC 2017. LNCS, vol. 10588, pp. 20–28. Springer, Cham (2017). https://doi.org/10.1007/978-3-319-68204-4_2
3. De Meester, B., Dimou, A.: The function ontology. Unofficial Draft, Ghent University - imec - IDLab (2016). https://w3id.org/function/spec
4. De Meester, B., Dimou, A., Verborgh, R.: Implementation-independent function reuse. Future Gener. Comput. Syst. (2019, under review)
5. Garijo, D., Gil, Y.: A new approach for publishing workflows: abstractions, standards, and linked data. In: Proceedings of the 6th Workshop on Workflows in Support of Large-Scale Science - WORKS 2011. ACM Press (2011)
6. Garijo, D., Gil, Y., Corcho, O.: Abstract, link, publish, exploit: an end to end framework for workflow sharing. Future Gener. Comput. Syst. **75**, 271–283 (2017)
7. Liew, C.S., Atkinson, M.P., Galea, M., Ang, T.F., Martin, P., Hemert, J.I.V.: Scientific workflows: moving across paradigms. ACM Comput. Surv. **49**(4), 661–6639 (2017)
8. Van Herwegen, J., Taelman, R., Capadisli, S., Verborgh, R.: Describing configurations of software experiments as linked data. In: Garijo, D., van Hage, W.R., Kauppinen, T., Kuhn, T., Zhao, J. (eds.) Proceedings of the First Workshop on Enabling Open Semantic Science (SemSci). CEUR Workshop Proceedings, vol. 1931, pp. 23–30, Aachen (2017)

---

[1] https://github.com/FnOio/function-handler-js and https://github.com/FnOio/function-handler-java are Function Handler proof-of-concept implementations for JavaScript and Java, respectively.

Knowledge Extraction from a Small Corpus of Unstructured Safeguarding Reports

Aleksandra Edwards[1,2]([✉]), Alun Preece[1,2], and Hélène de Ribaupierre[1]

[1] School of Computer Science and Informatics, Cardiff University, Cardiff, UK
edwardsai@cardiff.ac.uk
[2] Crime and Security Research Institute, Cardiff University, Cardiff, UK

Abstract. This paper presents results on the performance of a range of analysis tools for extracting entities and sentiments from a small corpus of unstructured, safeguarding reports. We use sentiment analysis to identify strongly positive and strongly negative segments in an attempt to attribute patterns on the sentiments extracted to specific entities. We use entity extraction for identifying key entities. We evaluate tool performance against non-specialist human annotators. An initial study comparing the inter-human agreement against inter-machine agreement shows higher overall scores from human annotators than software tools. However, the degree of consensus between the human annotators for entity extraction is lower than expected which suggests a need for trained annotators. For sentiment analysis the annotators reached a higher agreement for annotating descriptive sentences compared to reflective sentences, while inter-tool agreement was similarly low for the two sentence types. The poor performance of the entity extraction and sentiment analysis approaches point to the need for domain-specific approaches for knowledge extraction on these kinds of document. However, there is currently a lack of pre-existing ontologies in the safeguarding domain. Thus, in future our focus is the development of such a domain-specific ontology.

Keywords: Text mining · Sentiment analysis · Entity extraction

1 Introduction

The aim of this paper is to evaluate a range of text analysis tools and approaches for extracting knowledge from a small corpus of unstructured safeguarding reports. The purpose of these reports is to describe events prior to a crime, assess agencies and practices, and to reflect on lessons learned. The reports are lengthy and complex, so extracting information across the corpus by human inspection is a time-consuming and potentially bias-prone process. Moreover, the documents

We thank David Rogers and members of the Wales Safeguarding Repository research team for their assistance. http://orca.cf.ac.uk/111010/.

© Springer Nature Switzerland AG 2019
P. Hitzler et al. (Eds.): ESWC 2019 Satellite Events, LNCS 11762, pp. 38–42, 2019.
https://doi.org/10.1007/978-3-030-32327-1_8

are unstructured and contain a great deal of domain-specific terminology which makes them hard to analyse using automated methods. In an initial attempt at information retrieval we performed a sentiment analysis exercise hypothesising that strongly negative or positive sentences would contain key information. We also used entity extraction to identify key features in terms of individuals, organisations and locations. Further to this, we conducted a study comparing an 'inter-judgement agreement' between annotators and tools. Table 1 provides description for the text analysis tools.

Table 1. Text analysis tools

Tool	Sentiment analysis	Named entity extraction
Stanford Core NLP [2]	Recursive neural Tensor network	CRF classifier
Google Cloud API[a]	Deep learning models	Deep learning models
Gate [1]	Generic sentiment Analysis application	ANNIE dictionary look-up and rules
SentiStrength [3]	Dictionary look-up	NA
NLTK[b]	NA	MaxEnt chunker

[a] Google Cloud API: https://cloud.google.com/apis/
[b] NLTK: https://www.nltk.org

2 Results

Inter-human Agreement Versus Inter-machine Agreement. In this pilot study, conducted by the authors of this paper, we manually annotated sentences that were used as a baseline for comparing tool performance. The study used a *description* and a *reflection* set. Both sets consisted of 100 randomly-chosen sentences from different parts of the reports. The description set consisted of sentences describing the events of the safeguarding case—often involving one or more crimes—while the reflection set consisted of findings: lessons learned and recommendations. The two sets differed in the nature of how the sentiments of the sentences can be interpreted. The highlights of the descriptive set are the events; thus, the sentiment of the sentences will be judged by the sentiment of the event. An indicative (non-verbatim) example of a descriptive sentence is: "Prison staff found the subject had hanged himself". This sentence describes a negative event, i.e., a death. The highlights of the reflection sentences are the findings. Thus, the sentiment of the sentences will be judged by the sentiment of the comment. An indicative (non-verbatim) example of a reflective sentence is: "The key finding from the review of the agencies' involvement is that there was strong evidence of good inter-agency working and appropriate referrals between local services". This sentence express a positive reflection on inter-agency communication.

We measured the inter-annotator agreement and the inter-tool agreement for our sentiment analysis and entity extraction exercises (Table 2) using Fleiss' kappa. Fleiss' kappa scores for the sentiment analysis showed good agreement between the annotators but a significant disagreement between the tools.

The difference between the annotator scores for the two datasets suggests that humans find it easier to annotate the descriptive set rather than the reflective set while the tools did not differentiate between the two data sets. The vast majority of sentiment disagreement between the human annotators involved distinguishing between neutral vs positive/negative polarity. There was only a single instance of disagreement between positive vs negative polarity of a sentence: "The person disclosed at an appointment, that they had overdosed a month before and now felt stupid about it" (this example is paraphrased). However, the disagreement between the tools in terms of positive vs negative sentiment was considerably higher: 34% for the description and 36% for the reflections.

The Fleiss' kappa scores are low across all entity extraction categories for the software tools. Inter-human agreement for person and organisation are also low. Entities that humans disagreed on were: 'GP' (general practitioner), 'Coroner', 'Mental Health Teams', and 'Mental Health Tribunal', all of which tended to be labelled either as 'person' or 'organisation'. The low Fleiss' kappa scores show that the entity extraction task is challenging not only for software but also for non-specialist human annotators.

Table 2. Fleiss' kappa scores

	Annotators	Tools
Sentiment analysis		
Descriptions	0.6	0.1
Recommendations	0.4	0.1
Entity extraction		
Person	0.3	0.04
Organisation	0.3	0.3
Location	1.0	0.2

Sentiment Analysis. Figure 1 presents the average precision, recall, and F1 between the positive, negative, and neutral sentiment categories. These results show an unsatisfactory level of performance from the tools used. Overall, the tools performed better for descriptive sentences: SentiStrength performed the best for these with around 55% for precision, recall and F1. Gate performed best for reflective sentences with F1 of 48%. The poor performance of the tools can be attributed to the fact that they are trained on datasets very different to the safeguarding domain. For example, Stanford [2] is trained on movie reviews where a phrase such as "with recommendation" has positive sentiment while the

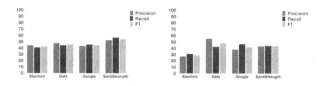

Fig. 1. Average precision, recall, F1 for sentiment analysis: description set (left), reflection set (right)

same phrase in the context of a safeguarding report might have a negative sentiment (e.g., "sentenced to life imprisonment *with recommendation* of years"). SentiStrength [3] is based on a dataset of MySpace content and uses a dictionary-based approach. It follows that sentences mentioning entities such as 'Specialist Dementia home' will match to the term dictionary 'special*' and thus have a positive sentiment.

Extracting Named Entities. Figure 2 shows poor performance across all categories with F1 lower than 60%. Precision and recall tend to be very unbalanced.

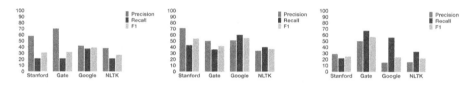

Fig. 2. Evaluation results for entity extraction: person (left), organisation (middle), location (right)

3 Conclusion and Future Work

The sentiment analysis results provide no evidence that off-the-shelf sentiment analysis tools can identify key parts of the safeguarding reports. In future we plan to focus on entity extraction. The unsatisfactory results of the entity extraction tools shows the need for more domain-targeted approaches, and for knowledge extraction such as the use of an ontology. However, existing semantic web resources to the best of our knowledge lacks ontologies relating to safeguarding and crime issues. A Swoogle search (conducted 1/3/19) on terms such as 'crime', 'safeguarding', and 'mental health' found no publicly-available ontologies fitting the purpose of our domain, pointing to a need for the creation of an ontology that models safeguarding issues. In the next stage of our work, we will use word and sentence vectors to discover main themes in documents. We will then use these themes as a base for the creation of an ontology.

References

1. Cunningham, H., Tablan, V., Roberts, A., Bontcheva, K.: Getting more out of biomedical documents with gate's full lifecycle open source text analytics. PLoS Comput. Biol. **9**(2), e1002854 (2013)
2. Manning, C.D., Surdeanu, M., Bauer, J., Finkel, J., Bethard, S.J., McClosky, D.: The Stanford CoreNLP natural language processing toolkit. In: Association for Computational Linguistics (ACL) System Demonstrations, pp. 55–60 (2014)
3. Thelwall, M., Buckley, K., Paltoglou, G., Cai, D., Kappas, A.: Sentiment strength detection in short informal text. J. Am. Soc. Inform. Sci. Technol. **61**(12), 2544–2558 (2010)

An Overview of the Festo Semantic Platform

Kathrin Evers[1], Thorsten Liebig[2], Andreas Maisenbacher[1], Michael Opitz[2], Jan R. Seyler[1], Gunther Sudra[1], and Jens Wissmann[1(✉)]

[1] Festo AG & Co. KG, Ruiter Str. 82, 73734 Esslingen, Germany
{kathrin.evers,andreas.maisenbacher,jan.seyler,gunther.sudra,
jens.wissmann}@festo.com
[2] derivo GmbH, Münchner Str. 1, 89073 Ulm, Germany
{liebig,opitz}@derivo.de

Abstract. We present an overview of the Festo Semantic Platform that is in productive usage at the automation company Festo to derive value adding information from product data. First we describe the current state of the platform. At its core OWL and SWRL reasoning is applied to infer compatibility relationships between products such as electric axes, mounting kits, motors and controllers. Further we outline an ongoing effort to establish a more well-defined data processing pipeline to gain more flexibility when integrating new knowledge domains. Finally, we discuss future directions, especially the role of the platform in skill based product search.

Keywords: Automation industry · Ontology · Knowledge graph · Reasoning

1 Current Application

Festo offers a wide spectrum of pneumatic and electric automation products to serve application domains ranging from microelectronics over food industry to heavy engineering. An electric automation solution is built from drivetrains which are composed of basic products: an axis, a mounting kit, optionally a gear, a motor and a controller. Festo's portfolio contains thousands of such products that are composable in many ways to meet a wide range of requirements. The modular design causes a combinatorial explosion resulting in millions of valid drivetrains. In the past, the product data and the compatibility information was maintained in relational databases. This approach was computationally expensive, time consuming and required a complex data maintenance and deployment management.

This challenge has been solved by an ontological approach [1] as part of the Festo Semantic Platform (FSP). The main goal is to compute all possible combinations of the aforementioned components in a drivetrain.

© Springer Nature Switzerland AG 2019
P. Hitzler et al. (Eds.): ESWC 2019 Satellite Events, LNCS 11762, pp. 43–46, 2019.
https://doi.org/10.1007/978-3-030-32327-1_9

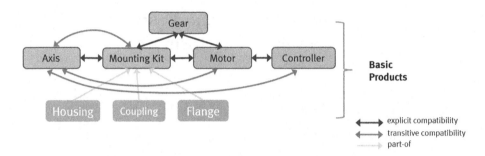

Fig. 1. Schema of the products and compatibilities in a drivetrain.

The direct compatibility of two neighbouring components depends on physical as well as electrical characteristics. These characteristics are expressed by so called interface codes. Each type of component has a set of in and outgoing interfaces that need a complementing code at its neighbour. To this end, two components are explicitly compatible when their respective interface codes match each other (cf. with Fig. 1). These dependencies are declaratively encoded with the help of a few dozen SWRL rules. We use RDFox [3] to derive the direct compatibility from interface codes. This approach is not only faster wrt. computation time and much better to maintain, it is also much easier to extend. In order to explicitly introduce indirect compatibility between components, such as between axes and controller, only a transitive super-property of the compatibility property is needed. Instead of writing a query or view – based on nested joins over relational data – this solution just requires one new property. All the rest is delegated to the RDFox inference engine that computes the necessary relations in seconds rather than hours as before.

2   Data Pipeline

As our application grows we face the challenge of dealing with more complex data ingestion scenarios. To be more flexible we are introducing a staged processing pipeline which is structured into four processing phases—change data capture, import selection, mapping and enrichment. Further we align our system with software engineering and continuous delivery practices such as *micro service architecture* and *container virtualization*.

Data is ingested from multiple SQL data sources. In the Change Data Capture phase we keep track of data changes, aggregate technical data of products and ignore irrelevant data. Technically, this is delivered by a layer of SQL databases that are in our sovereignty. We employ methods known from Data Warehousing [2] such as type 2 of the Slowly Changing Dimensions (SCD) method to detect changes and to historicize the data. In addition, the entity schema of the import database is geared toward the class model of the Knowledge Graph. Thus it makes the translation to a Knowledge Graph easier.

In the Import Selection phase product data from the import database are selected and unique identifiers to this data are added. Selection criteria such as data actuality are applied. The creation and lookup of identifier is performed by a separate service that acts as central authority. Typically, an identifier is computed from technical characteristics.

In the mapping phase relational data are transformed into instances of the Knowledge Graph, represented using RDF and OWL. The mapping was originally implemented in Java code, e.g. using the OWLAPI. We are in the process of moving to a declarative format such as (R2)RML. The intention is to clearly separate the business (mapping) logic from technical implementation details and to gain more flexibility in tool use.

In the final enrichment phase implicit information is made explicit by means of OWL and SWRL reasoning. Especially, categorization of Festo components according to product families or technical characteristics that are relevant for the subsequent services such as compatibility computation that was outlined previously.

To control and monitor the processing we intend to use a *workflow control* system. We use a micro service architecture and use the OpenAPI 3 standard to specify our REST interfaces. To enable continous delivery we use Maven and TeamCity for builds and Docker for containerization.

3   Future Directions

For plant manufacturers it can be time-consuming to find the components they need to realize a desired automation task. An information infrastructure that addresses this challenge needs to be based on well-curated and interlinked product data. But it is also desirable to enable plant manufacturers to find components based on their description of the desired task rather than having them deal with low level product details too early.

We want to approach these challenges from both sides. One aim is to improve the existing knowledge graph by adding more computations of complex products. Additional technical knowledge domains such as pneumatic products or accessory products may be included.

Another aim is to associate skills with resources such as our handling systems. These skills are in turn able to fulfill certain tasks. This would allow our customers (plant manufacturers) as well as our sales engineers to focus more on describing the plant manufacturer's handling needs and focus less on the mechanical and technical data. Technical data is in the ontology to back the skill based description of the plant manufacturer's needs but a first selection of all possible products is made easier by as skill and task based pre-selection.

The idea as sketched in Fig. 2 is to describe an application in terms of *tasks*. *Resources* such as a drivetrain can be annotated with *skills* such as a linear movement. Additional knowledge may be inferred such as the skills of a composed resource like a handling system (3D movement) based on the skills of its underlying resources.

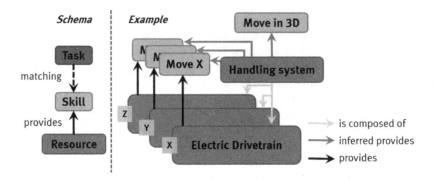

Fig. 2. Schema drivetrains in systems and tasks.

Related work with possible synergies is also done in other research and standardization efforts that Festo participates in such as BaSys 4.0[1] where the topic of capability based interoperability of manufacturing resources is explored [4].

Our current Semantic Platform can provide a shared data platform on which knowledge from different domains can be linked and maintained. Semantic Reasoning can be used to infer knowledge, check consistency and calculate compatibility. However, additional techniques will be necessary, for example, when dealing with complex numeric constraints or when applying objective functions to rank solutions.

References

1. Elmer, S., et al.: Ontologies and reasoning to capture product complexity in automation industry. In: Nikitina, N., Song, D., Fokoue, A., Haase, P. (eds.) Proceedings of the ISWC 2017 Posters & Demonstrations and Industry Tracks co-located with 16th International Semantic Web Conference (ISWC 2017). CEUR Workshop Proceedings, Vienna, Austria, 23–25 October 2017, vol. 1963 (2017). http://CEUR-WS.org
2. Kimball, R., Ross, M.: The Data Warehouse Toolkit: The Definitive Guide to Dimensional Modeling, 3rd edn. Wiley Publishing, Hoboken (2013)
3. Nenov, Y., Piro, R., Motik, B., Horrocks, I., Wu, Z., Banerjee, J.: RDFox: a highly-scalable RDF store. In: Arenas, M., et al. (eds.) ISWC 2015. LNCS, vol. 9367, pp. 3–20. Springer, Cham (2015). https://doi.org/10.1007/978-3-319-25010-6_1
4. Perzylo, A., et al.: Capability-based semantic interoperability of manufacturing resources: a basys 4.0 perspective. In: Proceedings of IFAC MIM 2019 (forthcoming) (2019)

---

[1] https://www.basys40.de/.

Semantic Relatedness as an Inter-facet Metric for Facet Selection over Knowledge Graphs

Leila Feddoul[1,2](✉) ⓘ, Sirko Schindler[2] ⓘ, and Frank Löffler[1] ⓘ

[1] Heinz Nixdorf Chair for Distributed Information Systems,
Friedrich Schiller University Jena, Jena, Germany
{leila.feddoul,frank.loeffler}@uni-jena.de
[2] Institute of Data Science, German Aerospace Center DLR, Jena, Germany
{leila.feddoul,sirko.schindler}@dlr.de

Abstract. Faceted Browsing is a wide-spread approach for exploratory search. Without requiring an in-depth knowledge of the domain, users can narrow down a resource set until it fits their need. An increasing amount of data is published either directly as Linked Data or is at least annotated using concepts from the Linked Data Cloud. This allows identifying commonalities and differences among resources beyond the comparison of mere string representations of metadata.

As the size of data repositories increases, so does the range of covered domains and the number of properties that can provide the basis for a new facet. Manually predefining suitable facet collections becomes impractical. We present our initial work on automatically creating suitable facets for a semantically annotated set of resources. In particular, we address two problems arising with automatic facet generation: (1) Which facets are applicable to the current set of resources and (2) which reasonably sized subset provides the best support to users?

Keywords: Faceted Browsing · Knowledge graph · Exploratory search

1   Introduction

Semantic annotations can considerably improve information retrieval by enriching resources with additional information. The Linked Data Cloud is a valuable source of such annotations. Its continuous growth in recent years, in both quantity of information and range of covered domains, enables applications to exploit semantic connections between resources, to ease information access, and to discover unexpected links across domains.

Consequently, semantic methods that are adapted to efficiently access Linked Data are gaining importance. Those methods allow to easily explore semantic data without expertise in the underlying technologies. In particular, non-expert users should not need to create complex queries to access this information.

© Springer Nature Switzerland AG 2019
P. Hitzler et al. (Eds.): ESWC 2019 Satellite Events, LNCS 11762, pp. 47–51, 2019.
https://doi.org/10.1007/978-3-030-32327-1_10

Faceted Browsing is a widely used technique to partition resource sets based on different dimensions. It provides a general overview of the characteristics of individual elements and allows exploring unknown data schemata. Users can leverage faceted interfaces to apply various filters, called *facets*, to incrementally refine the description of their information need. Possible tasks include searching for items with characteristic properties or exploring the whole set initially without specific goal in mind.

Considering a continuously changing and heterogeneous set of resources, manually predefining facets is often impractical. Furthermore, using concepts from *heterogeneous large scale* knowledge graph KGs, e.g., the Linked Data Cloud, for the semantic annotation of resources induces a large number of possible facets. Displaying all of them will negatively impact navigation efficiency. Hence, we require an automated method to select the most useful subset from any list of candidates matching a given collection of resources. For this purpose, we need to define metrics for measuring the "usefulness" of facets.

We focus on one component of this process that so far has not been extensively studied in the context of KGs: *inter-facet* metrics. In particular, we explore *semantic relatedness* as a measure to reduce the redundancy between selected facets while still maintaining a wide range of aspects. We adapt various techniques to develop a holistic system workflow for automatic facet generation over large scale KGs using the example of Wikidata [1].

2 Related Work

In the following, we give a short overview over selected publications on facet generation. Faceted Browsing over various data sources has been addressed by [2, 3]. In the context of Resource Description Framework (RDF) data, notable earlier research efforts include *BrowseRDF* [4], *mSpace* [5], and *Parallax* [6], followed by *gFacet* [7], and *Facete* [8]. Examples of recent works include *SemFacet* [9], and *GraFa* [10]. They focus on different aspects: *facet ranking* [4], *entity type pivoting* [6,9] *visualization* [7,8], or *indirect facet generation* [7,8].

Theoretical foundations of faceted search are defined in [9], while *performance issues* are described in [10]. Only few systems attempt to build facets over *large scale data* [6,10]. On the other hand, *domain heterogeneity* is disregarded by some approaches [4,5,8]. *Facetedpedia* [11] includes an inter-facet metric that relies on the category system of Wikipedia[1]. However, this does not provide the same generality as a generic *semantic relatedness* approach.

3 Automatic Facet Generation and Selection

Motivated by the idea that a faceted interface should not contain semantically overlapping facets, we consider the *semantic relatedness* as an inter-facet metric that can be used as an exclusion criterion. In effect, we want to prevent semantically close facets to appear together in the final result. For example, facets are

---

[1] https://www.wikipedia.org/.

semantically close when they are connected via an "is-a" relationship. The main reason behind this decision is to provide facets that partition the result space based on *different* aspects and thus helps avoid facets that generate the same subset of results.

In order not to overwhelm users, the number of shown facets should be limited. For this purpose, we need a ranking of candidate facets and, hence, a set of metrics to determine the degree of "usefulness". We categorize our metrics into two types: (i) *intra-facet metrics* rate the facets individually, and (ii) *inter-facet metrics* judge the relevance of a facet as part of a facet collection. Intra-facet metrics will be combined using a scoring function, mapping each facet to a score and providing an overall ranking. Inter-facet metrics will be used to decide which facets should not co-occur in the generated facet collection.

Figure 1 provides an overview of our proposed workflow for automatic facet generation and selection. It takes as input a *list of Internationalized Resource Identifiers*, e.g., the result of a keyword search, from which we generate a list of candidates using their direct properties and the first indirect ones. For example, considering an input list containing *universities*, both *location* and *location's country* are candidates, where *country* is linked to *location* and not to *university* itself.

Now, an initial filtering is performed to reduce the number of *candidates* and thereby the cost of subsequent ranking steps. For example, we remove candidates that apply only to a small subset of input IRIs. Details on this process are considered out of scope at this point.

To avoid co-occurrence of semantically related facets, we filter facets sharing a direct property. For this *selection of better categorization*, we group the facets by their direct property and only select the best-ranked candidate for further evaluation based on the already calculated intra-facet metrics. Considering the previous example, we select either *location* or *location's country*.

Fig. 1. Workflow for automatic facet generation and selection.

Out of the ranked list of candidates, a set of *facets that are semantically distant* from one another will be derived. For this, we consider solely the semantic relatedness of direct properties, even for facets based on indirect properties. We currently employ a structure-based relatedness measure [12] and use a selective approach: Let S be the final collection of suitable facets: (i) Initialize S with the best-ranked facet. (ii) Compare the next-best facet in terms of inter-facet metrics with the previous facets in S. (iii) Add it to S, iff it is not closely semantically related to previously chosen facets in S. (iv) Continue with Step (ii), until the desired number of facets is reached or there are no more candidates left.

After this process, S contains a collection of facets deemed suitable for the given set of resources, according to both our intra- and inter-facet metrics. These facets are now ready to be presented to users.

4 Conclusion

We propose a method for automatic facet generation including rankings based on intra- and inter-facet metrics. Our method also exploits indirect properties to find better categorizations and to create more useful facets. In particular, we focus on *semantic relatedness* as an inter-facet metric. This prevents facets in the final result that are too similar to one another and hence provide little additional assistance. Our goal is to automatically generate facets that are suitable for user navigation and consequently making a contribution in the improvement of accessibility to the semantic web for non-expert users.

In the future we aim to implement the proposed workflow, in a system that also scales with the size of big knowledge graphs like Wikidata. Furthermore, we plan an evaluation to test if our ranking approach provides facets that match user expectations and support them while browsing knowledge graphs.

References

1. Vrandečić, D., Krötzsch, M.: Wikidata: a free collaborative knowledgebase. Commun. ACM **57**(10), 78–85 (2014). https://doi.org/10.1145/2629489
2. Wei, B., Liu, J., Zheng, Q., Zhang, W., Fu, X., Feng, B.: A survey of faceted search. J. Web Eng. **12**(1–2), 41–64 (2013)
3. Tzitzikas, Y., Manolis, N., Papadakos, P.: Faceted exploration of RDF/S datasets: a survey. J. Intell. Inf. Syst. **48**(2), 329–364 (2016). https://doi.org/10.1007/s10844-016-0413-8
4. Oren, E., Delbru, R., Decker, S.: Extending faceted navigation for RDF data. In: Cruz, I., et al. (eds.) ISWC 2006. LNCS, vol. 4273, pp. 559–572. Springer, Heidelberg (2006). https://doi.org/10.1007/11926078_40
5. Schraefel, M.C., Smith, D.A., Owens, A., Russell, A., Harris, C., Wilson, M.: The evolving mSpace platform: leveraging the semantic web on the trail of the Memex. In: Proceedings of the Sixteenth ACM Conference on Hypertext and Hypermedia, HYPERTEXT 2005, pp. 174–183. ACM, New York (2005). https://doi.org/10.1145/1083356.1083391
6. Huynh, D., Karger, D.: Parallax and companion: set-based browsing for the data web. Technical report, Metaweb Technologies Inc. (2009)
7. Heim, P., Ziegler, J., Lohmann, S.: gFacet: a browser for the web of data. In: Proceedings of the International Workshop on Interacting with Multimedia Content in the Social Semantic Web (IMC-SSW 2008), Aachen (2008)
8. Stadler, C., Martin, M., Auer, S.: Exploring the web of spatial data with Facete. In: Proceedings of the 23rd International Conference on World Wide Web, WWW 2014 Companion, pp. 175–178. ACM, New York (2014). https://doi.org/10.1145/2567948.2577022
9. Arenas, M., Grau, B.C., Kharlamov, E., Marciuska, S., Zheleznyakov, D.: Faceted search over RDF-based knowledge graphs. Web Semant. Sci. Serv. Agents World Wide Web **37**, (2016). https://doi.org/10.2139/ssrn.3199228
10. Moreno-Vega, J., Hogan, A.: GraFa: scalable faceted browsing for RDf graphs. In: Vrandečić, D., et al. (eds.) ISWC 2018. LNCS, vol. 11136, pp. 301–317. Springer, Cham (2018). https://doi.org/10.1007/978-3-030-00671-6_18

11. Li, C., Yan, N., Roy, S.B., Lisham, L., Das, G.: Facetedpedia: dynamic generation of query-dependent faceted interfaces for wikipedia. In: Proceedings of the 19th International Conference on World Wide Web, WWW 2010, pp. 651–660. ACM, New York (2010). https://doi.org/10.1145/1772690.1772757
12. Li, Y., Bandar, Z.A., Mclean, D.: An approach for measuring semantic similarity between words using multiple information sources. IEEE Trans. Knowl. Data Eng. **15**(4), 871–882 (2003). https://doi.org/10.1109/TKDE.2003.1209005

How to Validate Ontologies with Themis

Alba Fernández-Izquierdo[(✉)] and Raúl García-Castro

Ontology Engineering Group, Universidad Politécnica de Madrid, Madrid, Spain
{albafernandez,rgarcia}@fi.upm.es

Abstract. Validating ontologies regarding the requirements they need to satisfy is a crucial activity during ontology development in order to assure, both to domain experts and ontology developers, that the ontologies are complete regarding their needs. The aim of this work is to present Themis, a web-based tool for validating ontologies by means of test expressions, which represent the desired behaviour expected in an ontology if a requirement is satisfied. The purpose of these test expressions is to ease the formalization of the requirements into test cases and, therefore, the validation process.

Keywords: Ontology testing · Ontology requirements · Ontology development

1 Introduction

The validation of ontologies, which deals with assessing the correct conceptualization that the ontologies need to specify [6], is a crucial activity for assuring the quality of the ontologies delivered and published on the Web. One of the main concerns in the validation of ontologies is to check whether the ontology requirements that need to be covered are satisfied, with the aim of assuring both the domain experts and the ontology developers that the ontologies they are building or using are complete regarding their needs.

The main problem in validating ontologies regarding their requirements is the ambiguity of such ontological requirements, which sometimes are difficult to formalize into tests and to translate into axioms. There are some testing tools, such as TDDOnto [5] or OntologyTest [4], that execute tests on an ontology. TDD is focused on checking the presence of axioms and added them to the ontology if they are absent while OntologyTest supports several types of tests related to the instances of an ontology.

In this context, the goal within this paper is to present a testing tool to help ontology practitioners and users to validate ontologies regarding their functional requirements, i.e., the requirements which define the knowledge the ontology has to represent [7]. This tool is called Themis[1] and can be used independently of the ontology development platform without any installation. Themis supports a

---

[1] http://themis.linkeddata.es/.

© Springer Nature Switzerland AG 2019
P. Hitzler et al. (Eds.): ESWC 2019 Satellite Events, LNCS 11762, pp. 52–57, 2019.
https://doi.org/10.1007/978-3-030-32327-1_11

collection of test expressions [2] which are extracted from a collection of lexico-syntactic patterns (LSPs) [1] collected by CORAL Corpus [3] in order to ease the requirements formalization into tests, and that represent the expected knowledge that should be added to an ontology.

The remainder of this paper is structured as follows. Section 2 presents the main features of Themis while Sect. 3 describes its architecture. Section 4 describes the demonstration that will be performed. Finally, Sect. 5 outlines some conclusions and future steps to improve this testing tool.

2   Themis Features

Themis supports and implements a set of 15 test expressions which were extracted from the existing LSPs related to ontological requirements collected by the CORAL corpus. These 15 test expressions allows to validate every type of requirement identified in such corpus. Among others, these test expressions include the validation of subsumption relations or cardinalities in the ontology. The complete test expression catalogue is available in the Themis web site, along with the requirement templates that are associated to each test expression[2] in order to help the translation of requirements into test cases. Each of these test expressions has an associated implementation in order to check whether the ontology satisfies a test. The implementation process of the test expressions is presented in [2]. Themis allows to execute the same test expressions on several ontologies, which can be used to check if there are ontological commitments between them.

By loading an ontology or a set of ontologies, Themis checks whether the test expressions are passed or not. Four possible results can be returned for each test expression and each ontology:

1. *Undefined terms*: The terms in the test expression are not defined in the ontology to be analysed.
2. *Passed*: The ontology includes the terms and relations defined in the test.
3. *Absent relation*: The expected relation is not modelled in the ontology.
4. *Conflict*: The addition of the axioms related to the test expression leads to a conflict with the information included in the ontology.

Figure 1 shows the Themis home page, where the users can enter the ontologies and the test expressions. Themis also allows to load test suites that are generated and published on the Web as RDF files following the Verification Test Case ontology[3] by entering the URL of such file.

After executing such test expressions, Themis generates a table that includes: (1) the test executed, (2) the result of each test and (3) the problem found after the execution of the test. Figure 2 shows the Themis interface with some examples of possible results for an ontology. Since each test expression can be

---

[2] http://themis.linkeddata.es/tests-info.html.
[3] https://w3id.org/def/vtc#.

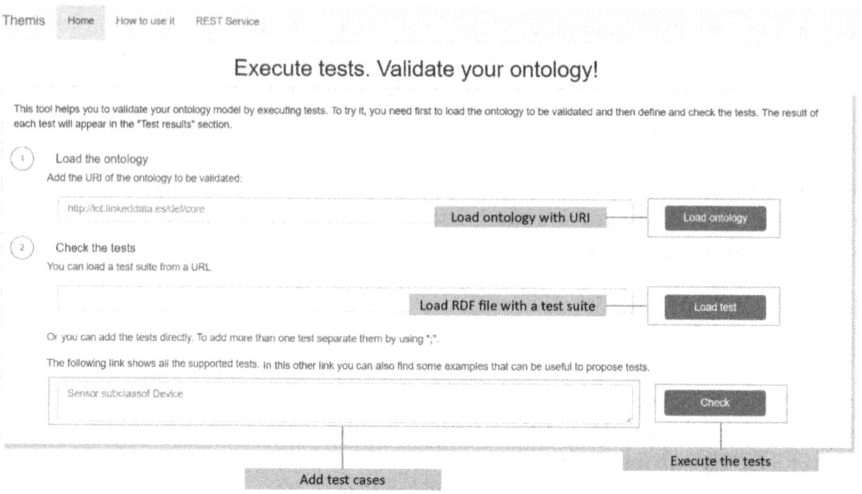

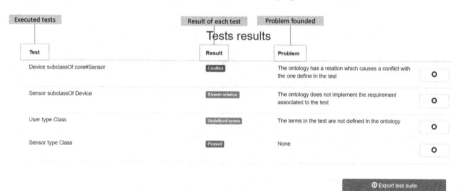

Fig. 1. Themis home page

Fig. 2. Example of results for an ontology

executed on more than one ontology, Themis displays each test expression result for each of the analysed ontologies. The collection of executed test expressions can be exported to an RDF file to allow its reuse on the same or other ontologies.

3 Architecture

Along this section the architecture of Themis, which is summarized in Fig. 3, is presented. Themis is a web-based tool based on JAVA,[4] HTML,[5] CSS,[6] and

---

[4] https://www.oracle.com/technetwork/java/javaee/overview/index.html.
[5] https://www.w3.org/html/wg.
[6] https://www.w3.org/Style/CSS.

jQuery[7] technologies. The user interface consists on a view where the user enters the URIs of the ontologies to be analysed, as well as the test expressions associated to a requirement. Then, the ontologies are parsed with the OWL API[8] and the associated implementation of the test expression is generated. To execute the test implementation on an ontology, Themis needs a glossary of terms to associate the generic terms in the test expression with a term in the ontology. For each ontology to be analysed, Themis automatically generates a glossary where the terms are the fragments of the URIs of each concept. For example, the term *http://iot.linkeddata.es/def/core#Device* will be represented as the term *Device* in the glossary. This glossary of terms provided by Themis can be modified by the users, since it is also displayed in the web user interface. Finally, the test execution results are displayed by means of the web user interface.

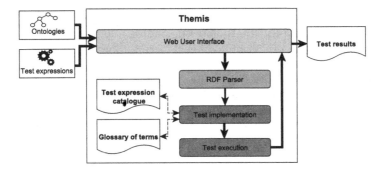

Fig. 3. Themis architecture

4   Demonstration

During the demonstration, two use cases will be analysed in order to show the participants all the features of Themis: (1) the validation of an ontology regarding its requirements and (2) the validation of two ontologies simultaneously to check whether there is an overlap of ontological commitments between them.

First, an ontology will be loaded in Themis and analysed by executing different types of test expressions. Additionally, such test expressions will be exported to an RDF file. Finally, a test suite that is publicly available on the Web in RDF will be loaded and executed on the analysed ontology.

Afterwards, another ontology will be loaded in Themis and several test expressions will be executed, which will allow the users to check whether the two loaded ontologies satisfy the same requirements.

---

[7] http://jquery.com.
[8] http://owlapi.sourceforge.net.

5   Conclusions

In this paper Themis is presented, along with its functionalities and its architecture, as a tool to validate ontologies through ontological requirements. This tool allows to: (1) execute a set of tests adding them directly in the web interface, (2) load a test suite in RDF and execute all its tests, (3) export the test suite to RDF, and (4) execute a test suite on one or several ontologies simultaneously.

Themis is currently being used by ontology engineers and it was also used in two European research projects, namely, the VICINITY[9] and the DELTA projects[10], where several ontologies are under development.

As part of the continuous process of improving Themis, if new types of requirements or LSPs are found, new tests associated to them are going to be included in the test expression catalogue supported by Themis. Furthermore, it is also planned to provide more types of results to the users, in addition to the four types that are provided so far. Finally, future work will be directed both to the addition of a feature to allow uploading a local ontology and to the integration of Themis in other ontology engineering tools, such as OnToology.[11]

Acknowledgments. This work is partially supported by the H2020 project VICIN-ITY: Open virtual neighbourhood network to connect intelligent buildings and smart objects (H2020-688467) and by a Predoctoral grant from the I+D+i program of the Universidad Politécnica de Madrid.

References

1. Aguado de Cea, G., Gómez-Pérez, A., Montiel-Ponsoda, E., Suárez-Figueroa, M.C.: Natural language-based approach for helping in the reuse of ontology design patterns. In: Gangemi, A., Euzenat, J. (eds.) EKAW 2008. LNCS (LNAI), vol. 5268, pp. 32–47. Springer, Heidelberg (2008). https://doi.org/10.1007/978-3-540-87696-0_6

2. Fernández-Izquierdo, A., García-Castro, R.: Requirements behaviour analysis for ontology testing. In: Faron Zucker, C., Ghidini, C., Napoli, A., Toussaint, Y. (eds.) EKAW 2018. LNCS (LNAI), vol. 11313, pp. 114–130. Springer, Cham (2018). https://doi.org/10.1007/978-3-030-03667-6_8

3. Fernández-Izquierdo, A., Poveda-Villalón, M., García-Castro, R.: CORAL: a corpus of ontological requirements annotated with lexico-syntactic patterns. In: European Semantic Web Conference (2019)

4. García-Ramos, S., Otero, A., Fernández-López, M.: OntologyTest: a tool to evaluate ontologies through tests defined by the user. In: Omatu, S., et al. (eds.) IWANN 2009. LNCS, vol. 5518, pp. 91–98. Springer, Heidelberg (2009). https://doi.org/10.1007/978-3-642-02481-8_13

5. Lawrynowicz, A., Keet, C.M.: The TDDonto tool for test-driven development of DL knowledge bases. In: Description Logics (2016)

---

[9] http://vicinity.iot.linkeddata.es.
[10] http://delta.iot.linkeddata.es.
[11] http://ontoology.linkeddata.es.

6. Suárez-Figueroa, M.C., Gómez-Pérez, A.: First attempt towards a standard glossary of ontology engineering terminology. In: International Conference on Terminology and Knowledge Engineering (2008)
7. Suárez-Figueroa, M.C., Gómez-Pérez, A., Villazón-Terrazas, B.: How to write and use the ontology requirements specification document. In: Meersman, R., Dillon, T., Herrero, P. (eds.) OTM 2009. LNCS, vol. 5871, pp. 966–982. Springer, Heidelberg (2009). https://doi.org/10.1007/978-3-642-05151-7_16

The Magic of Semantic Enrichment and NLP for Medical Coding

Nuria García-Santa[1]([✉]), Beatriz San Miguel[1], and Takanori Ugai[2]

[1] Fujitsu Laboratories of Europe, Camino Cerro de los Gamos,
28224 Pozuelo de Alarcón, Madrid, Spain
{nuria.garcia,beatriz.sanmiguelgonzalez}@uk.fujitsu.com
[2] Fujitsu Laboratories Ltd.,
4-1-1 Kamikodanaka, Nakahara-ku, Kawasaki 211-8588, Japan
ugai@fujitsu.com

Abstract. Artificial Intelligence technologies are every day more present in the medical domain. Several healthcare activities that were entirely done manually by experts in the past, now are reaching a high level of automatization thanks to a satisfactory integration between these technologies and the medical professionals. This is the case of the medical coding process, consisting on the annotation of clinical notes (free-text narrative reports) to standard medical classifications in order to align this information with the patients' records. This paper presents a combination of NLP and semantic enrichment techniques to generate an extended Biomedical Knowledge Graph in order to be exploited in the development of our automatic medical coding solution.

Keywords: Semantic enrichment · Natural Language Processing (NLP) · Knowledge graphs · Word embeddings · Medical coding

1 Introduction

The exponential increase of semi-structured and free-text narrative information in Electronic Health Records has created a recent need for automated tools to transform this data into valuable knowledge [3]. Currently, Knowledge Graphs and Semantic Web technologies in healthcare domain are expected to improve clinical outcomes [1]. The combination of Natural Language Processing (NLP) with semantic annotations has achieved crucial advances in the semi-automatization of data processing to build enriched knowledge bases for different healthcare use cases [5].

One healthcare use case of special interest is the medical coding. This is the process of annotating clinical notes directly with the codes of medical classifications/standards, such as the International Classification of Diseases (ICD)[1], for

---

[1] http://www.who.int/classifications/icd/en/.

© Springer Nature Switzerland AG 2019
P. Hitzler et al. (Eds.): ESWC 2019 Satellite Events, LNCS 11762, pp. 58–63, 2019.
https://doi.org/10.1007/978-3-030-32327-1_12

recording, diagnostic, billing and reporting purposes. Clinical notes are unstructured data related to patients created by healthcare professionals in a narrative form that contain medical terms which detail diagnosis, symptoms or procedures. As medical coding is usually performed manually by human medical coders, this can be extremely time-consuming and prone to errors [6].

The present paper proposes an approach using the combination of NLP and semantic enrichment to create automatically a Biomedical Knowledge Graph (BKG) that is the basis for our Medical Coding solution (our demonstration). Below, Sect. 2 describes our approach and demonstration, Sect. 3 the evaluation and results and finally Sect. 4 concludes and highlights future work.

2 Medical Coding Solution

2.1 Solution Overview

In this section we will describe our medical coding solution that is based on the generation and use of a proprietary BKG.

Figure 1 illustrates our workflow. First, an initial BKG is defined to store the medical classification for the coding (such as ICD-9 or ICD-10). Here, the nodes are the ICD entities with basic properties like code and description, and hierarchical relations among them. Next the BKG is semantically enriched in an automatic way with external resources such as medical vocabularies and scientific articles from PubMed.

With enriched BKG, we are able to carry out the medical coding task that involves Medical Named-Entity Recognition tools to identify diseases from clinical notes, string similarity comparison against our enriched BKG and heuristic approaches to return the outcome based on a scored ranking of potential ICD codes candidates.

2.2 The Semantic Enrichment of Biomedical Knowledge Graph

The semantic enrichment is focused on:

- Synonyms mapping from the Ontology of Consumer Health Vocabulary (OCHV)[2]: a tool has been developed to make a whole comparison over the descriptions of the ICD entities of our BKG with equivalent terms pointed by the above ontology. For those ICD entities annotated by the ontology, their synonyms are collected and included as other semantic feature within the specific ICD entity of the BKG. We used tokenization, noun chunk detection and string similarity techniques.
- Healthcare related terms extracted with Word Embedding techniques. This allows finding relationship between the descriptions of the ICD entities of the BKG and other new close medical terms (not synonyms). Word embeddings have been generated using the Word2Vec skip-gram algorithm[3] over a

---

[2] https://bioportal.bioontology.org/ontologies/OCHV.
[3] https://www.tensorflow.org/tutorials/representation/word2vec.

dataset created with the titles of PubMed medical articles. We have selected Word2Vec skip-gram because it works under low dimensional space representation of words and its architecture is focused on the probability calculation of the context of a given word. This provides a good approach to create related terms with good performance. Once the Word2Vec model is trained we use cosine-similarity measure to extract related terms. We make a whole comparison over ICD descriptions consulting each word against the model through cosine-similarity to retrieve the related terms and include them in the BKG.

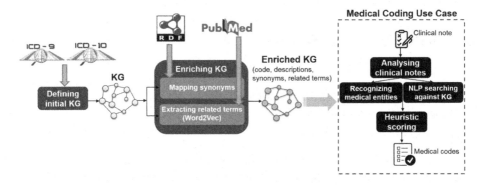

Fig. 1. Internal workflow of our approach

Next, a sample is shown for a specific medical entity in RDF. The data triples merge the origin information with enriched semantic data ('dbpedia-owl:synonym' and 'dbpedia-owl:related'). This semantic data is transformed to property-graph format to create our BKG for future exploitation. Property graphs provide compact models and express complex traversals queries with good performance. For the semantic data enrichment we have added other properties from Dbpedia[4] and the Human Disease Ontology[5] to define labels and relations of medical synonyms/related terms. Also we use the already mentioned OCHV ontology and Symptoms Ontology to codify specific symptom instances[6].

```
<http://fle.fujitsu.com/resource/med/J45>
    a dbpedia-owl:Disease ; rdfs:label "Asthma"@en, "Asma"@es ;
    dbpedia-owl:icd10 "J45" ; dbpedia-owl:icd9 "493" ;
    doid:has_symptom obo:SYMP_0019177 ; <!- fatigue ->
    dbpedia-owl:synonym "asthma bronchial"@en, "asthma disorders"@en ;
    rdfs:seeAlso <http://uth.tmc.edu/ontology/ochv#3972> ; <!- OCHV ->
    dbpedia-owl:related obo:SYMP_0000121 ; <!- rhinitis ->
```

---

[4] http://dbpedia.org/ontology/.
[5] http://purl.obolibrary.org/obo/doid.owl.
[6] http://purl.obolibrary.org/obo/symp.owl.

2.3   Demonstration

Our Medical Coding solution is developed in different languages (English, Spanish and Japanese). The enriched BKG is stored in Neo4j[7] because of its high performance in reading and writing thanks to the scalable architecture and the native graph storage, and because of its wide support. We provide a web-based interface to allow users to see clinical notes, its relevant entities, the associated standards codes, and to analyze texts dynamically. In Fig. 2 a screenshot of the demonstration is shown. Also we provide public access of a demo video[8].

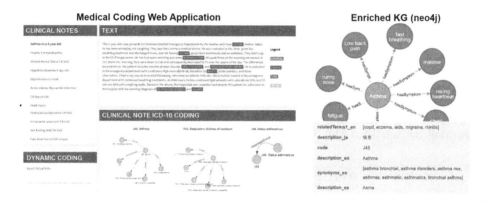

Fig. 2. Medical Coding system: (on the left) our web tool with a clinical note and its associated codes; (on the right) a part of the Enriched KG in neo4j

3   Preliminary Evaluation and Results

For evaluation, two main datasets have been used: (1) **MIMIC-III** [4], a publicly available clinical database that contains discharge summaries for English language with ICD-9 codes annotated by medical experts. We have selected 5000 random discharge summaries (**MIMIC-5000**) for the evaluation. (2) **200 private de-identified clinical notes** in English annotated manually by experts following the ICD-10 classification. We work with ~15000 ICD-10 codes and ~17000 ICD-9 codes. We demonstrate that our approach is able to manage different standards and there is no limitation to certain subsets. An advantage of our semantic approach is that there are no biases problems because there is no training over fixed target distribution. Our solution is based on semantic knowledge and covers all the codes distribution pointed out at the same level of coverage.

Medical coding is a multi-class, multi-label problem. We provide three potential codes for each clinical note, returning ICD-9 or ICD-10 codes depending on

---

7 https://neo4j.com/.

8 https://195.171.204.235/fujitsu-medical-coding.mp4.

the datasets. The F-score metric has been measured and the definition of the confusion matrix parameters are the next:

- True Positives = the codes assigned by the experts are among the selected ones by our method.
- False Positives = our method assigns codes to a text which does not have enough information to be coded according to the experts.
- False Negatives = the experts assign codes and our method is not able to assign any code, and our method assigns different codes from those selected by the experts.
- True Negatives = our method does not assign codes to a text which does not have enough information according to the experts.

The best metric performance to evaluate our approach is the F1-score which does a harmonic mean between precision and recall. We achieve good results with an F1-score of **0.75** for MIMIC-5000 and **0.72** for the 200 private clinical notes. In [2], the authors analyze current state-of-the-art methods for assigning ICD-9 codes to clinical notes and the best models achieve an F-score of 0.7233 returning the top 10 ICD-9. Our solution overcomes these results.

4   Conclusions and Future Work

We presented a prototype of an automatic Medical Coding solution that is based on semantic and NLP technologies. The evaluation results are very competitive with an F-score of 0.75 in the MIMIC-5000 dataset. Our work is easily adaptable to any medical classification, language and does not need pre-annotated datasets. The preliminary evaluation was just made for English language.

The exploitation of semantic enrichment and NLP techniques interlinked with the original data of the KG allows to build better mathematical models for the automatic medical coding, which means more context for resolving this problem and better performance and results [2].

For future work, we will compare our approach against different Neural Networks approaches. Additionally, we will provide further evaluation and comparisons between languages and methods. Moreover, we want to extend the system to more languages, apply cross-lingual approaches and analyze how to merge semantic and Deep Learning approaches.

References

1. Barisevičius, G., et al.: Supporting digital healthcare services using semantic web technologies. In: Vrandečić, D., et al. (eds.) ISWC 2018. LNCS, vol. 11137, pp. 291–306. Springer, Cham (2018). https://doi.org/10.1007/978-3-030-00668-6_18
2. Huang, J., Osorio, C., Sy, L.W.: An empirical evaluation of deep learning for ICD-9 code assignment using MIMIC-III clinical notes. arXiv preprint arXiv:1802.02311 (2018)

3. Jiang, F., et al.: Artificial intelligence in healthcare: past, present and future. Stroke Vasc. Neurol. **2**(4), 230–243 (2017)
4. Johnson, A.E., et al.: MIMIC-III, a freely accessible critical care database. Sci. Data **3**, 160035 (2016)
5. Lee, Y., Geller, J.: Semantic enrichment for medical ontologies. J. Biomed. Inform. **39**(2), 209–226 (2006)
6. Omalley, K.J., Cook, K.F., Price, M.D., Wildes, K.R., Hurdle, J.F., Ashton, C.M.: Measuring diagnoses: ICD code accuracy. Health Serv. Res. **40**(5p2), 1620–1639 (2005)

An Ontology of Finnish Historical Occupations

Lia Gasbarra[1]([envelope]), Mikko Koho[1], Ilkka Jokipii[3,4], Heikki Rantala[1], and Eero Hyvönen[1,2]

[1] Semantic Computing Research Group (SeCo), Aalto University, Espoo, Finland
lia.gasbarra@aalto.fi
[2] HELDIG – Helsinki Centre for Digital Humanities, University of Helsinki, Helsinki, Finland
[3] The National Archives of Finland, Helsinki, Finland
[4] Faculty of Arts, University of Helsinki, Helsinki, Finland

Abstract. Historical datasets often impose the need to study groups of people based on occupation or social status. This paper presents first results in creating an ontology of historical Finnish occupations, AMMO, that enables selection of groups of people based on their occupation, occupational groups, or socioeconomic class. For interoperability, AMMO is linked to the HISCO international historical occupation classification and to a late 20th century Finnish occupational classification. AMMO will be used as a component in two semantic portals for Finnish war history.

1 Introduction

The Finnish Civil War and the Second World War (WW2) are of great interest to historians and to the wider public: most Finns have relatives who died or participated in these wars as soldiers. For example, the WarSampo semantic portal [1] has had more than 400000 users since its opening in 2015.

An interesting piece of information in war-related datasets are the occupations and social statuses of the soldiers. For example, historians studying the Finnish Civil War are interested in learning why some people survived the prisoner camps and some did not—is this related to the occupation and social status of the prisoners? The problem is, however, that there are circa 1400 occupational labels in the Civil War data alone without any structure.

This paper presents the work done so far in studying, and harmonizing Finnish historical occupational labels, consisting mainly of manual expert work. AMMO, our historical Finnish occupation ontology under development, will be a fundamental resource containing Finnish historical occupational labels from 1914–1945, based on the War Victims[1] and WarSampo[2] datasets, in SKOS format. AMMO occupations are linked to the international historical classification

---

[1] http://www.ldf.fi/dataset/narc-sotasurmat1914-22.
[2] http://www.ldf.fi/dataset/warsa.

© Springer Nature Switzerland AG 2019
P. Hitzler et al. (Eds.): ESWC 2019 Satellite Events, LNCS 11762, pp. 64–68, 2019.
https://doi.org/10.1007/978-3-030-32327-1_13

of occupations HISCO [7] that is based on historical data collections from European and North American economies. HISCO provides a hierarchical backbone of occupational groups, as well as social stratification information through several measures like HISCLASS and HISCAM [3]. AMMO is also aligned with the Finnish Classification of occupations 1980 [6], a social stratification classification system in use in Finland.

This paper presents details on the manual harmonization work of national historical occupational labels in heterogeneous datasets. The AMMO ontology model and more detailed ontology creation process is presented in [2].

Related Work. Belgian occupational titles have been linked to early HISCO, with an overview of the common coding problems [4]. The Historical Sample of the Netherlands contains a representative sample of 78,000 people born in the Netherlands during 1812–1922, where occupational titles have been standardized and mapped to HISCO [8]. HISCO has been applied to the historical data of Catalonian population from the fifteenth to the twentieth century [5].

2   Occupations in Historical Datasets

The source datasets of AMMO are presented in Table 1, containing personal information of a total of 139 091 historical persons (soldiers) annotated with thousands of different occupation labels. The amount of people per dataset, and distinct occupational labels are shown. In the datasets, alternative or abridged forms of the same occupational title are often present (for example: 'hitsari' and 'hitsaaja' for welder). In some cases, the occupational title of a person is actually not an occupation but a social role or status, such as 'student', 'nobleman', 'child', or 'tenant'. Although occupations in HISCO are by definition solely activities that generate a remuneration, it is also possible to categorize these social roles or statuses (e.g., student) through HISCO relation and status coding.

The First World War (WW1) War Victims dataset contains the deceased of the WW1 era, which consist mostly of the Finnish Civil War. The data is gathered originally from various heterogeneous Finnish sources. It is not solely based on primary sources, but is a result of research, interpretation, and unification of nonhomogeneous data. The database presents the interpretation of sources provided by their compilers during different phases of archival work. These entries were gathered in many cases from parish records taken at the moment of death and/or other registers of parties, unions, local administrations and alike.

Table 1. Datasets providing Finnish historical occupations for AMMO.

Name	Data provider	Persons	Occupations
WW1 War Victims	National Archives	39 931	1391
WW2 Death Records	National Archives	94 700	2155
WW2 Prisoners of War	National Prisoners of War Project	4460	576

Both of the WW2 datasets shown in Table 1 are part of the WarSampo data. The Prisoners of War dataset contains the actual information source for most of the occupation annotations, whereas the death records lack this information. The WarSampo persons present a balanced sample of the Finnish male population during WW2, as all capable men had to take part in the war. Hence the occupation distribution is also well balanced among social classes. Female occupations are not well represented, as the datasets contain only about 1340 female records.

3   Transforming Occupational Labels into an Ontology

The occupation literals were extracted from the datasets, and easily recognizable various spellings of worker occupations are grouped together programmatically, as well as almost identical occupational labels based on a Jaro-Winkler string similarity distance. This resulted in a flat vocabulary of 2053 distinct occupation groups that contained 2977 distinct labels. This data was used as the starting point for manual harmonization, structuring, and linking work using a spreadsheet that is transformed into RDF.

The occupation labels were manually studied and different spellings of the same occupation were harmonized, while quantifying whether the label actually refers to an occupation, or to a title or a social role. Occupations were linked to HISCO basic codes, and if applicable, to relation, status and product codes. Linking was also done to the Finnish Classification of Occupations 1980 (COO1980), which was also used as a controlled vocabulary to help in the harmonization and as a source of information on occupations' details. COO1980 is based on, and compatible with, the Nordic classification of occupations from 1963, which is based on ISCO-58, and so shares the same roots with HISCO. COO1980 is compatible with several 20th century national censuses.

The attribution of a HISCO code to each occupational label was carried out without further insight into the individual person records. In some cases, the occupational label is too general [4] to really understand what a person with that occupation label has been doing. For example, the occupation "hioja" (grinder or polisher) might correspond to several different categories of activities, related to, e.g., glass, cement, wood, metal, stone, or tools production. In these cases, the 99999 HISCO code was assigned (the title is too vague or ambiguous).

The HISCO relation codes were used for the abundant occupations with a family relation, such as "driver's child", "driver's widow" or "training school teacher's wife": such entries have a historical foundation in a specific cultural context and therefore should be registered as such. Women were often registered as wives with only the husband's activity mentioned. For example, "butcher's wife" is linked to "butcher" HISCO occupation code with the corresponding relation code (11). The HISCO status codes add information regarding the status of workers and, with the basic code, is important for determining the socioeconomic status: master artisan, apprentice, etc.

4 Discussion

This paper presented the foundational work in creating an ontology of Finnish historical occupations. AMMO will enable answering research questions relating to occupations and social stratification in historical datasets. For example, the socioeconomic statuses of the two sides fighting in the Finnish Civil War can be compared. Combined with a historical place ontology, this can be further expanded to understand which social strata have joined either side in the war in different parts of the country.

The application of HISCO to a national reality presents complex tasks: creating a historical thesaurus of occupational names in the national language(s), possibly adapting the coding or creating additional coding to refine information. For example, for the Catalonian project [5] additional coding on institution was added to the administrative occupations, in order to distinguish between Colonial Administration, Army, Diplomacy, Local government administration, etc.

When assigning a HISCO code, it is important to find a balance between accuracy and generalization. In our case, HISCO coding is performed on secondary sources and therefore on occupational labels arranged into groups; the analysis is not performed on individual person records. In general, when an occupational label is too vague, further research on production activities in the place of residence and on familial occupational records should be done.

Our future work will study and analyze the aforementioned datasets with AMMO. AMMO is planned to be released in 2019, and will be used as a shared ontology for Finnish historical datasets in WarSampo and in an upcoming portal of the Finnish Civil War.

References

1. Hyvönen, E., et al.: WarSampo data service and semantic portal for publishing linked open data about the second world war history. In: Sack, H., Blomqvist, E., d'Aquin, M., Ghidini, C., Ponzetto, S.P., Lange, C. (eds.) ESWC 2016. LNCS, vol. 9678, pp. 758–773. Springer, Cham (2016). https://doi.org/10.1007/978-3-319-34129-3_46
2. Koho, M., Gasbarra, L., Tuominen, J., Rantala, H., Jokipii, I., Hyvönen, E.: AMMO ontology of finnish historical occupations. In: Proceedings of the First International Workshop on Open Data and Ontologies for Cultural Heritage (ODOCH 2019) (2019)
3. Mandemakers, K., et al.: HSN standardized, HISCO-coded and classified occupational titles, release 2018.01. IISG, Amsterdam (2018)
4. Matthijs, K., Peeters, H., Van den Troost, A., Van de Velde, I.: The coding of 19th century occupations from three different Belgian regions into ISCO68. KU Leuven, Departement Sociologie; Leuven (1998)
5. Pujadas-Mora, J.M., Marín, J.R., Villar, C.: Propuestas metodológicas para la aplicación de HISCO en el caso de Cataluña, siglos XV-XX. Revista de Demografía Histórica **32**, 181–219 (2014)
6. Statistics Finland: Classification of Occupations 1980. Statistics Finland (1981)

7. Van Leeuwen, M.H.D., Maas, I., Miles, A.: HISCO: Historical International Standard Classification of Occupations. Leuven University Press, Louvain (2002)
8. Zijdeman, R., Lambert, P.: Measuring social structure in the past: a comparison of historical class schemes and occupational stratification scales on dutch 19th and early 20th century data. J. Belg. Hist. **40**(1–2), 111–141 (2010)

Information Extraction in Editorial Setting. A Tale of PDFs

Anna Lisa Gentile$^{(\boxtimes)}$, Daniel Gruhl, Petar Ristoski, and Steve Welch

IBM Research Almaden, San Jose, CA, USA
{annalisa.gentile,petar.ristoski}@ibm.com
{dgruhl,welchs}@us.ibm.com

Abstract. In the last decade the Semantic Web initiative has promoted the construction of knowledge resources that are understandable by both humans and machines. Nonetheless considerable scientific and technical content is still locked behind proprietary formats, especially PDF files. While many solutions have been proposed to shift the publishing mechanism to more accessible formats, we believe that is paramount, especially in business scenarios, to be able to tap into this type of content and be able to extract machine readable semantic information from it.

In this demo we show how we can process and semantically annotate Medication Package Inserts, publicly available from the pharmaceutical companies in the form of PDF files. Our proposed solution is fully integrated with a standard PDF viewer and does not require the subject matter expert to use any external software.

1 Introduction

The Semantic Web community is constantly pushing the barrier on processing and producing knowledge that is understandable by both humans and machines. Nonetheless when it comes to scientific content, much of the information is conveyed by editorial publishers and locked behind proprietary formatting - e.g. in PDF files - which are not directly machine readable. In recent years many scientific publishers have been showcasing the benefit of augmenting scholarly content with semantic information, while academic initiatives have been encouraging the idea of "semantic publishing" [5] where the authors themselves augment their scientific papers with semantic annotations.

Despite many such initiatives, any information system that relies on scientific knowledge needs to extract information from various proprietary document formats, very often PDFs. Many approaches for information extraction start with the assumption that raw text is available and the task of obtaining such text from diverse sources (Web pages, text documents, PDF documents, etc.) is neglected. Nonetheless in many business applications it is extremely important to (i) assure ease and accuracy of extraction from whichever the input format and (ii) perform the annotation and extraction tasks directly on the input documents, without introducing costly (and often disruptive for the end user) format transformation.

© Springer Nature Switzerland AG 2019
P. Hitzler et al. (Eds.): ESWC 2019 Satellite Events, LNCS 11762, pp. 69–74, 2019.
https://doi.org/10.1007/978-3-030-32327-1_14

We propose a strategy to perform such information extraction tasks directly on the input documents, so as to be completely transparent for the end user. As our focus is on PDF documents, we add small task specific semantic annotators directly in to the PDF (and which are thus viewable with a standard PDF reader). These new semantic annotators are trained on demand, with a human-in-the-loop methodology, and modularly added to the document.

In the demo we showcase an application on extracting semantic information from medical documents, specifically from publicly available patient package inserts distributed in PDF format. We train and apply (i) an ontology-based Named Entity Recognition (NER) tool to recognize adverse drug events, (i) a sentence annotator that identify whole sentences that express a relation between a drug and its potential Adverse Drug Reaction, and (iii) a knowledge based lookup annotator to identify drugs in the text.

The advantage of our proposed solution is it's ability to unlock semantic information from proprietary documents - especially PDF - seamlessly, and allowing new annotators to be added modularly on demand, after a training interaction with the end user.

2   State of the Art

Much of today's scientific and technical content is locked behind proprietary document formats, making it difficult to consume for analytic systems.

In recent years many scientific publishers have been showcasing the benefit of augmenting scholarly content with semantic information. Examples are the Sci-Graph project[1] by Springer-Nature, the Dynamic Knowledge Platforms (DKP) by Elsevier[2] among others. Academic projects such as Biotea [3] pursue the same goal of creating machine readable and sharable knowledge extracted from scientific content in proprietary format (specifically XML files). Academic initiatives have been encouraging the idea of "semantic publishing" [5] where the authors themselves augment their scientific papers with semantic annotations, instead of relying on post-processing information extraction performed by third parties. Other initiatives aim at maintaining sharable knowledge about the metadata of scientific publication [4].

While significant effort has been put into extracting and maintaining semantic information from scientific publications, much of the content is still locked inside PDF files. This is even more true for technical documents that are not necessarily scientific papers, but which still contain extremely valuable information, e.g. as the use case of Medication Package Inserts that we are presenting in this demo. There are several efforts in the literature which explore extracting information from PDFs directly. Early examples [7,8] focus on parsing textual content and extracting structured information. They do so without maintaining the user interaction with the original files. This is undesirable, especially in cases where the layout of the text (e.g., tables) or ancillary information (e.g., chemical

---

[1] https://www.springernature.com/scigraph.

[2] http://data.elsevier.com/documentation/index.html.

structures or other illustrations) are critical context to the understanding of the text. More recent examples exploit the specific structure of certain PDF files, therefore also using specific visual clues of the documents to train the extraction models [1,2,6].

On the other hand we propose a solution that is agnostic of any specific structure of the input file and that is fully integrated within a PDF, and thus can be viewed with the PDF reader the subject matter expert is already using. Our solution allows the user to visually identify the information which is semantically relevant for their business case. Such information is used by the system to train semantic annotators, which are then integrated directly in the PDF viewer tool that the subject matter expert is already using.

3 Use Case: Extracting Semantics from Medication Package Inserts

During the demo we will showcase how we use the system to ingest, annotate and semantically enrich Medication Package Inserts.

A package insert (PI) is a document included in the package of a medication that provides information about that drug and its use. In U.S.A., annually all pharmaceutical companies must provide updated information about all their drugs to the U.S. Food and Drug Administration (FDA)[3], including the package inserts. All this information is then made publicly available on the FDA Web site. $DAILYMED$[4] provides access to $106,938$ drug listings including daily updates. Such daily updates can be very useful to monitor the changes in the package inserts. For example, new adverse drug reactions could be added, the dosage of the drug is changed, new drug interactions are discovered, etc. Such information is highly valuable to patients and medical practitioners. However, manual monitoring for such changes is not viable and automation is needed. With our tool, we can speed up the process of identifying the most relevant information in the updated documents and present it to the subject matter experts, e.g., drug names mentions, adverse drug reactions, dosage terms, and important textual changes.

3.1 Annotating Patient Package Inserts

The system takes as input a collection of documents $D = d_1, d_2, \ldots, d_n$ (PIs in this case) and enriches each document d_i with semantic annotations. In the instance of the system that we will demonstrate, the implemented semantic annotators include a set of entity types $E = e_1, e_2, ..., e_n$ and textual annotations $A = a_1, a_2, \ldots, a_n$. The entities e_i are either resolved to a specific Knowledge Base - as in the case of Adverse Drug Reactions (ADR) that we resolve using the MedDRA ontology[5] or simply typed - as in the case for Drugs where we

---

[3] https://www.fda.gov/.

[4] https://dailymed.nlm.nih.gov/dailymed.

[5] https://www.meddra.org.

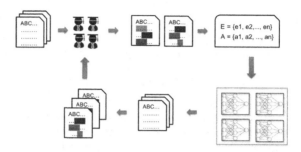

Fig. 1. Proprietary document annotation. System workflow.

use a dictionary lookup mechanism. The textual annotations a_i in this demo are sentences that identify salient information as defined by a subject matter expert. Specifically these are sentences that express a potential causal relation between a drug and an ADR. Figure 1 shows the overall workflow of the system. In essence the annotation process runs in 2 phases, i.e., (i) initialization and (ii) adjudication.

Initialization. The subject matter expert uploads the desired collection of documents to the system. The subject matter experts provides some seed annotation of the semantic information they want to extract and specifies external Knowledge Resources to be used, if any. Once a small number of annotations are provided, the system builds learning models for each type of annotations.

Adjudication. The initial models are applied to the whole document collection. The SME performs the adjudication of the produced semantic annotations and can (i) correct the mistakes and (ii) identify and add missing annotations. After each batch of corrections (where the batch size can be adjusted), the models are retrained and reapplied on the rest of the documents. New semantic annotations can be added at any time, i.e., once a new item is added the models are retrained and are able to identify the new item, being entity or textual annotation.

With such a system the SME has full control of what types of semantic annotations are going to be identified, and they can enforce that the accuracy of the system is always above a certain threshold (even 100% if they are willing or required to manually review the whole collection). The system simply assists the user to improve their efficiency in identifying the semantic annotations of interest, and reduce the human error. The produced semantic annotation enrich the initial document, without altering its layout (and potentially obscuring the context needed to understand the text). To realize that, we add semantic layers on top of the original document, where each layer contains the information for a specific semantic annotation. Figure 2 shows an example of annotated PI, as depicted in Adobe Acrobat Reader[6]. The results of the semantic annotators can be toggled on and off at will. For annotators that implement entity resolution, the recognized entities are linkable and refer to the external sources.

---

[6] https://get.adobe.com/reader/.

Fig. 2. Example of annotated Medication Package Insert.

4   Conclusions and Future Work

In this demo we showcase our solution to perform on-demand information extraction directly from PDF files. The key strengths of our solution are that the subject matter expert can train new semantic annotators which are directly integrated in their PDF viewer tool. Being able to semantically annotate PDF files is an extremely important capability in many business scenarios. In this demo we show an application with Medical Package Inserts, but one can envision many other scenarios, such as scientific publishing, legal contracts, the recruiting business - where many applicants' resumes are PDF files - just to mention a few. In all these scenarios it is crucial to be able to quickly train the extraction models and to deliver the results in a way that is familiar to the subject matter expert, without disrupting any existing workflow.

References

1. Abekawa, T., Aizawa, A.: SideNoter: scholarly paper browsing system based on PDF restructuring and text annotation. In: COLING 2016, pp. 136–140 (2016). http://www.aclweb.org/anthology/C16-2029
2. Ahmad, R., Afzal, M.T., Qadir, M.A.: Information extraction from PDF sources based on rule-based system using integrated formats. In: Sack, H., Dietze, S., Tordai, A., Lange, C. (eds.) SemWebEval 2016. CCIS, vol. 641, pp. 293–308. Springer, Cham (2016). https://doi.org/10.1007/978-3-319-46565-4_23
3. Garcia, A., Lopez, F., Garcia, L., Giraldo, O., Bucheli, V., Dumontier, M.: Biotea: semantics for pubmed central. PeerJ. **2018**, 1–26 (2018). https://doi.org/10.7717/peerj.4201
4. Nuzzolese, A.G., Gentile, A.L., Presutti, V., Gangemi, A.: Conference linked data: the ScholarlyData project. In: Groth, P., Simperl, E., Gray, A., Sabou, M., Krötzsch, M., Lecue, F., Flöck, F., Gil, Y. (eds.) ISWC 2016. LNCS, vol. 9982, pp. 150–158. Springer, Cham (2016). https://doi.org/10.1007/978-3-319-46547-0_16
5. Shotton, D.: Semantic publishing: the coming revolution in scientific journal publishing. Learn. Publish. **22**(2), 85–94 (2009). https://doi.org/10.1087/2009202
6. Staar, P.W.J., Dolfi, M., Auer, C., Bekas, C.: Corpus conversion service: a machine learning platform to ingest documents at scale. In: SIGKDD 2018, pp. 774–782. ACM (2018). https://doi.org/10.1145/3219819.3219834

7. Yuan, F., Liu, B.O.: A new method of information extraction from PDF files. In: ICMLC 2005, pp. 18–21. IEEE (2005)
8. Yuan, F., Liu, B., Yu, G.: A study on information extraction from PDF files. In: Yeung, D.S., Liu, Z.-Q., Wang, X.-Z., Yan, H. (eds.) ICMLC 2005. LNCS (LNAI), vol. 3930, pp. 258–267. Springer, Heidelberg (2006). https://doi.org/10.1007/11739685_27

An Open Source Dataset and Ontology for Product Footprinting

Agneta Ghose[1], Katja Hose[2], Matteo Lissandrini[2(✉)],
and Bo Pedersen Weidema[1]

[1] Department of Planning, Aalborg University, Aalborg, Denmark
{agneta,bweidema}@plan.aau.dk
[2] Department of Computer Science, Aalborg University, Aalborg, Denmark
{khose,matteo}@cs.aau.dk

Abstract. Product footprint describes the environmental impacts of a product system. To identify such impact, Life Cycle Assessment (LCA) takes into account the entire lifespan and production chain, from material extraction to final disposal or recycling. This requires gathering data from a variety of heterogeneous sources, but current access to those is limited and often expensive. The BONSAI project, instead, aims to build a shared resource where the community can contribute to data generation, validation, and management decisions. In particular, its first goal is to produce an open dataset and an open source toolchain capable of supporting LCA calculations. This will allow the science of lifecycle assessment to perform in a more transparent and more reproducible way, and will foster data integration and sharing. Linked Open Data and semantic technologies are a natural choice for achieving this goal. In this work, we present the first results of this effort (https://github.com/ BONSAMURAIS/): (1) the core of a comprehensive ontology for industrial ecology and associated relevant data; and (2) the first steps towards an RDF dataset and associated tools to incorporate several large LCA data sources.

1 Introduction

Life Cycle Assessment (LCA), also called "product footprinting", is concerned with analyzing the environmental impact of products, taking into account their complete production chain and lifespan [1]. For instance, assessing the impacts of operating a solar array goes beyond the pure manufacturing and assembly of the photo-voltaic modules. It also includes all impacts and emissions relative to the extraction of raw materials, transportation, installation, operation, and the final disposal. Hence, to produce an LCA in this case, it first requires the gathering of all relevant data from different sources into a so-called Life Cycle Inventory (LCI). Then, such data can be integrated and processed with state-of-the-art models and procedures. LCA is a highly complex and interdisciplinary field that

---

Authors are listed in alphabetical order.

© Springer Nature Switzerland AG 2019
P. Hitzler et al. (Eds.): ESWC 2019 Satellite Events, LNCS 11762, pp. 75–79, 2019.
https://doi.org/10.1007/978-3-030-32327-1_15

requires synthesizing information from a variety of discipline-specific studies. Nonetheless, it has a fundamental role in the realization of a sustainable world where human needs are met while minimizing the harm to the environment and without reducing the ability of future generations to meet their needs [4].

To a large extent, LCA currently exploits large background databases, often proprietary, which are expensive to access and consequently provide limited access to both the data and decisions on its management. Therefore, given the transversal importance of LCA, following the principles of Open and FAIR data [5], there is the requirement to establish an Open Source dataset for product footprinting. While past studies have outlined compact ontologies that formalize the spatio-temporal scope of activities in LCA [3,6], those are limited in their modeling of the domain [4] and have not resulted in the publication of open datasets. This work, led by the BONSAI (https://bonsai.uno) non-for-profit association, plans to overcome the limitation of previous initiatives. Here, we describe the first results of this effort, which involves experts and companies in the sector of environmental assessment and sustainability planning, and the long-term plan for the first open dataset and ontology for product footprinting.

2 Product Footprints: Development, Ontology, and Data

The BONSAI initiative has three main objectives: (1) the definition of a comprehensive ontology for industrial ecology (IE), (2) the publication and maintenance of an open source IE dataset for LCA, and (3) the development of a toolbox for data ingestion, integration, validation, and sharing to maintain such a dataset.

2.1   The BONSAI Ontology and Data

Domain and Purpose: The BONSAI dataset and its accompanying ontology describe entities that play important roles in representing the environmental impacts associated with all the stages of a product's life. To identify the entities and concepts that are expected, we defined a number of competency questions. Example competency questions include: (i) Is the flow x a determining flow for activity y (e.g., electricity from a power plant)? (ii) What is the amount of flow x emitted as output during the time period y (e.g., the emission of landfill gas)? (iii) What is the location of the agent performing activity y (e.g., where is the coal power plant located) and what other agents performing the same type of activity are present in the same location?

The competency questions highlight the centrality of two concepts: the Flow (e.g., some steel being produced, some coal being consumed) and the associated Activity (the production of steel). In LCA models, each activity is a *consequence* of a specific determining flow (e.g., the activity of steel production is a consequence of the demand for the flow of steel), while some other flows are subordinate (e.g., the consumption of coal and the CO_2 emission).

Ontology Building: To build the domain ontology we interacted with experts and analyzed existing datasets. We started from EXIOBASE (www.exiobase.eu), a well established database (with a tabular model) comprising, among others, 43 countries, 200 products, and 163 industries. Data published by international initiatives – Food and Agriculture Organization (FAO), United Nations Environment Programme (UNEP) – is also frequently used by LCA practitioners. We expanded existing ontologies drafted in the same context [3,6]. These original proposals did not provide (a) an adequate vocabulary for expressing all the required details of a flow and (b) clear linking to other relevant ontologies. We also identified a set of relevant ontologies and databases in complementary domains (e.g., units of measure[1], time[2], and GeoNames). In particular, we *identified important terms* like Flow, Activity, Input/Output, and Agent and we *defined classes and class hierarchies* with the most important terms being top-level classes (see Fig. 1). We note that we have explicitly established mappings with other interconnected ontologies and vocabularies (e.g., Schema.org) in order to foster data integration, discovery, and alignment. In the future, we plan to expand and integrate other vocabularies, e.g, vocabularies for data provenance[3] and statistical data[4]. We have *defined properties for each class*, specifying the instances of classes representing allowed domain and range values. Among others, an important aspect is that each Activity must be associated with at a least one Flow that is classified as Determining Flow.

Data Extraction, Ontology Evaluation, and Documentation: The appropriateness of the ontology has been tested by a technical evaluation where 12 domain experts assessed the correctness and expressive power of the available definition against the reference dataset. A conversion tool has been developed to process the EXIOBASE data and produce the corresponding RDF data. The set of competency questions were revised and used, with corresponding SPARQL queries, to verify the appropriateness of the model. The ontology and the dataset are accompanied with an external "living" documentation that describes among others, the ontology purpose, class definitions, description of class properties, and evaluation (at https://github.com/BONSAMURAIS).

Overview of the Ontology: The main classes Activity and Flow have broad definitions according to the literature [3,4], which facilitate their use with data supplied from external sources. Core concepts are defined as follows (Fig. 1).

Activity is the act of doing within a temporal interval, this includes both human activities (e.g., production, consumption, and market activities) and environmental mechanisms (e.g., radiative forcing, pollination). *Agent* is defined as an entity (person or thing) that performs an activity. An agent has a location and the location of the activity is also determined by the agent performing it. *Flow* is defined as an entity that is produced or consumed by activities or stored

---

[1] www.ontology-of-units-of-measure.org.

[2] www.w3.org/TR/owl-time/.

[3] www.w3.org/TR/prov-o/.

[4] www.w3.org/TR/vocab-data-cube/.

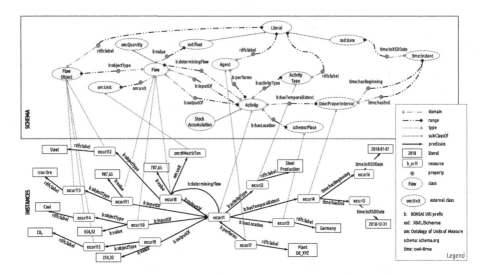

Fig. 1. The core of the ontology and an example instantiation.

within an activity (e.g., stock). *Determining Flow* is the flow of an activity determining its primary function. All other flows are co-produced by or demanded for in that specific activity but do not determine its existence. Usually, a change in the determining flow will affect the volume of all other flows involved.

2.2 Tools and Future Work

The long term plan is to allow the dataset to evolve and to third parties to contribute to it. Therefore, the project will provide tools building upon the state of the art [2] (i) to extract data from published studies and databases, (ii) to normalize to common industry and product classifiers, (iii) to assess data quality for many types of industrial ecology facts, and (iv) to build interpolation models for data across time and space.

3 Conclusions

Effective sustainability assessment requires access to data from a variety of heterogeneous sources. We believe that this effort will ensure low barriers for contributions from non-experts and for cross-dataset editing and that it will greatly benefit from the expertise and capabilities of the semantic web community.

Acknowledgments. This research was partially funded by the Danish Council for Independent Research (DFF) under grant agreement no. DFF-4093-00301B and Aalborg University's Talent Programme.

References

1. Curran, M.A.: Environmental life-cycle assessment. Int. J. Life Cycle Assess. **1**(3), 179–179 (1996)
2. Harth, A., Hose, K., Schenkel, R.: Linked Data Management. Chapman and Hall/CRC, Boca Raton (2014)
3. Janowicz, K., et al.: A minimal ontology pattern for life cycle assessment data. In: WOP. CEUR-WS.org (2015)
4. Weidema, B.P., Schmidt, J., Fantke, P., Pauliuk, S.: On the boundary between economy and environment in life cycle assessment. Int. J. Life Cycle Assess. **23**(9), 1839–1846 (2018)
5. Wilkinson, M.D., Dumontier, M., et al.: The FAIR Guiding Principles for scientific data management and stewardship. Sci. Data **3**, 160018 (2016)
6. Yan, B., et al.: An ontology for specifying spatiotemporal scopes in life cycle assessment. In: Diversity++@ ISWC, pp. 25–30 (2015)

IEDM: An Ontology for Irradiation Experiments Data Management

Blerina Gkotse[1,2(✉)], Pierre Jouvelot[1], and Federico Ravotti[2]

[1] MINES ParisTech, PSL University, Paris, France
[2] Experimental Physics Department, CERN, 1211 Geneva 23, Switzerland
Blerina.Gkotse@cern.ch

Abstract. Irradiation experiments (IE) are an essential step in the development of High-Energy Physics (HEP) particle accelerators and detectors. They are used to assess the radiation hardness of experimental devices by simulating, in a short time, the common long-term degradation effects due to energy loss in matter. Usually carried out with ionizing radiation, these complex processes require highly specialized infrastructures called "irradiation facilities". Aiming to promote knowledge sharing and digital management of IEs, we introduce IEDM, a new Irradiation Experiments Data Management ontology. This work presents an overview of the development of the key concepts and structure of IEDM while discussing possible applications.

Keywords: Ontology · OWL · Irradiation Experiment · Data Management

1 Introduction

In an irradiation experiment (IE), a piece of material (e.g., electronic chip, silicon detector, etc.) is purposefully exposed to radiation (of electromagnetic or corpuscular nature). IEs are often necessary, for instance, when designing and building High-Energy Physics (HEP) experiments. In HEP, the purpose of performing an IE is typically the qualification of detectors or electronic components in a radiation environment equivalent to the one these devices will encounter in actual HEP experiments, thus simulating, in a short time, long-term radiation-induced degradation effects [1]. Worldwide, IEs also find applications in other scientific and technical fields. For example, in space technology and avionics, the materials composing aircraft or spaceships are affected by radiation damage during their flights. Therefore, engineers need also to test components during their development projects. Other examples of IEs can be found in industry, where they are used for various purposes such as food sterilization or seed treatment. IEs are also performed on patients as part of radiotherapy treatments or for medical imaging in hospital environments. Even though these IEs are performed for a wide range of fields and in different infrastructures (e.g., hospitals, factories, and scientific institutes), they can all be assimilated, in an abstract manner, to what is called an "irradiation facility".

An earlier thorough survey about existing HEP irradiation facilities and their practices shows that at least hundreds of them are operational around the world [2]. Considering all the other IE-related fields of applications mentioned above, we estimate

© Springer Nature Switzerland AG 2019
P. Hitzler et al. (Eds.): ESWC 2019 Satellite Events, LNCS 11762, pp. 80–83, 2019.
https://doi.org/10.1007/978-3-030-32327-1_16

that these represent only a small subset of the facilities currently operating worldwide. Although these facilities use and produce knowledge of high scientific value, our survey shows that they often follow informal procedures for their overall data handling, storing data in spreadsheets or even only on paper. This practice makes irradiation facilities more prone to the risk of data errors and loss, hence the obvious need for a standardized approach in the data management of IEs.

Ontologies facilitate knowledge sharing and formalization of specific domains [3]. Thus, the main goal of this work is the formalization of the knowledge linked to the management of data associated to IEs by introducing a new ontology, called the Irradiation Experiments Data Management (IEDM) ontology[1]. IEDM has been built by investigating and analyzing the common elements and practices used in irradiation facilities around the world, building thus upon the knowledge of domain experts.

2 Related Work

In the literature, several ontologies attempt to formalize scientific knowledge. One example is the Knowledge Graph for Science, where the authors work on axiomatizing the knowledge present in the scientific literature [4]. However, this work describes mainly scientific documents rather than actual experimental information. Another example is the Web Physics Ontology [5], presenting physics equations and relationships among physical quantities; it is though limited to the domain of electromagnetism and mechanics. Another approach is the ontology design pattern proposed for particle physics analysis [6]. Although this work includes concepts that are typical in HEP experiments, it focuses mainly on the analysis of HEP data and not on the representation of experiments. Thus, to the best of our knowledge, an ontology dedicated to the formalization of the principles of irradiation experiments does not exist.

3 Methodology

Ontology Reuse. Following best practices in developing IEDM, we reuse existing ontologies that could partially describe IEs [7]. Specifically, we reused classes from the Ontology of Scientific Experiments (EXPO), the Units of Measure ontology (OM) and the Friend-of-a-Friend ontology (FOAF). EXPO is a general ontology for the formalization of scientific experiments. It introduces concepts specifically linked to the notions of experimental design, scientific methods, and other core principles of experiments [8]. In IEDM, EXPO is reused for describing abstract and physical concepts linked to the features of IEs. To ensure compatibility with the potential future enhancements of EXPO and other ontologies, one important design choice was to never copy, override or modify them. Instead, when more information was needed, we introduced IEDM-specific variants of existing classes, using the `iedm` namespace to avoid ambiguities.

---

[1] https://gitlab.cern.ch/bgkotse/iedm.

Since EXPO does not elaborate on physical quantities and units, restricting its key constructs to the logical structure of scientific experiments, OM [9] was instead used for their representation. OM describes entities from many physics-related domains, including concepts from particle physics. This ontology is thus necessary for the formalization of the physical quantities related to IEs.

The third imported ontology is the Friend-of-a-Friend ontology (FOAF) [10]. It aims to describe networks of people, their activities, and their relations. IEDM uses FOAF mostly to describe the characteristics of the various individuals involved in IEs. For example, the term "user" has a broad definition and can be a group, an organization, or a person. Therefore, we employed the definition of foaf:Agent, which contains, as subclasses, all these three types of entities.

IEDM Concepts. Since the domain of IEs is larger than those covered by the three foundational ontologies mentioned above, the second phase of the IEDM development required introducing concepts more specific to IEs. In this step, we followed a top-down approach: IE-specific concepts are added as subclasses of the upper ontologies' classes. We also added new relations created via IE-specific object properties. For example, the constraint iedm:hasFieldOfStudy some iedm:DomainOfExperiment is a superclass of the class iedm:IrradiationExperiment. A simplified illustration of some core classes is presented in Fig. 1. In total, IEDM consists of 115 classes and 941 annotations. Relations among the classes are represented with 24 object properties and 16 data properties.

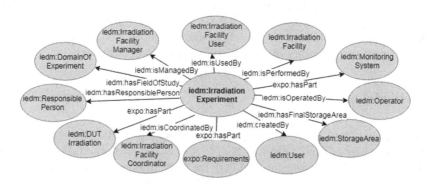

Fig. 1. Graph representation of some core IEDM entities and properties.

During the integration of IEDM with the upper ontologies, we came across several issues. One of them was that a concept could appear in more than one of the three upper ontologies (e.g., expo:Quantity and om:Quantity). In that case, we used the concept whose definition better fits the model. We also noticed cases where two concepts were in fact complementary to each other (e.g., expo:Agent and foaf:Agent), and hence we decided to create another IEDM class (iedm:User) that would be the subclass of both, taking advantage of Web Ontology Language (OWL) multiple inheritance. Finally, given the importance of documentation in ontology development and usage, dedicated annotations are used as internal elements providing information for each new IEDM entity, while external documentation is provided online[2].

IEDM Example. To assess the coherence of IEDM, the data of an actual IE were represented in IEDM. The IE taken as an example (*FCC-RadMon*) is testing a new technology of particle fluence monitors, performed at the CERN proton irradiation facility (IRRAD). For this specific experiment example, 43 instances of IEDM classes were inserted. Moreover, the ontology was also tested with the Pellet reasoner [11] in order to ensure its consistency.

4 Conclusion and Future Work

In this paper, we presented IEDM, a new ontology describing the data management of irradiation experiments. Concepts from EXPO, OM and FOAF are adopted and extended with new ones relevant to IEs. Moreover, an actual experiment is represented with IEDM as a proof-of-concept test, providing evidence of the ontology's validity.

Beyond its use as a knowledge formalization effort for the whole HEP community, our vision for IEDM is to use it as a model for web application generation. Another application of IEDM could be to annotate the HEP data available in the Irradiation Facilities online database [2].

References

1. Leo, W.R.: Techniques for Nuclear and Particle Physics Experiments: A How-to Approach. Springer, Heidelberg (1994). https://doi.org/10.1007/978-3-642-57920-2
2. Irradiation Facilities Database. https://irradiation-facilities.web.cern.ch
3. Fensel, D.: Ontologies. Springer, Heidelberg (2001). https://doi.org/10.1007/978-3-662-04396-7
4. Sören, A., et al.: Towards a knowledge graph for science. In: WIMS 2018 Proceedings of the 8th International Conference on Web Intelligence, Mining and Semantics, pp. 1–6. ACM, New York (2018)
5. Cvjetkovic, V.: Web physics ontology: online interactive symbolic computation in physics. In: 4th Experiment@ International Conference, Faro, Portugal. IEEE (2017)
6. Carral, D., et al.: An ontology design pattern for particle physics analysis. In: Workshop on Ontology and Semantic Web Patterns (WOP2015), Pennsylvania, USA (2015)
7. Janowicz, K., et al.: Five stars of linked data vocabulary use. Semant. Web **5**, 173–176 (2014)
8. Soldatova, L.N., King, R.: An ontology of scientific experiments. J. R. Soc. Interface **3**, 795–803 (2006)
9. Rijgersberg, H., van Assem, M., Top, J.: Ontology of units of measure and related concepts. Semant. Web **4**(1), 3–13 (2013)
10. Brickley, D., Miller, L: FOAF vocabulary specification 0.91 (2010)
11. Sirin, E., et al.: Pellet: a practical OWL-DL reasoner. J. Web Semant. **5**(2), 51–53 (2007)

---

[2] http://cern.ch/iedm.

CALVADOS: A Tool for the Semantic Analysis and Digestion of Web Contents

Govind[✉], Amit Kumar, Céline Alec, and Marc Spaniol

Department of Computer Science, Université de Caen Normandie,
Campus Côte de Nacre, 14032 Caen Cedex, France
{govind,amit.kumar,celine.alec,marc.spaniol}@unicaen.fr

Abstract. Web users these days are confronted with an abundance of information. While this is clearly beneficial in general, there is a risk of "information overload". To this end, there is an increasing need of filtering, classifying and/or summarizing Web contents automatically. In order to help consumers in efficiently deriving the semantics from Web contents, we have developed the CALVADOS (Content AnaLytics ViA Digestion Of Semantics) system. To this end, CALVADOS raises contents to the entity-level and digests its inherent semantics. In this demo, we present how entity-level analytics can be employed to automatically classify the main topic of a Web content and reveal the semantic building blocks associated with the corresponding document.

Keywords: Entity-level web analytics · Semantic content digestion · Web semantics · Analytics interface

1 Introduction

Celebrating the Web's 30th anniversary in 2019, we still observe a gigantic growth in Web contents being created and, at the same time, being available for consumption. This novel data source is a blessing and curse at the same time. On the one hand, we benefit from a vast amount of information accessible 24/7 all over the planet. On the other hand, we might be overwhelmed by the sheer amount of data. To this end, efficient and smart approaches are required, in order to help us to "digest" this huge quantity of data in a "healthy manner". Our hypothesis - therefore - is, that the named entities contained in a Web content carry its inherent semantics. In order to do so, we combine named entity disambiguation (e.g., AIDA [6] or DBpedia Spotlight [10]) with freely available knowledge bases (KBs) such as DBpedia [1] or YAGO [5]. As a result, we have previously introduced `semantic fingerprinting` [3,4] as a general purpose approach towards Web content classification.

In this paper, we introduce the CALVADOS (Content AnaLytics ViA Digestion Of Semantics) system as an extension of `semantic fingerprinting`. CALVADOS is a novel approach that aims at distilling and visualizing semantics of

© Springer Nature Switzerland AG 2019
P. Hitzler et al. (Eds.): ESWC 2019 Satellite Events, LNCS 11762, pp. 84–89, 2019.
https://doi.org/10.1007/978-3-030-32327-1_17

documents by exploiting entity-level analytics for a user-friendly "digestion". To this end, our demonstration paper makes the following salient contributions:

- use of `semantic fingerprinting` to capture content's (inherent) semantics
- visualization & exploration of (inter-) dependencies among entities contained
- provisioning of contextual KB data (e.g., types) supporting data digestion

2   Related Work

Most of the approaches dealing with analytics of Web contents focus on automatic classification of text into predefined categories [7]. Document classification using machine learning methods has been studied by [11]. Recent approaches employ deep neural networks requiring a vast amount of training data. Examples include utilizing the word order of the textual data [8] or a hierarchical attention network [12]. In contrast to these works, our approach exploits entity-level semantics to capture a better document representation (i.e., the `semantic fingerprint` [3]).

Exploiting entity-level semantics is possible thanks to recent named entity recognition and disambiguation (NERD) systems. Several tools, like AIDA [6] or DBpedia Spotlight [10] (also employed in CALVADOS system), identify the mentions of named entities in a text and map them onto their canonical entities in a knowledge base (KB), for instance YAGO [5] or DBpedia [1]. There are recent works, such as EARL [2] and FALCON[1], which aim to disambiguate entities in short text. Further, information from the linked KBs can be utilized.

To the best of our knowledge, the approach most similar to our work is TagTheWeb [9]. This tool aims at identifying topics associated with documents. It relies on the knowledge expressed by the taxonomic structure of Wikipedia, based on the generation of a fingerprint through the semantic relation between nodes of the Wikipedia Category Graph. Compared to this work, our `semantic fingerprint` is based on more fine-grained categories. Besides, our tool also allows to semantically compare two documents.

3   Conceptual Approach Overview of CALVADOS

The goal of CALVADOS is to digest the semantics of a Web content and provide visualizations to facilitate content consumption. The backbone of the CALVADOS system is `semantic fingerprinting`, a fine-grained type classification approach based on the hypothesis that "*You know a document by the named entities it contains*". The general approach is briefly explained in this section, more details can be found in [4]. In short, the semantics of a document is captured by the use of a `semantic fingerprint`, i.e., a vector that encodes the core semantics of the document based on the type information of

---

[1] https://labs.tib.eu/falcon/.

entities contained. The ambiguity among named entities is handled using afore-mentioned standard NERD systems. The actual fine-grained type prediction via `semantic fingerprinting` can be described in the following two steps. First, the document's `semantic fingerprint` is computed. For this purpose, we perform entity-level analytics of the entities contained and, in particular, exploit the type information from the knowledge base YAGO. Second, we employ a random forest classifier to predict the top-level type of our prediction. Once identified, the system aims to find the most suitable fine-grained sub-type. In order to do so, the cosine similarity between the `fingerprint` of the document and the representative vectors of the sub-types are computed, and the one with the highest score being selected. For example, an article about some football game can be predicted as an `event` in the top-level prediction, and further aligned to the more specific type `game` in the second step. CALVADOS utilizes the aforementioned `semantic fingerprints` to semantically analyze and digest Web contents.

4   Demonstration

The goal of CALVADOS is to help users in digesting documents via entity-level analytics. To this end, entity information are extracted and visualized. In particular, various interactive visualizations are provided:

- the `semantic fingerprint` of a document
- the tag cloud based on the named entities contained
- statistics about similarity with other types showcasing the document's "flavor"
- an opportunity to compare two documents based on their inherent semantics

As such, this demo comprises two use cases of the CALVADOS system (cf. Figure 2 for a screenshot of the Web interface or https://calvados.greyc.fr/ for an online demonstrator). The first use case facilitates content digestion of an individual document (cf. Subsect. 4.1). The second use case allows users to compare the semantics of two different documents (cf. Subsect. 4.2).

The overall pipeline of CALVADOS works in four stages. In the first stage, the user inputs the document, and preprocessing (boilerplate removal, NERD via DBpedia Spotlight, etc.) on the document content is performed. The following stage then involves the computation of the `semantic fingerprint` for the concerned document. Subsequently, in the third stage, the relevant fine-grained types for the document are predicted. Finally, the `semantic fingerprint` and predictions generated in previous stages are visualized to serve the overall goal of a simplified content digestion based on a semantic distillation. Visualizations are constructed by utilizing the JavaScript library Data-Driven Documents[2] (D3.js). Figure 1 depicts the overview of aforementioned stages.

---

[2] D3.js https://d3js.org/.

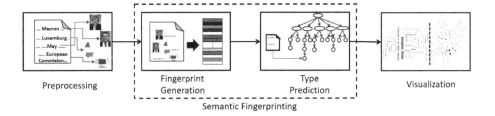

Fig. 1. Conceptual overview of the CALVADOS pipeline

4.1   Use Case I: Content Digestion via Semantic Distillation

The first use case of CALVADOS is content digestion via semantic distillation. The user can input the content by providing a reference URL to the document or by uploading the raw text itself. CALVADOS performs the entity-level analytics on the document via `semantic fingerprinting`. As a result, the system offers various visualization in order to provide a user-friendly content consumption. Focal point here is the visualization of the `semantic fingerprint` depicting the associated types based on the underlying type hierarchy. This graphical metaphor allows the user to understand the document's constituents on a semantic level. For example, a news article about Theresa May[3] comprises a combination of various political parties, administrative districts, skilled workers, etc. Further, CALVADOS also provide an "entity cloud" based on the named entities contained, and highlights those types that are conceptually similar on the entity-level. Figure 2a displays a screenshot of the previously mentioned news article in CALVADOS.

4.2   Use Case II: Comparison of Documents Semantics

The second use case of CALVADOS is a semantic document comparison. To this end, we enable the end user to analyze the overlap and differences between two documents at the semantic level. This is achieved by visualizing the `semantic fingerprints` of both documents simultaneously as "overlay". Further, an entity cloud on the intersecting named entities is provided. Here, it can be easily observed, that the `semantic fingerprints` provide more insights in contrast to the plain entity mentions. In addition, information about the most similar types associated with both documents are provided in order to disclose their overall "flavor". For example, when comparing the previous news article about Theresa May with a Manchester City FC article, there are visible differences. The former article being aligned towards political parties, skilled workers, etc. whereas the later one towards contests, clubs, etc. (cf. Figure 2b). Finally, the quantified value of similarity based on the `semantic fingerprints` is indicated, as well.

---

[3] https://www.bbc.com/news/uk-politics-47627744.

(a) Semantic digest of a Web page   (b) Semantic comparison of Web pages

Fig. 2. Screenshots of CALVADOS

5   Conclusion and Outlook

In this paper, we introduced CALVADOS, a tool for the semantic analysis and digestion of Web contents. CALVADOS lifts document analysis to the entity-level and utilizes `semantic fingerprints` in order to capture the inherent semantics of a Web content. In future work, we aim at two directions. Since entity-level analytics is language-agnostic in itself, we aim at transferring CALVADOS into other languages (e.g., French). In addition, we will study the aspect of document similarity on the entity-level, e.g., in the context of fake news detection.

Acknowledgements. This work was supported by the RIN RECHERCHE Normandie Digitale research project ASTURIAS contract no. 18E01661. We thank our colleagues for inspiring discussions.

References

1. Auer, S., Bizer, C., Kobilarov, G., Lehmann, J., Cyganiak, R., Ives, Z.G.: DBpedia: a nucleus for a web of open data. In: ISWC/ASWC, pp. 722–735 (2007)
2. Dubey, M., Banerjee, D., Chaudhuri, D., Lehmann, J.: EARL: joint entity and relation linking for question answering over knowledge graphs. In: Vrandečić, D., et al. (eds.) ISWC 2018. LNCS, vol. 11136, pp. 108–126. Springer, Cham (2018). https://doi.org/10.1007/978-3-030-00671-6_7

3. Govind, Alec, C., Spaniol, M.: Semantic fingerprinting: a novel method for entity-level content classification. In: Mikkonen, T., Klamma, R., Hernández, J. (eds.) ICWE 2018. Lecture Notes in Computer Science. Springer, Cham (2018). https://doi.org/10.1007/978-3-319-91662-0_21

4. Govind, Alec, C., Spaniol, M.: Fine-grained web content classification via entity-level analytics: the case of semantic fingerprinting. J. Web Eng. (JWE) **17**(6&7), 449–482 (2019)

5. Hoffart, J., Suchanek, F.M., Berberich, K., Weikum, G.: YAGO2: a spatially and temporally enhanced knowledge base from wikipedia. Artif. Intell. **194**, 28–61 (2013)

6. Hoffart, J., et al.: Robust disambiguation of named entities in text. In: Conference on EMNLP, Edinburgh, Scotland, UK, pp. 782–792 (2011)

7. Jindal, R., Malhotra, R., Jain, A.: Techniques for text classification: literature review and current trends. Webology **12**, 1–28 (2015)

8. Johnson, R., Zhang, T.: Effective use of word order for text categorization with convolutional neural networks. CoRR abs/1412.1058 (2014)

9. Medeiros, J.F., Pereira Nunes, B., Siqueira, S.W.M., Portes Paes Leme, L.A.: TagTheWeb: using wikipedia categories to automatically categorize resources on the web. In: Gangemi, A., et al. (eds.) ESWC 2018. LNCS, vol. 11155, pp. 153–157. Springer, Cham (2018). https://doi.org/10.1007/978-3-319-98192-5_29

10. Mendes, P.N., Jakob, M., García-Silva, A., Bizer, C.: DBpedia spotlight: shedding light on the web of documents. In: I-Semantics 2011, pp. 1–8. ACM, New York (2011)

11. Sebastiani, F.: Machine learning in automated text categorization. ACM Comput. Surv. **34**(1), 1–47 (2002)

12. Yang, Z., Yang, D., Dyer, C., He, X., Smola, A., Hovy, E.: Hierarchical attention networks for document classification. In: NAACL-HLT, pp. 1480–1489 (2016)

Efficient Retrieval of Knowledge Graph Fact Evidences

Dhruv Gupta[1,2(✉)] and Klaus Berberich[1,3]

[1] Max Planck Institute for Informatics, Saarbrücken, Germany
{dhgupta,kberberi}@mpi-inf.mpg.de
[2] Graduate School of Computer Science, Saarbrücken, Germany
[3] htw saar, Saarbrücken, Germany

Abstract. We report preliminary results on the problem of efficient retrieval of evidences for knowledge graph (KG) facts from large document collections. KGs are rich repositories of human knowledge and real-world events. To verify and validate facts about entities, it is often required to spot their evidences in large news archives or on the Web. To do so, KG facts can be translated to their natural language equivalent by using surface forms. Naïvely, attempting to search for all combinations of the aliases in large document collections is a time-consuming solution. We show that by using a combination of inverted indexes over n-grams and skip-grams we can return evidences in the form of sentences for KG facts within seconds.

1 Introduction

Knowledge graphs (KGs) are rich repositories of information about entities and real-world events. KGs such as Wikidata allow users to create new entries for emerging entities and establish their relations to other prominent entities in the KG. Often, such new facts about emerging entities in the KG are left without any references. Establishing provenance for KG facts is a problem of high interest, as shown by many recent works in the Semantic Web community [1,3,5]. Provenance information in the form of textual evidences from news articles and web pages can help put a KG fact into context. Most importantly, journalists and scholars in humanities often rely on such provenance information to verify and validate facts concerning emerging entities in news and real-world events [2].

In this work, we solve the problem of efficiently retrieving sentences from large document collections that establish provenance for a given KG fact. KG facts $\langle$(S)UBJECT, (P)REDICATE, (O)BJECT$\rangle$ can be translated to their natural language equivalent by substituting aliases and surface forms underlying the $\langle$S, P, O$\rangle$ triple from paraphrase dictionaries (e.g., Wikidata labels). For example, $\langle$BILL-GATES, SPOUSE, MELINDA-GATES$\rangle$, can be transformed to its natural language equivalent using surface forms underlying the fact arguments as:

$$\left\langle \left\{ \begin{array}{c} \textit{bill gates} \\ \textit{william gates} \\ \textit{william henry gates iii} \\ \textit{william henry bill gates iii} \end{array} \right\}, \left\{ \begin{array}{c} \textit{married to} \\ \textit{marry} \\ \textit{wedded to} \\ \textit{married} \end{array} \right\}, \left\{ \begin{array}{c} \textit{melinda gates} \\ \textit{melinda ann french} \\ \textit{melinda french gates} \\ \textit{melinda ann gates} \end{array} \right\} \right\rangle.$$

© Springer Nature Switzerland AG 2019
P. Hitzler et al. (Eds.): ESWC 2019 Satellite Events, LNCS 11762, pp. 90–94, 2019.
https://doi.org/10.1007/978-3-030-32327-1_18

Three key challenges arise when attempting to retrieve sentences as evidences for KG facts from large document collections. First, we must be able to quickly retrieve all documents that mention at least one surface form from each argument of the KG triple. Second, we must be able to ascertain that the surface forms corresponding to each argument of the triple occur in the order specified. This is to assure that the retrieved sentences are semantically meaningful. Third and finally, we must be able to determine that all three surface forms appear within sentence boundaries. This is done to avoid retrieving text regions or passages that are irrelevant as they may contain mentions of the entities in isolation (e.g., as part of compound or different sentences). We next describe our approach, that builds on our prior work [4], to address these challenges.

2 Approach

Notation. Consider a large document collection $\mathcal{D} = \{d_1, d_2, \ldots, d_{|\mathcal{D}|}\}$. Each document in the collection $d \in \mathcal{D}$ consists of a sequence of sentences $d = \langle s_1, s_2, \ldots, s_{|d|} \rangle$. Further, each sentence in the document $s \in d$ is a sequence of words $s = \langle w_1, w_2, \ldots, w_{|s|} \rangle$ drawn from the vocabulary of the document collection Σ. Let, $\mathcal{K}$ denote a knowledge graph containing facts F in the form of triples: $\langle$(S)UBJECT, (P)REDICATE, (O)BJECT$\rangle$. A fact in the knowledge graph F $\in \mathcal{K}$ can be translated to its natural language equivalent using surface forms (e.g., labels from Wikidata) corresponding to each triple argument:

$$\mathsf{F} \equiv \langle \mathsf{S}, \mathsf{P}, \mathsf{O} \rangle \equiv \langle \{\mathsf{S}_1, \mathsf{S}_2, \ldots, \mathsf{S}_m\}, \{\mathsf{P}_1, \mathsf{P}_2, \ldots, \mathsf{P}_n\}, \{\mathsf{O}_1, \mathsf{O}_2, \ldots, \mathsf{O}_l\} \rangle. \quad (1)$$

Problem Statement. For a given KG fact F $\in \mathcal{K}$ as an input query, we are required to output sentences $s \in d$ from the document collection $\mathcal{D}$. Each sentence s output contains at least one surface form from each phrase set representing $\langle \mathsf{S}, \mathsf{P}, \mathsf{O} \rangle$ *and* the surface forms appear in order. For example, for the query representing the fact $\langle$ BILL-GATES, SPOUSE, MELINDA-GATES $\rangle$ (see Sect. 1), the sentence $\langle$ *william gates married, in 1994, his company's employee melinda ann french*$\rangle$ is considered a match.

Inverted Indexes. To support efficient retrieval of sentences, we create indexes for word sequences, that record their positional span and their sentence identifiers. We create two types of inverted indexes: n-gram and skip-gram indexes. The n-gram indexes help us determine the sentences that contain the surface forms of the triples. The skip-gram indexes help us in two ways. First, skip-grams help us determine whether surface forms belonging to two different triple arguments co-occur (e.g., $\langle \mathsf{S}, \mathsf{P} \rangle$). Second, skip-grams give us a cardinality estimate on the number of positional spans that must be inspected to determine a match within a sentence. Concretely, we created n-gram indexes that record unigrams, bigrams, and trigrams. We created skip-gram indexes that record skip-grams of words that occur within a window of ten words.

Query Processing and Optimization. Given a natural language representation of a KG fact (see Eq. 1) as a query, we retrieve sentences in three steps. In the first step, we determine the positional spans corresponding to each surface form in the fact F using the n-gram indexes. This is done by decomposing all the surface forms into overlapping

Table 1. Document collection statistics.

COLLECTION	#DOCUMENTS	#WORDS	#SENTENCES
NYT	1,855,623	1,058,949,098	54,024,146
GIGAWORD	9,870,655	3,988,683,648	181,386,746

Table 2. Index sizes in Gigabytes (GB).

	NYT	GIGAWORD
COLLECTION SIZE	3.00	9.10
INDEX TYPE	NYT	GIGAWORD
WORD INDEX	5.80	22.30
N-GRAM INDEXES	45.90	154.40
SKIP-GRAM INDEX	56.10	203.60

Table 3. Testbed statistics.

CATEGORY	PREDICATES	#QUERIES	AVG. #WORDS
WRITERS	AWARD RECEIVED, NOTABLE WORK	684	57.95
MEDICINE LAUREATES	AWARD RECEIVED, EMPLOYER	410	55.02
PHYSICS LAUREATES	AWARD RECEIVED, EMPLOYER	406	58.48
CHEMISTRY LAUREATES	AWARD RECEIVED, EMPLOYER	348	56.04
MOVIES	CAST MEMBER, FILMING LOCATION	114	75.51
ALL US ELECTIONS	CANDIDATE	1	1081.00
ALL WORLD WAR I BATTLES	LOCATION	1	1669.00
ALL WORLD WAR II BATTLES	LOCATION	1	2563.00
ALL SUMMER OLYMPICS	LOCATION	1	717.00
ALL WINTER OLYMPICS	LOCATION	1	407.00
TOTAL QUERY INSTANCES: 1,977			

n-grams (up to trigrams) and looking up their positional spans in the corresponding n-gram indexes. Alternatively, we can determine the same set of positional spans using the skip-gram index by decomposing the surface forms as overlapping skip-grams.

In the second step, we inspect that the positional spans corresponding to each fact argument, occur in the sequence specified by the fact. For the fact $F \equiv \langle S, P, O \rangle$ all positional spans corresponding to the predicate P come after subject S. To minimize time, we choose to examine those fact argument combinations first that will result in a minimum number of resulting positional spans. This cardinality estimate of the *join* can be determined by looking at frequencies of skip-grams built using surface forms belonging to different fact arguments. In the third step, we verify that the positional spans corresponding to surface forms from each fact argument are within the same sentence. This is done by checking the sentence identifier retrieved along with the positional spans from the inverted indexes.

3 Evaluation

Document Collection and Indexes. We consider two news archives as our test document collections: the New York Times (NYT) Annotated corpus[1] and the Fifth Edition of English Gigaword[2]. Statistics for both collections are reported in Table 1. For each document collection we created n-gram indexes and skip-gram indexes as discussed in Sect. 2. To put the n-gram and skip-gram index sizes into perspective, we also show sizes of a word only (unigram) index and the size of the document collection in GB (Table 2).

Queries for KG Facts were constructed using the Wikidata KG. Concretely, to construct the queries, we picked prominent entities from categories such as medicine, physics, and chemistry laureates. For each prominent entity we then considered those predicates where multiple objects could be associated. For instance, all employment positions for Nobel laureates. For each fact instance, we translated them to their natural language equivalent using their Wikidata labels for items and properties. Details of the query testbed are shown in Table 3.

Setup. We preprocessed the document collections using Stanford CoreNLP to determine sentences, words, and their positional spans in each document. We then instantiated their n-gram and skip-gram indexes in HBase, a distributed extensible record store on our Hadoop cluster. Our cluster consists of twenty machines equipped with Intel Xeon CPUs at 3.50 GHz, up to 128 GB of RAM, and up to eight 4 TB secondary storage. We execute the runtime experiments on a high-memory compute node equipped with 1.48 TB of RAM and 96 core Intel Xeon CPU at 2.66 GHz.

Baselines and Systems. We consider three baselines. The first baseline, B_{SCAN}, simply establishes the time needed to scan the entire document collection on our Hadoop cluster once. This gives us an upper bound on how long a query should take to process. The second baseline, B_{BIGRAM}, processes each phrase in the query using only the unigram and bigram indexes. We can not solely use unigram indexes as we do not index stopwords for them. The third baseline, B_{NGRAM} processes each query using all of the n-gram indexes. That is, for each phrase in the query B_{NGRAM} makes use of unigram, bigram, and trigram indexes. We consider two variations of our system: $A_{HALF-OPT}$ and $A_{CMPLT-OPT}$. The system $A_{HALF-OPT}$ performs the query processing without estimating the join cardinalities. Whereas, $A_{CMPLT-OPT}$ performs all three steps of the query processing and optimization described in Sect. 2. We evaluate the baselines and our system using a sample of 100 queries for three rounds in a cold-cache setting. To simulate cold caches we shuffle the order of queries in between rounds. We also measure the statistical significance of the results using the Student's paired t-test at significance level $\alpha = 0.05$. Statistically significant results with respect to the baselines B_{BIGRAM} and B_{NGRAM} are marked by the symbols △ and ▲, respectively.

Results for the baselines and systems are shown in Tables 4 and 5. From Table 4, we see that naïvely scanning the document collection can be quite expensive, in the order of minutes, to spot KG facts. From Table 5, we see that the B_{BIGRAM} baseline also performs

---

[1] https://catalog.ldc.upenn.edu/LDC2008T19.
[2] https://catalog.ldc.upenn.edu/LDC2011T07.

Table 4. Results for B_{SCAN} (secs).

SYSTEM	NYT	GIGAWORD
B_{SCAN}	111.00	396.00

Table 5. Runtime results (secs).

SYSTEM	NYT	GIGAWORD
B_{BIGRAM}	7.77 ± 12.91	41.24 ± 62.94
B_{NGRAM}	1.80 ± 2.82	7.89 ± 7.16
$A_{HALF\text{-}OPT}$	$^\triangle 1.92 \pm 3.63$	$^\triangle 7.74 \pm 7.30$
$A_{CMPLT\text{-}OPT}$	$^{\triangle\blacktriangle} 1.41 \pm 2.42$	$^{\triangle\blacktriangle} 6.45 \pm 6.50$

poorly in retrieving sentences for KG facts as it only leverages n-grams of up to length two for query processing. The B_{NGRAM} baseline benefits by leveraging trigrams that further help bring down the query-processing cost. Among our two systems, $A_{HALF\text{-}OPT}$ and $A_{CMPLT\text{-}OPT}$, we see that by leveraging skip-grams for cardinality estimation we can see significant speedups over the baselines B_{BIGRAM} and B_{NGRAM}.

References

1. Bhatia, S., Dwivedi, P., Kaur, A.: That's interesting, tell me more! finding descriptive support passages for knowledge graph relationships. In: Vrandečić, D., et al. (eds.) ISWC 2018. LNCS, vol. 11136, pp. 250–267. Springer, Cham (2018). https://doi.org/10.1007/978-3-030-00671-6_15
2. Cohen, S., et al.: Computational journalism: a call to arms to database researchers. In: CIDR (2011)
3. Ercan, G., Elbassuoni, S., Hose, K.: Retrieving textual evidence for knowledge graph facts. In: Hitzler, P., et al. (eds.) ESWC 2019. LNCS, vol. 11503, pp. 52–67. Springer, Cham (2019). https://doi.org/10.1007/978-3-030-21348-0_4
4. Gupta, D., Berberich, K.: GYANI: an indexing infrastructure for knowledge-centric tasks. In: CIKM (2018)
5. Gerber, D., et al.: DeFacto - temporal and multilingual deep fact validation. J. Web Semant. **35**, 85–101 (2015)

SAD Generator: Eating Our Own Dog Food to Generate KGs and Websites for Academic Events

Pieter Heyvaert[1]([⊠]) [iD], David Chaves-Fraga[2] [iD], Freddy Priyatna[2] [iD], Juan Sequeda[3] [iD], and Anastasia Dimou[1] [iD]

[1] IDLab, Dept of Electronics and Information Systems,
Ghent University – imec, Ghent, Belgium
`{pheyvaer.heyvaert,anastasia.dimou}@ugent.be`
[2] Ontology Engineering Group, Universidad Politécnica de Madrid, Madrid, Spain
`{dchaves,fpriyatna}@fi.upm.es`
[3] Capsenta, Austin, USA
`juan@capsenta.com`

Abstract. Nowadays, a website is used to disseminate information about an event (e.g., location, dates, time). In the academic world, it is common to develop a website for an event, such as workshops or conferences. Aligning with the "Web of data", its dissemination should also happen by publishing the information of the event as a knowledge graph, e.g., via RDF that is available through a SPARQL endpoint or a Triple Patterns Fragment server. However, the RDF generation and website development is not always straightforward and can be time-consuming. In this demo, we present the Semantic Academic-event Dissemination (SAD) Generator for generating RDF and websites for academic events. The generator allows to (i) annotate CSV files that contain academic event data and use the annotations to generate a knowledge graph and (ii) generate a website with the information for the event querying the knowledge graph. We used our generator to generate the RDF and website of a real workshop, the KGB workshop. It can be easily reused by organizers of other academic events by simply providing the event's information in CSV files.

Keywords: RML · RDF · GraphQL · SPARQL · YARRRML

1 Introduction

In many domains, a website is one of the most frequent dissemination tools used to reach a wide range of audiences. Typically, a website is generated when an event is organized, containing useful information for potential attendees, such as the location, the dates or its main description. In the academic world, different kinds of event are usually organized, such as conferences, workshops, research schools or seminars where a corresponding website may be provided.

© Springer Nature Switzerland AG 2019
P. Hitzler et al. (Eds.): ESWC 2019 Satellite Events, LNCS 11762, pp. 95–99, 2019.
https://doi.org/10.1007/978-3-030-32327-1_19

In the context of workshops and conferences, the information showed by their websites has usually the same structure. The website may show general information about the event (name, dates, location), call for papers together with corresponding topics, organizers, important dates and program committee. This data can be easily defined using semi-structured data formats, such as CSV files or Excel files.

The resources of the event should also be published as a knowledge graph to be aligned with the "Web of data", following the Semantic Web/Linked Data approach: instances are identified by URLs and their types and properties are properly annotated. However, this step is usually seen as an additional feature for the dissemination, so it is avoided and, even if done, it remains unrelated to the website generation process. In fact, many of these websites obtain the data from isolated data sources where the used format is selected by the Web developer (e.g., databases, JSON or XML) and the data model is specific for each case. Recommendations, like RDFa, provide mechanisms to solve some of these issues, but its uptake is low, as it needs a manual intensive effort.

In this demo paper, we propose the SAD Generator[1], a Semantic Academic-event Dissemination Generator that uses Semantic Web technologies to generate a knowledge graph and website for academic events. This knowledge graph provides the data for generating the website. Furthermore, the knowledge graph can be made available via, e.g., a SPARQL endpoint or a Triple Pattern Fragments (TPF) server. We use this generator to build the knowledge graph and website of Knowledge Graph Building Workshop 2019[2] (co-located with ESWC2019).

2   The SAD Generator

When using our generator two main steps are executed: (i) the **knowledge graph** is built based on the raw data and, then, (ii) the **website** is generated based on this graph (see Fig. 1). To achieve that, our generator considers the following data: (i) **CSV files** provided by the organizers of the event and describe the workshop itself, the organizers, programme committee (PC), topics, subtopics, and important dates; (ii) the **knowledge graph** that is generated based on the CSV files; and (iii) **HTML pages** of the website that are generated based on the knowledge graph. In the remaining, we discuss the two steps in more details: in Sect. 2.1, we discuss how the knowledge graph is built and, in Sect. 2.2, we elaborate on the website's generation.

2.1   Building the Knowledge Graph

In this section, we discuss the data model used for the knowledge graph, and the YARRRML rules [1], created based on the data model, that are executed to build the knowledge graph based on the CSV files.

---

[1] Available online at: https://github.com/kgb-workshop/sad-generator.

[2] http://kgb-workshop.org/.

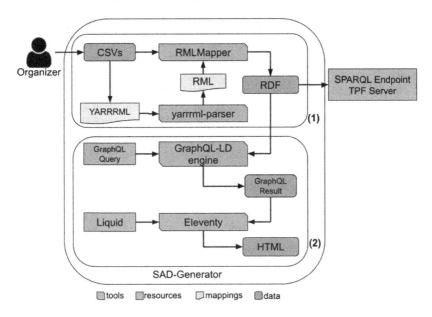

Fig. 1. SAD Generator workflow

Data Model. We annotate the different entities defined in the raw data semantically mostly using the Schema.org vocabulary to increase their reusability and shareability. A workshop is annotated as an event with the class `schema:Event`. The name, duration, conference co-located event, location, start date and end date are added as datatype properties. The organizers, program committee, (sub)topics, and important dates are added as object properties. Organizers and PC members are annotated as a person with the class `schema:Person`. Important dates are annotated as events with the class `schema:Event` and for the sub(topics) we use the class `schema:CreativeWork`.

Listing 1.1. YARRRML rules for the PC members

```
sources :
  − [ "csv/pc.csv∼csv " ]
s :  https ://kgb−workshop.org/resources/ProgramCommittee/$(id )
po :
  − [a,  schema:Person ]
  − [schema:name,  $(name )]
  − [schema:memberOf,  $(organization )]
  − [schema:performerIn ,
     https ://kgb−workshop.org/resources/Event/kgb2019∼iri ]
```

YARRRML Rules. Based on the structure of the CSV files and the data model, we use Matey[3] to define the corresponding YARRRML rules to build the knowledge

---
[3] http://rml.io/yarrrml/matey/.

graph[4]. These rules converted to RML rules [2] using the YARRRML Parser[5]. Initially, the RML rules are executed using the RMLMapper[6], which outputs the first version of the knowledge graph as RDF. If the data is updated, we execute the RML rules again and a new knowledge graph is build. If the structure of the CSV files or the data model is updated, we update the YARRRML rules and convert them to RML rules, and execute the latter to build a new knowledge graph. The YARRRML rules that define how to generate RDF describing the PC members can be found in Listing 1.1. They state that the relevant CSV file can be found in the folder `csv`, the URL of PC member is generated based on the `id` of a member, and that members are annotated with the class `schema:Person`, their name, organization and event they are performing in.

2.2 Generating the Website

In this section, we discuss how we use an existing static site generator, Eleventy[7], to generate a website based on our knowledge graph: how the graph is queried and how the results of the queries are used to generate the HTML. We use a static site generator to reduce complexity, i.e., only a static file server is needed to host the website, and improve scalability, i.e., the website can be easily replicated.

We need to query the knowledge graph for the relevant data to be used in the HTML pages. We use a Comunica engine to execute GraphQL-LD queries on the RDF file. Comunica [3] is a highly modular and flexible meta query engine for the Web that allows executing queries across different RDF data sources, including RDF files, SPARQL endpoints, and TPF servers. GraphQL-LD [4] brings GraphQL to RDF: GraphQL-LD queries are translated to SPARQL queries. We use GraphQL-LD because of the Web developer-friendly approach of GraphQL and because the output of these queries are JSON arrays, which can then be used by template languages, such as Liquid[8], to build HTML pages. Comunica allows building a query engine that supports these GraphQL-LD queries on RDF files, which we use with Eleventy to query our knowledge graph[9].

Listing 1.2. GraphQL-LD query to retrieve the list of PC members

```
{ ... on Person
  {
    name
    affiliation
    event(_:workshop)
  }
}
```

Listing 1.3. Result of GraphQL-LD query

```
[ { name: "Amrapali Zaveri",
    affiliation:
      "Maastricht University"
  }, ...
]
```

---

[4] https://github.com/kgb-workshop/sad-generator/blob/master/kg/mapping.yml.
[5] https://github.com/rmlio/yarrrml-parser.
[6] https://github.com/rmlio/rmlmapper-java.
[7] https://11ty.io.
[8] https://shopify.github.io/liquid/.
[9] https://github.com/pheyvaer/graphqlld-on-file.

Listing 1.4. Using the results in HTML

```
<ul>
  {% for person in programcommittee %}
    <li >{{person.name}}, {{person.affiliation}}</li >
  {% endfor %}
</ul>
```

In Listing 1.2 the GraphQL-LD query that returns the PC members can be found. We only look for persons in our knowledge graph that have a name, affiliation, and that perform in a specific workshop. The URL of the workshop is assigned to **workshop**. The result is a JSON array containing an object for each PC member (see Listing 1.3). These objects are used in an HTML template with Liquid to list all the PC members (see Listing 1.4).

During the demo, we show how users can easily use the generator for their own events and how the changes to the CSV files result in an updated knowledge graph and website. Furthermore, we have already used this generator to build the knowledge graph[10] and the website[11] of Knowledge Graph Building Workshop 2019 (co-located with ESWC2019).

Acknowledgements. The described research activities were funded by Ghent University, imec, Flanders Innovation & Entrepreneurship (AIO), the Research Foundation – Flanders (FWO), and the European Union. The work presented in this paper is partially supported by the Spanish Ministerio de Economía, Industria y Competitividad and EU FEDER funds under the DATOS 4.0: RETOS Y SOLUCIONES - UPM Spanish national project (TIN2016-78011-C4-4-R) and by an FPI grant (BES-2017-082511).

References

1. Heyvaert, P., De Meester, B., Dimou, A., Verborgh, R.: Declarative rules for linked data generation at your fingertips!. In: Gangemi, A., et al. (eds.) ESWC 2018. LNCS, vol. 11155, pp. 213–217. Springer, Cham (2018). https://doi.org/10.1007/978-3-319-98192-5_40
2. Dimou, A., et al.: RML: a generic language for integrated RDF mappings of heterogeneous data. In: LDOW (2014)
3. Taelman, R., Van Herwegen, J., Vander Sande, M., Verborgh, R.: Comunica: a modular SPARQL query engine for the web. In: Vrandečić, D., et al. (eds.) ISWC 2018. LNCS, vol. 11137, pp. 239–255. Springer, Cham (2018). https://doi.org/10.1007/978-3-030-00668-6_15
4. Taelman, R., Vander Sande, M., Verborgh, R.: GraphQL-LD: linked data querying with GraphQL. In: The 17th International Semantic Web Conference, ISWC 2018 (2018)

---

[10] https://github.com/kgb-workshop/data.
[11] https://github.com/kgb-workshop/website.

OECM: A Cross-Lingual Approach for Ontology Enrichment

Shimaa Ibrahim[1,2]($\boxtimes$), Said Fathalla[1,3], Hamed Shariat Yazdi[1],
Jens Lehmann[1,4], and Hajira Jabeen[1]

[1] Smart Data Analytics (SDA), University of Bonn, Bonn, Germany
{ibrahim,fathalla,shariat,jens.lehmann,jabeen}@cs.uni-bonn.de
[2] Institute of Graduate Studies and Research, University of Alexandria,
Alexandria, Egypt
[3] Faculty of Science, University of Alexandria, Alexandria, Egypt
[4] Enterprise Information Systems Department, Fraunhofer IAIS,
Sankt Augustin, Germany

Abstract. Due to the rapid expansion of multilingual data on the web, development of approaches to enrich ontologies has become an interesting and active subject of research. In this paper, we propose a cross-lingual matching approach for ontology enrichment (OECM) in order to enrich an ontology using another one in a different natural language. A prototype for the proposed approach has been implemented and evaluated using the MultiFarm benchmark. Evaluation results show higher precision and recall in comparison to other four state-of-the-art approaches.

Keywords: Cross-lingual matching · Ontology enrichment · Machine translation

1 Introduction

The increasing amount of multilingual data on the Semantic Web has motivated many researchers to develop ontologies in various natural languages. In fact, ontologies can be enriched by adding additional classes and/or relations extracted from other resources, even in another natural language [7]. Such enrichment is a resource demanding and time-consuming task. Therefore, automated or semi-automated ontology enrichment approaches are highly desired. Most research efforts pay attention to enrich English ontologies from English resources rather than non-English ones, by applying ontology matching techniques [7]. This raises a key question; How can an ontology be enriched using another ontology in a different natural language? In order to enrich ontologies from multilingual resources, most of the recent efforts in developing different techniques for cross-lingual ontology matching focus on one-to-one translation between ontology concepts [8]. Consequently, inappropriate translations negatively affect the quality of the matching process [8]. Therefore it is important to develop innovative approaches which are capable of enriching ontologies by selecting the best

© Springer Nature Switzerland AG 2019
P. Hitzler et al. (Eds.): ESWC 2019 Satellite Events, LNCS 11762, pp. 100–104, 2019.
https://doi.org/10.1007/978-3-030-32327-1_20

translation among all available translations (i.e. one-to-many translations) for a particular term. To the best of our knowledge, only our previous work [1] has addressed the problem of enriching ontologies from multilingual text. In this paper, we propose a new approach (OECM) to enrich an ontology, i.e. the target ontology T, using another one, i.e. the source ontology S, in a different natural language. The prominent feature of the proposed approach is the selection of the best translation between all available translations when matching classes among ontologies. This selection significantly improves the quality of the matching process. Furthermore, the usage of ontologies as the source for the enrichment process can significantly reduce the cost of data pre-processing and parsing of the data used being used for the enrichment. To evaluate OECM, we compare the cross-lingual ontology matching process with four state-of-the-art approaches. The implementation of OECM and the datasets used for evaluation are publicly available at https://github.com/shmkhaled/OECM.

2   The Proposed Approach

Goal: Given two ontologies S and T, in two different natural languages L_1 and L_2 respectively, as RDF triples $\langle s, p, o \rangle \in \mathcal{C} \times \mathcal{R} \times (\mathcal{C} \cup \mathcal{L})$ where $\mathcal{C}$ is the set of ontology domain entities (i.e. classes), $\mathcal{R}$ is the set of relations, and $\mathcal{L}$ is the set of literals. We aim at finding the complementary information $\mathcal{T}_e = S - (S \cap T)$ from S in order to enrich T. The methodology of the proposed approach comprises three phases: (1) pre-matching, (2) matching, and (3) enrichment. We have considered only class labels, or local names, and three standard relations: rdfs:subClassOf, owl:equivalentClass, owl:disjointWith.

(1) Pre-matching: T and S are prepared before starting the matching phase by performing two tasks: **(a) Pre-processing:** The aim of this task is to prepare the local names and/or labels of classes of S and T by employing several natural language processing techniques, such as tokenization, normalization, stop words removal and POS-tagging. The output of this task is two sets of pre-processed classes $\mathcal{C}'_S$ and $\mathcal{C}'_T$ for S and T respectively, **(b) Translation:** Each class in $\mathcal{C}'_S$ is translated using Google Translator to the language of T (i.e. L_2). A list of translations is associated with each class, for example, the class label "Thema" in German, has a list of two English translations: "Subject" and "Topic". The best translation will be selected in the next phase.

(2) Matching: In order to identify which, and where the new information will be added to T, potential matches between S and T should be identified. We use two types of matching: *Terminological matching* and *Structural matching*. **(a) Terminological matching:** This task is used to identify which information can be added to T. In order to choose the best translation for each class that matches the corresponding one in T, we perform a pairwise string matching between them. We chose Jaccard similarity as a string similarity metric because it has achieved the best score in terms of precision in the experiments conducted

Table 1. State-of-the-art comparison results

Approaches	Conference$_{de}$ × Ekaw$_{en}$			Conference$_{de}$ × Edas$_{en}$		
	Precision	Recall	F-measure	Precision	Recall	F-measure
AML [3]	0.56	0.20	0.29	0.86	0.35	0.50
KEPLER [6]	0.33	0.16	0.22	0.43	0.18	0.25
LogMap [5]	0.71	0.20	0.31	0.71	0.29	0.42
XMap [9]	0.18	0.16	0.17	0.23	0.18	0.20
OECM	**0.75**	**0.67**	**0.71**	**0.93**	**0.76**	**0.84**

for the ontology alignment task in the MultiFarm benchmark[1] [2]. We consider similarity scores greater than or equal to a specific threshold θ to get the best matches. After running the experiments for ten times, we obtained the best value of θ which gives the best matching results. If no match is found, this class is considered as a new class, which is added to T. At the end, matched classes are validated by experts in order to confirm that the best translation is selected for each class. **(b) Structural matching:** It is used to identify where the new information can be added to T. Each class in S is replaced by its best translation found in the previous matching in order to get a translated ontology S_{trans}. We apply a pairwise triple comparison between S_{trans} and T to get the set of triples to be enriched $\mathcal{T}_e$, which is represented by $\langle s, p, o, F \rangle$. Each triple is associated with a flag F, with a value either 'E' for enrichment or 'A' for addition. For a particular triple, if $s \in \mathcal{C}'_T$ and $o \notin \mathcal{C}'_T$, then $F = $ 'E', i.e. this triple is needed to enrich the existing information in T, while if $s \notin \mathcal{C}'_T$ and $o \in \mathcal{C}'_T$, then $F = $ 'A', i.e. this triple is needed to add a new class to T.

(3) Enrichment: $\mathcal{T}_e$ is used to enrich T according to the flags associated with each triple. We enrich the Scientific Events Ontology (SEO$_{en}$) [4], which has 49 classes in English, using the Conference$_{de}$ ontology from the MultiFarm dataset (see Sect. 3), which has 60 classes in German. OECM has identified new 15 triples to enrich SEO$_{en}$. For instance, `<ConferenceContributor, subClassOf, Person, 'A'>` is used to add a new class `ConferenceContributor`, as a `subClassOf Person`, to SEO$_{en}$. In addition, `<KeynoteSpeaker, subClassOf, ConferenceContributor, 'E'>` is used to enrich SEO$_{en}$ with additional information, i.e. adding a new relation `subClassOf` between the two classes. The complete 15 triples can be found at the GitHub repository. We have successfully enriched SEO$_{en}$ by 93.75% of the triples identified by an expert.

3   Evaluation

We use ontologies in the MultiFarm benchmark to measure the quality of the cross-lingual matching process. MultiFarm consists of seven ontologies, their

---

[1] https://www.irit.fr/recherches/MELODI/multifarm/.

translation into nine languages, and the corresponding cross-lingual alignments between them (i.e. the gold standard). We compare our results with four state-of-the-art approaches (see Table 1) for matching Conference$_{de}$ with Ekaw$_{en}$ and Conference$_{de}$ with Edas$_{en}$ ontologies. OECM outperforms all other systems in terms of precision, recall, and F-measure. For AML [3], authors include pre-computed dictionaries with translations, to overcome the query limit of Microsoft Translator which decrease the efficiency of their approach. LogMap [5] depends mainly on the initial mappings to discover new mappings, which decreased after performing the translation. XMap [9] did not achieve satisfactory results because of many internal exceptions. Surprisingly, we found seven new alignments, which did not exist in the gold standard, when matching Conference$_{de}$ with Ekaw$_{en}$, for instance, (`<LeiterDerWorkshops>`$_{de}$, `<Workshop_Chair>`$_{en}$).

4   Conclusion

We present a new approach (OECM) for enrichment of ontologies using other ontologies in different natural languages. Terminological and structural matching have been used in order to identify which, and where, information from the source ontology, can be used to enrich the target ontology. We consider all available translations for each term and select the best translation that matches the corresponding term in the target ontology. Such selection has significantly improved the quality of the matching process. It is worth to mentioning that OECM has also found new alignments, which were missing in the gold standard. OECM outperforms most of the state of the art systems in terms of precision, recall, and F-measure. We are in the process of investigating the usage of semantic similarity between terms in the matching process, in addition to considering other non-standard semantic relations and individuals in the enrichment process.

References

1. Ali, M., Fathalla, S., Ibrahim, S., Kholief, M., Hassan, Y.: Cross-lingual ontology enrichment based on multi-agent architecture. Proc. Comput. Sci. **137**, 127–138 (2018)
2. Cheatham, M., Hitzler, P.: String similarity metrics for ontology alignment. In: Alani, H., et al. (eds.) ISWC 2013. LNCS, vol. 8219, pp. 294–309. Springer, Heidelberg (2013). https://doi.org/10.1007/978-3-642-41338-4_19
3. Faria, D., et al.: Results of AML participation in OAEI 2018. In: Proceedings of the 13th International Workshop on Ontology Matching, pp. 125–131. CEUR-WS (2018)
4. Fathalla, S., Vahdati, S., Auer, S., Lange, C.: The scientific events ontology of the openresearch.org curation platform. In: Proceedings of the 34th ACM/SIGAPP Symposium on Applied Computing, pp. 2311–2313. ACM (2019)
5. Jiménez-Ruiz, E., Grau, V.C.: LogMap family participation in the OAEI 2018. In: Proceedings of the 13th International Workshop on Ontology Matching, pp. 187–191. CEUR-WS (2018)

6. Kachroudi, M., Diallo, G., Yahia, S.B.: OAEI 2018 results of KEPLER. In: Proceedings of the 13th International Workshop on Ontology Matching, pp. 173–178. CEUR-WS (2018)
7. Petasis, G., Karkaletsis, V., Paliouras, G., Krithara, A., Zavitsanos, E.: Ontology population and enrichment: state of the art. In: Paliouras, G., Spyropoulos, C.D., Tsatsaronis, G. (eds.) Knowledge-Driven Multimedia Information Extraction and Ontology Evolution. LNCS (LNAI), vol. 6050, pp. 134–166. Springer, Heidelberg (2011). https://doi.org/10.1007/978-3-642-20795-2_6
8. Trojahn, C., Fu, B., Zamazal, O., Ritze, D.: State-of-the-art in multilingual and cross-lingual ontology matching. In: Buitelaar, P., Cimiano, P. (eds.) Towards the Multilingual Semantic Web, pp. 119–135. Springer, Heidelberg (2014). https://doi.org/10.1007/978-3-662-43585-4_8
9. Djeddi, W.E., Yahia, S.B., Khadir, M.T.: XMap results for OAEI 2018. In: Proceedings of the 13th International Workshop on Ontology Matching, pp. 210–215. CEUR-WS (2018)

How Diverse Are Federated Query Execution Plans Really?

Anders Langballe Jakobsen, Gabriela Montoya[(✉)], and Katja Hose

Aalborg University, Aalborg, Denmark
{alja,gmontoya,khose}@cs.aau.dk

Abstract. Federated query engines optimize and execute SPARQL queries over the data accessible via SPARQL endpoints; even in the absence of information about which sources provide relevant data. Different query optimization strategies may produce different execution plans, which in many cases explains the huge differences in performance that we encounter with state-of-the-art federated query engines. Related work has so far mainly focused on execution time and number of selected sources, overlooking the importance of the execution plans themselves. In this demonstration paper, we therefore present PIPE, a tool that allows for comparing federated query engines in terms of performance, execution plans, and query answers. Currently, PIPE supports five state-of-the-art federated query engines; we provide a Java library for straightforward integration of additional federated query engines.

1 Introduction

The efforts of the Semantic Web community have led to the publication of billions of RDF triples organized into thousands of datasets. A key element of Linked Data is that the datasets are not isolated but they include links to other datasets, which allows users to pose queries that cannot be answered using a single dataset alone. Instead, such *federated* queries require data from multiple datasets. In this paper, we consider federated queries that do not include hints about where the triple patterns should be executed but rely on a federated query engine to optimize the query, i.e., select relevant sources, decompose the query into subqueries, delegate those subqueries to the appropriate sources, combine the partial answers, and compute the final result to the original query. We assume that a source provides access to a dataset via a SPARQL endpoint, i.e., an RDF interface that supports full SPARQL expressiveness.

Several federated query engines, such as [1–3,6], have been proposed in the last decade. Even if these engines have many differences, including different implementations of the SPARQL operators, the most important difference is their query optimization strategies. Different strategies produce quite different execution plans, and in many cases the huge differences in performance are mainly due to key differences in the execution plans produced by the engines. So far, comparisons among these engines have been mainly based on execution

© Springer Nature Switzerland AG 2019
P. Hitzler et al. (Eds.): ESWC 2019 Satellite Events, LNCS 11762, pp. 105–110, 2019.
https://doi.org/10.1007/978-3-030-32327-1_21

time and to some extent on the number of selected sources, but comparisons that take the diversity of execution plans into consideration have been very limited and mainly used for motivating examples.

In this paper, we therefore present PIPE, Performance Inspector and Plan Explorer, a tool that allows for comparing different federated query engines in terms of their performance, i.e., planning and execution time, computed execution plans, and query answers. A key novelty of PIPE is providing a uniform framework for studying the impact of optimization strategies used by the engines on the shapes of the produced execution plans. Supporting the analysis of these plans allows for easing the understanding of query optimization strategies, including the identification of their limitations and the proposal of novel query optimization strategies.

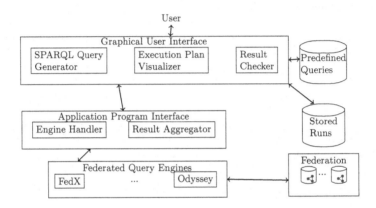

Fig. 1. PIPE's architecture

2   System Architecture

Figure 1 illustrates PIPE's architecture. The user interacts with our system through a Graphical User Interface (GUI) that relies on an Application Program Interface (API) to interact with the federated query engines, and provide an abstract representation of the engines' execution plans, results, and performance measurements. In the remainder of this section, we sketch purpose and core functionality of each system component.

GUI. It allows to load a predefined SPARQL query or provide a new query using the *simple* and *advanced* query interfaces. These query interfaces allow for creating queries with different trade-offs between expressiveness, e.g., possible operators, and usability for novice users, e.g., well-defined query structure. It also allows for choosing the endpoints for the federation, the federated query engines to study, and a timeout value. It visualizes the execution plans as trees and allows to explore the complete answers. If two or more engines produce the same plan, they are combined in order to ease the comparison of the plans that are actually different. Further functionality includes saving executions for later study and checking if the answers obtained by different engines are consistent. Currently, consistency of the answers is limited to checking the number of answers.

API. Given an analysis request, consisting of a query, federated engines, and sources to use, the API creates an execution job in which it sequentially runs each engine to avoid any interference between different executions. Once a query has been executed on all engines, the API aggregates the results and makes them available to the user. When execution jobs are created, users are provided with a unique token that can be used to cancel the execution job at any time. As the API does not rely on any specific implementation detail from the query engines, it can work with any federated query engine as long as the engine outputs a JSON object that adheres to the expected structure.

Federated Query Engine. It identifies relevant sources, decomposes the query into subqueries, and combines the subquery answers to produce the query answer. Minor changes were done to the engines to homogenize the output of the query optimization (execution plan), query execution (query results), and the measurement of relevant metrics. To minimize the code changes and ease the inclusion of other engines, our changes are mainly provided as a Java library that can be used to integrate federated query engines that rely on the RDF4J framework[1] into our comparison tool. In addition to performing serialization, the library automatically converts the execution plans into a canonical abstract version that is supported by our GUI. PIPE currently supports FedX [6], HiBIS-CuS [4], Odyssey [3], SemaGrow [1], and SPLENDID [2].

```
SELECT DISTINCT * WHERE {
    ?film dbo:director ?director .              (tp1)
    ?film rdf:type dbo:Film .                   (tp2)
    ?movie owl:sameAs ?film .                   (tp3)
    ?movie movie:film_subject film_subject:444 .  (tp4)
    ?movie dcterms:title ?title                 (tp5)
}
```

Listing 1.1. Q1: find the time travel film's directors (subject 444)

3   Processing Federated SPARQL Queries

Consider query Q1 (Listing 1.1), which asks for directors of time travel films, and a federation of SPARQL endpoints composed of ChEBI, KEGG, Drugbank, Geonames, DBpedia, Jamendo, NYTimes, SWDF, and LMDB. The execution plans computed by PIPE's currently supported federated query engines are depicted in Fig. 2. FedX, HiBISCuS, SemaGrow, and SPLENDID identify eight endpoints as relevant for tp3 because there is at least one triple in each of these endpoints that has the same predicate as tp3, i.e., owl:sameAs. Even if these engines select the same sources for all the triple patterns, SemaGrow computes a considerably better execution plan at the tradeoff of spending more time during planning (Fig. 3(b)). Semagrow relies on voiD statistics to correctly estimate

---

[1] http://rdf4j.org.

that **tp4** is the most selective triple pattern, and as such, it is better to execute **tp4** first. FedX and HiBISCuS rely solely on heuristics to assess selectivity, e.g., **tp1** and **tp2** are identified as the most selective triple patterns because they can be executed exclusively by one endpoint. Similarly to SemaGrow, Odyssey relies on statistics to identify that **tp4** is the most selective triple pattern. Differently from SemaGrow, Odyssey uses its federated statistics to identify that from all the endpoints that could be relevant for **tp3** and **tp5**, only LMDB has triples that describe entities that also have the property used as predicate in the triple pattern **tp4**, and therefore is the only one that is actually relevant for the execution of this query. A video of PIPE and its functionality is available at http:// qweb.cs.aau.dk/pipe.

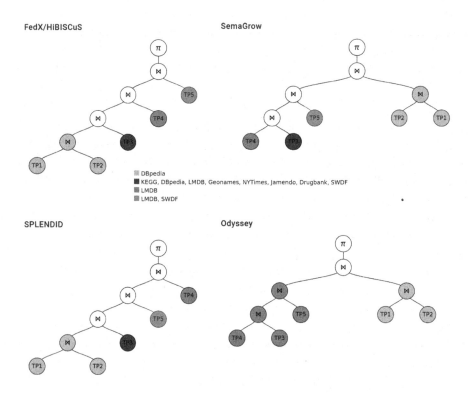

Fig. 2. Execution plans for **Q1**

4   Demonstration

At the conference, PIPE will be used to compare state-of-the-art federated query engines: FedX [6], HiBISCuS [4], Odyssey [3], SemaGrow [1], and SPLENDID [2].

Conference attendees will be able to formulate arbitrary SPARQL queries if they are experts or use the simple query interface to compose a basic graph pattern component by component. Moreover, users can choose a predefined query among the 25 queries defined in the FedBench benchmark [5] and focus on using PIPE to study how diverse the produced execution plans and their impact on the engines' performances are.

For the purposes of the demonstration, a federation of nine SPARQL endpoints as defined in the General Linked Open Data Collection and the Life Science Data Collection of the FedBench benchmark [5] will be available locally to avoid any network connectivity issues during the demonstration.

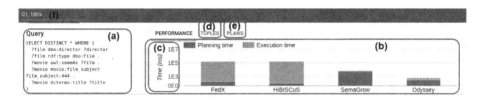

Fig. 3. Performance of the federated query engines for `Q1`

Figure 3 shows PIPE's GUI following the execution of `Q1` (Fig. 3(a)). It shows the performance of the engines that did not time out after 180 s (Fig. 3(b)) using a logarithmic scale on the vertical axis (Fig. 3(c)). Using PIPE's GUI, conference attendees can also choose to look at the execution plans (as shown in Fig. 2) by clicking on "PLANS" (Fig. 3(d)) or examine the query answers by clicking on "TUPLES" (Fig. 3(e)). The analysis of Q1 is saved to the browser's local storage after giving it a name (Fig. 3(f)).

5   Conclusion

In this paper, we have presented PIPE, a tool for comparing federated query engines in terms of performance, computed execution plans, and query answers. PIPE allows for inspecting the query optimization result, i.e., the execution plans, and in many cases, it allows for explaining the huge differences observable in terms of execution time. Notably, PIPE allows to assess how diverse the query execution plans produced by the federated query engines are. Currently, the query execution plans represent the operations as logical operators; as part of our future work, we plan to also depict physical operators. In addition, we plan to introduce additional performance measures, such as the number of requests made to the endpoints and the amount of transferred data.

Acknowledgments. This research was partially funded by the Danish Council for Independent Research (DFF) under grant agreement no. DFF-4093-00301B and Aalborg University's Talent Programme.

References

1. Charalambidis, A., Troumpoukis, A., Konstantopoulos, S.: SemaGrow: optimizing federated SPARQL queries. In: SEMANTICS 2015, pp. 121–128 (2015)
2. Görlitz, O., Staab, S.: SPLENDID: sparql endpoint federation exploiting VOID descriptions. In: COLD (2011)
3. Montoya, G., Skaf-Molli, H., Hose, K.: The Odyssey approach for optimizing federated SPARQL queries. In: d'Amato, C., et al. (eds.) ISWC 2017. LNCS, vol. 10587, pp. 471–489. Springer, Cham (2017). https://doi.org/10.1007/978-3-319-68288-4_28
4. Saleem, M., Ngonga Ngomo, A.-C.: HiBISCuS: hypergraph-based source selection for SPARQL endpoint federation. In: Presutti, V., d'Amato, C., Gandon, F., d'Aquin, M., Staab, S., Tordai, A. (eds.) ESWC 2014. LNCS, vol. 8465, pp. 176–191. Springer, Cham (2014). https://doi.org/10.1007/978-3-319-07443-6_13
5. Schmidt, M., Görlitz, O., Haase, P., Ladwig, G., Schwarte, A., Tran, T.: FedBench: a benchmark suite for federated semantic data query processing. In: Aroyo, L., et al. (eds.) ISWC 2011. LNCS, vol. 7031, pp. 585–600. Springer, Heidelberg (2011). https://doi.org/10.1007/978-3-642-25073-6_37
6. Schwarte, A., Haase, P., Hose, K., Schenkel, R., Schmidt, M.: FedX: optimization techniques for federated query processing on linked data. In: Aroyo, L., et al. (eds.) ISWC 2011. LNCS, vol. 7031, pp. 601–616. Springer, Heidelberg (2011). https://doi.org/10.1007/978-3-642-25073-6_38

Open Data Chatbot

Sophia Keyner, Vadim Savenkov[(✉)], and Svitlana Vakulenko

Institute for Information Business, Vienna University of Economics and Business, Vienna, Austria
sophia.keyner@s.wu.ac.at
{vadim.savenkov,svitlana.vakulenko}@wu.ac.at

Abstract. Recently, chatbots received an increased attention from industry and diverse research communities as a dialogue-based interface providing advanced human-computer interactions. On the other hand, Open Data continues to be an important trend and a potential enabler for government transparency and citizen participation. This paper shows how these two paradigms can be combined to help non-expert users find and discover open government datasets through dialogue.

Keywords: Open Data · Conversational search

1 Introduction

Open Data is often used to create new services and applications. The major source of Open Data, remain government Open Data portals designed to provide more transparency and enable the general public to monitor the state of affairs and exercise control over the actions of government bodies. Open Data access is expected to encourage public awareness and citizen participation.

Chatbot is a software providing a conversational interface. One of the applications for chatbots in conversational search providing access to an information source, such as a database. Chatbots have a number of advantages as well as associated challenges in comparison with other graphical interfaces:

- Light-weight and inexpensive to deploy, especially in comparison with custom visualizations;
- Engaging and intuitive, do not require user training.

In this paper we present an implementation of a chatbot that provides conversational search interface to an Open Data repository utilizing geo-entity annotations. Our code is open-source[1] and the web interface is publicly available[2].

---

[1] https://git.ai.wu.ac.at/sophiakeyner/open_data_chatbot.
[2] https://odbot.communidata.at.

© Springer Nature Switzerland AG 2019
P. Hitzler et al. (Eds.): ESWC 2019 Satellite Events, LNCS 11762, pp. 111–115, 2019.
https://doi.org/10.1007/978-3-030-32327-1_22

2 Related Work

Chatbots were introduced as an alternative interface able to provide a more user-friendly and engaging experience, while also serving as an effective information access point to structured data sources, such as Open Data repositories [2,6,7] and knowledge graphs [1]. DBpedia chatbot [1], for example, relies on a handful of pre-defined rules, which prevents from a more fine-grained query analysis, requires continuous engineering efforts and makes the approach difficult to scale and incorporate new conversational patterns. The approach we describe in this paper leverages machine-learning models that can be further improved by continuously learning from interactions with end-users. We show how machine-learning-based dialogue systems can benefit from explicit semantics, such as geographic entities (locations) annotations, that assist in natural language interpretation.

Open Data makes a perfect use case for the integration of the spatial linked data source, as it was previously shown to heavily rely on the geographic dimensions to enable effective search and discovery [3,5]. We leverage these insights and demonstrate how semantic geo-information linked data sources can help to enhance user experience with automated dialogue systems. Our work is a follow-up on the previously proposed Open Data chatbot architectures [2,6]. The main difference to the previously proposed architecture [6] is providing support for dataset discovery functionality beyond conversational search towards enabling conversational browsing of the underlying data structures. The mode switch is triggered by the intent detection component of our system.

Our implementation also utilizes the results of the semantic annotation approach proposed by Neumaier et al. [5] similar to the chatbot for geo-search and visualization by Heil and Neumaier [2]. We make a step further by training a supervised model for intent detection and entity recognition from the user natural-language input.

3 Chatbot Architecture

Our architecture design is based on the Rasa framework[3], which also provides an open-source Python library that implements several models for training customized dialogue systems. The chatbot architecture integrates different components into a single processing pipeline that takes an input from the user and produces a response. Figure 1 depicts the main steps of the processing pipeline across the components.

3.1 Message Interpretation

The message interpretation module includes separate machine learning models for entity recognition and intent classification tasks. We hand-crafted 250 sample messages to train these models.

---

[3] https://rasa.com.

Entity Recognition. Our proof-of-concept prototype can recognize two types of entities: topic keywords and geo-entities. The first step, entity mention extraction, is an instance of the sequence labeling task [4]. Its input is the text of the user utterance represented as a sequence of words. Then, a supervised machine learning model, conditional random fields (CRF) in our implementation, is trained to assign labels to words. 121 of the sample messages, which were used for training the model, included one of the topic keywords and 18 samples contained one of the geo-entities. These labels are then used to extract entity mentions. By entity mention we mean a text span that refers to one of the entities, e.g. "schools" or "Graz". Entity mentions are then used in the search query to retrieve and rank relevant datasets from our Open Data repository. We found out that the pre-trained model often fails to extract geo-entities that were absent from the training dataset. To mitigate this issue we implemented a look-up table that contains a list of geo-entities as an alternative unsupervised approach for entity mention extraction.

Intent Classification was trained with a support vector machine (SVM) classifier to recognize nine intents: greeting, good-bye, add keyword, add location, search, explore, thank you, affirm, deny. We designed at least six sample messages for each of the intents.

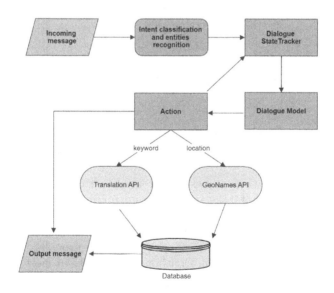

Fig. 1. Open Data Chatbot architecture.

3.2 Dialogue Management

The sequence of selected actions is tracked and determines the current dialogue state. Our set of available actions includes 10 hand-crafted utterance-templates and a custom action to access the database. The dialogue management component receives the entities and the intent detected at the previous step of message interpretations and selects the next action from the predefined set of actions. This selection is made by a neural network model, which was trained on 14 hand-crafted stories, based on the user's intent and the current dialogue state.

4   Dialogue Flow

After greeting the user, Chatbot requests User to make a choice between two interaction modes: search and explore (see Fig. 2). The mode can be switched at any time with an ad-hoc user utterance (e.g. "Could I go back to explore?") that should be classified with the corresponding intent.

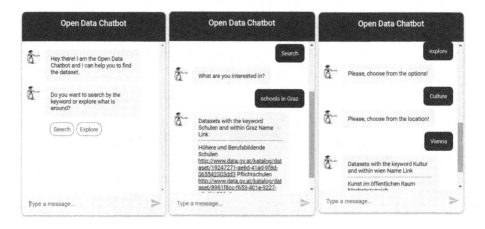

Fig. 2. Example of the search and exploratory modes.

In search mode, Chatbot requests User to define the topic of interest. In exploratory mode, Chatbot asks two follow-up questions which the available options displayed as buttons. The first question is the topic of interest, such as education and health care, the second is the geo-location that defines the scope of the dataset. User then can choose one of the options provided by Chatbot or enter a custom query instead. Then, Chatbot answers with at most five matching dataset titles and links to the original Open Data portal.

5   Conclusion

We implemented a novel prototype of an Open Data chatbot by integrating state-of-the-art parsing and semantic technologies. This demonstration showcases a conversational search application for a repository of publicly available datasets, but the design approach we described is not limited to this specific use case and can be transferred to other domains, such as cultural heritage or e-commerce, where users can benefit from more engaging and compact interfaces for search and discovery. The main limitation for training dialogue models using machine learning techniques is the need for annotated conversational data. We showed that it is possible to develop such models using only a handful of examples, but it is important to look further for more scalable solutions that can help to gradually extend these models beyond the initial built-in assumptions about the dialogue structure.

Demonstration Plan. We will engage conference participants in the evaluation of our system designed as a user study. The task is given a broad topic, such as Nature, find relevant datasets using our chatbot interface. The participants will be encouraged to fill out a small questionnaire in the end, which includes rating of their experience, providing additional feedback and a wish list.

Acknowledgements. This work was supported by the Austrian Research Promotion Agency (FFG) under the project CommuniData (grant no. 855407).

References

1. Athreya, R.G., Ngomo, A.N., Usbeck, R.: Enhancing community interactions with data-driven chatbots-the dbpedia chatbot. In: Companion of the The Web Conference 2018 on The Web Conference 2018, WWW 2018, Lyon, France, 23–27 April 2018, pp. 143–146 (2018)
2. Heil, E., Neumaier, S.: reboting.com: towards geo-search and visualization of austrian open data. In: Gangemi, A., et al. (eds.) ESWC 2018. LNCS, vol. 11155, pp. 105–110. Springer, Cham (2018). https://doi.org/10.1007/978-3-319-98192-5_20
3. Kacprzak, E., Koesten, L., Tennison, J., Simperl, E.: Characterising dataset search queries. In: Companion of the The Web Conference 2018, WWW 2018, Lyon, France, 23–27 April 2018, pp. 1485–1488 (2018)
4. Lafferty, J.D., McCallum, A., Pereira, F.C.N.: Conditional random fields: probabilistic models for segmenting and labeling sequence data. In: Proceedings of the Eighteenth International Conference on Machine Learning (ICML 2001), Williams College, Williamstown, MA, USA, 28 June - 1 July 2001, pp. 282–289 (2001)
5. Neumaier, S., Savenkov, V., Polleres, A.: Geo-semantic labelling of open data. In: Proceedings of the 14th International Conference on Semantic Systems, SEMANTICS 2018, Vienna, Austria, 10–13 September 2018, pp. 9–20 (2018)
6. Neumaier, S., Savenkov, V., Vakulenko, S.: Talking open data. In: The Semantic Web: ESWC 2017 Satellite Events - ESWC 2017 Satellite Events, Portorož, Slovenia, 28 May - 1 June 2017, pp. 132–136 (2017)
7. Porreca, S., Leotta, F., Mecella, M., Vassos, S., Catarci, T.: Accessing government open data through chatbots. In: Garrigós, I., Wimmer, M. (eds.) ICWE 2017. LNCS, vol. 10544, pp. 156–165. Springer, Cham (2018). https://doi.org/10.1007/978-3-319-74433-9_14

Question Answering for Link Prediction and Verification

Maria Khvalchik[✉], Artem Revenko, and Christian Blaschke

Semantic Web Company, Vienna, Austria
{maria.khvalchik,artem.revenko,christian.blaschke}@semantic-web.com

Abstract. In this work we tackle the link prediction task in knowledge graphs. Following recent success of Question Answering systems in outperforming humans, we employ the developed tools to identify and verify new links. To identify the gaps in a knowledge graph, we use the existing techniques and combine them with Question Answering tools to extract concealed knowledge. We outline the overall procedure and discuss preliminary results.

Keywords: Link prediction · Knowledge graph completion · Question answering · Relation extraction

1 Introduction

Knowledge graphs (KGs) contain knowledge about the world and provide a structured representation of this knowledge. Current KGs contain only a small subset of what is true in the world [7]. There are different types of information that could be incomplete, for example, incomplete set of entities (not all movies are mentioned in the movies KG), incomplete set of predicates, or missing links between existing entities. Different types of incompleteness are usually addressed with different methods. For example, Named Entity Recognition is successfully applied to find new entities of given classes [10]. In this work we consider the latter problem of link prediction (LP), i.e. finding triples (subject s, predicate p, objects o), where p is defined in the schema of the KG and s and o are known instance contained in the existing KG.

LP approaches can roughly be subdivided into two classes:

Leveraging the knowledge from the existing KG

- The rule induction methods [3,6] learn rules over KG that capture patterns in data. In a generic domain one can learn, for example, that a

This work has been partially funded by the project LYNX. The project LYNX has received funding from the European Union's Horizon 2020 research and innovation programme under grant agreement no. 780602. More information is available online at http://www.lynx-project.eu.

P. Hitzler et al. (Eds.): ESWC 2019 Satellite Events, LNCS 11762, pp. 116–120, 2019.
https://doi.org/10.1007/978-3-030-32327-1_23

person has a home address or that a consumer good has a price. These rules help to identify potential gaps in an incomplete KG. In order to fill in the gaps one needs to verify the veracity of the potential new triple.

– Embeddings project symbolic entities and relations into continuous vector space. The vector arithmetic is used to predict new links [8,12].

Extracting the knowledge from other sources.

– Transformation of the information from some structured source[1].
– Relation Extraction (RE) methods [11] employ trained models to recognize triples in the text and add those triples to the existing KG.

In this work we consider combining both approaches. Given a KG we use rules and heuristics to identify potential gaps in the KG. Then we employ a Question Answering (QA) framework to find and/or verify new triples. Therefore, for each new triple we can demonstrate supporting piece of text. It is interesting to compare with the paper [1] describing a ranking method to provide descriptive explanations for relationships in the KG. In our paper we look for relationships expressed in the text that are not yet in the KG.

The difference of the introduced methodology from the existing approaches:

LP typically considers only the KG itself and not the textual data.
RE lacks in finding new relations not presented in the training set.

2   Approach

After applying the learned rules or heuristics we obtain a set of pairs (s,p) and triples (s,p,o). In case of having pairs, the task is to find objects O such that $\{(s,p,o) \mid o \in O\}$ is a set of valid triples. In case of having triples, the task is to verify the provided triples. Our approach consists of the following steps:

1. Question formulation,
2. Retrieving documents potentially containing answers from the corpus,
3. Employing QA over documents to get candidate answers and their scores,
4. Choosing correct answers.

Question Formulation. The goal is to go from a pair (s,p) to such a question that a correct answer o defines a valid triple (s,p,o). In order to articulate this natural language question q we employ lexicalization techniques [5].

Retrieving Documents. Given a question q we use query expansion techniques [2] and formulate a search query to retrieve relevant document from the corpus.

---

[1] https://www.w3.org/TR/r2rml/.

Question Answering. Our end-to-end QA system accepts a natural language question and a set of documents as input and outputs a set of pairs (answer, confidence score). The score indicates the confidence of the system that the answer is correct. The QA systems are usually computationally demanding, therefore it is not feasible to send the whole corpus as an input to the QA system.

We use an implementation of BERT [4] that we trained on a large set of question-answer pairs of SQuAD dataset [9]. BERT is a deep learning based system that outperforms previous approaches and reaches close to human performance in QA tasks.

Verification and Integration. Given the answers produced by the QA system we try to match each answer to an instances in the KG. If an answer could not be matched then it is discarded. For the undiscarded answers we check if the class of the matched instances complies with the range restrictions of the predicate definition in the schema. If the range restriction is satisfied we add the triple (subject, predicate, matched instances) to the KG.

In the special case when we know that at most one triple is allowed for a pair (subject, predicate) we choose the answer yielding the highest score of the QA system if it satisfies the range restriction.

3   Preliminary Results and Conclusion

The first used corpus is a collection of over 3300 biomedical paper abstracts from "PubMed"[2] containing term "BRCA1". Questions and first 3 answers are provided in the Table 1. For the first question: "Which diseases does niraparib treat?" it is possible to check the following triple (niraparib, treatsDisease, BRCA-mutant ovarian cancer). If this triple fails the verification stage, we continue to verify other candidates for their existence. In this case the answer satisfies the verification as "BRCA-mutant ovarian cancer" is indeed a disease.

In all three examples we asked what kind of disease is treated by such drugs as niraparib, rucaparib, and olaparib. All these drugs are anti-cancer agents, the system can successfully match these drugs with treating cancer. Moreover, the system is able to identify the specific types of cancer and additional details.

The second dataset is a collection of paper abstracts containing the term "rs1045642", the identifier of a single-nucleotide polymorphism (SNP) in the human genome. We intend to observe data about mutations, the KG of which we expect not to be complete as the database of mutations is not up-to-date. To add such frequently updated data one should inspect corresponding literature. That being said, it is clear that an automated system could come as a benefit.

Conclusion. We considered an important practically relevant task of LP in KGs. In our approach we combine existing techniques to identify potential gaps with QA system to extract concealed knowledge from a text corpus and to

---

formulate new triples. The first experiments show promising results even for domain specific datasets.

Table 1. Questions and answers.

Question	Answers, confidence score
PubMed dataset with term "BRCA1"	
Which diseases does niraparib treat?	1. BRCA-mutant ovarian cancer, 0.259
	2. Tumors with Defective Homologous Recombination, 0.226
	3. ovarian cancer, 0.223
Which diseases does rucaparib treat?	1. Advanced ovarian and breast cancer, 0.204
	2. nausea, vomiting, asthenia/fatigue, anemia and transient transaminitis, 0.136
	3. Patients with Deleterious BRCA Mutation-Associated Advanced Ovarian Cancer, 0.114
Which diseases does olaparib treat?	1. ovarian cancer and BRCA mutations, 0.446
	2. ovarian cancer, 0.111
	3. specific forms of ovarian cancer and BRCA mutations, 0.063
PubMed dataset with term "rs1045642"	
What is rs1045642 associated with?	1. risk of mucositis, 0.366
	2. increased abdominal fat mass and decreased appendicular skeletal muscle mass, 0.236
	3. time to allograft failure, 0.211
What does rs1045642 modulate?	1. Office Blood Pressure, 0.780
	2. Blood Pressure, 0.081
	3. Office Blood Pressure at 1-Year Post Kidney Transplantation, 0.061

References

1. Bhatia, S., Dwivedi, P., Kaur, A.: That's interesting, tell me more! Finding descriptive support passages for knowledge graph relationships. In: Vrandečić, D., et al. (eds.) ISWC 2018. LNCS, vol. 11136, pp. 250–267. Springer, Cham (2018). https://doi.org/10.1007/978-3-030-00671-6_15
2. Bhogal, J., Macfarlane, A., Smith, P.: A review of ontology based query expansion. Inform. Process. Manage. **43**(4), 866–886 (2007)
3. d'Amato, C., Staab, S., Tettamanzi, A.G.B., Minh, T.D., Gandon, F.: Ontology enrichment by discovering multi-relational association rules from ontological knowledge bases. In: ACM, vol. 31, pp. 333–338 (2016)

4. Devlin, J., Chang, M., Lee, K., Toutanova, K.: BERT: pre-training of deep bidirectional transformers for language understanding. CoRR abs/1810.04805 (2018)
5. Ell, B., Harth, A.: A language-independent method for the extraction of RDF verbalization templates. In: INLG 2014, pp. 26–34 (2014)
6. Ho, V.T., Stepanova, D., Gad-Elrab, M.H., Kharlamov, E., Weikum, G.: Rule learning from knowledge graphs guided by embedding models. In: Vrandečić, D., et al. (eds.) ISWC 2018. LNCS, vol. 11136, pp. 72–90. Springer, Cham (2018). https://doi.org/10.1007/978-3-030-00671-6_5
7. Ji, G., He, S., Xu, L., Liu, K., Zhao, J.: Knowledge graph embedding via dynamic mapping matrix. In: ACL 2015, Volume 1: Long Papers, pp. 687–696 (2015)
8. Lin, Y., Liu, Z., Sun, M., Liu, Y., Zhu, X.: Learning entity and relation embeddings for knowledge graph completion. In: Proceedings of the Twenty-Ninth AAAI Conference on Artificial Intelligence, pp. 2181–2187 (2015)
9. Rajpurkar, P., Jia, R., Liang, P.: Know what you don't know: unanswerable questions for squad. In: Proceedings of the 56th Annual Meeting of the Association for Computational Linguistics, pp. 784–789 (2018)
10. Sanchez-Cisneros, D., Aparicio Gali, F.: UEM-UC3M: an ontology-based named entity recognition system for biomedical texts. In: SemEval 2013, pp. 622–627. Association for Computational Linguistics (2013)
11. Schutz, A., Buitelaar, P.: RelExt: a tool for relation extraction from text in ontology extension. In: Gil, Y., Motta, E., Benjamins, V.R., Musen, M.A. (eds.) ISWC 2005. LNCS, vol. 3729, pp. 593–606. Springer, Heidelberg (2005). https://doi.org/10.1007/11574620_43
12. Wang, Z., Zhang, J., Feng, J., Chen, Z.: Knowledge graph embedding by translating on hyperplanes. In: AAAI 2014, pp. 1112–1119 (2014)

Extracting Genealogical Networks of Linked Data from Biographical Texts

Petri Leskinen[1(✉)] and Eero Hyvönen[1,2]

[1] Semantic Computing Research Group (SeCo), Aalto University, Espoo, Finland
{petri.leskinen,eero.hyvonen}@aalto.fi
[2] HELDIG – Helsinki Centre for Digital Humanities, University of Helsinki,
Helsinki, Finland
http://seco.cs.aalto.fi, http://heldig.fi

Abstract. This paper presents the idea and our work of extracting and reassembling a genealogical network automatically from a collection of biographies. The network can be used as a tool for network analysis of historical persons. The data has been published as Linked Data and as an interactive online service as part of the in-use data service and semantic portal *BiographySampo—Finnish Biographies on the Semantic Web*.

1 Introduction

Extracting and inferring social or genealogical networks from historical documents can provide new information for biographical and prosopographical [1] research. However, genealogical data is often available only in textual form providing challenges for knowledge extraction: How to identify persons and their gender by different name forms? How to disambiguate namesakes in different times? How to extract the genealogical relations between the mentions? This paper presents a case study for extracting the explicit genealogical network implicit in the national collection of 13 144 Finnish biographies[1]. The methodological idea is to combine regular expression identification, imprecise proper name matching, gender information, and data about expected lifespans for more accurate results. The system was evaluated with promising results, and a tool was constructed, based on Linked Data, for examining the underlying network of ~81 000 extracted basic relations "parent", "spouse", and "child". On top of the Linked Data service, a new application was created for studying the networks interactively as a new part of the in-use BiographySampo[2] system [2].

Related Work. Extracting and studying biographical networks has been researched in the *Six Degrees of Francis Bacon* [3] project and *BiographyNet* [4]. Articles [5,6] discuss extracting genealogical networks from multi-source vital records. For the large public there are many crowd-sourcing-based commercial

---

[1] https://kansallisbiografia.fi/, accessed 20 March 2019.
[2] Online at: http://biografiasampo.fi; cf. project homepage for further information and publications: https://seco.cs.aalto.fi/projects/biografiasampo/en/.

© Springer Nature Switzerland AG 2019
P. Hitzler et al. (Eds.): ESWC 2019 Satellite Events, LNCS 11762, pp. 121–125, 2019.
https://doi.org/10.1007/978-3-030-32327-1_24

genealogy websites, such as ancestry.com, myheritage.com, and geni.com. This paper extends our earlier papers about BiographySampo [2] and network analysis based on biographical link references into extraction of genealogical networks [7,8], and presents an application view for studying such networks interactively.

2   Extracting Genealogical Networks from Texts

Dataset. BiographySampo is a semantic portal based on a knowledge base that has been created using natural language processing methods, linked data, and semantic web technologies. It contains 13 144 biographies of notable Finns that can be browsed through a faceted search application and using tools for Digital Humanities research. [9] In addition to the genealogical network discussed in this paper, the data been a source for reference network extraction [7,8].

Pattern-Based Knowledge Extraction. Many biographies in the dataset include semi-formal textual descriptions of family relations of the protagonist. As an example, the description of baroness *Elisabeth Järnefelt*[3] is given below:

> Jelizaveta Konstantinovna Clodt von Jürgensburg from year 1857 known as Järnefelt, Elisabeth S 11.1.1839 Pietari, K 3.2.1929 Helsinki.
> *V* Baron, major general Konstantin Karlovitsh Clodt von Jürgensburg and Catharine Vigné.
> *P* 1857– senator, governor, lieutenant general August Alexander Järnefelt *S* 1833, *K* 1896, *PV* bailiff Gustaf Adolf Järnefelt and Aurora Fredrika Molander.
> *Children:* Caspar (Kasper) Woldemar *S* 1859, *K* 1941, critic, translator, Russian language teacher, painter, *P* Emma Ahonen; Edvard Armas *S* 1869, *K* 1958, conductor, composer, professor, *P1* songstress Maikki Pakarinen, *P2* songstress Olivia (Liva) Edström; Aina (Aino) *S* 1871, *K* 1969, *P* composer Jean Sibelius;

The semi-formal expressions here have uniformity in structure that can be used effectively for pattern-based information extraction: First, the given and family names are mentioned and after that the years of birth S and death K. The description provides information about the parents (marked with V), spouses (P), parents-in-law (PV), children, and children-in-law of the protagonist.

One major problem in knowledge extraction here is recognizing the same person, here *Elisabeth Järnefelt*, referenced with different names: *Jelizaveta Konstantinovna Clodt von Jürgensburg, Elisabeth Clodt von Jürgensburg* or most commonly *Elisabeth Järnefelt*. On the other hand, same names are used in families over and over again. For example, there is a case of four people with name *Christian Trapp*, a grandfather, a father, a son[4], and a grandson. They cannot be distinguished without additional information about their known lifespans.

Data Processing. In our knowledge extraction pipeline, the genealogical textual description of the protagonist is first divided into the parts describing his/her parents, spouses (wife/husband distinction is not known at this point), and children. The division is based on using regular expressions matching the punctuation and the tokens V, P, PV.

---

[3] http://biografiasampo.fi/henkilo/p3148.
[4] http://biografiasampo.fi/henkilo/p10013.

The years of birth, death, or marriage are easily separated from the text sequence. To separate occupational descriptions from the proper names, we used the ARPA service[5] together with vocabularies of Finnish female, male, and family names[6]. The extracted names were used to reason the gender of the person, which was used to refine relations, e.g., to specify a *parent* as a *mother* or a *father*. For the network, the spouses were linked with the children by the known years of marriage and child birth.

To gain detailed vital information for disambiguation, we reasoned lifetime estimates, e.g., the missing years of birth of the parents based on the known birth year of their child. The estimates were constructed by first collecting the years of births of a parent and a child from the known cases in data. The distributions of parent ages at child birth are depicted in Fig. 1. To reason the ages of spouses, a similar study was performed with the result that 99% of differences between the births of a husband and wife is in the range of -18–+35 years. The more relatives with known records a person has, the more precise the estimates are.

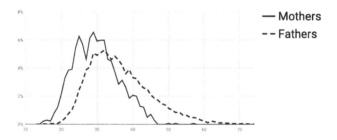

Fig. 1. Distribution of parent ages at a child birth

3   Evaluation

For evaluation we randomly chose 50 biographies, and manually compared the texts with the extracted results. The test set had mentions of 170 people. We compared the data fields of person names, years of birth and death, gender, occupation, and relation type. According to our evaluation 94.5% of the extracted people records were mentioned only in a single biography; the accuracy was 97.3%. For people mentioned in multiple biographies the accuracy was 80.4%; our system could not identify all mentions referring to same people.

For an example of the extracted network, a part of genealogical network of Elisabeth Järnefelt[7] is depicted in Fig. 2. She is in the largest connected component in our network. This component contains 2694 family relation links and

---

[5] http://seco.cs.aalto.fi/projects/dcert/, accessed: 9 March 2019.
[6] https://www.avoindata.fi/data/en_GB/dataset/none, accessed: 20 March 2019.
[7] http://biografiasampo.fi/henkilo/p3148/sukulaiset.

connects 1835 people in 250 biographies. To further enrich the web portal, the immediate family relations were used to reasons[8] like siblings, cousins, uncles, aunts, grandparents, grandchildren, and relatives-in-law.

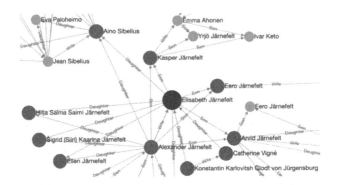

Fig. 2. Genealogical network around Elisabeth Järnefelt as seen in a BiographySampo view

Acknowledgements. Thanks to Business Finland for financial support and CSC – IT Center for Science, Finland, for computational resources.

References

1. Verboven, K., Carlier, M., Dumolyn, J.: A short manual to the art of prosopography. In: Prosopography approaches and applications. A handbook. Unit for Prosopographical Research (Linacre College), pp. 35–70 (2007)

2. Hyvönen, E., et al.: BiographySampo – publishing and enriching biographies on the semantic web for digital humanities research. In: Hitzler, P., et al. (eds.) ESWC 2019. LNCS, vol. 11503, pp. 574–589. Springer, Cham (2019). https://doi.org/10.1007/978-3-030-21348-0_37

3. Finegold, M., Otis, J., Shalizi, C., Shore, D., Wang, L., Warren, C.: Six degrees of Francis Bacon: a statistical method for reconstructing large historical social networks. Digit. Hum. Q. **10**(3) (2016)

4. Ockeloen, N., et al.: BiographyNet: managing provenance at multiple levels and from different perspectives. In: Proceedings of the 3rd International Conference on Linked Science (LISC 2013), vol. 1116, pp. 59–71. CEUR Workshop Proceedings (2013)

5. Efremova, J., et al.: Multi-source entity resolution for genealogical data. In: Bloothooft, G., Christen, P., Mandemakers, K., Schraagen, M. (eds.) Population Reconstruction, pp. 129–154. Springer, Cham (2015). https://doi.org/10.1007/978-3-319-19884-2_7

6. Malmi, E., Rasa, M., Gionis, A.: AncestryAI: a tool for exploring computationally inferred family trees. In: Proceedings of the 26th International Conference on World Wide Web Companion, pp. 257–261. International World Wide Web Conferences Steering Committee (2017)

---

[8] http://biografiasampo.fi/henkilo/p3148.

7. Tamper, M., Leskinen, P., Apajalahti, K., Hyvönen, E.: Using biographical texts as linked data for prosopographical research and applications. In: Ioannides, M., et al. (eds.) EuroMed 2018. LNCS, vol. 11196, pp. 125–137. Springer, Cham (2018). https://doi.org/10.1007/978-3-030-01762-0_11

8. Tamper, M., Hyvönen, E., Leskinen, P.: Visualizing and analyzing networks of named entities in biographical dictionaries for digital humanities research. In: Proceedings of the 20th International Conference on Computational Linguistics and Intelligent Text Processing (CI-Cling 2019). Springer, April 2019, accepted

9. Hyvönen, E., Leskinen, P., Tamper, M., Tuominen, J., Keravuori, K.: Semantic National Biography of Finland. In: Proceedings of the Digital Humanities in the Nordic Countries 3rd Conference (DHN 2018), vol. 2084, pp. 372–385. CEUR Workshop Proceedings (2018). http://www.ceur-ws.org/Vol-2084/short12.pdf

Entity Embedding Analogy for Implicit Link Discovery

Nada Mimouni$^{(\boxtimes)}$, Jean-Claude Moissinac, and Anh Tuan Vu

Telecom ParisTech, Institut Mines Telecom, 46 Rue Barrault, 75013 Paris, France
{nada.mimouni,jean-claude.moissinac,anh.vu}@telecom-paristech.fr
https://www.telecom-paristech.fr/

Abstract. In this work we are interested in the problem of knowledge graph (KG) incompleteness, which we propose to solve by discovering implicit triples using observed ones in the incomplete graph leveraging analogy structures deducted from a KG embedding model. We use a language modelling approach that we adapt to entities and relations. The first results show that analogical inferences in the projected vector space is relevant to a link prediction task.

1 Introduction

General purpose knowledge bases (KB) such as Yago, Wikidata and DBpedia are valuable background resources for various AI tasks, for example recommendation, web search and question answering. However, using these resources bring to light several problems which are mainly due to their substantial size and high incompleteness [5]. Recently, vector-space embedding models for KB completion have been extensively studied for their efficiency and scalability and proven to achieve state-of-the-art link prediction performances [1,3,7]. Numerous KB completion approaches have also been employed which aim at predicting whether or not a relationship not in the KG is likely to be correct. An overview of these models with the results for link prediction and triple classification is given in [6]. KG embedding models learn distributed representations for entities and relations, which are represented as low-dimensional dense vectors, or matrices, in continuous vector spaces. These, in turn, are intended to preserve the information in the KG.

In this work we are particularly interested in adapting the language modelling approach proposed by [4] where relational similarities or linguistic regularities between pairs of words are captured. They are represented as translations in the projected vector space where similar words appear close to each other and allow for arithmetic operations on vectors of relations between word pairs. For instance, the vector translation $v(Germany) - v(Berlin) \approx v(France) - v(Paris)$ (1) shows relational similarity between countries and capital cities. It highlights clear-cut the analogical properties between the embedded words expressed by the analogy "*Berlin* is to *Germany* as *Paris* is to *France*".

© Springer Nature Switzerland AG 2019
P. Hitzler et al. (Eds.): ESWC 2019 Satellite Events, LNCS 11762, pp. 126–129, 2019.
https://doi.org/10.1007/978-3-030-32327-1_25

We propose to apply this property to entities and relations in KGs as represented by diagrams (a) and (b) in Fig. 1. The vector translation example is likely to capture the *capital* relationship that we could represent by a translation vector $v(capital)$ verifying the following compositionality [4]: $v(France) + v(capital) - v(Paris) \approx 0$. We use the analogical property for KB completion and show that it is particularly relevant for this task. Our intuition is illustrated by diagrams (b) and (c) in Fig. 1 where an unobserved triple can be inferred by mirroring its counterpart in the parallelogram [3]. Our approach is described in Sect. 2 and the initial results are given in Sect. 3.

2   Approach

First, we adapt the language modelling approach to KG embedding[1]. We transform the entities and relations in the graph as paths that are considered as sequences of words in natural language. To extract RDF graph substructures, we use the breath-first algorithm to get all the graph walks or random walks for a limited number N. Let

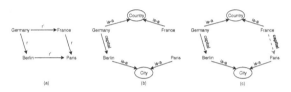

Fig. 1. (a) Analogy relation diagram (parallelogram) between countries and capital cities. In KGs (b) and (c), r corresponds to the relation *capital* and r' is decomposed into two type relations (*is-a*) to concepts *Country* and *City*.

$G = (V, E)$ be an RDF graph where V is the set of vertices and E is the set of directed edges. For each vertex v we generate *all* or N graph walks P_v of depth d rooted in the vertex v by exploring direct outgoing and incoming edges of v and iteratively direct edges of its neighbours v_i until depth d is reached. The paths after the first iteration follow this pattern $v \rightarrow e_i \rightarrow v_i$ where $e_i \in E$. The final set of sequences for G is the union of the sequences of all the vertices $\bigcup_{v \in V} P_v$.

Next, we train a neural language model which estimates the likelihood of a sequence of entities and relations appearing in the graph and represents them as vectors of latent numerical features. To do this, we use the CBOW (continuous bag of words) and Skip-Gram models as described in [4]. CBOW predicts target words w_t from context words within a context window c while Skip-Gram does the inverse and attempts to predict the context words from the target word. The probability $p(w_t | w_{t-c}...w_{t+c})$ is calculated using the *softmax* function.

Finally, we extract analogical properties from the feature space to estimate the existence of new relationships between entities. We use the following arithmetic operation on the feature vectors (entities of Fig. 1): $v(Berlin) - v(Germany) + v(France) = v(x)$ which we consider is solved correctly if $v(x)$ is most similar to $v(Paris)$ as in equality (1). On the left-hand side of (1), entities with the same type contribute positively to the similarity, for example,

---

[1] A similar approach is described in [8]. Although ours differs in several aspects, it is not discussed here due to space constraints.

Germany and *France* having the same type *Country*. Whereas *Berlin* of a different *City* type contribute negatively. The right-hand side of the equation contains the missing corner of the diagram which remains to be predicted. We then use cosine similarity measures between the resulting vector $v(x)$ and vectors of all other entities of the same type in the embedding space (discarding the original ones of the equation) in order to rank the results.

3   Experimental Evaluation

We test our approach on a sub-graph of DBpedia representing a target domain: here we chose museums of Paris. We propose to address the scalability issue by contextualizing the input graphs assuming that more relevant information is centralized within a perimeter of α hops around main entities of this domain (we used $\alpha = 2$ as suggested by [2]). We build our KG as the union of individual contextual graphs of all entities representing the input data from the cultural institution *Paris Musées* (13 sites). We identify each site by its URI on DBpedia-fr after an entity resolution task[2]. The final graph contains 448309 entities, 2285 relations and 5122879 triples. To generate sequences of entities and relations we use random graph walks with $N = 1000$ for depth $d = \{4, 8\}$. We also consider for each entity all walks of depth $d = 2$ (direct neighbours). We then train the Skip-Gram word2vec model on the corpus of sequences with the following parameters: window size = 5, number of iterations = 10, negative samples = 25 (for the purpose of optimisation) and dimension of the entities' vectors = 200.

To evaluate the approach we build a ground-truth for analogy between entities in the KG. Each entry corresponds to a parallelogram as described in Fig. 1 with one unobserved triple in the KG. For each entity, we collect a list of well-known artists for this site as follows: find in DBpedia-fr the list of artists (dbo:Artist) or otherwise, individuals (dbo: Person) who are associated with the site. For some sites, we manually create the list, for example by searching for well-known artists for a museum on the website http://parismuseescollections. paris.fr/fr/recherche.

We use conventional metrics: Mean Reciprocal Rank (MRR) and the number of correct responses at a fixed rate (Hits@). The evaluation protocol is as follows: for each $Muri_i$, URI of a museum, consider all $Muri_j \mid j \neq i$, find the top most similar entities of the predicted vectors with positives $= [Muri_i, Muri_j]$ and negative $= [Auri_k]$, URI of the first artist identified for $Muri_i$, filtered by type *Artist*. In the list of results, we then examine the intersection with artists $Auri_l$ associated with $Muri_j$. Table 1 shows results of MRR and Hits@$\{3, 5, 10\}$ (%) for $d = \{4, 8\}$ and $N = 1000$. The final row of the table shows the impact of considering longer paths on the performances of the approach. In fact, longer paths capture richer contexts for entities and results in better vectors estimation by the neural language model.

---

[2] In the following, we denote the URI http://fr.dbpedia.org/resource/entity shortly as dbr:entity.

Table 1. MRR and Hits@$\{3, 5, 10\}$ (%) of a subset of representative examples of *Paris Musées* data for $d = \{4, 8\}$ and $N = 1000$.

Entity	MRR		Hits@3		Hits@5		Hits@10	
	d = 4	d = 8	d = 4	d = 8	d = 4	d = 8	d = 4	d = 8
dbr:Musée_Bourdelle	0,39	0,43	0,50	0,42	0,50	0,42	0,66	0,50
dbr:Musée_Carnavalet	0,43	0,59	0,58	0,67	0,66	0,75	0,83	0,75
dbr:Musée_Zadkine	0,43	0,44	0,41	0,42	0,50	0,50	0,50	0,50
dbr:Musée_Cernuschi	0,42	0,50	0,50	0,58	0,58	0,67	0,75	0,67
dbr:Petit_Palais	0,38	0,63	0,50	0,75	0,66	0,75	0,66	0,75
dbr:Maison_de_Balzac	0,23	0,44	0,25	0,58	0,41	0,58	0,41	0,58
dbr:Musée_Cognacq-Jay	0,33	0,49	0,33	0,58	0,33	0,58	0,33	0,58
dbr:Musée_d'art_moderne_de_Paris	0,36	0,71	0,41	0,75	0,50	0,83	0,58	0,83
dbr:Musée_de_la_Vie_Romantique	0,34	0,48	0,41	0,50	0,41	0,58	0,50	0,58
dbr:Palais_Galliera	0,36	0,48	0,50	0,50	0,50	0,58	0,50	0,58
dbr:Maison_de_Victor_Hugo	0,38	0,55	0,50	0,58	0,58	0,58	0,58	0,67
dbr:Musée_de_Grenoble	0,34	0,33	0,41	0,33	0,50	0,33	0,50	0,33
All entities in *Paris Musées*	0,37	**0,52**	0,44	**0,58**	0,51	**0,62**	0,57	**0,64**

4   Conslusion

In this paper, we presented an approach for link discovery in KBs based on the neural language embedding of RDF graphs and leveraging analogical structures extracted from relational similarities which could be used to infer new unobserved triples from the observed ones. The test of our approach on a domain-specific ground-truth shows promising results. We will continue to expand upon the research and compare it with state-of-the-art approaches for KB completion on the standard baselines.

References

1. Bordes, A., Usunier, N., García-Durán, A., Weston, J., Yakhnenko, O.: Translating embeddings for modeling multi-relational data. In: NIPS (2013)
2. Hulpus, I., Hayes, C., Karnstedt, M., Greene, D.: Unsupervised graph-based topic labelling using DBpedia. In: Proceedings of WSDM, pp. 465–474 (2013)
3. Liu, H., Wu, Y., Yang, Y.: Analogical inference for multi-relational embeddings. In: Proceedings of ICML, pp. 2168–2178 (2017)
4. Mikolov, T., Sutskever, I., Chen, K., Corrado, G.S., Dean, J.: Distributed representations of words and phrases and their compositionality. In: NIPS (2013)
5. Min, B., Grishman, R., Wan, L., Wang, C., Gondek, D.: Distant supervision for relation extraction with an incomplete knowledge base. In: Proceedings of NAACL-HLT, pp. 777–782 (2013)
6. Nguyen, D.Q.: An overview of embedding models of entities and relationships for knowledge base completion. CoRR abs/1703.08098 (2017)
7. Nickel, M., Rosasco, L., Poggio, T.A.: Holographic embeddings of knowledge graphs. In: AAAI (2016)
8. Ristoski, P., Paulheim, H.: RDF2Vec: RDF graph embeddings for data mining. In: Groth, P., et al. (eds.) ISWC 2016. LNCS, vol. 9981, pp. 498–514. Springer, Cham (2016). https://doi.org/10.1007/978-3-319-46523-4_30

A License-Based Search Engine

Benjamin Moreau[1,2(✉)], Patricia Serrano-Alvarado[1], Matthieu Perrin[1], and Emmanuel Desmontils[1]

[1] Nantes University, LS2N, CNRS, UMR6004, 44000 Nantes, France
{Benjamin.Moreau,Patricia.Serrano-Alvarado,Matthieu.Perrin,
Emmanuel.Desmontils}@univ-nantes.fr
[2] OpenDataSoft, Paris, France
Benjamin.Moreau@opendatasoft.com

Abstract. The reuse of licensed resources to produce new ones is very common and encouraged on the Web. But producing resources whose licenses are compliant with all reused resource licenses is not easy. It is necessary to know (1) the set of licenses with which the license of the produced resource is compliant and (2) what are the available resources whose licenses are part of this set. With CaLi, we provide an answer to the first concern. CaLi is a lattice-based model that partially orders licenses in terms of compatibility and compliance. In this demonstration, we illustrate the usability of CaLi through a prototype for the second concern. That is, based on a CaLi ordering of licenses we implement a license-based search engine which can answer questions such as *"find licensed resources that can be reused under a given license"* or *"find licensed resources that can reuse a resource that has a particular license"*.

1 Introduction and Motivation

To facilitate reuse on the Web, resource producers should systematically associate licenses with resources before sharing or publishing them [3]. Licenses specify precisely the conditions of reuse of resources, i.e., what actions are *permitted, obliged* and *prohibited* when using the resource.

For a resource producer, choosing the appropriate license for a combined resource or choosing the appropriate licensed resources for a combination involves choosing a license compliant with all the licenses of combined resources as well as analysing the reusability of the resulting resource through the compatibility of its license.

We consider simplified definitions of compliance and compatibility [1], *a license l_j is compliant with a license l_i if a resource licensed under l_i can be licensed under l_j without violating l_i.* If a license l_j is compliant with l_i then we consider that l_i is compatible with l_j and that resources licensed under l_i are reusable with resources licensed under l_j. In general, if l_i is compatible with l_j then l_j is more (or equally) restrictive than l_i. We also consider that *a license l_j is more (or equally) restrictive than a license l_i if l_j allows at most the same permissions and has at least the same prohibitions/obligations than l_i.*

© Springer Nature Switzerland AG 2019
P. Hitzler et al. (Eds.): ESWC 2019 Satellite Events, LNCS 11762, pp. 130–135, 2019.
https://doi.org/10.1007/978-3-030-32327-1_26

But producing resources whose licenses are compliant with all reused resource licenses is difficult. It is necessary to know (1) the set of licenses with which the license of the produced resource is compliant and (2) what are the pertinent and available resources whose licenses are part of this set.

With CaLi [1], we provide an answer to the first concern. CaLi is a lattice-based model to define compatibility and compliance relations among licenses. It is based on a restrictiveness relation that is refined with constraints to take into account the semantics of actions existing in licenses.

For the second concern, imagine a license-based search engine that can answer questions such as *"find all resources that can be reused under the CC BY-NC license"*. The answer must contain resources licensed under licenses such as CC BY and CC BY-NC itself that are less or as restrictive as CC BY-NC and compatible with it.

There exist search engines in services such as GitHub[1], APISearch[2], CC search[3], LODAtlas[4], DataHub[5], Google Dataset Search[6] or OpenDataSoft[7] that can find resources licensed under a particular license. However they can not find resources whose licenses are compatible or compliant with a particular license.

We illustrate the usability of CaLi by answering the second concern. We developed a prototype of a search engine based on a CaLi ordering of licenses, *ODRL_CaLi*. The goal is to be able find resources whose licenses are compatible or compliant with a particular license. Our prototype can answer questions such as: *"find licensed resources that can be reused under a given license"* or *"find licensed resources that can reuse a resource that has a particular license"*.

In our search engine, resources (linked data and source code) are associated to licenses. Licenses are described in RDF with the ODRL vocabulary[8] and ordered in terms of compatibility according to the *ODRL_CaLi* ordering. In addition to indexing licenses, the titles, descriptions and uri of each licensed resources are also indexed to enable full-text search. We remark that we are not interested in implementing ODRL. We use the ODRL vocabulary because it is the most complete vocabulary for licenses and it is well accepted by the community.

In the following, Sect. 2 overviews the CaLi model and the *ODRL_CaLi* ordering used in our search engine, and Sect. 3 describes the demonstration.

2   Modelling the Compatibility of Licenses

Inspired by lattice-based access control models, we propose a CaLi model as a tuple $\langle \mathcal{A}, \mathcal{LS}, C_{\mathcal{L}}, C_{\rightarrow} \rangle$ that partially orders licenses, such that [1]:

---

[1] https://github.com/.

[2] http://apis.io/.

[3] https://ccsearch.creativecommons.org/.

[4] http://lodatlas.lri.fr/.

[5] https://datahub.io/.

[6] https://toolbox.google.com/datasetsearch.

[7] https://data.opendatasoft.com/.

[8] https://www.w3.org/TR/odrl-model/.

1. $\mathcal{A}$ is a set of *actions* (e.g., *read, modify, distribute*, etc.);
2. $\mathcal{LS}$ is a *restrictiveness lattice of status* that defines (i) all possible status (e.g., permissions, obligations, prohibitions, etc.) of an action in a license and (ii) the restrictiveness relation among status denoted by $\leqslant_S$;
3. $C_\rightarrow$ is a set of *compatibility constraints* to identify if a restrictiveness relation between two licenses is also a compatibility relation; and
4. $C_\mathcal{L}$ is a set of *license constraints* to identify non-valid licenses.

In CaLi, $\mathcal{L}_{\mathcal{A},\mathcal{LS}}$ defines the set of all licenses that can be expressed with $\mathcal{A}$ and $\mathcal{LS}$. $(\mathcal{L}_{\mathcal{A},\mathcal{LS}}, \leqslant_\mathcal{R})$ is the restrictiveness lattice of licenses that defines the restrictiveness relation $\leqslant_\mathcal{R}$ over the set of all licenses $\mathcal{L}_{\mathcal{A},\mathcal{LS}}$. With $C_\mathcal{L}$ non-valid licenses are identified. We consider a license l_i as non-valid if a resource can not be licensed under l_i. If two valid licenses have a restrictiveness relation then it is possible that they have a compatibility relation too. To identify the compatibility among licenses, CaLi refines the restrictiveness relation with compatibility constraints $C_\rightarrow$.

$ODRL\_CaLi$, is a CaLi ordering $\langle \mathcal{A}, \mathcal{LS}, C_\mathcal{L}, C_\rightarrow \rangle$ such that:

- $\mathcal{A}$ is the set of 72 actions considered by ODRL[9];
- $\mathcal{LS}$ is the restrictiveness lattice of status where (i) the possible status are Permission, Duty, Prohibition[10] or Undefined (for actions that do not appear in the license), and (ii) the restrictiveness relation is $Undefined \leqslant_S Permission \leqslant_S Duty \leqslant_S Prohibition$; and
- $C_\mathcal{L}, C_\rightarrow$ are the sets of constraints, inspired from the ODRL information model, defined below.

$C_\mathcal{L} = \{\omega_{\mathcal{L}_1}, \omega_{\mathcal{L}_2} \omega_{\mathcal{L}_3}\}$ allows to invalidate a license (1) when *cc:Commercial Use* is required, (2) when *cc:ShareAlike* is prohibited and (3) when the semantics of a permitted or obliged action is included in a prohibited action (e.g. if *CommercialUse* is permitted then *use* should not be prohibited because *CommercialUse* implies *use*):

$$\omega_{\mathcal{L}_1}(l_i) = \begin{cases} False \text{ if } l_i(cc:CommercialUse) = \text{Duty}; \\ True \text{ otherwise.} \end{cases}$$

$$\omega_{\mathcal{L}_2}(l_i) = \begin{cases} False \text{ if } l_i(cc:ShareAlike) = \text{Prohibition}; \\ True \text{ otherwise.} \end{cases}$$

$$\omega_{\mathcal{L}_3}(l_i) = \begin{cases} False \text{ if } a_i \text{ odrl:includedIn } a_j \\ \qquad \text{AND } (l_i(a_i) = \text{Permitted OR } l_i(a_i) = \text{Duty}) \\ \qquad \text{AND } l_i(a_j) = \text{Prohibition}; \\ True \text{ otherwise.} \end{cases}$$

$C_\rightarrow = \{\omega_{\rightarrow_1}, \omega_{\rightarrow_2}\}$ allows to identify (1) when *cc:ShareAlike* is required and (2) when *cc:DerivativeWorks* is prohibited. That is because *cc:ShareAlike* requires that the distribution of derivative works be under the same license only,

---

[9] https://www.w3.org/TR/odrl-vocab/#actionConcepts.
[10] https://www.w3.org/TR/odrl-model/#rule.

and *cc:DerivativeWorks*, when prohibited, does not allow the distribution of a derivative resource, regardless of the license.

$$\omega_{\rightarrow_1}(l_i, l_j) = \begin{cases} False \text{ if } l_i(cc:ShareAlike) = \text{Duty}; \\ True \text{ otherwise.} \end{cases}$$

$$\omega_{\rightarrow_2}(l_i, l_j) = \begin{cases} False \text{ if } l_i(cc:DerivativeWorks) = \text{Prohibition}; \\ True \text{ otherwise.} \end{cases}$$

Other constraints could be defined to be closer to the ODRL information model but for the purposes of this demonstration these constraints are enough.

The size growth of CaLi orderings is exponential $|\mathcal{LS}|^{|\mathcal{A}|}$, so the size of $ODRL\_CaLi$ is 4^{72}, which makes it impossible to build. Nevertheless, it is not necessary to explicitly build a lattice to use it. Our search engine uses a sorting algorithm that can sort any set of licenses according to the $\mathcal{LS}$ defined above, in approximatively $n^2/2$ comparisons of restrictiveness, n being the number of licenses to sort, i.e., $O(n^2)$. This algorithm is able to insert a license in a graph in linear time $O(n)$ without sorting again the graph (see [1] for more details). Thus, our algorithm produces compatibility graphs of licenses conform to the $ODRL\_CaLi$ ordering of licenses. This algorithm is available on GitHub under the MIT license[11].

3   Demonstration

Using $ODRL\_CaLi$ and the sorting algorithm described in the previous section, we generated two compatibility graphs of licences. One for licenses that are the most used in DataHub[12] and another for the most used licenses in GitHub.

Licenses are in RDF. We use the dataset of licenses proposed by [2].

Resources associated to licenses refer to some licensed RDF datasets from DataHub, from OpenDataSoft[13] and from licensed repositories from GitHub.

The source code of the search engine is available on GitHub[14] under the MIT license. Our demonstration is available online at http://cali.priloo.univ-nantes. fr.

Both compatibility graphs of licences are visually available. Figure 1a shows the compatibility graph of the CaLi ordering for some licensed RDF datasets. Blue nodes are licenses, grey arrows are compatibility relations among licenses and orange nodes are RDF datasets associated to licenses. Licenses that have the same actions in the same status are represented in the same node. In the graph, licenses that are compatible with a particular license l_i are below l_i and licenses that are compliant with l_i are above l_i. We recall that the ordering relations of compatibility and compliance that we define are reflexive, transitive and asymmetric.

---

[11] https://github.com/benjimor/CaLi.
[12] https://old.datahub.io/.
[13] https://data.opendatasoft.com/pages/home/.
[14] https://github.com/benjimor/CaLi-Search-Engine.

During the demonstration, attendees will be able to search for resources licensed under licenses compliant or compatible with a particular license. Figure 1b shows the search bar of our search engine. It enables full-text and license-compliant searches over each graph, for RDF datasets[15] or repositories[16]. For example, users can search for *datasets about 'bikes' whose licenses are compatible with the CC BY-NC license* (i.e. datasets about 'bikes' that can be reused under the CC BY-NC license). The result contains all RDF datasets indexed in the search engine where title or description contains the word 'bikes' and whose license is compatible with CC BY-NC (e.g. CC BY, MIT, CC-Ze, etc.).

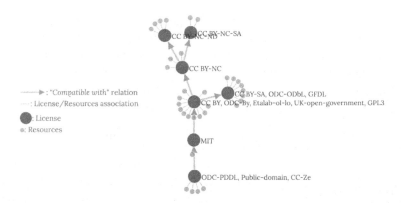

(a) Compatibility graph of the *ODRL_CaLi* ordering for some licensed RDF datasets.

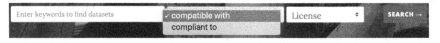

(b) Search bar of the license-based search engine.

Fig. 1. Screenshoots of the license-based search engine. (Color figure online)

Both compatibility graphs of licences are available online through a documented API. Finally, these graphs are also accessible through a TPF server[17,18] or can be exported in RDF (turtle, xml, n3 and json-ld).

A possible extension of our search engine is to allow the collaborative addition of licenses and licensed resources. That is, to allow users to add new licenses and resources to increase the size and therefore the interest of these two graphs.

---

[15] http://cali.priloo.univ-nantes.fr/ld/.

[16] http://cali.priloo.univ-nantes.fr/rep/.

[17] http://cali.priloo.univ-nantes.fr/api/ld/tpf.

[18] http://cali.priloo.univ-nantes.fr/api/rep/tpf.

References

1. Moreau, B., Serrano-Alvarado, P., Perrin, M., Desmontils, E.: Modelling the compatibility of licenses. In: Hitzler, P., et al. (eds.) ESWC 2019. LNCS, vol. 11503, pp. 255–269. Springer, Cham (2019). https://doi.org/10.1007/978-3-030-21348-0_17
2. Rodríguez Doncel, V., Gómez-Pérez, A., Villata, S.: A dataset of RDF licenses. In: Legal Knowledge and Information Systems Conference (ICLKIS) (2014)
3. Seneviratne, Oshani, Kagal, Lalana, Berners-Lee, Tim: Policy-aware content reuse on the web. In: Bernstein, A., et al. (eds.) ISWC 2009. LNCS, vol. 5823, pp. 553–568. Springer, Heidelberg (2009). https://doi.org/10.1007/978-3-642-04930-9_35

HistorEx: Exploring Historical Text Corpora Using Word and Document Embeddings

Sven Müller[1], Michael Brunzel[1], Daniela Kaun[1], Russa Biswas[1,2], Maria Koutraki[3], Tabea Tietz[1,2(✉)], and Harald Sack[1,2]

[1] Institute AIFB, Karlsruhe Institute of Technology, Karlsruhe, Germany
{uodlt,ubebi,ugebn}@student.kit.edu
[2] FIZ Karlsruhe – Leibniz Institute for Information Infrastructure,
Karlsruhe, Germany
{Russa.Biswas,Tabea.Tietz,Harald.Sack}@fiz-karlsruhe.de
[3] L3S Research Center, Leibniz University Hannover, Hanover, Germany
koutraki@l3s.de

Abstract. Written text can be understood as a means to acquire insights into the nature of past and present cultures and societies. Numerous projects have been devoted to digitizing and publishing historical textual documents in digital libraries which scientists can utilize as valuable resources for research. However, the extent of textual data available exceeds humans' abilities to explore the data efficiently. In this paper, a framework is presented which combines unsupervised machine learning techniques and natural language processing on the example of historical text documents on the 19*th* century of the USA. Named entities are extracted from semi-structured text, which is enriched with complementary information from Wikidata. Word embeddings are leveraged to enable further analysis of the text corpus, which is visualized in a web-based application.

Keywords: Word embeddings · Document vectors · Wikidata ·
Cultural heritage · Visualization · Recommender system

1 Introduction

Humanities as well as social sciences, historical sciences and political sciences are essentially text-based sciences, i.e. philologies, and hence strongly depend on the diligent analysis of text corpora. Cultural heritage text data grants researchers from these text-based sciences precious insights into past and present cultures and social structures. However, the extent of information available in the form of unstructured text provides a difficult challenge for researchers to fully grasp the content of the documents in a cultural heritage data collection, the interrelations between the documents as well as the places and figures they involve in a reasonable amount of time and work effort. As a result, the meaning of these

© Springer Nature Switzerland AG 2019
P. Hitzler et al. (Eds.): ESWC 2019 Satellite Events, LNCS 11762, pp. 136–140, 2019.
https://doi.org/10.1007/978-3-030-32327-1_27

data for the societies they describe often remains uncharted. This problem calls for interdisciplinary work between technical and non-technical researchers with the goal to process these documents in a way that they can be explored, understood, and placed into the context of the time and culture they were authored in [1]. To achieve this, the data has to be analyzed and enriched with machine understandable information before it is presented to the user in a comprehensible interface for exploration [2].

The presented work also addresses this challenge and contributes a framework that combines unsupervised Machine Learning techniques with Natural Language Processing (NLP) with the goal to uncover semantic connections among collections of textual documents on the example of a historical text corpus on the $19th$ century USA[1]. The data was originally published by the Humboldt Chair for Digital Humanities of the University of Leipzig and made available by the Coding da V1nc1 hackathon[2]. In total the collection comprises 334 documents with various types of literary works including local reports on the American Civil War to biographies and novels. As part of the presented framework, named entities are extracted and partially enriched with additional information from the Wikidata knowledge graph. Furthermore semantic representations of the documents are obtained using word vectors and document vectors. The framework also includes an interface that exploits the results from the proposed approach and enables users on the web to explore the text collection.

2   Description of HistorEx

The proposed workflow, as illustrated in Fig. 1, follows two separate pipelines: (1) Entity extraction is performed using Beautiful Soup[3]. The persons and locations mentioned in the text are directly imported into Dash[4]. The extracted authors are enriched with additional information from the Wikidata knowledge base. (2) After preprocessing, semantic representations of each document are obtained by a neural net approach. In the final step, all data from both the pipelines is integrated into an interactive web application for data exploration.

2.1   Vector Representation

The semantic representations of the documents, i.e. the word and document vectors are generated using the Distributed Memory Model of Paragraph Vectors (PV-DM) [3]. The word and the document vectors are initialized randomly. The document vector is unique to a document, whereas the word vectors are shared among all the documents. Therefore, the word vectors learned from all the documents in the collection. Noise-contrastive estimation (NCE) is used for

---

[1] http://www.perseus.tufts.edu/hopper/collection?collection=Perseus:collection:cwar.

[2] https://codingdavinci.de/about/, last retrieved: March 05, 2019.

[3] https://www.crummy.com/software/BeautifulSoup/bs4/doc/.

[4] https://plot.ly/products/dash/.

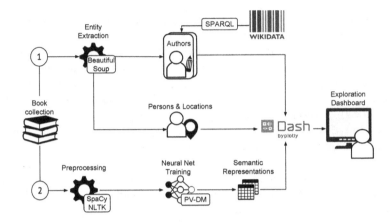

Fig. 1. Structure of the proposed double tracked pipeline.

optimization of the neural network. The quality of the trained representations is assessed during the training by manually monitoring the most-similar words to a corresponding set of selected tokens which leads to a training for eight epochs with a batch size of 512 and a context window-size of six (three on each side of the target-token).

2.2   Data Exploration Dashboard

The results of the proposed approach are presented in an interactive dashboard, depicted in Fig. 2a and b. It provides the user with several entry points to explore the text collection visually. It was implemented with Dash. The exploration dashboard and its user interaction possibilities are described in the Demo (Sect. 3) of this paper.

3   Demo

The HistorEx dashboard provides the user with several entry points to the content of the collection. Figure 2a presents an initial overview of the entire collection. A T-SNE plot ① lets the user explore the similarity between the documents in the corpus through visualized clusters. In the presented plot, each dot represents one book. Here, the user can also zoom in to the graph to get a closer look on the data and hovering each dot reveals its title. A table ② shows the collection of books overall and a bar chart let's the user explore the most common persons mentioned in the collection ③. Hovering individual bars reveals their quantity of occurrence. The places mentioned in the texts are visualized in a map view ④ which are plotted using GeoPy. Next to the general overview, the user can systematically explore the content by searching for specific entities or documents using the search bar ⑤ implemented with an autosuggestion feature.

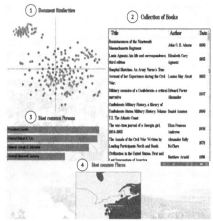

(a) Dashboard: Data collection overview with (1) T-SNE plot of document similarities, an overview of (2) books in the collection, (3) mentioned persons, (4) mentioned places. Due to space efficiency, the screenshots only show part of the information given in the dashboard.

(b) Book exploration with (5) a search bar (6) book author information, (7) common persons bar chart, (8) similar documents.

Fig. 2. HistorEx demo interface

Figure 2b shows the result of a book search. Next to its title, the author information (6), automatically retrieved from Wikidata, is given along with a link to the original Wikidata page. The user can furthermore explore persons occurring in the book (7) and receive document recommendations based on similarity (8). A map view (not pictured), similarly to (4) presented in Fig. 2a reveals the places named in the explored document. The HistorEx demo is publicly available[5].

4 Experiments and Results

In this section, the experiments conducted on 308 historical books which amounts to roughly 30 million tokens are described. First, the word vectors generated by PV-DM method are evaluated against SimLex-999[6]. Secondly, the document vectors generated by PV-DM are compared against the document vectors generated by averaging the Google pre-trained word vectors. Thirdly, most similar top-k documents are retrieved based on cosine similarity for both types of document vectors. Also, both types of document vectors are projected to a low dimensional space to gain better insight of the similar documents using t-Stochastic Neighbor Embedding (t-SNE)[7].

---

[5] https://ise-fizkarlsruhe.github.io/CourseProjects2019#historex.

[6] https://fh295.github.io/simlex.html.

[7] https://lvdmaaten.github.io/tsne/.

It has been observed that these two different types of document vectors exhibit different orientation in the low dimensional space and also in top-k recommendation of most similar documents. This is due to the usage of different set of vocabularies in Wikipedia and historical text. Moreover, Wikipedia is an open encyclopedia consisting of information from various domains whereas historical data is restricted to a specific geographical location in a certain era. A few results from the experiments and the t-SNE plot have been provided at Github[8].

5   Conclusion

In this paper, HistorEx, a framework to analyze and explore semi-structured historical text collections on the example of a historical text corpus on the 19th century of the USA was presented. HistorEx includes the extraction of named entities from the text corpus and enrichment of document authors with knowledge from Wikidata. Furthermore, semantic representations of the documents are obtained using word vectors and document vectors. The results are integrated into an interactive dashboard to facilitate document exploration.

Experiments to assess the quality of the word and document vectors show that the application of the PV-DM model provides promising results on the example text collection. Furthermore, evidence is provided that the approach seems especially useful for the analysis of unstructured historical English text collections, as long as the amount of text is sufficiently large in order to train meaningful semantic representations with the neural net. Future work will focus on enriching not only document authors with additional information from the Wikidata knowledge graph but also persons and locations mentioned in the documents to improve the exploration environment of the framework and enrich the collection with further context.

Acknowledgement. This paper is motivated by the the first German open cultural data hackathon, Coding da V1nc1. It supports interdisciplinary work on cultural heritage data by bringing together GLAM institutions, programmers and designers to develop ideas and prototypes for the cultural sector and for the public.

References

1. Gold, M.K.: Debates in the Digital Humanities. University of Minnesota Press, Minneapolis (2012)
2. Jänicke, S., Franzini, G., Cheema, M.F., Scheuermann, G.: Visual text analysis in digital humanities. In: Computer Graphics Forum, vol. 36, pp. 226–250. Wiley Online Library (2017)
3. Le, Q.V., Mikolov, T.: Distributed representations of sentences and documents. CoRR abs/1405.4053 (2014). http://arxiv.org/abs/1405.4053

---

[8] https://github.com/ISE-FIZKarlsruhe/HistorEx.

Ordia: A Web Application for Wikidata Lexemes

Finn Årup Nielsen[✉]

Cognitive Systems, DTU Compute, Technical University of Denmark,
Kongens Lyngby, Denmark
faan@dtu.dk

Abstract. Since 2018, Wikidata has had the ability to describe lexemes, and the associated SPARQL endpoint *Wikidata Query Service* can query this information and visualize the results. *Ordia* is a Web application that displays the multilingual lexeme data of Wikidata based on embedding of the responses from the Wikidata Query Service via templated SPARQL queries. Ordia has also a SPARQL-based approach for online matching of the words of a text with Wikidata lexemes and the ability to use a knowledge graph embedding as part of a SPARQL query. Ordia is available from https://tools.wmflabs.org/ordia/.

1 Introduction

The multilingual collaboratively editable and freely-licensed knowledge base *Wikidata*[1] [7] was set up in October 2012. On this website users can describe items and links between the items via properties, as well as add qualifiers and sources to support the individual claims. The Wikidata data—originally formatted in a nested JSON-like structure—is translated to a Semantic Web representation and continuously updated and made available via a SPARQL endpoint: The *Wikidata Query Service* (WDQS)[2] and as such part of the Linked Open Data cloud.

In 2016, the Wikidata developers announced dictionary support in Wikidata [4], and in May 2018, Wikidata enabled the entering of basic data about *lexemes* and their *forms*. Later that year, Wikidata also switched on support for *senses*, and links to the Q-items from senses[3] can be established. As the rest of Wikidata, the lexeme part of Wikidata is multilingual and ontological definitions in one language are available in other languages.

---

[1] https://www.wikidata.org.

[2] https://query.wikidata.org.

[3] The "ordinary" Wikidata items are referred to by an identifier consisting of the letter 'Q' and an integer, while the properties are identified by the letter 'P' and an integer. Lexemes are identified by the initial letter 'L'.

This work is funded by the Innovation Fund Denmark through the projects DAnish Center for Big Data Analytics driven Innovation (DABAI) and Teaching platform for developing and automatically tracking early stage literacy skills (ATEL).

© Springer Nature Switzerland AG 2019
P. Hitzler et al. (Eds.): ESWC 2019 Satellite Events, LNCS 11762, pp. 141–146, 2019.
https://doi.org/10.1007/978-3-030-32327-1_28

Below I will describe the *Ordia* Web application that takes advantage of the Wikidata lexeme data, aggregating the information via WDQS and presenting it on a website with added functionality in the form of lexeme extraction from a text and SPARQL integration of knowledge graph embedding information.

2   Ordia Web Application

Ordia is available from GitHub at http://github.com/fnielsen/ordia developed under the Apache 2.0 licens. It may be cloned from that repository and run locally. The canonical homepage for the Web application is at https://tools.wmflabs. org/ordia/ under the *Toolforge* cloud service provided by the Wikimedia Foundation.

As a Web application and Python package, Ordia is heavily inspired from our other current Wikidata Web application projects: Scholia [3], cvrminer[1] and Wembedder [2]: Ordia uses the Flask web framework together with Javascript and SPARQL templates in Jinja[2] to dynamically build webpages. The constructed SPARQL queries are sent to the WDQS SPARQL endpoint and the responses are added to the generated HTML pages, either

Fig. 1. Screenshot of the page in Ordia for the Danish lexeme *fyr* at https://tools. wmflabs.org/ordia/L33928.

with HTML embedding or via Javascript and the *DataTables* library.[3] The library provides means for sorting table rows and for drill down via a search field. The SPARQL queries used to generate the tables in Ordia are all linked from an anchor in the lower left corner of the tables, making a SPARQL-knowledgeable user able to inspect and modify the queries.

Ordia creates separate pages for Q-items, lexemes, forms and senses, and makes panels with tables on each of them. Figure 1 shows an example for a lexeme. Ordia uses a URL scheme for Q-items inspired from Scholia's notion of *aspects* and shows aspects for language, lexical category, grammatical features, propeties and references, e.g., the link /language/Q809 will show Polish (Q809)

---

[1] Descriptions of cvrminer at https://tools.wmflabs.org/cvrminer/ has not been published. The Web application displays information about organizations as listed in Wikidata.

[2] http://flask.pocoo.org/ and http://jinja.pocoo.org/.

[3] https://datatables.net/.

lexemes, while /Q809 shows Polish as a semantic concept in its own right. Some of the aspects show graphs for the ontology, e.g., the page for noun as a lexical category at /lexical-category/Q1084.

For searching after lexemes and forms, Ordia uses the MediaWiki API of Wikidata: The user types in a search in the Ordia interface and Ordia makes an API call to Wikidata and presents the results in the Ordia interface.

Wembedder, a Wikidata-based knowledge graph embedding Web service [2], works with a simplified RDF2Vec approach implemented with Gensim's word2vec model [1, 5,8]. As Ordia, Wembedder runs as part of Toolforge.[4] The current implementation only handles the Q-items and properties of Wikidata,— not lexemes, forms nor senses. The only functionality implemented in the Wembedder Web service so far is a *most similar* service that returns the most similar items and properties based on a query item. Wembedder has no SPARQL endpoint capability, so federated SPARQL queries cannot be made. Instead Ordia calls the REST interface of Wembedder via a Javascript Ajax call from the server side and formats the received JSON with Wikidata identifier and similarity values as two-tuple values for the SPARQL VALUES construct. The VALUES construct is then interpolated into a SPARQL template and sent off to WDQS with the response formatted in Ordia in a table with the DataTable library.

Fig. 2. Screenshot of Ordia's page for the *Thursday* Wikidata concept (Q129). The top panel shows the associated lexemes and senses in the languages that link to the concept, while the lower panel displays the result from the Wembedder knowledge graph embedding similarity computation.

Ordia uses the Wembedder queries on pages for Q-items, where a table displays related Q-items sorted according to similarity and augmented with information from the lexeme part of Wikidata. Figure 2 shows an example of the output on the page for the concept *Thursday* corresponding to the page https:// tools.wmflabs.org/ordia/Q129, where the top panel displays lexemes for languages linked (e.g., jeudi, Donnerstag, Thursday) and the lower panel shows the result from WDQS with Wembedder-included results. Here Wednesday and Saturday are the most related concepts to Thursday.

---

[4] https://tools.wmflabs.org/wembedder/.

The **text-to-lexeme** facility in Ordia at https://tools.wmflabs.org/ordia/text-to-lexemes enables the user to write a short text into an HTML text area on the client side, and send it off to Ordia. Ordia then makes a simple sentence detection and lowercases the first letter of the sentences before word tokenization with a simple regular expression pattern. Identified words are interpolated into a WDQS query via the VALUES keyword to search for matching forms, and the response from the SPARQL endpoint is shown in a table in the Ordia interface. The language of the input sentence must be specified. Currently, Ordia only handles a small number of selected languages, but in principle every language in Wikidata lexemes could be supported.

Figure 3 displays the result after the Danish sentence "Regeringen spiser grønne æbler om vinteren" ("The government is eating green apples during winter") has been submitted to Ordia. The result of the WDQS query here shows the word and—if matched—the form, lexeme, lexical category, lexical feature, sense and image associated with the sense. If a word matches several forms in a

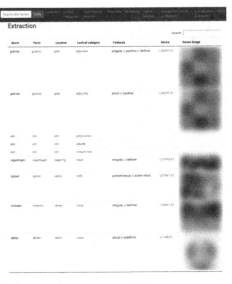

Fig. 3. Screenshot of Ordia's text-to-lexeme facility, where the sentence "Regeringen spiser grønne æbler om vinteren" ("The government is eating green apples during winter"): https://tools.wmflabs.org/ordia/text-to-lexemes?text=Regeringen+spiser+gr%C3%B8nne+%C3%A6bler+om+vinteren&language=da. (Color figure online)

language, they are all shown, i.e., no word sense disambiguation is performed. Ordia's text-to-lexemes responds within seconds. Usually Ordia responds with the HTML within 300 ms for a sentence like the above. The SPARQL query sent by the client to WDQS completes typically between 1.5 and 2 s after the user submitted the original query. The further download and rendering of the images from Wikimedia Commons—as shown in Fig. 3—may take an extra second. If the SPARQL query does not find a matching form, a link is created to Ordia's search page, which links further on to lexeme creation to ease the setup of new lexemes.

3 Discussion

I have shown Ordia, a Web service that uses the WDQS SPARQL endpoint to build a site with lexicographic data from Wikidata. Compared to the Wiktionary-based DBnary [6], Ordia needs no extractor and presents the lexicographic information graphically and up-to-date via WDQS as changes occur in Wikidata.

The conceptual choices that has been made in designing Ordia are: (1) A user should easily be able to perform powerful SPARQL queries by navigating the Ordia interface and without using any knowledge of SPARQL; (2) the URL pattern for each page should be easy to understand and predict; (3) Each page should link to other pages and in such a way let the user discover new lexemes, concepts, forms etc., and (4) the interface should use graphics when possible, e.g., graphs of word and concept relations and for displaying images associated with senses of words.

Other Wikidata lexeme Web applications beyond Ordia are available: Lucas Werkmeister has created *Wikidata Lexeme Forms* which enables easy HTML-form-based set up of lexemes and their lexical forms for a range of languages. In November 2018, Werkmeister found that this tool has been used for the creation of 10'827 lexemes out of a total of 37'886.[5] Alicia Fagerving has created *Wikidata Senses* which eases the setup of senses associated with lexemes. While the above tools focuses on input, Léa Lacroix' *DerDieDas* game, tasks a language learner to guess and learn the grammatical gender of presented nouns. It uses the data in Wikidata via a WDQS query. Originally in German, it now has derived versions in French and Danish. Another of Werkmeister's online tools, *Wikidata Lexeme Graph Builder*, constructs a graph based on a specified Wikidata item and a Wikidata property. These and further Wikidata lexicographical tools are listed at https://www.wikidata.org/wiki/Wikidata:Tools/Lexicographical_data.

Ordia can be used in a variety of ways: A copy-and-paste of a text into Ordia's text-to-lexeme tool will quickly return an overview of missing lexeme data in Wikidata. Most words from a typical English news article are usually matched to a Wikidata lexeme,—except for proper nouns. Another useful overview that Ordia gives is the ontology of lexical categories. For instance, https://tools.wmflabs.org/ordia/lexical-category/Q36224 shows a graph with subconcepts and superconcepts of the pronoun concept independent of language. Such an overview is convenient to consult when entering lexeme data in Wikidata. The use of Ordia as, e.g., a translation or synonymy dictionary is still constrained by the yet low number of lexemes that have been entered and linked.

References

1. Mikolov, T., Chen, K., Corrado, G.S., Dean, J.: Efficient estimation of word representations in vector space, January 2013. https://arxiv.org/pdf/1301.3781v3
2. Nielsen, F.Å.: Wembedder: Wikidata entity embedding web service, October 2017. https://arxiv.org/pdf/1710.04099
3. Nielsen, F.Å., Mietchen, D., Willighagen, E.: Scholia, scientometrics and Wikidata. In: Blomqvist, E., Hose, K., Paulheim, H., Lawrynowicz, A., Ciravegna, F., Hartig, O. (eds.) ESWC 2017. LNCS, vol. 10577, pp. 237–259. Springer, Cham (2017). https://doi.org/10.1007/978-3-319-70407-4_36
4. Pintscher, L.: Let's move forward with support for Wiktionary. Wikidata mailing list, September 2016. https://lists.wikimedia.org/pipermail/wikidata/2016-September/009541.html

---

[5] https://quarry.wmflabs.org/query/28791.

5. Ristoski, P., Paulheim, H.: RDF2Vec: RDF graph embeddings for data mining. In: Groth, P., et al. (eds.) ISWC 2016. LNCS, vol. 9981, pp. 498–514. Springer, Cham (2016). https://doi.org/10.1007/978-3-319-46523-4_30

6. Sérasset, G.: DBnary: Wiktionary as a lemon-based multilingual lexical resource in RDF. Semant. Web **6**(4), 355–361 (2015). https://doi.org/10.3233/SW-140147

7. Vrandečić, D., Krötzsch, M.: Wikidata: a free collaborative knowledgebase. Commun. ACM **57**, 78–85 (2014)

8. Řehůřek, R., Sojka, P.: Software framework for topic modelling with large corpora. In: New Challenges For NLP Frameworks Programme, pp. 45–50, May 2010

Towards Cataloguing Potential Derivations of Personal Data

Harshvardhan J. Pandit[1]([✉]), Javier D. Fernández[2,3], Christophe Debruyne[1], and Axel Polleres[2,3]

[1] ADAPT Centre, Trinity College Dublin, Dublin, Ireland
{pandith,debruync}@tcd.ie
[2] Vienna University of Economics and Business, Vienna, Austria
[3] Complexity Science Hub Vienna, Vienna, Austria
{jfernand,axel.polleres}@wu.ac.at

Abstract. The General Data Protection Regulation (GDPR) has established transparency and accountability in the context of personal data usage and collection. While its obligations clearly apply to data explicitly obtained from data subjects, the situation is less clear for data derived from existing personal data. In this paper, we address this issue with an approach for identifying potential data derivations using a rule-based formalisation of examples documented in the literature using Semantic Web standards. Our approach is useful for identifying risks of potential data derivations from given data and provides a starting point towards an open catalogue to document known derivations for the privacy community, but also for data controllers, in order to raise awareness in which sense their data collections could become problematic.

Keywords: Personal data · Derived data · GDPR · Semantic web

1 Introduction

The General Data Protection Regulation (GDPR) [5] provides several obligations that require transparency regarding collection and processing of personal data. Compliance towards these obligations requires data controllers to explain the processing of data and its purpose in understandable terms, such as through privacy policies, where it is made clear which categories of personal data are collected, and for which purpose. However, these categories are limited to data collected from the data subject and do not contain information on data derived from collected data. Thus, data subjects are often left unclear about the nature and usage of their personal data, which is still not described explicitly in terms of derived and potentially sensitive features. A well-known example of this is inferring personality types and political opinions from social media interactions [4]. Likewise, even good-willing data controllers may not be aware of what additional data can be inferred from data they collect.

In this paper we propose to address the issue of understanding risks about potential derivations of additional information from collected personal data by

© Springer Nature Switzerland AG 2019
P. Hitzler et al. (Eds.): ESWC 2019 Satellite Events, LNCS 11762, pp. 147–151, 2019.
https://doi.org/10.1007/978-3-030-32327-1_29

making these derivations explicit and machine-readable. We collect examples of derivations from literature and formalise them as machine-readable inference rules using semantic web technologies. To demonstrate its usefulness, we present a proof-of-concept illustrating how such a formalisation can be used to highlight potentially problematic derivations of sensitive features within a dataset.

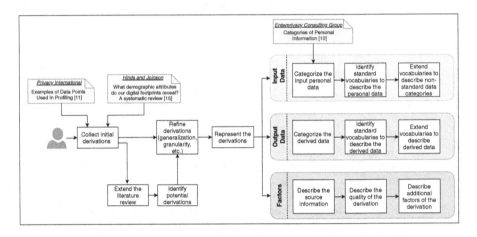

Fig. 1. Key stages of our methodology to represent inferred data.

2   Methodology

Figure 1 illustrates our methodology to arrive at a machine-readable catalog of personal data derivations based on a systematic and extended literature survey comprising of four main steps. We first **collect initial derivations** from two primary input sources: (i) a report by Privacy International [1] that describes documented derivations with references to source literature, and (ii) a recent survey [2] that reviews 327 studies that infer demographic attributes (mainly gender, age, location and political orientation) from "digital traces" (mainly social media, blogs and websites).

Starting from the two initial reports, we **extend our literature review to cover a wider spectrum of derivations**. Initially, we performed a keyword-based literature review based primarily on the topics of personalisation and user modelling. We then identified relevant derivations to select 13 additional papers[1]. In the future, we plan to open our catalog as a collaborative resource for the community. Then, we **refine selected derivations**. First, the collected derivations are represented using generation rules of the form $\{input \rightarrow output[source]\}$, where source is a reference to the paper, study, tool, or report documenting the derivation. We found that most collected derivations contain ambiguous or coarse descriptions that do not necessarily detail automatic, machine-processable

---

[1] https://github.com/coolharsh55/personal-data-inferences/.

inferences. We clean and refine this data to prepare the derivation for semantic representation in the next step. Finally, we **represent derivations in RDF and OWL** to allow automatic, machine-processable inferences and querying of our corpus. A proof of concept prototype of the model is presented in Sect. 3. Methodologically, we (i) categorize input and output data, (ii) identify standard vocabularies to represent them, or extend/create vocabularies to cover novel needs, and (iii) represent additional meta-data for factors that influence or determine the derivation such as quality of derivation (e.g. methods that produce derivations with some percentage of confidence), and input requirements (e.g. minimum input data rate or frequency needed to perform the derivation). We focus on (i), whereas (ii) and (iii) are part of future work.

3   Proof-of-Concept Implementation

We present a proof-of-concept implementation (see footnote 1) that takes given data categories and identifies potential data derivations based in literature. We define personal data categories and their characteristics as an ontology using OWL2, starting with the taxonomy by Enterprivacy Consulting Group[2], and then adding additional data categories from literature. We also define 'dimensions' such as source, medium, and format which are relevant to the method that derives data. Each inference is linked to the literature identifying its source for transparency.

In our ontology, data derivations identified from literature are defined as logical inferences using the class *InferenceVector*. The input data categories to the inference are specified using *usesData*, and the additional data categories produced as output are specified using *infersData*, with the source literature specified using *rdfs:isDefinedBy*. To define a derivation based in literature, we create a sub-class of *InferenceVector* using *rdfs:subClassOf* and associate it with data categories and relevant dimensions using these properties. To identify potential data derivations for a given set of personal data categories, we first represent derivations found in literature using *InferenceVector*. We then define a new instance of *InferenceVector* using *rdf:type* and associate it with given data categories using *usesData*. We then use a semantic reasoner such as HermiT[3] to identify potential inferences for given data categories. The reasoner identifies defined derivations by matching their inputs (*usesData*) with given data categories (or their parent categories), and associates them with the instance using *rdf:type* relation. We then use a SPARQL query to retrieve the applicable derivations. A simplified example (single source, no dimensions) representing the derivation of demographic data from twitter [3] is visualised in Fig. 2.

---

[2] https://enterprivacy.com/2017/03/01/categories-of-personal-information/.
[3] http://www.hermit-reasoner.com/.

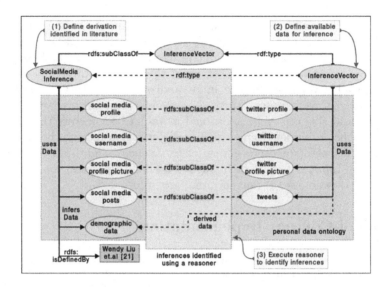

Fig. 2. Identifying derivations using OWL2 ontology and reasoner

4   Conclusion and Future Work

This paper addresses the issue of transparency regarding how additional information can be derived from collected personal data. Our proposed approach assists in identification of potential data derivations using rule-based formalisation using semantic web technologies of derivations in literature. We presented feasibility of this approach using a proof-of-concept that uses an OWL2 ontology for representing personal data characteristics and derivations, and a semantic reasoner to identify potential derivations for given data categories. Our approach is useful in the identification of risks of such potential data derivations, and is aimed as a starting point for an open catalogue that documents known derivations of personal data towards raising awareness. As for future work, the foremost challenge lies in representing personal data information to sufficiently express its complexity, where we expect to use rule-based approaches such as SWRL. Also, to incorporate literature from Sect. 2, adding attributes such as identifiers, and recording use of techniques such as machine learning. The aim is to create an open community resource for documenting derivations for transparency.

Acknowledgements. This work is supported by funding under EU's Horizon 2020 research and innovation programme: grant 731601 (SPECIAL), the Austrian Research Promotion Agency's (FFG) program "ICT of the Future": grant 861213 (CitySPIN), and ADAPT Centre for Digital Excellence funded by SFI Research Centres Programme (Grant 13/RC/2106) and co-funded by European Regional Development Fund.

References

1. Examples of data points used in profiling. Privacy International, April 2018
2. Hinds, J., Joinson, A.N.: What demographic attributes do our digital footprints reveal? A systematic review. PLoS One **13**(11), e0207112 (2018)
3. Liu, W., Al Zamal, F., Ruths, D.: Using social media to infer gender composition of commuter populations. In: Proceedings of the When the City Meets the Citizen Workshop at ICWSM, p. 4 (2012)
4. Quercia, D., Kosinski, M., Stillwell, D., Crowcroft, J.: Our twitter profiles, our selves: predicting personality with twitter. In: Proc of PASSAT and SocialCom, pp. 180–185 (2011)
5. Regulation (EU) 2016/679 of the european parliament and of the council of 27 April 2016 (general data protection regulation). Off. J. Eur. Union **L119**, 1–88 (2016–05)

DAFO: An Ontological Database System with Faceted Queries

Tadeusz Pankowski$^{(\boxtimes)}$ and Jarosław Bąk

Institute of Control and Information Engineering, Poznań University of Technology, Poznań, Poland
{tadeusz.pankowski,jaroslaw.bak}@put.poznan.pl

Abstract. We present an ontology-based data access provided with a faceted interface. The underlying relational database is perceived through an ontological schema. Queries against the ontology are formulated using a hierarchical faceted interface. We show main ideas of DAFO and discuss how it relates to well-known OBDA systems.

1 Introduction

DAFO (*Data Access based on Faceted queries over Ontology*) [6,7] is an ontological database system, where the conceptual schema is specified as an ontology and the extensional part is stored in a relational database. Queries in DAFO are formulated by end-users by means of an interactive graphical faceted interface. Queries expressible in DAFO are equivalent to concept expressions in description logic (DL):

$$\text{DL-PE} \subseteq \text{DL-GN} \subseteq \text{DL-GN}^{\theta k},$$

where DL-PE is a class of *positive existential* queries, DL-GN is a class of queries with *guarded negation*, and DL-GN$^{\theta k}$ is an extension of DL-GN with *number restriction* (*count aggregation restriction*) [2]. Description logic is a natural base for faceted queries since queries in both cases are monadic and tree-shaped [1].

In OBDA (*Ontology-Based Data Access*) systems [8], queries are formulated in SPARQL, and mappings are defined from a relational database schema to the ontological schema using GAV (Global As View) approach. As a consequence, the unfolding based on mappings can be used in query rewriting. Like in OBDA, DAFO ontology is based on OWL 2 QL. In DAFO, we follow LAV (Local As View) approach, i.e., the ontological schema is mapped to an underlying relational database schema. Then the translating queries into SQL is more complex than in OBDA but ensures more flexibility. In faceted-based approach [5], a user can gradually refine her/his query using an interactive faceted query interface. The challenging issues are then: (a) presenting the relevant part of the underlying ontological schema in a form of a hierarchical faceted interfaces, (b) expressiveness of faceted queries which are formulated using only click operations on the faceted interface, (c) rewriting faceted queries into SQL.

Further on, we will describe and illustrate some main features of DAFO referring to a running example based on the example discussed in [3].

© Springer Nature Switzerland AG 2019
P. Hitzler et al. (Eds.): ESWC 2019 Satellite Events, LNCS 11762, pp. 152–155, 2019.
https://doi.org/10.1007/978-3-030-32327-1_30

2   Ontology in DAFO

In Fig. 1, there is a sample *Staff* ontology (see [3]) specifying an application domain of a project company. Nodes are labeled by types (unary predicates), and edges are labeled by object properties (binary predicates). Data properties are neglected in the figure. Extensional predicates (solid lines) are those that are mapped to a relational database, while intensional (dotted lines) are defined by means of some rules.

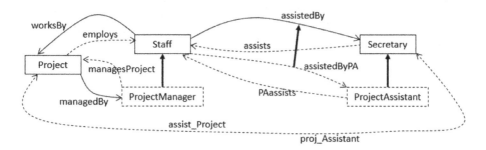

Fig. 1. *Staff* ontology graph: solid and dotted lines denote extensional and intensional predicates, respectively; fat arrows denote subsumptions between types and properties.

Domains and ranges of binary predicates, as well as subtype and subproperty relationships, can be deduced from the graph. Some other rules are shown below:

$(R1)$ $\forall x$ $(ProjectManager(x) \rightarrow \exists y\ assistedByPA(x,y))$
$(R2)$ $\forall x$ $(\exists y\ managesProject(x,y) \rightarrow ProjectManager(x))$
$(R3)$ $\forall x,y$ $(managedBy(x,y) \leftrightarrow managesProject(y,x))$
$(R4)$ $\forall x,y,z$ $(managedBy(x,z) \wedge assistedBy(z,y) \rightarrow proj\_Assistant(x,y))$

3   Query Formulation and Rewriting in DAFO

Assume that we are interested in staff members assisted by secretaries. In DAFO, instead of trying to write a query, a user starts with providing a sequence of types (a *keyword query*). The first type in the sequence denotes the type of answers, and the others are intended to be used in defining restrictions (in faceted queries, Fig. 2(e)). In this case, the keyword query is $(Staff, Secretary)$, Fig. 2(a).

The reasoning engine in DAFO uses the set of rules in the ontology to find all possible associations between *Staff* and *Secretary*. In result, an initial query $q(x)$ is produced and displayed in a form of faceted interface, Fig. 2(b). The query, denoted by checked nodes in Fig. 2(b), is the union of monadic conjunctive tree-shaped queries (of the class DL-PE):

$$q(x) = Staff(x) \wedge \exists y\ assistedBy(x,y) \wedge Secretary(y) \vee$$
$$Staff(x) \wedge \exists y\ assistedBy(x,y) \vee \qquad (1)$$
$$ProjectManager(x) \vee \exists y\ managesProject(x,y)$$

$ProjectManager(x)$ is in $q(x)$ in force of $(R1)$ stating that $assistedByPA$ is total on $ProjectManager$ (i.e., on a subset of its domain) so, every project manager must be assisted by at least one project assistant. $\exists y\ managesProject(x,y)$ is in $q(x)$ since, in force of $(R4)$, is a subset of $ProjectManager$.

A user can accept the query, uncheck some nodes or refine the query by performing some operations on the interface displayed in the context menu in Fig. 2(c). The query in Fig. 2(d) asks for members of staff who are assisted by more than one secretary (query of the class DL-GN$^{\theta k}$). A SQL form of this query is shown in Fig. 2(f). The query in Fig. 2(e) asks for members of staff who are not assisted by secretaries with job equal to '$ADMAs$' (query of the class DL-GN). The corresponding SQL query is in Fig. 2(g). In Fig. 2(h), there is a relational database schema the $Staff$ ontology is mapped to.

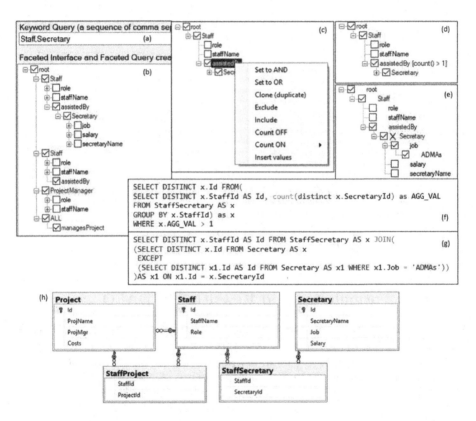

Fig. 2. Screenshots of DAFO system during operating on faceted interface (a)–(d), SQL forms of faceted queries (f)–(g), and schema of the underlying relational database (h).

Like in OBDA, queries in DAFO are processed in two stages: (a) the *ontology-mediated query* (OMQ) rewriting is used to produce a first-order query, (b) the query is translated into SQL. In general, the rewriting in OBDA produced by the rewriting algorithm PerfectRef [4] can be prohibitively large and complex [8]. For example, query (1) seems to be unnecessarily complex. Indeed, the second disjunction in $q(x)$ subsumes the first one. Techniques used in query rewriting depend on the assumption concerning preservation of consistency in the underlying database. Because of a dynamic character of the system, some updates may not be propagated making the database inconsistent. Moreover, due to the presence of rules like $(R1)$, the database can be incomplete. These facts must be taken into account in the rewriting process. In consequences, the final query can have a large number of unions. If we assume that the underlying database is consistent, i.e., all ontology rules are satisfied, we can use optimization techniques based on conjunctive query containment. Then the final form of query (1) can be simpler, like that in Fig. 2(c). In DAFO, both alternatives are available.

4 Summary

We presented DAFO system, which combines: (a) a user friendly, yet expressive, faceted-oriented approach to query formulation over ontologies, (b) usage of an ontology to semantic enrichment of relational database, and (c) utilization of the mature relational DBMS engine offering advanced optimization capabilities to store data (the extensional part of the ontology) and answer queries.

Acknowledgement. We acknowledge the support from the grant 04/45/DSPB/0185.

References

1. Arenas, M., Grau, B.C., Kharlamov, E., Marciuska, S., Zheleznyakov, D.: Faceted search over ontology-enhanced RDF data. In: ACM CIKM 2014, pp. 939–948. ACM (2014)
2. Baader, F., Calvanese, D., McGuinness, D., Nardi, D., Petel-Schneider, P. (eds.): The Description Logic Handbook: Theory, Implementation and Applications. Cambridge University Press, Cambridge (2003)
3. Bienvenu, M., Kikot, S., Kontchakov, R., Podolskii, V.V., Zakharyaschev, M.: Ontology-mediated queries: combined complexity and succinctness of rewritings via circuit complexity. J. ACM **65**(5), 28:1–28:51 (2018)
4. Calvanese, D., Giacomo, G., Lembo, D., Lenzerini, M., Rosati, R.: Tractable reasoning and efficient query answering in description logics: the DL-lite family. J. Autom. Reasoning **39**(3), 385–429 (2007)
5. Ferré, S., Hermann, A.: Semantic search: reconciling expressive querying and exploratory search. In: Aroyo, L., et al. (eds.) ISWC 2011. LNCS, vol. 7031, pp. 177–192. Springer, Heidelberg (2011). https://doi.org/10.1007/978-3-642-25073-6_12
6. Pankowski, T.: Exploring ontology-enhanced bibliography databases using faceted search. In: Kamps, J., Tsakonas, G., Manolopoulos, Y., Iliadis, L., Karydis, I. (eds.) TPDL 2017. LNCS, vol. 10450, pp. 27–39. Springer, Cham (2017). https://doi.org/10.1007/978-3-319-67008-9_3
7. Pankowski, T.: Schema transformations and query rewriting in ontological databases with a faceted interface. In: Rensink, A., Sánchez Cuadrado, J. (eds.) ICMT 2018. LNCS, vol. 10888, pp. 76–91. Springer, Cham (2018). https://doi.org/10.1007/978-3-319-93317-7_3
8. Xiao, G., et al.: Ontology-based data access: a survey. In: 27-th Joint Conference on Artificial Intelligence, IJCAI 2018, pp. 5511–5519 (2018)

A Configurable Evaluation Framework
for Node Embedding Techniques

Maria Angela Pellegrino[1]([⊠]), Michael Cochez[2,3,4] [ID], Martina Garofalo[1],
and Petar Ristoski[5]

[1] Department of Computer Science, University of Salerno, Fisciano, Italy
mapellegrino@unisa.it, margar1994@gmail.com
[2] Fraunhofer FIT, Sankt Augustin, Germany
michael.cochez@fit.fraunhofer.de
[3] Information Systems and Databases, RWTH Aachen University, Aachen, Germany
[4] Faculty of Information Technology, University of Jyvaskyla, Jyvaskyla, Finland
[5] IBM Research Almaden, San Jose, CA, USA
petar.ristoski@ibm.com

Abstract. While Knowledge Graphs (KG) are graph shaped by nature, most traditional data mining and machine learning (ML) software expect data in a vector form. Several node embedding techniques have been proposed to represent each node in the KG as a low-dimensional feature vector. A node embedding technique should preferably be task independent. Therefore, when a new method has been developed, it should be tested on the tasks it was designed for as well as on other tasks. We present the design and implementation of a ready to use evaluation framework to simplify the node embedding technique testing phase. The provided tests range from ML tasks, semantic tasks to semantic analogies.

Keywords: Evaluation framework · Node embedding · Machine learning · Semantic tasks

1 Introduction

While a Knowledge Graph (KG) is graph shaped by nature, most traditional data mining and Machine Learning (ML) algorithms expect data to be in vector form. To perform the *vectorization* process, several vector space embedding algorithms have been proposed. They represent each node (and often relations) in a graph as a low-dimensional vector; often preserving semantic properties (e.g., keep similar entities close together) and/or geometric properties. Preferably, these vectors would be task independent, meaning that they can be reused for other applications as they were created for. Therefore, it is useful to test the vectors in different settings to find out which information they preserve. Even if other evaluation frameworks [2,8,9] tested embedding algorithms on link prediction, graph reconstruction, visualisation, classification, and clustering tasks, systematic comparative evaluations of different approaches are scarce. Moreover,

P. Hitzler et al. (Eds.): ESWC 2019 Satellite Events, LNCS 11762, pp. 156–160, 2019.
https://doi.org/10.1007/978-3-030-32327-1_31

recent node embeddings have extended neural embedding techniques, traditionally introduced only for natural language word sequences. Thus, it is interesting to evaluate vectors also on semantic tasks by adapting them to work on entities since the node embedding approaches do not work on words.

Therefore, we present an open-source *evaluation framework*[1] which includes ML tasks (classification, regression, and clustering), semantic tasks (entity relatedness and document similarity), and semantic analogies to simplify the evaluation phase of node embedding techniques and to enable a fair comparison. To the best of our knowledge, it is one of the most extensive evaluation framework, and the most extensive one specifically for large Knowledge Graphs like DBpedia.

2   Evaluation Framework

The framework can be useful for scientists who create new embedding techniques and for users in detecting the best embedded vectors based on the task they will be used for. To start the evaluation the user has to provide an input file containing the embedded entities and their vector representations. The input can be provided in a text file format or as HDF5. The tasks can be run either sequentially or in parallel. In Table 1, we report for each task (i) the parameters which can be customised, (ii) the data set(s) used as gold standard, (iii) the trained method(s) (and their configurations), and (iv) the evaluation metric(s). By default, we use the *cosine* as distance function. However, it can be customised according to the inherent properties of the embedded space. The *Classification, Regression, Entity Relatedness*, and *Document similarity* tasks are based on RDF2Vec [6] and KGloVe [1]; the *Semantic Analogies* task is inspired by Word2Vec [5]; the *Clustering* task is completely new. The provided tasks assume DBpedia identifiers.

Classification and Regression. They are evaluated on data sets described by Ristoski et al. [7]. Besides the methods reported in Table 1, for the SVM classifier we optimize the parameter C in the range $\{10^{-3}, 10^{-2}, 0.1, 1, 10, 10^2, 10^3\}$. Each task performs (i) the inner join between the input file and each data set, (ii) trains each model on these values, and (iii) computes the evaluation metric.

Clustering. The *Cities & Countries* gold standard is created by querying the DBpedia endpoint asking for `dbo:City` and `dbo:PopulatedPlace`, both considering all the cities and balancing the two clusters. The *Sports teams* gold standard contains the *Football* and *Basketball* teams retrieved from the DBpedia endpoint, querying the `dbo:SportsTeam` whose URLs contain 'Football/ Basketball_team'. The task performs the inner join between the input file and each data set. Then, it trains each model on these values asking for 5 clusters in the first case and 2 in the other ones. In all the used models but K-means, the distance metric can be customised. For each entity missing in the input file or not assigned to a cluster, we create a new cluster which contains only that entity. We call these extra

---

[1] https://github.com/mariaangelapellegrino/Evaluation-Framework.

Table 1. For each implemented task we report the customizable *parameters*; the data set(s) used as *gold standard*, the adopted *method(s)* and *evaluation metrics*. The cells filled by * mean that the used approach is clarified into the body of this article.

Task	Params	Data set(s)	Methods and configurations	Evaluation metric(s)
Classification		Cities, AAUP, forbes, metacritic movies, matacritic albums	GaussianNB, K-NN k=3, SVM, C45	Accuracy
Regression		As classification	LR, M5, K-NN k=3	RMSE
Clustering	Distance function	1. Cities, AAUP, forbes, metacritic movies, metacritic albums; 2. Cities & countries; 3. Sports teams	k-means, DBSCAN, ward hierarchical and agglomerative clustering	Adjusted rand index, fowlkes mallows score, homogeneity score, completeness score,v_measure score
Entity relatedness	Distance function	KORE (21 main entities for 20 ranked entities)	*	Kendall's tau correlation
Semantic analogies	Analogy function	Data sets provided by Word2Vec	*	Accuracy
Document similarity	Distance function	LP50	*	Pearson and Spearman scores, and their harmonic mean

clusters *singleton cluster*. The evaluation metrics are computed on the clusters returned by the clustering model and all the singletons.

Entity Relatedness. Two entities are related if they often appear in the same context, such as "Facebook" and " Zuckerberg" [6]. We consider two entities related if they appear close to each other in the feature space. Therefore, the problem of calculating the relatedness between two instances in the graph is a matter of calculating the distance between the two instances in the given feature space. The words in KORE [3] have been manually linked to DBpedia entities. For each main entity, we rank the related entities according to the distance score and we compute the Kendall's tau correlation between the actual ranking and the one in KORE. If one *main entity* is missing, the related group is simply ignored. All the missing *right entities* referred to the same *main entity* are put randomly in the tail of the ranking and then the evaluation metric is calculated.

Document Similarity. Starting from the LP50 data set [4], for each pair of documents we compute the average of the assessed rates and used it as gold standard. Each document is represented by a set of entities: X-LiSA links the words in the document to entities in Knowledge Bases. For each document, the task ranks all the other documents using the similarity score. X-LiSA also provides weights, hence the previous procedure is repeated by averaging the entities distances by these weights to compute the document similarity score.

Semantic Analogies. This task takes in input quadruplets of entities (e_1, e_2, e_3, e_4) - given that between e_1 and e_2 exists the same analogy which occurs between e_3 and e_4 - and checks whether it is possible to predict the last entity based on the first three ones. A well known example provided by Word2Vec [5] is (*king, queen, man, woman*). We evaluate how vector(*queen*)-vector(*king*) + vector(*man*) is close to the vector(*woman*). In some embedding spaces, the operation to find analogies is different and can hence be customised. We substituted each words in the Word2Vec data sets with its corresponding DBpedia entity. For each quadruplet, if the input file does not contain any of the entities, the whole quadruplet is discarded. The accuracy is calculated only on the effective tested quadruplets.

3 Evaluation

We evaluated the performance of the framework on embeddings generated by RDF2Vec using the uniform weighting technique - both in text[2] and HDF5[3] format. The experiments are performed on a system with an Intel(R) Xeon(R) E5-2640 v4 CPU at 2.40 GHz and 256 GB RAM. In Table 2 we report (i) the running times of each task run separately, (ii) the whole task set run in sequential and (iii) in parallel. The sequential time does not match the sum of individual tasks because in the sequential time the input file is read only once, while performing each task separately the reading step is repeated by each run. The times are related to a single run. However, the Classification & Regression tasks perform a 10-fold cross validation. As future direction, we also aim to verify its correctness by comparing our results with those returned by other tools (e.g. GEM).

Table 2. Running time for each task run separately is reported. The times are in the format h:mm:ss or m:ss and they are obtained by the command */usr/bin/time*.

File format	Classification & regression	Clustering	Semantic analogies	Document similarity	Entity relatedness	Reading time	Sequential time	Parallel time
txt	36:26	9:16	6:30	22:22	3:15:54	5:39	4:07:42	3:20:26
HDF5	25:31	7:04	0:10	0:05	3:25:04	33:49	3:56:44	3:26:00

References

1. Cochez, M., Ristoski, P., Ponzetto, S.P., Paulheim, H.: Global RDF vector space embeddings. In: 16th International Semantic Web Conference ISWC (2017)
2. Goyal, P., Ferrara, E.: Graph embedding techniques, applications, and performance: a survey. Knowl.-Based Syst. **151**, 78–94 (2018)
3. Hoffart, J., Seufert, S., Nguyen, D.B., Theobald, M., Weikum, G.: KORE: keyphrase overlap relatedness for entity disambiguation. In: Proceedings of the 21st ACM International Conference on Information and Knowledge Management (2012)

---

[2] https://doi.org/10.5281/zenodo.1318146.
[3] https://doi.org/10.5281/zenodo.2017356.

4. Lee, M.D., Welsh, M.: An empirical evaluation of models of text document similarity. In: XXVII Annual Conference of the Cognititive Science Society (2005)
5. Mikolov, T., Sutskever, I., Chen, K., Corrado, G.S., Dean, J.: Distributed representations of words and phrases and their compositionality. In: 27th Annual Conference on Neural Information Processing Systems (2013)
6. Ristoski, P., Rosati, J., Di Noia, T., De Leone, R., Paulheim, H.: RDF2Vec: RDF graph embeddings and their applications. Semant. Web J. **10**(4), 721–752 (2018). in press
7. Ristoski, P., de Vries, G.K.D., Paulheim, H.: A collection of benchmark datasets for systematic evaluations of machine learning on the semantic web. In: Groth, P., et al. (eds.) ISWC 2016. LNCS, vol. 9982, pp. 186–194. Springer, Cham (2016). https://doi.org/10.1007/978-3-319-46547-0_20
8. Rulinda, J., de Dieu Tugirimana, J., Nzaramba, A., Aila, F.O., Langat, G.K.: An integrated platform to evaluate graph embedding. Int. J. Sci. Eng. Res. **9**, 665–676 (2018)
9. Wang, D., Cui, P., Zhu, W.: Structural deep network embedding. In: Proceedings of the 22nd International Conference on Knowledge Discovery and Data Mining (2016)

Querying the Edit History of Wikidata

Thomas Pellissier Tanon[(✉)] and Fabian Suchanek

Télécom ParisTech, Paris, France
`ttanon@enst.fr`

Abstract. In its 7 years of existence, Wikidata has accumulated an edit history of millions of contributions. In this paper, we propose a system that makes this data accessible through a SPARQL endpoint. We index not just the diffs done by a revision, but also the global state of Wikidata graph after any given revision. This allows users to answer complex SPARQL 1.1 queries on the Wikidata history, tracing the contributions of human vs. automated contributors, the areas of vandalism, the big schema changes, or the adoption of different values for the "gender" property across time.

1 Introduction

Recent years have seen the rise of Wikidata [13], a generalist collaborative knowledge base. The project started in 2012. As of July 2018, it has collected 5B statements about 50M entities. More than 700M revisions have been done by 56k contributors.

Wikidata provides a SPARQL endpoint[1] to query this data. However, this endpoint emits only the latest version of the data, and is blind to the edit history of the knowledge base. Therefore, users cannot even ask simple queries such as "What was the number of people in Wikidata two years ago?". This poses a problem for Wikidata contributors who wish to trace the progress of Wikidata over time, measure the amount of contributions by bots, identify areas of vandalism, or learn corrections from the data [9]. All these analyses require easy access to historical data.

The only way to access the full historical revisions of Wikidata is to download a 250 GB set of compressed XML dumps, which contain a JSON blob for each revision. This dump is hard to manipulate, and even harder to index. It would be prohibitively expensive to create one RDF graph for each of the 700 million revisions, each with billions of triples. If one indexes only the differences between the revisions, one loses the global state at each revision.

In this paper, we propose a system that smartly indexes the revisions, so that the full history of Wikidata edits becomes usable in a SPARQL endpoint. Our endpoint is able to:

1. Retrieve the diff, i.e. the set of added and/or removed triples, for any Wikidata revision.

---

[1] https://query.wikidata.org.

© Springer Nature Switzerland AG 2019
P. Hitzler et al. (Eds.): ESWC 2019 Satellite Events, LNCS 11762, pp. 161–166, 2019.
https://doi.org/10.1007/978-3-030-32327-1_32

2. Evaluate any triple pattern against the global state of Wikidata after a given revision.
3. Retrieve the revisions that have added/removed triples matching a given triple pattern.

With this, we can answer questions such as "How many cities existed in Wikidata across time?", "How many entities were modified exclusively by bots?", or "How were different values for the gender property used across time in Wikidata?". All these queries can be asked in standard SPARQL, without any additions to the language.

2   Related Work

SPARQL endpoints for versioned RDF datasets have been proposed by several authors. [5] first discussed the problem of querying linked data archives. [6] provides an extensive discussion of known solutions. Our work is concerned with an actual implementation of such a versioned RDF store for Wikidata. This causes practical problems of size that have not been considered in previous works.

There are several systems that allow storing versioned RDF: Quad stores (e.g., [1]) and archives (e.g., [4]) could be used to store each triple annotated with their revision. However, this would mean that each triple would have to be stored once for every revision in which it appears. In the case of Wikidata, this would amount to quadrillions of triples to be stored. tgrin [10] allows annotating RDF triples with a timestamp. However, the system does not provide time range support or, indeed, an available implementation. R&Wbase [12] is a wrapper on top of a SPARQL 1.1 endpoint that provides a git-like system for RDF graphs. However, it stores only the diff between different revisions. Therefore, it does not allow efficient querying of the full graph state at a given point of time. x-RDF-3X [8] is a SPARQL database that annotates each triple with the timestamp at which it was added or remove. It annotates triples with validity ranges, thus permitting queries for any state of the database. It also provides advanced consistency features. However, by design, it does not allow loading data with already known timestamps or version IDs. Thus, it is not usable in our case. v-RDFCSA [2] allows efficient storage and retrieval of versioned triples. However, it does not allow subsequent additions of revisions, and does not support revision ranges. Therefore, the system is hard to use with the huge number of revisions that Wikidata brings. OSTRICH [11] allows storing version annotated triples, as well as querying them based on the version ID. It uses a HDT file for storing the base version and then stores a changeset with respect to this initial version. This system is not tailored to the case of Wikidata, where the base version is empty. Thus, the system would have to store the full global state for each revision.

3   System Overview

Our goal is to provide a SPARQL endpoint that allows querying not just for the differences between Wikidata revisions, but also for the global state after each revision. At the same time, we want to use only existing SPARQL features. For this purpose, we designed the following data model:

Global State Graph: We will have one named graph per revision, which contains the global state of Wikidata after the revision has been saved.

Addition Graph: For each revision, we will have one graph that contains all the triples that have been added by this revision.

Deletion Graph: In the same spirit, we will have one graph for each revision that stores the triples that were removed.

Default Graph: The default graph contains triples that encode metadata about each revision: the revision author, the revision timestamp, the id of the modified entity, the previous revision of the same entity, the previous revision in Wikidata, and the IRIs of the additions, deletions, and global state graphs.

This data model allows us to query both the global state of Wikidata after each revision and the modifications brought by reach revision – without any change of the SPARQL 1.1 semantics or syntax [7]. We use the same schema as the official Wikidata dumps [3].

To store our data model, we cannot just load it as is into a triple store. The revision graphs alone would occupy exabytes of storage. Therefore, we use RocksDB[2]. RocksDB is a scalable key value store, optimized for a mixed workload between query and edits. This choice anticipates the possibility of live updates from Wikidata in the future. We create the following indexes:

Dictionary Indexes: Following a well-known practice in RDF storage systems, we represent every string by an integer id. We use one dictionary index to map the strings to their ids, and another one to map the ids to the strings.

Content Indexes: Each triple (s, p, o) appears in three content indexes. The indexes have as keys the permutations spo, pos and osp, respectively, and as value a set of revision ranges. Each range is of the form $[start, end[$, where $start$ is the id of the revision that introduced the triple, and end is the id of the revision that removed it (or $+\infty$ if the triple has not been removed).

Revision indexes: We use two revision indexes, which give the set of triples that have been added or removed by a given revision. Since the Wikidata edits affect only a single entity and usually only a single statement, the number of triples added and removed per edit is small. Therefore, we can easily store all of them in the value part of the key-value store.

Meta indexes: We use several metadata indexes to store, for each revision, its author, the previous revision, etc.

Thanks to the content indexes, it is easy to retrieve for a given triple pattern when the triples have been added and, if relevant, when they have been removed. The indexes can also be used to evaluate a triple pattern against the global state graph, by filtering the results against the revision ranges. This is efficient because out of the 4931M triples that have existed in the Wikidata history as of July 1st 2018, only 475M have been removed. Therefore, the largest revision contains 90% of the total number of Wikidata triples that ever existed.

---

[2] https://rocksdb.org/.

These indexes allow us to evaluate all possible quad patterns. If the quad pattern targets revision metadata, we use the metadata indexes. If it targets the content triples, we proceed as follows:

1. If the graph name is set to an addition graph or a deletion graph, we use the revision indexes to retrieve all the triples that were added or deleted, and we evaluate the triple pattern on them.
2. Otherwise, we do a prefix search in one of the content indexes, building the prefix from the bound parts of the triple pattern and choosing the index that allows us to have the longest prefix, and so the highest selectivity.
   (a) If the graph name is set and is a global state graph, we filter the triples that are returned from the prefix search by using the revision range as a filter.
   (b) Otherwise, we iterate through the matching triples, and build quads by using, for each triple, the revision range to find the ids of the addition graphs and the deletion graphs in which the triple appears. We do not return the ids of the global state graphs, because a query for the graph ids of a single triple pattern could return hundreds of millions of ids.

This storage system allows us to answer queries for a single quad pattern. To answer SPARQL queries, we plug our quad pattern evaluator into Eclipse RDF4J[3]. This system evaluates an arbitrary SPARQL 1.1 query by repeated calls to our quad pattern evaluator. It supports a wide range of query optimizations, including join reordering with static cardinality estimations that are based on the structure of the RDF dataset. For example, every revision has exactly a single author, and the number of triples per Wikidata entity is usually small.

Due to storage space constraints on the server provided by the Wikimedia Foundation, only the direct claim relations are loaded in our demo endpoint. We cover the range from the creation of Wikidata to July 1st, 2018. Our demonstration instance stores more than 700M revisions and 390M content triples about 49M items. The RocksDB indexes are using 64Go on disk with the RocksDB gzip compression system, after having compacted the database.

4   Demonstration Setting

Our system allows users to query the entire Wikidata edit history. For example, Listing 1 asks for the 10 most frequent replacements for the value of the "gender" property. The query retrieves first the set of triples with the gender property (wdt:P21) (Line 2), annotated with the name of addition graphs. Then, it retrieves the names of the deletion graphs for each revision that have seen such additions (Line 3). Finally, it retrieves any deleted triple with the same subject and predicate (Line 4). After that it uses the usual SPARQL 1.1 features to compute the final result (Lines 1 and 5).

Such an analysis yields a number of interesting insights: First, we can observe that users correct erroneous gender values (such as "man") by their intended variants ("male"). Second, a slightly modified variant of the query allows us

---

[3] http://rdf4j.org/.

```
1   SELECT ?addedGender ?deletedGender (COUNT(?revision) AS ?count) WHERE {
2     GRAPH ?addGraph { ?s wdt:P21 ?addedGender }
3     ?revision hist:additions ?addGraph ; hist:deletions ?delGraph .
4     GRAPH ?delGraph { ?s wdt:P21 ?deletedGender }
5   } GROUP BY ?addedGender ?deletedGender ORDER BY DESC(?count) LIMIT 10
```

Fig. 1. Retrieving the most common replacements of a "gender" value.

to quantify the gender gap in Wikidata over time: while the absolute difference between the number of men and women in Wikidata keeps increasing over time, the relative difference actually decreases. Finally, a similar query allows us to trace the increasing presence of non-traditional sex/gender values, such as "trans-male" or "non-binary" in the dataset.

5 Conclusion

In this paper, we propose a system that efficiently indexes the entire Wikidata edit history, and that allows users to answer arbitrary SPARQL 1.1 queries on it. Our system allows queries on both the revision diffs and the global state of Wikidata after each revision. Our system is available online at https://wdhqs.wmflabs.org. For future work, we plan to update the content of our system live based on the Wikidata edit stream.

Acknowledgement. Partially supported by the grant ANR-16-CE23-0007-01 ("DICOS").

References

1. Bishop, B., Kiryakov, A., Ognyanoff, D., Peikov, I., Tashev, Z., Velkov, R.: OWLIM: a family of scalable semantic repositories. Semantic Web **2**(1), 33–42 (2011)
2. Cerdeira-Pena, A., Fariña, A., Fernández, J.D., Martínez-Prieto, M.A.: Self-indexing RDF archives. In: DCC, pp. 526–535 (2016)
3. Erxleben, F., Günther, M., Krötzsch, M., Mendez, J., Vrandečić, D.: Introducing wikidata to the linked data web. In: ISWC, pp. 50–65 (2014)
4. Fernández, J.D., Martínez-Prieto, M.A., Polleres, A., Reindorf, J.: HDTQ: managing RDF datasets in compressed space. In: ESWC, pp. 191–208 (2018)
5. Fernández, J.D., Polleres, A., Umbrich, J.: Towards efficient archiving of dynamic linked open data. DIACRON @ ESWC **1377**, 34–49 (2015)
6. Fernández, J.D., Umbrich, J., Polleres, A., Knuth, M.: Evaluating query and storage strategies for RDF archives. In: SEMANTICS, pp. 41–48 (2016)
7. Harris, S., Seaborne, A., Prud'hommeaux, E.: SPARQL 1.1 query language (2013)
8. Neumann, T., Weikum, G.: x-RDF-3X: fast querying, high update rates, and consistency for RDF databases. PVLDB **3**(1), 256–263 (2010)
9. Pellissier Tanon, T., Bourgaux, C., Suchanek, F.: Learning how to correct a knowledge base from the edit history. In: WWW (2019)
10. Pugliese, A., Udrea, O., Subrahmanian, V.S.: Scaling RDF with time. In: WWW, pp. 605–614 (2008)

11. Taelman, R., Sande, M.V., Verborgh, R.: OSTRICH: versioned random-access triple store. In: WWW, pp. 127–130 (2018)
12. Vander Sande, M., Colpaert, P., Verborgh, R., Coppens, S., Mannens, E., Van de Walle, R.: R&wbase: git for triples. LDOW @ WWW 996 (2013)
13. Vrandečić, D., Krötzsch, M.: Wikidata: a free collaborative knowledgebase. Commun. ACM **57**(10), 78–85 (2014)

A New Tool for Linked Data Visualization and Exploration in 3D/VR Space

Razdiakonov Daniil[1,2], Gerhard Wohlgenannt[1(✉)], Dmitry Pavlov[2],
Yury Emelyanov[2], and Dmitry Mouromtsev[1]

[1] Faculty of Software Engineering and Computer Systems, ITMO University,
St. Petersburg, Russia
wohlg@ai.wu.ac.at, gwohlg@corp.ifmo.ru
[2] Vismart Ltd., St. Petersburg, Russia

Abstract. Linked data and knowledge graphs have become widely used in the last years. As the interest in linked data and ontologies grows, so does the interest in means of studying, presenting, developing and storing ontologies. Here, we introduce a first version of novel tool for presenting and studying ontologies and linked data which visualizes the semantic graph structure in the natural form for humans – in form of 3D objects in space. The use of 3D space provides additional means to visualize and annotate objects, and for the user to explore. The presented tool builds on an existing ontology visualization system (Ontodia), and extends it with the ability to display ontologies in 3D and virtual reality space.

Keywords: Semantic data visualization · Visual data exploration · Knowledge graphs · 3D graph · Virtual reality

1 Introduction

Ontologies and linked data, as a means of knowledge representation, are typically hard to understand for lay users if serialized in RDF or similar formats. Visualization tools can make the semantic data more easily accessible. In visual data consumption, different users will prefer different representations. Depending on the use case, some find it convenient to work with a table views, others prefer flat trees, others again graph views, etc. Therefore, visualization tools often take the complex approach of multi-faceted graph visualization by implementing several representations of the same data at once with the possibility of seamless switching between representations [2].

In this work, we build on a semantic graph visualization platform called *Onto-dia*[1] [4,5]. *Ontodia3D* is an extension of the Ontodia in order to visualize ontologies and linked data in 3D and VR space. We chose Ontodia as underlying framework, as it is (a) published under an open license (GNU LGPL), (b) it is build on a modern technology stack and under active development, (c) offers a wide range of functionalities and potential use cases [1].

---

[1] ontodia.org.

© Springer Nature Switzerland AG 2019
P. Hitzler et al. (Eds.): ESWC 2019 Satellite Events, LNCS 11762, pp. 167–171, 2019.
https://doi.org/10.1007/978-3-030-32327-1_33

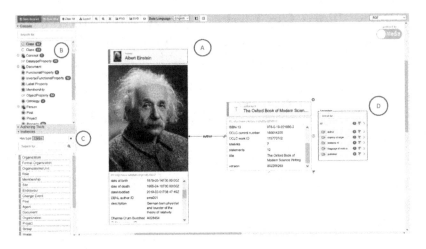

Fig. 1. Ontodia - visualization example from the DBPedia dataset

Figure 1 shows an example of a simple visualization within the Ontodia interface, which is inherited by Ontodia3D. The interface includes the ontology panel
(Class panel, Fig. 1B) and the data panel (Instances panel, Fig. 1C), as well as
the Connections panel, (Fig. 1D), which allows users to add elements to a graph
by searching them by types and by direction of relations.

To the best of our knowledge, there has been little work in 3D visualization
of ontologies and linked data – restricted to visualization plugins for the desktop
versions of Protege and Eclipse (see Sect. 2). In contrast, Ontodia3D[2] is a scalable
Web-based tool built on a recent technology stack. In the demo track at ESWC
we plan to present the latest version of the Ontodia3D prototype, including its
main features of visual customization of various graph components by their type
(see Sect. 3), and the 3D exploration of small but also large graph structures. We
aim to use the potential offered by the addition dimension to improve semantic
graph exploration and understanding. A short video presenting the prototype is
available here: https://cl.ly/bdb3919f4fac.

2   Related Work

In contrast to 2D visualization of ontologies and linked data, there has been
little work on 3D visualization and making use of VR technologies. VR systems
become a mass product only recently, and interactive 3D visualization of large
graphs poses very high demands on the available hardware. Existing work on 3D
visualization of ontologies includes OntoSphere3D [6] and Harmony information
landscape (HIL) [3]. Originally designed for hypertext document, HIL provides
landscapes with color-encoded documents on a 3D plane with relations between

---

[2] Prototype demo available at: https://ontodia3d.herokuapp.com/wikidata.html.

them. OntoSphere3D can be used as plugin for either the Protege[3] environment or for Eclipse[4]. The tool uses a multi-faceted approach to ontology visualization and supports four types of diagrams: taxonomy view, concept detailing view, instances view and a main view for smoother navigation.

In contrast to existing work, the tool presented here is Web-based and uses a modern technology stack. While OntoSphere3D is restricted to the 3D visualization of specific parts of ontologies with a limited number of nodes, Ontodia3D is limited only by the amount of memory available on the machine, and can potentially render graphs with thousands of nodes – depending on a complexity of shapes which are representing elements. Finally, the current technology stack (three.js/WebGL) allows Ontodia3D to implement VR support with little extra effort.

3 Ontodia3D

Ontodia3D currently is a fork of the original Ontodia repository. We support seamless switching between React/SVG and Three.js/WebGL/CSS3D stacks within the UI. With "seamless" we mean that elements from the 2D-graph can occupy the corresponding position in the 3D-graph, which prevents a user from losing the display context. Ontodia provides *Element Templates* for flexible annotation of elements and for embedding of content into a graph scene. Ontodia3D element templates in turn expand the basic Ontodia templates allowing to define the 3D-shapes that represent the selected elements. 3D-shapes can be

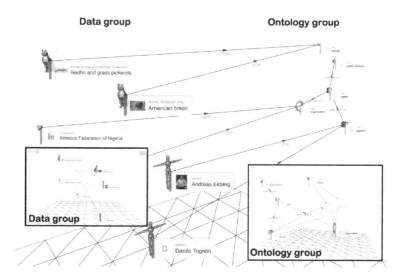

Fig. 2. Ontodia3D - an example of grouping elements via the 3rd dimension

---

[3] protege.stanford.edu.

[4] www.eclipse.org.

loaded from files or as one of the predefined primitives, incl. sphere, cube, ring, pyramid, octahedron, and dodecahedron (see Fig. 2).

Additionally to the customization of shapes, Ontodia3D supports setting object colors, and templates selected by annotation type. The user of the library can determine the rules to select certain element styles. For example, all the vertices of the graph that are instances of the http://dbpedia.org/ontology/ Agent class can be rendered in a shape of a 3D person, and the annotations to this vertex can be represented as a page from a social network (see e.g. Fig. 3). The annotation templates are based on the original templates from Ontodia, which allow setting the color and style of annotations, as well as to integrate almost any content that can be rendered on a Web page, from SVG-images to videos from YouTube.

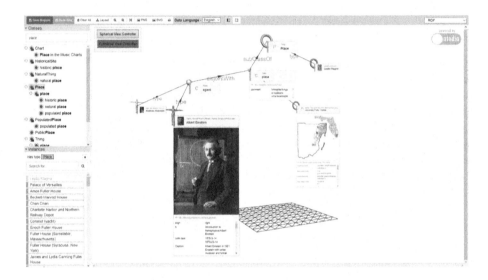

Fig. 3. Ontodia3D - an example from the DBPedia dataset

The 3D representation of graphs provides multiple benefits and opportunities as compared to 2D. Firstly, we have another spacial dimension for expressing and grouping data. In 2D space we can differentiate elements of an ontology by color, text, template design (annotations), as well as by the shape and size of an object – in order to express certain properties. In 3D space the depth of space allows for a more meaningful placement and grouping of objects, and for 3D object shapes and textures.

A frequent challenge faced by graph visualization tools is the difficulty to draw links between nodes so that links do not overlap with each other. This problem is mitigated in 3D space, esp. when using stereo vision (VR helmet). In addition, the 3rd dimension gives the ability to group elements more effectively. For example, all elements of one data set can be placed farther from the user, elements from another dataset closer. While using the Ontodia3D navigation tools, a user can change the position of the viewpoint when switching between data sets. Moreover, links between two data sets will be easily noticed by turning the view-port in a position perpendicular to the data placement planes (see Fig. 2).

Finally, as a more concrete use case, it is possible e.g. to make an ontology of kitchen furniture and, at the same time, place real 3D models of kitchen furniture in 3D space, so that the ontological graph will look like a 3D scene equipped with annotations that provide important characteristics of each class or instance.

4   Conclusion

We introduce a prototype of a new tool for 3D linked data visualization. Ontodia3D is a Web-based application with a modern technology stack that extends an existing ontology visualization framework. The tool aims to make use of the additional visual dimension in order to improve semantic graph exploration by providing new features to customize object and link shapes and annotations, to allow visual distinctions for example by object type, navigation in 3D space, and supports flexible integration of different types of content into the visualization. In contrast to existing work, Ontodia3D aims to display large graphs.

Future work will improve the prototype in various directions: (a) Tighten the integration with the Ontodia base platform, esp. regarding UI interaction, (b) import and export of 3D scenes in various formats, (c) extend the number of supported layout-algorithms for 3D-graphs, (d) align and group nodes using 3D shapes in space (layers, etc), (e) enhance the support for VR devices, (f) 3D features such as camera movement animation, scene customization, lighting configuration, and the ability to use textures on objects. After the implementation of these and other features, we plan a user study to empirically study the benefits and drawbacks of 3D visualization in semantic graph exploration.

Acknowledgments. This work was supported by the Government of the Russian Federation (Grant 074-U01) through the ITMO Fellowship and Professorship Program.

References

1. Dudas, M., Lohmann, S., Svatek, V., Pavlov, D.: Ontology visualization methods and tools: a survey. Knowl. Eng. Rev. Forthcom. **33**(e10), 1–39 (2018)
2. Hadlak, S., Schumann, H., Schulz, H.J.: A survey of multi-faceted graph visualization. In: EuroVis Conference. The Eurographics Association (2015)
3. Katifori, A., Halatsis, C., Lepouras, G., Vassilakis, C., Giannopoulou, E.: Ontology visualization methods - a survey. ACM Comput. Surv. **39**(4), 10 (2007)
4. Mouromtsev, D., Pavlov, D., Emelyanov, Y., Morozov, A., Razdyakonov, D., Galkin, M.: The simple web-based tool for visualization and sharing of semantic data and ontologies. In: International Semantic Web Conference (Posters & Demos) (2015)
5. Wohlgenannt, G., Klimov, N., Mouromtsev, D., Razdyakonov, D., Pavlov, D., Emelyanov, Y.: Using word embeddings for visual data exploration with ontodia and wikidata. In: BLINK/NLIWoD3@ISWC, ISWC, vol. 1932. CEUR-WS.org (2017)
6. Zamazal, O., Svátek, V.: The ten-year ontofarm and its fertilization within the onto-sphere. Web Semant. **43**, 46–53 (2017)

Open Cultural Heritage Data in University Programming Courses

Tabea Tietz[1,2(✉)] and Harald Sack[1,2]

[1] Karlsruhe Institute of Technology, Institute AIFB, Karlsruhe, Germany
[2] FIZ Karlsruhe – Leibniz Institute for Information Infrastructure,
Eggenstein-Leopoldshafen, Germany
{tabea.tietz,harald.sack}@fiz-karlsruhe.de

Abstract. Cultural heritage data are not only an important research subject for the semantic web community, but also provide interesting material for practical programming courses in universities. In this paper, four projects created by master students at Karlsruhe Institute of Technology (KIT) show how open cultural heritage data can be used to develop creative and ambitious applications which improve the students' knowledge and experience working with semantic web technologies, linked data, natural language processing techniques and machine learning. Furthermore, challenges and lessons learned are discussed.

Keywords: Education · Cultural heritage · Semantic web · Linked data · Data exploration · Machine learning · Natural language processing

1 Introduction

Cultural heritage data have become an important subject of research in many domains. Especially in the field of semantic web research, the possibilities of providing means to explore the growing amount of these data and the tasks for knowledge engineering and knowledge mining are numerous [6,7]. At the same time, students of semantic web (and related) courses in bachelor and master programs at universities need to be provided with interesting topics and projects to build their skills and spark their enthusiasm for the field. The idea to combine real world research problems with university-level education has been implemented widely as it not only provides students with realistic insights into the academic life but also allows tutors to integrate results obtained into their own research efforts. The presented poster paper follows this line of argumentation. In the paper, outcomes of a master student course are presented in which student groups chose open cultural heritage datasets, developed and evaluated their own web-based applications, thereby utilizing and improving their knowledge in semantic web technologies, natural language processing (NLP), and machine learning (ML). The presented results consist of an exploration framework for historical texts, a gamification approach for history lessons enriched with linked

© Springer Nature Switzerland AG 2019
P. Hitzler et al. (Eds.): ESWC 2019 Satellite Events, LNCS 11762, pp. 172–175, 2019.
https://doi.org/10.1007/978-3-030-32327-1_34

data, a content-based book recommendation system and a museum chatbot. A specialty about this particular programming course is the use of open cultural heritage datasets made available by the Coding da Vinci initiative, which confronted the students with interesting and mostly uncharted data to explore [1]. Coding da Vinci is the first German open cultural data hackathon, founded in 2014. Its goal is to bring together cultural heritage institutions with the hacker & designer community to develop ideas and prototypes for the cultural sector as well as for the public. The paper furthermore provides lessons learned from the practical seminar including challenges the student groups have dealt with.

2   Course Structure and Data

The seminar project course 'Information Service Engineering' (ISE) was held at KIT for master students of information management. As a prerequisite, all students previously attended the ISE lecture, which prepared them with foundations in linked data engineering, ML, and NLP. The goal of the project course was to work on a common research problem in groups of 3 students each and to come up with and implement a web-application using state-of-the art scientific research methods. All groups received the tasks to select datasets part of Coding da Vinci and to implement their own project idea, supported by at least 2 tutors from the teaching team. Coding da Vinci originally is a German hackathon which supports interdisciplinary work on cultural heritage data. However, the hackathon concept does not really fit the university curriculum, i.e. with a timeframe of 5 weeks for the current edition of Coding da Vinci, the obtained workload would significantly influence the students' other courses. Therefore, it was decided to decouple the Coding da Vinci competition from the 14 weeks' course work. However, the goal was nevertheless to establish a competitive environment with the student teams working on real world datasets, comparing their achieved results also with the original hackathon results. In general, the experimental ISE programming course was conducted to give proof that current research problems of the cultural heritage and digital humanities domain can successfully be integrated into the teaching curriculum by the development of semantic web based solutions.

3   Applications

Overall, 4 cultural heritage data projects have been implemented (cf. Fig. 1). All applications can be accessed on the web [2]

① **Exploring Historical Text using Word and Document Embeddings.** In this project a framework is presented which combines unsupervised ML techniques and NLP on the example of historical text documents on the $19th$ century USA. Named entities are identified and extracted from semi-structured text, which is enriched with complementary information from Wikidata. Word embeddings are leveraged to enable the analysis of the text corpus, which is visualized in a web-based application. Experiments provide evidence that the method used

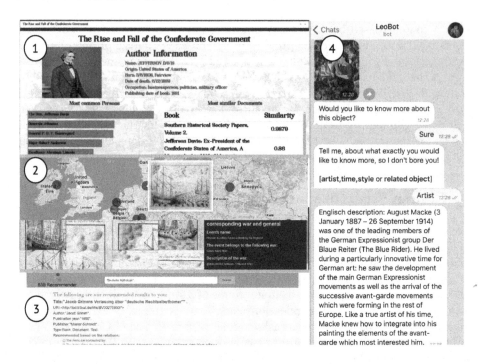

Fig. 1. Screenshots of the four presented ISE applications

to create the semantic representations using word and document vectors are especially promising for the analysis of unstructured historical English text collections, as long as the amount of text is sufficiently large to train meaningful semantic representations with the neural net.

(2) **Learning History Through Gamification.** This project contributes to the area of improving history lessons through gamification. Users interested in studying historical wars in Europe can select from a set of pictures presented on a map. Once chosen, a puzzle game based on historical pictures of European wars opens. Upon completion, the user receives complementary information automatically generated from DBpedia and Wikidata about the event and persons involved. The maps and landscapes used are part of the Hessian State Archives [4]. An evaluation of the game involved 37 participants and revealed that the users are interested in the presented combination of solving a game and receiving further knowledge about historical events, especially in the context of history lessons in schools and museums. The main challenge for the students involved the often sparse amount of data available for historical wars and battles.

(3) **Content-based Book Recommender System.** A content-based book recommender system was developed using a dataset published by the Bavarian State Library [3]. A main challenge for the students was handling the large size of the 135 GB dataset consisting of more than 100 million entities. Recommendations are generated based on semantic similarities of the documents and on relatedness of specific entities in the corpus being connected to Wikidata.

④ **A Linked Data Enhanced Museum Chatbot.** In this project, a chatbot for the Städel Museum Frankfurt, Germany [5] was developed to make museum visits more interesting for younger generations. The application is based on the Telegram messenger app and lets the user converse with a chatbot to receive information about art pieces and background information about artists, places or paintings integrated using Wikidata and DBpedia.

4   Lessons Learned and Conclusion

In this paper, the outcomes of a university programming course are presented, where methods have been developed to successfully explore cultural heritage data collections using semantic web and linked data technologies, as well as NLP and ML techniques. An evaluation of the course performed by the university reveals that the students genuinely enjoyed the course. It is especially welcomed that the students implemented their own ideas using the data they have chosen themselves. The evaluation also reveals that the workload the students encountered was very high, which is a disadvantage of the groups choosing the project topics on their own, because the amount of work to be completed was always underestimated. This will be counteracted in the future by examining the datasets more closely before the seminar and pointing out possible problems with concrete solutions. The most valuable lessons learned in this course are that the open nature of the course fostered refreshing and interesting ideas and perspectives from students who are not yet part of the semantic web research community. The seminar enabled to build bridges between traditional GLAM institutions who own the data and young researchers who provide the necessary ideas on how to explore these data using scientific methods and new technologies. Last but not least, the seminar helped to increase the students' interest in semantic web technologies, because the application on cultural heritage data revealed a broader context on why these technologies are important after all.

Acknowledgement. We would like to thank all seminar students and tutors, who invested a great amount of work to make each project a successful one, and the Coding da Vinci initiative for providing the extensive amount of data.

References

1. Coding da Vinci (2014). Accessed 19 Mar 2019. https://codingdavinci.de/
2. Course Projects. Accessed 23 Apr 2019. https://ise-fizkarlsruhe.github.io/CoursePr ojects2019
3. Bavarian St. Library. Accessed 19 Mar 2019. https://www.bsb-muenchen.de/
4. Hessian St. Archives. Accessed 19 Mar 2019. https://landesarchiv.hessen.de/
5. Städel Museum. Accessed 19 Mar 2019. https://www.staedelmuseum.de/en
6. Dragoni, M., Tonelli, S., Moretti, G.: A knowledge management architecture for digital cultural heritage. JOCCH **10**(3), 15 (2017)
7. Simou, N., Chortaras, A., Stamou, G., Kollias, S.: Enriching and publishing cultural heritage as linked open data. Mixed Reality and Gamification for Cultural Heritage, pp. 201–223. Springer, Cham (2017). https://doi.org/10.1007/978-3-319-49607-8_7

Using an Existing Website as a Queryable Low-Cost LOD Publishing Interface

Brecht Van de Vyvere$^{(\boxtimes)}$, Ruben Taelman, Pieter Colpaert ,
and Ruben Verborgh

IDLab (imec – Ghent University), Technologiepark-Zwijnaarde 122,
9052 Ghent, Belgium
{brecht.vandevyvere, ruben.taelman, pieter.colpaert,
ruben.verborgh}@ugent.be

Abstract. Maintaining an Open Dataset comes at an extra recurring cost when it is published in a dedicated Web interface. As there is not often a direct financial return from publishing a dataset publicly, these extra costs need to be minimized. Therefore we want to explore reusing existing infrastructure by enriching existing websites with Linked Data. In this demonstrator, we advised the data owner to annotate a digital heritage website with JSON-LD snippets, resulting in a dataset of more than three million triples that is now available and officially maintained. The website itself is paged, and thus hydra partial collection view controls were added in the snippets. We then extended the modular query engine Comunica to support following page controls and extracting data from HTML documents while querying. This way, a SPARQL or GraphQL query over multiple heterogeneous data sources can power automated data reuse. While the query performance on such an interface is visibly poor, it becomes easy to create composite data dumps. As a result of implementing these building blocks in Comunica, any paged collection and enriched HTML page now becomes queryable by the query engine. This enables heterogenous data interfaces to share functionality and become technically interoperable.

This is a print-version of a paper first written for the Web. The Web-version is available at https://brechtvdv.github.io/Article-Using-an-existing-website-as-a-queryable-low-cost-LOD-publishing-interface/.

Keywords: JSON-LD data snippets · Hypermedia web APIs · Intelligent agents · Digital humanities · Linked Open Data · Semantic web

1   Introduction

The Flemish Institute for Audiovisual Archiving (VIAA) is a non-profit organization that preserves petabytes of valuable image, audio or video files. These files and accompanying metadata are covered by distinct licenses, but some can be made accessible under an Open Data license. One initiative is opening up historical newspapers of the first World War with the open platform hetarchief.be. In 2017, the raw data of these newspapers have been published as a Linked Open Data [1]

© Springer Nature Switzerland AG 2019
P. Hitzler et al. (Eds.): ESWC 2019 Satellite Events, LNCS 11762, pp. 176–180, 2019.
https://doi.org/10.1007/978-3-030-32327-1_35

(LOD) dataset using the low-cost Triple Pattern Fragments [2] (TPF) interface. Although this interface is still accessable[1], no updates from the website have been exported to the TPF interface due to absence of automatisation.

Maintaining an up-to-date LOD interface brings besides technical resources also an organizational challenge. Content editors often work in a seperate environment such as a Content Management System (CMS) to update a website. The raw data gets exported from that system and published in a dedicated environment leaving the source of truth to the CMS. The question rises whether the data can be published closer to the authorative source in a more sustainable way.

Website maintainers are currently using JSON-LD structured data snippets to attain better search result ranking and visualisation with search engines. These snippets are script tags inside a HTML webpage containing Linked Data in JSON format (JSON-LD) compliant with the Schema.org [3] datamodel. Not only search engine optimization (SEO), but also standard LOD publishing is possible. The data should be representative with the main content of the subject page, such as newspaper metadata, to be aligned with the structured data guidelines of search engines. In order that Linked Data user agents such as Comunica [4] can query a website as a dataset, the webpages should be linked together through hypermedia controls [5].

First we give a short background of the Comunica tool and the Hydra partial collection views. We then describe how hetarchief.be is enriched with JSON-LD snippets. Next, we explain how we allow Comunica to query over this and other sources by adding two building blocks. After this, we demonstrate how a custom data dump can be created by an end-user that wants to further analyze this data, for instance in spreadsheet software. The online version of this paper embeds this demo and can be tested live. Finally, we conclude the demonstrator with a discussion and perspective on future work.

2   Background

2.1   Comunica

Comunica [4] is a Linked Data user agent that can run federated queries over several heterogeneous Web APIs. This engine has been developed to make it easy to plug in specific types of functionality as separate modules.

A bus module is used as communication channel to solve one problem, e.g. to extract hypermedia controls from a Web API. Multiple actor modules can subscribe to a bus and extract one or more hypermedia controls according to their implementation. A mediator module wraps around the bus to select the most appropriate results. As such, by supporting multiple hypermedia controls more intelligent user agents can be created.

---

[1] http://linkeddatafragments-qas.viaa.be/.

2.2 Hydra Partial Collection Views

Open Data is filled with collections of items (hotel amenities, road works etc.). Using the Hydra vocabulary for hypermedia-driven Web APIs, not only the relations between items and collections can be expressed, but also how different parts of the collection can be retrieved, so called partial collection view controls (e.g. a next page link). This way, a collection can be split in multiple documents while a Web client can still query over the collection by retrieving its view controls.

3 Implementation

3.1 hetarchief.be

Every newspaper webpage is annotated with JSON-LD snippets containing domain-specific metadata and hypermedia controls. The former metadata is described using acknowledged vocabularies such as Dublin Core Terms (DCTerms), Friend of a Friend (FOAF), Schema.org etc. The latter is described using the Hydra vocabulary for hypermedia-driven Web APIs. Although hetarchief.be contains several human-readable hypermedia controls (free text search bar, search facets, pagination for every newspaper) only Hydras partial collection view controls are implemented: hydra:next describes the next newspaper, vice versa hydra:previous. Also an estimate of the amount of triples on a page is added using hydra:totalItems and void:triples. This helps user agents to build more efficient query plans.

3.2 Building Blocks Comunica

To make Comunica work with hetarchief.be, two additional actors were needed. First, we needed a generic actor to support pagination over any kind of hypermedia interface. Secondly, an actor was needed to parse JSON-LD data snippets from HTML documents. We will explain these two actors in more detail hereafter.

BusRdfResolveHypermedia is a bus in Comunica that resolves hypermedia controls from sources. Currently, this bus only contains an actor that resolves controls for TPF interfaces. We added a new actor (*ActorRdfResolveHypermediaNextPage*) to this bus that returns a search form containing a next page link.

The parsing of most common Linked Data formats (Turtle, RDF/XML, JSON-LD…) are already supported by Comunica. However, no parser for extracting data snippets from HTML documents existed yet. That is why we added an actor (*ActorRdfParseHtmlScript*) for parsing such HTML documents. This intermediate parser searches for data snippets and forwards these to their respective RDF parser. In case of a JSON-LD snippet, the body of a script tag <script type="application/ld +json"> will be parsed by the JSON-LD parse actor.

By adding these two actors to Comunica, we can now query over a paged collection that is declaratively described with data snippets. As federated querying comes out-of-the-box with Comunica, this cultural heritage collection can now be queried together with other knowledge bases (cfr. Wikidata). For example, retrieving basic information such as title, publication date etc. from 17 newspaper pages requires 1.5 min until all results are retrieved. This is caused by deficiency of indexes where all pages need examination before having a complete answer.

In next section we will demonstrate how SPARQL-querying can be applied for extracting a spreadsheet.

4   Demonstrator

This demonstrator shows that a non-technical user can create a data dump from the cultural heritage website hetarchief.be. More specifically, a spreadsheet can be extracted using SPARQL-querying from embedded paged collection views. The application is written with the front-end playground Codepen[2]. A browser compatible library of Comunica is built using a custom configuration that can be found on Github[3] under an Open License.

First, a user can insert a URL of a hypermedia-enabled LOD interface. For example, a user can go to hetarchief.be and select a newspaper as starting point. After pressing Generate, Comunica fetches the document located on the given URL and follows the embedded pagination controls. While querying, user feedback is provided with request logs, the amount of processed CSV records and bytes. Next, the user can Copy the CSV output to its clipboard. Finally, a SPARQL-query can be configured to customize the desired outcome (Fig. 1).

Fig. 1. A spreadsheet is generated by entering a URL of a newspaper from hetarchief.be.

---

[2] https://codepen.io/brechtvdv/pen/ebOzXB.

[3] https://github.com/brechtvdv/hetarchief-comunica.

5 Conclusion

Data owners can publish their LOD very cost-efficient on their website with JSON-LD snippets. After an initial cost of adding this feature to their website, they can have an always up-to-date dataset with negligible maintenance costs, however, machine clients that query and harvest over websites can introduce unforeseen spikes of activity. Data owners will need to extend their monitoring capabilities to not only focus on human interaction (e.g. Google Analytics) and apply a HTTP caching strategy for stale resources.

Linked Data services (HDT [6] file, TPF interface…) with a higher maintenance cost can be created on top of JSON-LD snippets, but these would suffer from scalability problems: OCR texts have bad compression rates, and thus require gigabytes of disk space. With our solution, these OCR texts are published in a seperate document keeping the maintenance cost low while harvesting in an automated way is still possible.

The LOD interfaces of the European cultural heritage platform Europeana take an opposite approach from this work: every subject page contains a title and description annotation for SEO, but the actual machine-readable data is exposed through a separate record API with API key protection and publicly available SPARQL endpoint. Supporting JSON-LD snippets as explained in this work would make the record API obsolete and more importantly, Open Data reusers would have a starting point for querying the SPARQL endpoint.

In future work, extending Comunica for harvesting Hydra collections would help organizations to improve their collection management. These collections could be defined on their main page of their website improving Open Data discoverability.

References

1. Berners-Lee, T.: 5 Star Data (2009). https://5stardata.info/en/
2. Verborgh, R., et al.: Triple pattern fragments: a low-cost knowledge graph interface for the web. J. Web Semant. **37**, 184–206 (2016)
3. Mika, P.: On Schema.org and why it matters for the web. IEEE Internet Comput. **19**, 52–55 (2015)
4. Taelman, R., Van Herwegen, J., Vander Sande, M., Verborgh, R.: Comunica: a modular SPARQL query engine for the web. In: Vrandečić, D., et al. (eds.) ISWC 2018. LNCS, vol. 11137, pp. 239–255. Springer, Cham (2018). https://doi.org/10.1007/978-3-030-00668-6_15
5. Fielding, R.T., Taylor, R.N.: Architectural Styles and the Design of Network-Based Software Architectures. University of California, Irvine (2000)
6. Fernández, J.D., Martínez-Prieto, M.A., Gutiérrez, C., Polleres, A., Arias, M.: Binary RDF representation for publication and exchange (HDT). J. Web Sem. **19**, 22–41 (2013)

A Tagger for Glossary of Terms Extraction from Ontology Competency Questions

Dawid Wisniewski[1]([✉])[iD] and Agnieszka Ławrynowicz[1,2][iD]

[1] Faculty of Computing, Poznan University of Technology, Poznań, Poland
{dwisniewski,alawrynowicz}@cs.put.poznan.pl
[2] Center for Artificial Intelligence and Machine Learning (CAMIL),
Poznan University of Technology, Poznań, Poland

Abstract. Competency Questions (CQs) are questions expressed in natural language aimed to indicate ontology's scope, which are later formalized according to the language used to represent the ontology. One intermediate step that facilitates formalizing CQs, proposed in ontology engineering methodologies, is to extract so-called Glossary of Terms from them, which is so far a manual process. To automate this intermediate step, we propose a tagger, which for the given sequence of words, in a CQ, decides whether it should be considered as a suggestion of vocabulary (a class, an instance or a property) in the created ontology, and in this way being a good candidate entry to the Glossary of Terms. We also report about preliminary evaluation of the tagger.

Keywords: Ontology engineering · Competency Questions · Knowledge extraction

1 Introduction

Competency Questions (CQs) are questions expressed in natural language aimed to indicate the scope of an ontology, and which are later formalized according to the language used to represent the ontology. One step that facilitates formalizing CQs is to extract from them so-called *Glossary of Terms* (the list of terms and objects included in the CQs), an artefact proposed in the NeON methodology for ontology engineering [4] and part of so-called Ontology Requirements Specification Document.

The contributions of this poster paper are as follows: (i) We present a tagger, which for the given sequence of words, in a competency question, decides whether it should be considered as a suggestion of vocabulary (a class, an instance or a property) in the created ontology. Such suggestions indicate that the sequence may be a good candidate to become an entry addition to the Glossary of Terms. (ii) We present a preliminary evaluation of the tagger.

P. Hitzler et al. (Eds.): ESWC 2019 Satellite Events, LNCS 11762, pp. 181–185, 2019.
https://doi.org/10.1007/978-3-030-32327-1_36

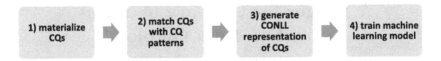

Fig. 1. Proposed method.

2   Related Work

Analysis of CQs. Ren et al. [3] analysed CQs and determined patterns in the form of CQ archetypes (e.g., "Which [CE1] [OPE] [CE2]?") containing place-holders for presupposed ontology elements. Bezerra et al. [1] also proposed CQ patterns with placeholders for ontology elements, a form of templates for CQs e.g. "Does <class>+ <property><class>?", functioning as Controlled Natural Language. We do not presuppose slots for specific ontology vocabulary, since we assume that the same phrase in a CQ may be modelled in an ontology either via a property or by a class. Instead, we are focused on a linguistic analysis of the natural language text in CQs themselves. Furthermore, no automatic tagger has been proposed so far for the purpose of extracting terms and objects from CQs.

Preliminaries. In our previous work [5], we presented a set of CQs with the set of ontologies and described generation of CQ patterns which are ontology vocabulary agnostic. Those CQ patterns contain two kinds of placeholders for phrases that may describe elements that are likely to be part of ontology specific vocabulary: (i) Entity Chunk (EC): fragment of text describing an object (entity) that is likely to be represented in the ontology. (ii) Predicate Chunk (PC): fragment of text being a simple predicate that represents relations between entities that are likely to be represented in the ontology. Consider, for instance, the following CQ: "What software can perform Genome assembly?". In this case it is transformed to a pattern: "What EC1 PC1 EC2?".

The phrase 'likely to be represented' refers to situations in which we cannot be sure how ontology engineer models knowledge in an ontology. Consider CQ: "Which components of model are there?, in that case both components and model can be modelled as separate entities, but also, they can be modelled as for instance one components of model class. EC and PC mark in the patterns the shortest spans of text which can be interpreted as entities or relations.

3   Proposed Method

The proposed method consists of the following steps (depicted also in Fig. 1):

1. **Materialize CQs to increase the training data size.** This step consists of replacing CQs containing placeholders (we call them *dematerialized* CQs) such as "What software can perform [task x]?", where "[task x]" is a placeholder. We replace all CQs with placeholders with their *materialized* equivalents (i.e., we populate the placeholder with subclasses of an adequate class from the

Table 1. The features used to train the machine learning model.

(1)	Lowercased representation of token
(2)	Flag indicating if token is an auxiliary verb
(3)	The last 3 characters of token
(4)	Flag indicating if token begins with a capital letter
(5)	Flag indicating if token contains many capital letters
(6)	Number of verbs in the CQ
(7)	Flag indicating if token is a digit
(8)	Part of speech tag of token
(9)	Last two characters of part of speech tag of token
(10)	The dependency parse tree label of token
(11)	The dependency parse tree label of dependency tree parent of token

ontology and we generate as many new CQs as there are such subclasses). For instance, to populate [task x] with the appropriate classes from the SWO ontology, where [task x] represents tasks in this case, we consider every class that is a subclass of task.

2. **Match CQs with CQ patterns and detect where entities and relations occur.** The CQ patterns (generated in [5], see: Sect. 2) are matched to materialized CQs, i.e., they are used to search in materialized CQs for sequences of words, which are associated with the EC and PC tags, and in this way extract either classes and individuals (EC) or properties (PC). The EC and PC tags constitute our golden standard annotations which are used in the training process.

3. **Generate CONLL representation of CQs containing features of every token.** This step consists of generating the CONLL representation (http://ufal.mff.cuni.cz/conll2009-st/task-description.html) of CQs to define features required by the classifier and mark where entities and relations start and end. Each token from the CQ is written in a separate line and described by the features such as the token content, part of speech tag, name of the relation in the dependency tree, etc. Entities and relations are marked in two last columns, utilizing the IOB format: B-E denotes a beginning of an entity, I-E its continuation, B-R denotes a beginning of a relation and I-R the continuation. O denotes a token that is neither a part of entity nor relation.

4. **Train machine learning model.** We propose a model, based on Conditional Random Fields (CRFs) [2], where every token is represented with features

Table 2. An example of the execution of a trained model.

Competency question:	What	software	can	perform	Genome	assembly	?
Predicted labels:	O	B-E	B-R	I-R	B-E	I-E	O

Table 3. Preliminary evaluation.

Label	B-E	I-E	B-R	I-R
Precision	0.86	0.73	0.38	0.8
Recall	0.76	0.86	0.34	0.55
F1	0.81	0.79	0.36	0.65

describing current and context tokens jointly. Current token is represented using a vector of 11 features defined in Table 1 which is concatenated with vectors of features (1, 4, 5, 8, 9, 10, 11) describing two previous and later context tokens.

Table 2 presents an example of the execution of a trained model. Each token from the competency question receives a label, and by interpreting the labels we arrive in a one candidate for a property ('can perform') and two candidates for classes/instances ('software', 'Genome assembly').

4   Evaluation

Materials. We used the set described in [5], where the details of the particular ontologies are included. The dataset consists of CQ sets defined against selected ontologies: SWO (with 88 CQs materialied into 46465 forms), Stuff (11 CQs materialized into 90 forms), AWO (14 CQs materialized into 47 forms), Dem@Care (107 CQs materialized into 107 forms) and OntoDT (14 CQs materialized into 482 forms). In order to prevent overfitting and check how our method generalizes to work on different domains and CQ styles, we trained a CRF model on the largest dataset (SWO) and evaluated it against the separate test set consisting of union of CQs defined against Dem@Care, OntoDT, AWO, Stuff. We set regularization: $L1 = 1$, $L2 = 0.001$ and max iterations $= 100$ as hyperparameter values and measured the quality of model using precision, recall and F1 scores.

Results. Table 3 contains a preliminary evaluation of our system. It occurs that it can predict where entities occur with a good overall quality (average F1 $=$ 0.8) and quite good relation quality (average F1 $=$ 0.505). The source code of the application can be found on: https://bit.ly/2LtXPpD.

5   Conclusions

The obtained evaluation results prove that our method trained on one dataset can generalize to work well on different datasets, which is a promising observation for future work. We hope that broad feature selection and increasing the training set size can lead to even better results in the future.

References

1. Bezerra, C., Santana, F., Freitas, F.: CQChecker: a tool to check ontologies in OWL-DL using competency questions written in controlled natural language. Learn. Nonlinear Models **12**(2), 115–129 (2014)
2. Lafferty, J.D., McCallum, A., Pereira, F.C.N.: Conditional random fields: probabilistic models for segmenting and labeling sequence data. In: Proceedings of ICML (2001)
3. Ren, Y., Parvizi, A., Mellish, C., Pan, J.Z., van Deemter, K., Stevens, R.: Towards competency question-driven ontology authoring. In: Presutti, V., d'Amato, C., Gandon, F., d'Aquin, M., Staab, S., Tordai, A. (eds.) ESWC 2014. LNCS, vol. 8465, pp. 752–767. Springer, Cham (2014). https://doi.org/10.1007/978-3-319-07443-6_50
4. Suarez-Figueroa, M.C., et al.: NeOn methodology for building contextualized ontology networks. NeOn Deliverable D5.4.1, NeOn Project (2008)
5. Wisniewski, D., Potoniec, J., Lawrynowicz, A., Keet, C.M.: Competency questions and SPARQL-OWL queries dataset and analysis. Technical report 1811.09529, November 2018. https://arxiv.org/abs/1811.09529

I Know Where to Find What You Want: Semantic Data Map from Silos

Sungmin Yi$^{(\boxtimes)}$, Soo-Hyung Kim$^{(\boxtimes)}$, Jungho Park$^{(\boxtimes)}$, Taeho Hwang, Jaehun Lee, and Yunsu Lee

Samsung Research, Samsung Electronics, Seoul, South Korea
{sungmin.yi, sooh0721.kim, j0106.park, taeho.hwang, jaehun20.lee, yunsu16.lee}@samsung.com

Abstract. Data-driven analysis is critically important for creating new insights and values; however, data silos prevent a full utilization of existing data. To overcome this issue, we propose *Semantic Data MAP* (SD-MAP). SD-MAP utilizes a virtual graph and conceptual groups to bypass a physical integration of databases while allowing users to access data using intuitive queries. In order to show our system's effectiveness, we introduce a plausible scenario with a data structure from real world. A demonstration video of SD-MAP is available at: https://youtu.be/i7U_8763Ogk.

Keywords: Virtual graph · Data integration · Silo effect · Semantic Data Map · Intuitive queries · SPARQL

1 Introduction

With the growth of AI and data science, many companies understand the importance of deriving new insights and values from data [1]. However many companies rely on legacy databases that are fragmented and ill-suited for modern data analytics [2]. For instance, most companies partitions a business unit into smaller functional groups, and each group creates and maintains a separate database that is best suited for each individual use cases. As a result, data are kept in silos. If a user wants to find relevant data for an application, the user has to explore each silo one at a time. Many attempted to address the silo issue by data integration, but physical data integration is often prohibitively expensive.

To address the silo effect, we introduce a novel end-to-end semantic data integration system, called the *Semantic Data MAP* (SD-MAP) (see Fig. 1). SD-MAP utilizes a virtual graph which contains database schemas as nodes and their relationships as edges. Owing to a virtual graph, SD-MAP virtually integrates databases and finds data locations quickly. In addition, our user interface supports intuitive queries. In other words, users do not need to know details of data (e.g. exact database name, table name, column name, and so on) and how to construct SQL query or SPARQL query. Users only have to know about the concepts such as "*id*", "*country code*", and so on.

S. Yi, S.-H. Kim and J. Park—These authors contributed equally.

P. Hitzler et al. (Eds.): ESWC 2019 Satellite Events, LNCS 11762, pp. 186–190, 2019.
https://doi.org/10.1007/978-3-030-32327-1_37

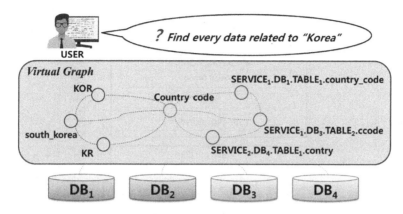

Fig. 1. Semantic Data Map (SD-MAP)

The contributions of the system are as follows:

1. Intuitive query interface: users are able to build queries using only concepts, since SD-MAP forms groups of conceptually-related data automatically.
2. Finding data location: the system can find an exact location of target data because the siloed databases are automatically collected and expressed in a data map.
3. Virtual integration: it gets rid of a need for physical integration.

The rest of the paper is organized as follows. Section 2 presents an overview of SD-MAP, and Sect. 3 describes a detail explanation of a use case.

2   SD-MAP System Overview

SD-MAP is an end-to-end semantic data integration system (see Fig. 2). When a user provides databases information you want to integrate, SD-MAP generates Virtual Graph automatically and a user can extract target data by intuitive query. SD-MAP consists of three main components: a Virtual Graph Engine, a Federated DB, and a web UI. First of all, the Virtual Graph Engine has three modules: Virtual Graph, OBDA (Ontology-based Data Access) [3], and SPARQL-to-SQL. The Virtual Graph is a semantic graph made by an ontology which consists of databases schemas, schema mappings [4], and entity mappings [5]. The Virtual Graph Engine converts SPARQL to SQL using an OBDA. In other words, the Virtual Graph Engine integrates multiple databases and constructs SQL queries to get targeted data from multiple databases. In order to generate the virtual graph from multiple databases, SD-MAP adopts a Federated DB. It controls the connections of multiple databases. Lastly, the web UI provides a Data Map Search and a Query Generator. Users can find exact locations of target data through the Data Map Search. In addition, users can use intuitive queries due to the Query Generator that can convert those queries to SPARQL queries.

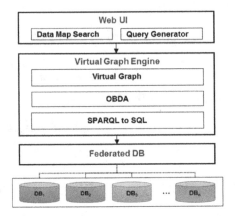

Fig. 2. SD-MAP system architecture overview

To develop SD-MAP, we utilize several OSSs in our system. *vis.js* [6] is used for data map visualization and *Spring Boot* is used for Web UI and *Ontop* [3] is used for Virtual Graph Engine and *Teiid* [7] is used for Federated DB.

3   Demonstration of SD-MAP

3.1   Background

Supply chain management (SCM) oversees the flow of products and services from raw materials into final products [1]. SCM usually includes a wide range of sub processes that cover an entire life cycle of products: procurement of raw materials and components, assembly, shipping, sales, and customer care, each with its own set of standard operation procedures.

In real world, SCM data, amassed in each point of the flow, are closely related to each other. However, the generated data is stored in different silos (i.e., different database with different schemas) and managed separately using different schemas. This fragmentation renders siloed data not well-suited for data analytics. For instance, aggregating number of sales from each retailer requires numerous steps in a data silo. First of all, a user must identify every database that store relevant information: sales, distribution, etc. Second, the user has to obtain access privilege by contacting administrators of each database. Then, the user need to understand schemas and relationships among multiple databases for the analysis. This traditional approach is inefficient and time-consuming. To demonstrate the utility of SD-MAP, we define a demo scenario as follows.

Scenario 1. The scenario is *"Extract the sell-out data by retailer in BURNABY for BEST BUY in 2018"*. In order to get its results, we need to get both *Wholesaler* and *Channel* data in *DISTRIBUTION* database and *Sell-out* and *Retailer* data in *SALE* database (Fig. 3).

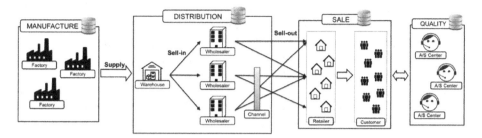

Fig. 3. The figure shows the general flow in SCM for our scenario. The data generated in this flow is separately stored in separate databases of four departments.

3.2 Demonstration of Scenario

In this section, we introduce how to use SD-MAP in our SCM scenario. When a user enters the SD-MAP system, the system shows Data Map graph, constructed from selected databases. The graph nodes are composed of DBs, tables, columns and semantic concepts (Fig. 4(a)). The semantic concepts are created from a schema mapping. The graph edges are composed of DB-table-column schema relations and schema mapping relations (red colors). Data Map shows schema mapping relations as potential JOIN keys. The user can easily understand whole data in fragmented databases through Data Map.

The user can extract data by semantic concepts query. The user input concepts values corresponding to the scenario in SELECT and WHERE clauses. In this scenario we input *"Wholesaler name, Retailer Name, SellOut"* concepts in SELECT and *"Wholesaler Name=BEST BUY, SellOut Date=2018, Retailer Cit =BURNABY"* in WHERE clauses (Fig. 4(b)). Then, our system automatically creates FROM clauses from the information in SELECT and WHERE clauses and constructs a concept query.

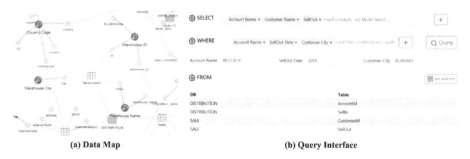

| (a) Data Map | (b) Query Interface |

Fig. 4. Data Map (left) and Query Interface (right). Data Map is described from selected DB schemas and their mappings. In Query Interface, user input concepts in SELECT and WHERE clauses. Concepts are created form Data Map. (Color figure online)

SD-MAP consumes the request in the following manner. Firstly, the concept query is transformed to a SPARQL query by Query Generator. Secondly, the SPARQL query is transformed to a SQL query by a Virtual Graph Engine. Finally, the SQL query is executed in a Federated DB. The system returns the query results to the user. In the Virtual Graph Engine, the system uses information from entity mapping to aggregate semantically equivalent records (e.g. KOR and KR both indicate Korea). As a result, our system removes semantically duplicated results.

As we demonstrated, SD-MAP can quickly extract the target data by semantic concepts without a detailed knowledge of multiple schemas from siloed databases. A video demonstrating is available at: https://youtu.be/i7U_8763Ogk.

4   Conclusion and Future Work

In this work, we introduced *Semantic Data MAP* (SD-MAP) which is a full-stack data integration system that addresses the silo effect. We showed the utility and practicality of SD-MAP through a plausible scenario. The SD-MAP virtual graph approach can reduce time and resources for a conventional data integration process.

To enhance our system, we will add more query operations such as range, group by, and so on (in present, the SD-MAP only consider the SELECT-WHERE clause). In the future, we are going to support additional database types: NoSQL and XML.

References

1. Tiwari, S., Wee, H., Daryanto, Y.: Big data analytics in supply chain management between 2010 and 2016: insights to industries. Comput. Ind. Eng. **115**, 319–330 (2018)
2. Dong, X.L., Halevy, A., Yu, C.: Data integration with uncertainty. VLDB J. **18**(2), 469–500 (2009)
3. Calvanese, D., et al.: Ontop: answering SPARQL queries over relational databases. Semant. Web **8**(3), 471–487 (2017)
4. Renée, M., Laura, H., Mauricio, H.: Schema mapping as query discovery. In: Proceedings of the 26th International Conference on Very Large Data Bases, VLDB 2000, pp. 77–88 (2000)
5. Shen, W., Wang, J., Han, J.: Entity linking with a knowledge base: issues, techniques, and solutions. IEEE Trans. Knowl. Data Eng. **27**(2), 443–460 (2015)
6. vis.js Homepage. http://visjs.org/
7. Teiid Homepage. http://teiid.io/

Extensible Visualizations of Ontologies in OWLGrEd

Kārlis Čerāns[✉], Jūlija Ovčiņņikova, Renārs Liepiņš,
and Mikus Grasmanis

Institute of Mathematics and Computer Science, University of Latvia,
Raina blvd. 29, Riga 1459, Latvia
{karlis.cerans, julija.ovcinnikova, renars.liepins,
mikus.grasmanis}@lumii.lv

Abstract. OWLGrEd is a visual editor for OWL 2.0 ontologies that combines
UML class diagram notation and textual OWL Manchester syntax for expressions. We review the basic OWLGrEd options for ontology presentation customization and consider the framework of OWLGrEd extensions that enables introducing rich use-case specific functionality to the editor. A number of available OWLGrEd extensions offering rich ontology management features to their end-users are described, as well.

Keywords: OWL · OWLGrEd · Custom ontology visualization

1 Introduction

Presenting OWL ontologies [1] in a comprehensible form is vital for ontology designers and their users alike. Several approaches and tools, including OWLViz [2], VOWL [3], OntoDia [4], ODM [5], TopBraid Composer [6] and OWLGrEd [7] have been developed to present the ontologies visually so that ontologically related constructs are linked together in the presentation (e.g. an object property can be depicted as a line connecting its domain and range classes, or a sub-class can be linked to its super-class). A recent extensive and in-depth overview of the ontology visualization methods and tools is [8].

The OWLGrEd ontology editor[1] [7] stands out in the ontology visualization tools family by combining the ontology visualization and editing facilities. So, an ontology or its fragment can be adjusted after its initial automatic visualization, or an ontology can be even created from scratch within the editor and then saved into some standard textual serialization format. We describe here the options for and experience with custom/extended ontology presentation in OWLGrEd. These can be viewed also as an initial response to the call for "ontology visualization framework implementing a core set of visual and interactive features that can be extended and customized" in [8].

The OWLGrEd notation [7] comprising extended UML class diagrams [9] combined with OWL Manchester syntax [10] for textual expression encoding allows to express all OWL 2.0 [1] ontology constructs. Should an ontology be used as a data

---

[1] http://owlgred.lumii.lv/.

© Springer Nature Switzerland AG 2019
P. Hitzler et al. (Eds.): ESWC 2019 Satellite Events, LNCS 11762, pp. 191–196, 2019.
https://doi.org/10.1007/978-3-030-32327-1_38

model within some context, it may be convenient to store an important part of the model contents within the ontology entity annotations. To facilitate custom handling of designated annotation properties, ontology visualization profiles extending the diagram element structure have been introduced to OWLGrEd in [11], cf. also [12]; the sharing and development of the profiles is described here for the first time.

The practical usage of visualization profiles in custom-annotated ontology engineering has shown that it is convenient to consider such a profile within a context of a more "heavy-weight" ontology editor extension (an editor "plugin" in terms of [13]) which, besides the profile itself, may contain programmable editor functionality extensions.

We shall describe in the paper and show in the demonstration the following:

(1) Review of the OWLGrEd notation and its basic options for presentation tuning,
(2) The list of available existing and novel OWLGrEd extensions together with the instructions how to install an extension into a users' OWLGrEd project, and
(3) The means (advanced) to create new extensions for OWLGrEd editor (extension architecture, custom fields and views, outline of the programmable data model).

2 Basic Tuning of Presentation in OWLGrEd

Figure 1 shows an OWL ontology example in the OWLGrEd notation, we refer to e.g. [7, 13] or the OWLGrEd home page for its more detailed explanation.

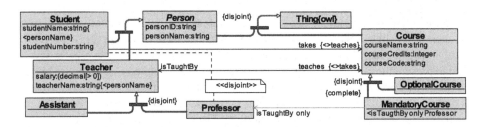

Fig. 1. A simple mini-University ontology in OWLGrEd

The UML notation [9] allows for presenting a property either graphically as an association role, or textually as an attribute. OWLGrEd supports alternative visual ways of the same semantic construct expressing for properties and restrictions, as well as e.g. for subclass, equivalent classes and disjoint classes notation. A line connecting two classes shows visually their connectivity, while the textual form may be preferable to reduce the graph overloading with lines, or eventually may enable splitting a large connected graph into separate fragments. The ***RefactoringServices*** extension (cf. Sect. 3) provides built-in ontology presentation re-shaping services.

There are options to configure the inclusion and initial shaping (e.g. visual or textual) of ontology constructs in the ontology diagram created during the ontology loading (import) phase by means of ontology import parameters, as described in [13].

There are two options to change the presentation style (including visibility) of an element present in an ontology diagram. The "shallow" (ad-hoc) option is provided by the GRTP platform [14] the OWLGrEd editor is built upon and is available on a per-symbol basis (e.g. it is possible to change the color of a diagram element). The structure-based definition of the presentation style (e.g. make all superclass-to-subclass lines the left-to-right flow lines) is also available in the default OWLGrEd configuration (cf. the "*Style palette*" context menu option and toolbar icon).

3 OWLGrEd Extensions

An OWLGrEd extension can add custom (domain-specific) data structures and functionality to the editor. The principal components of an OWLGrEd extension are:

(1) **custom information fields** for ontology diagram symbols, each with possible visual appearance and/or semantics (e.g. annotation assertion) specification, and

(2) high-level programmable **functionality extensions** (tied e.g. to context menu or palette elements, or to explicit extension points in the existing procedures).

In addition, **ontology presentation views** [11] can be specified within each OWLGrEd extension; a view can define the style (including visibility) of visual element types, with an option for conditionally applied styles based on data field values.

Any user of the OWLGrEd editor can download extensions e.g. from the Extensions section of the OWLGrEd home page; then add them (de-compressed first) to the project via "*Extensions*" context menu command within a project diagram.

The currently available extensions include:

(1) **OWLGrEd_UserFields**, historically the first extension [11], part of default OWLGrEd configuration, providing the basic mechanisms of both creation and run-time support for custom information fields and ontology presentation views;

(2) **RefactoringServices**, supports transformations among ontology element visual presentation options (e.g. an object property presentation can be switched between the graphical and textual form); the transformations are added to the context menus of the ontology diagram elements to be transformed;

(3) **OWLGrEd_Schema**, a novel (work in progress) extension supports assertions of a property applicability within a given class context; the property domain is then computed as the union of all classes for which the property is applicable (cf. Fig. 2);

(4) **OWLGrEd_OBIS,** supports the annotation framework [15] for automated ontology-based information system generation [16]. Parts of it have been also refactored into separate extensions, including **UML_Plus** (introduction of UML-style elements for modeling notation: a composition, an enumerated class, an abstract class and a derived property) and **DefaultOrder** (recording of attribute ordering information within a class node).

(5) **OWLCNL_LanguageFields**, an experimental framework for adding verbal forms to ontology entities to enable contextual verbalization of ontologies [17].

The OWLGrEd extensions currently are actively developed further and applied in practical use cases. For instance, for the ontology development for the existing (legacy) data structure of the Latvian Enterprise Registry registers the UML_Plus, OWL-GrEd_Schema and RefactoringServices custom extensions have been important[2].

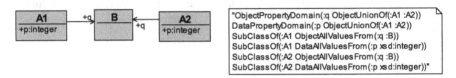

Fig. 2. Outline of property applicability assertions: visual form and OWL Functional Syntax

4 Create Your Own Extension

An OWLGrEd extension is a data folder that can be added to a project by placing it under the Plugins sub-folder within the projects' folder and then re-opening the project. The principal elements of the contents of an OWLGrEd extension folder are:

(1) info.lua – a text file stating the extensions' identifier, name and version;
(2) load.lua – the code to be executed upon installing the extension (e.g. introducing the custom fields, and other editor configuration updates);
(3) unload.lua – the code to be executed upon uninstalling the extension;
(4) other data and functionality information, referred to from the loading and unloading programs, including the code to be attached to e.g. newly created menu and toolbar items, or pre-defined extension points within the editor code.

The OWLGrEd editor is built upon the GRTP platform [14], whose data model is best described in [18] and augmented by the custom fields part in [11]. The "live" data model diagram is available also from within the editor itself under the *Show→Meta-model* global menu item. The programming environment is based on Lua programming language and uses library lQuery [19] for data model management. Examples of loading and unloading transformations can be seen e.g. in the code of **UML_Plus** extension.

The definitions of custom fields are typically stored in textual form within extension's AutoLoad sub-folder and must be loaded by the code in load.lua. The custom field definition file can be created using the OWLGrEd style palette environment (to be opened from the project diagram): under *'Manage views and profiles'* select *'New profile'*, give it a name, add custom fields (views can be added, as well), then save the profile. The abstract profile structure follows [11]; the OWLGrEd style palette allows to "fill in" the instances of the profile metamodel.

Each custom field is defined within editor structure context (a field can be ascribed to e.g. a class, a role or an attribute) and can have basic appearance properties, functional translates and semantic tags defined. A semantic tag typically is a template for

---

OWL Functional Syntax [1] assertion associated with the field, as, for example, AnnotationAssertion(obis:textPattern $subject $value) in ***OWLGrEd_OBIS*** extension is, where the $subject and $value variables refer to the context and the contents of the field respectively. The semantic tags and style effects can be attached to the choice items of check-box or drop-down type editor fields, as well.

5 Conclusions

OWLGrEd offers a wide range of customization options for presentation of an ontology loaded or created within the editor.

The OWLGrEd editor extensions are playing a major role in supporting ontology development and custom presentation in use cases that typically come up with their own requirements for extra add-on functionality to the standard editor features.

The source code of the OWLGrEd extensions is included within OWLGrEd distribution (their code is interpreted during the run-time, so any changes to it are effective immediately) and is free to be amended, modified and used (as is OWLGrEd itself).

The OWLGrEd extension architecture is suitable also for eventual migration into the web environment, as is envisaged for the OWLGrEd editor itself; it admits the user role separation allowing the system administrators to define and install the extensions, while letting the end-users to choose which extensions to activate within a project.

References

1. Motik, B., Patel-Schneider, P.F., Parsia, B.: OWL 2 web ontology language structural specification and functional-style syntax (2012). https://www.w3.org/TR/owl2-syntax/
2. OWLViz. http://www.co-ode.org/downloads/owlviz/
3. Lohmann, S., Negru, S., Haag, F., Ertl, T.: Visualizing ontologies with VOWL. Semant. Web 7(4), 399–419 (2016)
4. Mouromtsev, D., Pavlov, D., Emelyanov, Y., Morozov, A., Razdyakonov, D., Galkin, M.: The simple, web-based tool for visualization and sharing of semantic data and ontologies. In: ISWC P&D 2015, CEUR, vol. 1486 (2015). http://ceur-ws.org/Vol-1486/paper_77.pdf
5. ODM UML profile for OWL. http://www.omg.org/spec/ODM/1.0/PDF/
6. TopBraid Composer. http://www.topquadrant.com/tools/modeling-topbraid-composer-standard-edition/
7. Bārzdiņš, J., Bārzdiņš, G., Čerāns, K., Liepiņš, R., Sproģis, A.: UML style graphical notation and editor for OWL 2. In: Forbrig, P., Günther, H. (eds.) BIR 2010. LNBIP, vol. 64, pp. 102–114. Springer, Heidelberg (2010). https://doi.org/10.1007/978-3-642-16101-8_9
8. Dudáš, M., Lohmann, S., Svátek, V., Pavlov, D.: Ontology visualization methods and tools: a survey of the state of the art. Knowl. Eng. Rev. **33**, E10 (2018). https://doi.org/10.1017/S0269888918000073
9. Unified Modeling Language Specification. https://www.omg.org/spec/UML/2.5
10. OWL 2 Manchester Syntax. http://www.w3.org/TR/owl2-manchester-syntax/
11. Čerāns, K., Ovčiņņikova, J., Liepiņš, R., Sproģis, A.: Advanced OWL 2.0 ontology visualization in OWLGrEd. In: Caplinskas, A., Dzemyda, G., Lupeikiene, A., Vasilecas, O. (eds.) Databases and Information Systems VII. Frontiers in Artificial Intelligence and Applications, vol. 249, pp. 41–54. IOS Press (2013)

12. Cerans, K., Liepins, R., Sprogis, A., Ovcinnikova, J., Barzdins, G.: Domain-specific OWL ontology visualization with OWLGrEd. In: Simperl, E., et al. (eds.) ESWC 2012. LNCS, vol. 7540, pp. 419–424. Springer, Heidelberg (2015). https://doi.org/10.1007/978-3-662-46641-4_38

13. Ovčiņņikova, J., Čerāns, K.: Advanced UML style visualization of OWL ontologies. In: Proceedings of VOILA 2016. CEUR, vol. 1704, pp. 136–142 (2016). CEUR-WS.org, 2016

14. Bārzdiņš, J., et al.: GrTP: transformation based graphical tool building platform. In: Proceedings of MDDAUI-2007. CEUR, vol. 297 (2007). http://ceur-ws.org/Vol-297/paper6.pdf

15. Čerāns, K., Romāne, A.: OBIS: ontology-based information system framework. In: Proceedings of CAiSE FORUM 2015. CEUR, vol. 1367 (2015). http://ceur-ws.org/Vol-1367/paper-09.pdf

16. Zviedris, M., Romane, A., Barzdins, G., Cerans, K.: Ontology-based information system. In: Kim, W., Ding, Y., Kim, H.-G. (eds.) JIST 2013. LNCS, vol. 8388, pp. 33–47. Springer, Cham (2014). https://doi.org/10.1007/978-3-319-06826-8_3

17. Liepiņš, R., Bojārs, U., Grūzītis, N., Čerāns, K., Celms, E.: Towards self-explanatory ontology visualization with contextual verbalization. In: Arnicans, G., Arnicane, V., Borzovs, J., Niedrite, L. (eds.) DB&IS 2016. CCIS, vol. 615, pp. 3–17. Springer, Cham (2016). https://doi.org/10.1007/978-3-319-40180-5_1

18. Bārzdiņš, J., et al.: An MDE-based graphical tool building framework. In: 2010 Scientific Papers. University of Latvia, vol. 756, pp. 121–138 (2010)

19. Liepiņš, R.: Library for model querying: lQuery. In Proceedings of Workshop on OCL and Textual Modelling, pp. 31–36 (2012)

PhD Symposium

Developing a Knowledge Graph
for a Question Answering System
to Answer Natural Language
Questions on German Grammar

Stefan Falke[(⊠)] [ID]

Leibniz-Institut für Deutsche Sprache, Mannheim, Germany
`falke@ids-mannheim.de`

Abstract. Question Answering Systems for retrieving information from Knowledge Graphs (KG) have become a major area of interest in recent years. Current systems search for words and entities but cannot search for grammatical phenomena. The purpose of this paper is to present our research on developing a QA System that answers natural language questions about German grammar.

Our goal is to build a KG which contains facts and rules about German grammar, and is also able to answer specific questions about a concrete grammatical issue. An overview of the current research in the topic of QA systems and ontology design is given and we show how we plan to construct the KG by integrating the data in the grammatical information system *Grammis*, hosted by the Leibniz-Institut für Deutsche Sprache (IDS). In this paper, we describe the construction of the initial KG, sketch our resulting graph, and demonstrate the effectiveness of such an approach. A grammar correction component will be part of a later stage. The paper concludes with the potential areas for future research.

Keywords: Knowledge Graph · Ontology development · German grammar · Question Answering System

1   Introduction

Questions about german grammar reach the Leibniz-Institut für Deutsche Sprache (IDS)[1] by e-mail every day. The answers are mostly more than just a *Yes* or *No*, but rather give some more information about the case, sometimes with empirical data from a corpus analysis or the latest research results as referenced papers.

For the department of grammar, the online information system *Grammis*[2] is an important source of information to answer these questions. *Grammis* is the online information system on German grammar of the IDS with more than

---

[1] Leibniz-Institute for the German Language.
[2] http://grammis.ids-mannheim.de [25].

© Springer Nature Switzerland AG 2019
P. Hitzler et al. (Eds.): ESWC 2019 Satellite Events, LNCS 11762, pp. 199–208, 2019.
https://doi.org/10.1007/978-3-030-32327-1_39

3,000 descriptive texts and about 2,000 dictionary entries [25]. The information in *Grammis* is taken mostly from the three-volumes book "Grammatik der Deutschen Sprache (GDS)"[3] [30] written by the IDS. Even though most information to answer these questions is in *Grammis*, the user cannot find it or cannot apply it to his concrete case. The *user* is usually a professional writer (author, journalist), teacher or student (school teacher, german as a foreign language, linguistic student) or professional linguist.

To find information in *Grammis*, the user can either use the navigation menus or a full-text search. Both have their limitations, because to use the navigation menu the user should know in which grammatical field his question is located, e.g., to find information on the word class noun, one had to follow the navigation path: *Forschung → Systematische Grammatik → Ausdruckskategorien und Ausdrucksformen → Wortarten → Nomen*[4]. This path leads to a descriptive text about nouns. One could also use the full-text search, in which the user enters a few keywords, in this case *Nomen* (noun). The result is a ranked result list with more than 100 documents.

Both ways lead to documents, that only provide general rules on German grammar. It can be frustrating or confusing for the user to apply these rules to his specific case. It would improve the users' experience if the user could ask the system a question in his own words (i.e. in natural language) and *Grammis* would provide a concrete answer. Therefore *Grammis* should be reconstructed to handle natural language questions about grammatical problems and retrieve a specific answer from the data already available in *Grammis*.

In this paper, we describe the development of a Question Answering (QA) system that allows the user to ask a question about German grammar in natural language and to receive a specific answer to his question. To build a QA system that can answer those questions, we plan to construct a knowledge graph (KG) that is able to represent grammatical information about the German language. The KG should be able to represent data from different sources within the IDS, so that the system can retrieve the information for the answers out of the KG.

The remainder of this paper is organized as follows: In the following section we describe state of the art QA systems, ontology design, and automated grammar correction. In Sect. 3 we state the problem and the research question. Our research methodology is described in Sect. 4. Section 5 contains an evaluation of our KG. Preliminary results are presented in Sect. 6. The paper closes with a summary of our findings and potential areas of future research.

2   State of the Art

In this section, we define the terminology to distinguish *knowledge graph* and *ontology*. This is followed by a discussion of QA systems in the Semantic Web and methodologies for ontology design.

---

[3] Grammar of the German Language.

[4] *Research → Systematic Grammar → Categories and Forms of Expressions → Word Classes → Nouns*.

2.1 Terminology

This paper follows Paulheim's [22] definition of *knowledge graph* (for other definitions of knowledge graph, cf. [8]). According to Paulheim a KG consists of the schema (T-box) and the actual instances (A-box), but with a clear focus on the instances. We use the term *ontology* to refer to the schema of a knowledge graph (T-box) and *knowledge graph* to refer to the actual graph filled with instances (A-box) in which the schema is included, but only plays a minor role.

2.2 Question Answering in the Semantic Web

A QA system receives a question in natural language and provides the user with a concrete answer to their question rather than just a list of ranked documents [12]. In recent years, the research on QA systems querying the semantic web has grown rapidly [13,15,27]. With an increasing amount of knowledge as linked data, the need to access this data has also grown. Semantic Question Answering (SQA) bridges the gap between semantic data and the end user [13]. Höffner et.al. [13] surveyed 62 systems using linked data as data source, and identified and described seven challenges that such systems face. Two of these challenges are complex queries and the type of questions. While factual or yes-no questions directly conform to SPARQL, more complex queries are still not solved [13]. They also mention the system HAWK [28], which is a hybrid source system that retrieves the answers from both linked data and textual representation. Current QA systems retrieve the information following semantic entities, but they do not search for information following grammatical phenomena [12].

Using semantic data as data source makes the QA system independent from the underlying ontology, meaning that it is possible to extend the KG with additional information over time and that it is possible to handle unknown vocabulary in the query [15,27,31]. Ambiguities are also challenging but they are manageable, since there are a variety of disambiguation methods that have already been established [13].

Some ontologies are specially designed for linguistic purposes, like the Lemon Model [19] and LexInfo [4]. The Lemon Model is an important model for creating KGs on linguistic knowledge. Lemon represents lexical information in context with concepts and terms [19].

LexInfo provides classes and properties for linguistic cases like word classes (noun, verb, etc.) or relations (hyperonym, hyponym, etc.) [4].

2.3 Ontology Design

The design of ontologies should follow a methodology in order to prevent chaotic constructions and low quality ontologies [6]. There are several frameworks for designing ontologies [9,10,29].

We will look at the methodology by Grüninger and Fox [10] in more detail. It consists of six phases: (1) First, the Motivation Scenarios should be outlined which gave the impulse for developing the ontology. (2) With a set of Informal

Competency Questions, which are questions in natural language, the scope of the ontology should be determined. (3) The First-Order Logic Terminology will be extracted with these questions. (4) After this a set of Formal Competency Questions, which are questions in a query language, will be created. (5) With these questions the First-Order logic Axioms will be defined. (6) At last the ontology will be evaluated by using Completeness Theorems which are conditions under which the solutions to the questions are complete.

2.4 Automated Grammar Correction

Automated Grammar Correction exists for a variety of languages [2,26]. There are different approaches to grammar correction: rule-based, statistical, and syntactical [16]. Syntax-based approaches are language dependent and need much handwork till they can predict a sentence as correct or incorrect. Although rule-based techniques require many handwritten rules, this approach is language dependent. Statistic-based techniques are also language independent, but they require a large corpus to be trained on, and the test and training set need to be similar to provide good results. While the first two approaches provide error messages with the found error, the statistic-based approach does not provide an error message [16]. Since each correction system focuses on one or a handful of error classes, none of the systems is able to detect all possible error classes [2,26].

Only a handful of Grammar Correction systems exist for German grammar [7,21,24], and all of the existing Grammar Correction systems solely check a given text for grammatical errors. The Language Tool [21] is rule-based, so only implemented rules are applied and a short explanation on the found error is given. But none of these tools is embedded in a QA system and none provides deeper explanations on the found error.

3   Problem Statement and Contributions

The overall task for developing the QA system, described in this paper, is to answer concrete questions about specific grammatical phenomena. The IDS has a database of the questions that users send to the IDS and the corresponding answers that the users receive. There are currently about 50,000 entries. A subset of 500 of those questions has been manually categorized [23] into one of the five categories listed in Table 1.

About three quarters of the questions that the IDS receives fall into question categories QC1 and QC5 (see Table 1). These questions could potentially be handled automatically, but only if the factual questions (question categories QC2, QC3, and QC4) are answered first.

While current QA and Information Retrieval (IR) Systems search for the entered words or entities, respectively [12,17], our QA System will be searching for grammatical phenomena. For example, if one search string is *meiner Schwester Auto* (my sister's car), the user presumably wants to know something about the genitive, not about family relations (indicated by *Schwester* (sister)) or cars (indicated by *Auto* (car)). So it would not be helpful to the user, to

Table 1. Question categories [23]

Category	Title (with examples[a])	Ratio
QC1	Correction question / Alternative question Example: Ist *a* richtig? (engl. Is *a* correct?)	52%
QC2	Grammatical category Example: Wie ist der Plural von *a*? (engl. What is the plural of *a*?)	4%
QC3	Grammatical definition / Rule question Example: Wie lautet die Regel für *C*? (engl. What is the rule for *C*?)	9%
QC4	Lexical question example: Wie lautet das Synonym für *a*? (engl. What is a synonym for *a*?)	11%
QC5	Punctuation example: Ist das Komma im folgenden Satz richtig *a*? (engl. Is the comma in the following sentence correct *a*?)	24%

[a] represents a language object (word, phrase, term), *C* a grammatical category (Tense, Case).

present any page on which one of those words appear, because there could be pages where these words appear in another context. Instead the QA System should provide the user with information about the genitive, maybe other ways to express the given sentence, like *das Auto meiner Schwester* (the car of my sister). The user could also be presented with information about the genitive, since *Grammis* contains a genitives database, which could present more background information on the genitive use of the German language.

Therefore a KG will be used to organize the data. One advantage of semantic web technologies is that one can include different resources [1]. Since answering questions about German grammar requires a large amount of data, integrating the different resources in one KG connects the data from different sources and for different aspects. These resources can either be from within the IDS but might also be external resources like GermaNet [11].

Since there are many research projects at the IDS, their collected data could be integrated into the KG as well, to find better answers or to enrich the answers with recent research. This should be considered when designing the ontology.

We derived the following main research question from our described problem.

RQ1. How does the knowledge graph need to be built to support a Question Answering System for questions about German grammar?

In addition to the main question, there are several secondary research questions, which should also be considered during the implementation of the system.

SRQ1. What entities and relations does the ontology need to consist of?
SRQ2. Can existing QA system frameworks be extended to answer questions about German grammar?

SRQ3. Could additional (external) resources be used to improve the question answering?

The goal is to construct a QA system that is able to process the different question types and present an answer to them. The system's main purpose is to measure the effectiveness of the question answering and the proposed techniques and processes.

4   Research Methodology and Approach

In this section we discuss our construction of the QA system, and our design for the ontology of the KG.

4.1   Question Answering System

The development of the QA system will follow the principles of agile software development [5]. Starting with a prototype to explore the KG, more features will be added over time. The first version will only be able to navigate through the KG. In later versions, the question and answer components will be added. The advantages of prototyping are that at an early stage a running software is available, so that basic functionality can be tested [3]. The QA system will have a modular structure, so every component can be developed and maintained independently from the other modules.

There are some frameworks, that can serve as a starting point [13], e.g., openQA [18]. The focus on developing the QA system is on the question and data component. Different approaches exist for answer retrieval, e.g., graph exploration or machine learning approaches [27]. These should be taken into account since answering questions about grammar is a complex task. The system should also be able to find the answer in linked and textual data, c.f. the HAWK QA system [28].

4.2   Ontology Design

The ontology is designed following the methodology of Grüninger and Fox [10]. The Informal Competency Questions are based on the IDS questions database [23].

For every question category (see Table 1), the required classes and relations are defined. For example, a question out of category QC2 that asks for the plural of a word would make it necessary to have the information about the plural form in the ontology. Therefore a relation could be formulated like this: $plural(L, P)$, where l is a class for a lexical entry $l \in L$, p is the plural form of l ($p \in P$) and l and p are connected via the relation $plural(l, p)$.

The ontology will not be limited by the data that is currently available in *Grammis*. Even if entities and relations are needed that are not extractable from *Grammis*, the ontology will contain these entities. If there are existing classes and relations in other ontologies, these will be included by importing and using these ontologies, e.g., Lemon [20] and LexInfo [4].

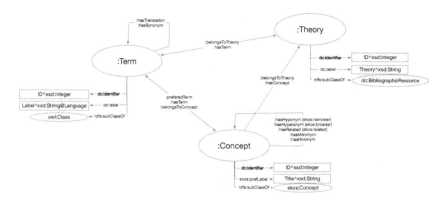

Fig. 1. Terminological classes and relations of the Ontology

5   Evaluation Plan

The evaluation will focus on achieving high precision values, while recall values are less important. This is because in order to extract the answer from the found documents, it is more important to get many true positives, than to retrieve all relevant documents but also some non-relevant documents in the result set.

Performance and scalability will be measured using the query time for a set of predefined queries. Also the query time will be measured when filling the KG with more and more facts, to compare the performance of these queries with a growing number of facts (e.g. 50 k, 100 k, 150 k facts).

Depending on the category, the questions can either be answered qualitatively or quantitatively. Since the categories QC2, QC3, and QC4 are mostly factual questions, the correct answer can be extracted from *Grammis*. These answers can be compared to the answers given by the QA system and then be categorized as *correct*, *false*, and *not answered*. In case of qualitative answers, like categories QC1 and QC5, the question database [23] works as a base for the gold standard. A set of questions and answers out of the given categories will be revised by human experts. The answers of the QA system are then categorized manually as *correct*, *incomplete*, *false*, or *not answered*.

At different stages of the development of the application, different types of questions will be possible to answer, so that in an early stage only questions from category QC2 can be answered, since these are factual questions. As the project progresses more and more questions out of the different categories should be answered correctly.

6   Preliminary Results

A web application using Flask[5] has been developed, which loads the prototype KG and lets the user navigate through it. So far, the dictionary of grammatical

---

[5] Flask – A Python Microframework, http://flask.pocoo.org.

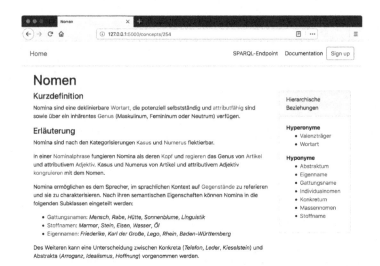

Fig. 2. Front end of Flask Application showing the entry *Nomen* (noun)

terms[6] and the orthographical dictionary[7] have been transferred into RDF and build a KG with 48,924 triples. Figure 1 shows the classes and relations of the grammatical terminology. A *concept* is a representation of an entity, while a *term* is an actual name for it. Every concept can have multiple terms. In a *theory*, a whole representation of several concepts together with their relations is defined, as well as which terms are assigned to each concept [14].

It is possible to navigate through the hierarchical relations from one concept to the other. Figure 2 shows the front end of the application. Title and description of the concept *Nomen* (noun) are in the center of the screen, on the right side there are listed the hyperonyms and hyponyms to this concept. The linked terms lead to the entry of the selected concept.

The application has a SPARQL endpoint, with which one can validate freely entered SPARQL queries against the KG. Thus it is possible to retrieve information from the KG, which later will be used to answer the factual questions. There is currently no interface to actually ask a question in natural language.

7   Conclusions

Our goal is to build a KG that is able to answer natural language questions on German grammar. Current QA systems search information by semantical entities rather than by grammatical phenomena. In addition, most grammatical

---

[6] Wissenschaftliche Terminologie, https://grammis.ids-mannheim.de/terminologie.

[7] Datenbank Rechtschreibwortschatz, https://grammis.ids-mannheim.de/rechtschreibwortschatz.

correction tools have been developed for English, with only a handful of German examples, all of which are not integrated into a QA system. The approach describe in this paper contributes to filling these gaps.

The main challenge will be to answer high level questions like in the categories QC1 and QC5. Currently, the system only has a web front end with which one can navigate through the graph, and a SPARQL endpoint. The prototype can currently retrieve answers to a few low level questions, but not react to actual questions, since the question component has not yet been implemented.

The grammar correction will be part of the later stage of this project, since answering factual questions is a fundamental prerequisite for grammar correction. Also, the extension to a multilingual system is taken into account. Although the system is designed for german grammar, every module will be checked for its language dependence. Every module which is language independent can be reused, while the other modules need to be adjusted.

Acknowledgments. I would like to thank Prof. Heiko Paulheim for his valuable feedback and support in the realization of this work.

References

1. Berners-Lee, T., Hendler, J., Lassila, O., et al.: The semantic web. Sci. Am. **284**(5), 28–37 (2001)
2. Bhirud, N., Bhavsar, R., Pawar, B.: Grammar checkers for natural languages: a review. Int. J. Nat. Lang. Comput. **6**(4), 1–13 (2017)
3. Bischofberger, W.R., Pomberger, G.: Prototyping-Oriented Software Development: Concepts and Tools. Springer, Heidelberg (2012). https://doi.org/10.1007/978-3-642-84760-8
4. Cimiano, P., Buitelaar, P., McCrae, J., Sintek, M.: Lexinfo: a declarative model for the lexicon-ontology interface. Web Seman. Sci. Serv. Agents World Wide Web **9**(1), 29–51 (2011)
5. Cockburn, A.: Agile Software Development, vol. 177. Addison-Wesley, Boston (2002)
6. Corcho, O., Fernández-López, M., Gómez-Pérez, A.: Ontological engineering: what are ontologies and how can we build them? In: Semantic web services: Theory, tools and applications, pp. 44–70. IGI Global (2007)
7. Crysmann, B., Bertomeu, N., Adolphs, P., Flickinger, D., Klüwer, T.: Hybrid processing for grammar and style checking. In: Proceedings of the 22nd International Conference on Computational Linguistics, vol. 1, pp. 153–160. Association for Computational Linguistics (2008)
8. Ehrlinger, L., Wöß, W.: Towards a definition of knowledge graphs. In: SEMANTiCS (Posters, Demos, SuCCESS) (2016)
9. Fernández-López, M., Gómez-Pérez, A., Juristo, N.: Methontology: from ontological art towards ontological engineering (1997)
10. Grüninger, M., Fox, M.S.: Methodology for the design and evaluation of ontologies (1995)
11. Hamp, B., Feldweg, H.: Germanet-a lexical-semantic net for German. In: Automatic Information Extraction and Building of Lexical Semantic Resources for NLP Applications (1997)

12. Hirschman, L., Gaizauskas, R.: Natural language question answering: the view from here. Nat. Lang. Eng. **7**(4), 275–300 (2001)
13. Höffner, K., Walter, S., Marx, E., Usbeck, R., Lehmann, J., Ngonga Ngomo, A.C.: Survey on challenges of question answering in the semantic web. Seman. Web **8**(6), 895–920 (2017)
14. Lang, C., Schwinn, H., Suchowolec, K.: Grammatische Terminologie am IDS-ein terminologisches Online-Wörterbuch als ein vernetztes Begriffssystem. Sprachreport (2018)
15. Lopez, V., Uren, V., Sabou, M., Motta, E.: Is question answering fit for the semantic web?: a survey. Seman. Web **2**(2), 125–155 (2011)
16. Manchanda, B., Athavale, V.A., Kumar Sharma, S.: Various techniques used for grammar checking. Int. J. Comput. Appl. Inf. Technol. **9**(1), 177 (2016)
17. Manning, C.D., Raghavan, P., Schütze, H., et al.: Introduction to Information Retrieval, vol. 1. Cambridge University Press, Cambridge (2008)
18. Marx, E., Usbeck, R., Ngomo, A.C.N., Höffner, K., Lehmann, J., Auer, S.: Towards an open question answering architecture. In: Proceedings of the 10th International Conference on Semantic Systems, pp. 57–60. ACM (2014)
19. McCrae, J., et al.: Interchanging lexical resources on the semantic web. Lang. Resour. Eval. **46**(4), 701–719 (2012)
20. McCrae, J., Spohr, D., Cimiano, P.: Linking lexical resources and ontologies on the semantic web with lemon. In: Antoniou, G., et al. (eds.) ESWC 2011. LNCS, vol. 6643, pp. 245–259. Springer, Heidelberg (2011). https://doi.org/10.1007/978-3-642-21034-1_17
21. Naber, D.: A rule-based style and grammar checker (2003)
22. Paulheim, H.: Knowledge graph refinement: a survey of approaches and evaluation methods. Seman. web **8**(3), 489–508 (2017)
23. Ripp, S., Falke, S.: Questions categories on German grammar information systems and their operability, article in preperation
24. Schmidt-Wigger, A.: Grammar and style checking for German. In: Proceedings of CLAW, vol. 98, pp. 76–86. Citeseer (1998)
25. Schneider, R., Schwinn, H.: Hypertext, Wissensnetz und Datenbank: die Webinformationssysteme Grammis und ProGr@mm, pp. 337–346. Ansichten und Einsichten, Institut für Deutsche Sprache, Mannheim (2014)
26. Sharma, S.K.: Rule based grammar checking systems. Int. J. Comput. Appl. Inf. Technol. **10**(1), 217–220 (2016)
27. Unger, C., Freitas, A., Cimiano, P.: An introduction to question answering over linked data. In: Koubarakis, M., et al. (eds.) Reasoning Web 2014. LNCS, vol. 8714, pp. 100–140. Springer, Cham (2014). https://doi.org/10.1007/978-3-319-10587-1_2
28. Usbeck, R., Ngomo, A.-C.N., Bühmann, L., Unger, C.: HAWK – Hybrid question answering using linked data. In: Gandon, F., Sabou, M., Sack, H., d'Amato, C., Cudré-Mauroux, P., Zimmermann, A. (eds.) ESWC 2015. LNCS, vol. 9088, pp. 353–368. Springer, Cham (2015). https://doi.org/10.1007/978-3-319-18818-8_22
29. Uschold, M., King, M.: Towards a methodology for building ontologies. In: Workshop on Basic Ontological Issues in Knowledge Sharing (IJCAI) (1995)
30. Zifonun, G., Hoffmann, L., Strecker, B., Ballweg, J.: Grammatik der deutschen Sprache, vol. 1. Walter de Gruyter, Berlin (1997)
31. Zou, L., Huang, R., Wang, H., Yu, J.X., He, W., Zhao, D.: Natural language question answering over rdf: a graph data driven approach. In: Proceedings of the 2014 ACM SIGMOD International Conference on Management of Data, pp. 313–324. ACM (2014)

Quality-Driven Query Processing
over Federated RDF Data Sources

Lars Heling[(✉)]

Institute AIFB, Karlsruhe Institute of Technology (KIT), Karlsruhe, Germany
`heling@kit.edu`

Abstract. The integration of data from heterogeneous sources is a common task in various domains to enable data-driven applications. Data sources may range from publicly available sources to sources within data lakes of companies. The added value generated by integrating and analyzing the data greatly depends on the quality of the underlying data. As a result, querying heterogeneous data sources as a way of integrating data enabling such applications needs to consider quality aspects. Quality-driven query processing over RDF data sources aims to study approaches which consider data quality description of the data sources to determine optimal query plans. In contrast to most federated query approaches, in quality-driven query processing the quality of an optimal plan and thus of the retrieved data, not only depends on efficiency typically measured as execution time but also on other quality criteria. In this work, we present the challenges associated with considering multiple quality criteria in federated query processing and derive our problem statement accordingly. We present our research questions to address the problem and the associated hypotheses. Finally, we outline our approach including an evaluation plan and provide preliminary results.

Keywords: Federated querying · Linked Data · Data quality · SPARQL

1 Introduction

Driven by Linked Open Data (LOD) initiatives, an increasing amount of data is being published as Linked Data (LD) on the web[1]. Due to different origins and publishers of the data, the datasets are heterogeneous with respect to various properties, such as schema, data access, and data quality. Data quality may greatly vary due to the procedure and context in which the data is generated and intended to be used for. For instance, automatically extracted data based on crowd-curated data sources such DBpedia[2] is likely to yield a different data quality than expert-curated datasets which are used in the life science applications such as Drugbank[3] [22]. Consequently, the value generated by applications

---

[1] https://lod-cloud.net/.
[2] https://wiki.dbpedia.org/.
[3] http://drugbank.bio2rdf.org/.

© Springer Nature Switzerland AG 2019
P. Hitzler et al. (Eds.): ESWC 2019 Satellite Events, LNCS 11762, pp. 209–219, 2019.
https://doi.org/10.1007/978-3-030-32327-1_40

querying the data from such federations of RDF data sources highly depends on the quality of the sources. A variety of heterogeneous data sources differing in quality are not merely encountered on the web but are also a phenomenon within business organizations. In the era of Big Data, companies increasingly maintain their data in its native, often schema-less format in large repositories, so-called *data lakes*. As a result, employing data analysis over such data lakes requires querying a plethora of heterogeneous data sources differing in schema and data quality. As the effectiveness of analyses depends on the quality of the underlying data, it is desirable to consider data quality aspects when querying the sources [12]. Hence, providing high quality data is an important task in query processing over heterogeneous data sources and it yields three major questions: *(i)* how can the data quality of independent and heterogeneous sources be measured, *(ii)* which sources should be included when processing a query to provide answers of high quality, and *(iii)* how can the quality of a query plan be assessed to be used as a proxy for the quality of the answers it provides?

Several challenges arise when addressing these questions. First, quality assessment approaches retrieving quality descriptions while considering the dynamics and access restriction (i.e., interface to query the data) of the data sources are required. Moreover, in order to find query plans retrieving high quality answers when processing a query, source selection, query decomposition, and query planning need to consider these quality descriptions as well as the fact that the data sources may contain overlapping, replicated or disjoint data. Finally, in contrast to quality-driven query processing over a single data source, the query planning in a federated scenario needs to consider both quality metrics on the data level (e.g., conciseness) as well as on the data source level (e.g., accessibility).

The proposed doctoral thesis aims to address open research questions related to quality-driven querying processing over federations of RDF data sources. In particular, we address the challenges of *(i)* retrieving quality descriptions for data provided via web querying interfaces for RDF, *(ii)* determining the quality of a query plan with respect to various quality dimensions, and *(iii)* finding a quality maximizing query plan to be executed over the federation.

2   State of the Art

Data quality is essential for a large variety of applications in many domains. Data quality is commonly defined as the "fitness for use" [21] which underpins the importance of context when assessing data quality. Federated RDF query processing investigates approaches for querying a federation of RDF data sources and SPARQL is the de facto language to express such queries [1]. Due to the heterogeneity of data sources involved in such federations, data quality may strongly vary across these sources. Extensions of the SPARQL query language which allow considering additional data properties, such as the trustworthiness of statements, have been proposed and quality-driven query processing has been studied in the area of relational databases. However, thus far few research has focused on quality-driven query processing for federated RDF data sources.

Linked Data Quality. Assessing quality for Linked Data has been addressed by various authors [4, 7, 22]. In their survey, Zaveri et al. [22] identify 18 data quality dimensions for Linked Data and group them into four major dimensions: accessibility, representation, contextual and intrinsic data quality. For each dimension, there are several data quality metrics which are procedures for measuring a certain dimension. Along those lines, RDF dataset profiling, which includes data quality aspects as well, has been proposed to facilitate dataset discovery and selection for tasks such as distributed querying, search and question answering [4]. However, most current distributed query processing approaches merely consider data summaries which do not include quality information of the data sources to decide on the relevancy of data sources [8, 9].

Federated RDF Query Processing. Federated SPARQL query engines provide means for integrating RDF data sources by allowing to query a federation of SPARQL endpoints via a unique interface. The initial version of SPARQL does not provide features for querying federations of data sources, however a myriad of approaches to allow for federated query processing have been proposed [3, 6, 17–19]. The prevalent definition for the result of executing a query over a federation has been that the results should be the same as querying the union of all RDF data provided by the federation members, i.e. *complete* answers [1]. As a result, the proposed approaches aim to provide complete answers while minimizing the processing cost and they devise different strategies to achieve this goal. In contrast, our work aims to address additional quality dimensions besides completeness and especially, the potential trade-off between these dimensions.

Quality-Driven RDF Query Processing. Previous works have focused on enhancing the quality of answers when querying RDF. Darari et al. [5] focus on the quality dimension of data completeness in query processing. They propose the concept of completeness statements which allows to decide whether a query returns complete answers with respect to an ideal graph containing all facts that hold in this world. Acosta et al. [2] propose HARE, a hybrid query processing system leveraging crowd sourcing to improve query results by identifying missing values in a data set and completing them using the crowd. Based on a model for completeness, the system detects parts of the query which potentially yield incomplete results and uses the crowd to augment the missing answers.

SPARQL Extensions. Hartig [10] proposes tSPARQL which is an extension allowing to query trust weighted RDF graphs. Such graphs consist of an RDF graph G and a trust function tv^C mapping all triples in G to a trust value. Furthermore, trust weighted solution mappings assigning a trust value to each solution mapping based on the trust weighted graph. The keywords TRUST AS and ENSURE TRUST are introduced to make use of the assigned trust values within a query. The keywords allow for assigning trust values to variables and for filtering of solution mappings according to their trust value.

Similarly, AnQL [14] is an extension of SPARQL for querying annotated RDFS. Annotated RDFS is an extension of the RDF data model providing means for annotations of triples. An annotated triple is an expression $\pi : \lambda$ with π a triple and λ an annotation value. Hence, it is a more generic approach than the trust weighted RDF graph by allowing to annotate triples with any meta information, such as trust, temporal validity, or provenance. To allow for querying such annotated graphs, the syntax of SPARQL is extended by annotated triple pattern and the semantics of evaluating an AnQL graph pattern are defined accordingly. Moreover, the keywords ASSIGN, ORDERBY and GROUPBY are introduced for variable assignment, projections, aggregates and solution modifiers.

Quality-Driven Query Processing in Databases. Previous work in the area of relational databases has studied how data quality may be considered when querying heterogeneous data sources. Naumann et al. [15] describe a framework that includes quality information in query processing over multiple databases. The goal of their work is using the quality information about the data sources in the query planning process and they argue that "the goodness of a plan depends primarily on the expected quality of the results and not on pure technical criteria such as response time" [15]. First, the authors determine a set of information quality measures which they categorize into *source-specific, query correspondence assertion (QCA[4])-specific* and *user query-specific* criteria. Thereafter, these source-specific quality metrics are used to filter out sources in the source selection phase and the QCAs are used in the plan creation phase to create all plans for a user query. Lastly, in the plan selection phase, each plan is given an overall quality value by first calculating the quality values for the QCA-specific and user query-specific criteria, and by finally aggregating the information quality of a plan into a single value using simple additive weighting.

Summarizing, Linked Data quality assessment and federated query processing have been studied extensively in the Semantic Web community. In addition, enhancing the quality of query answers by identifying and completing missing information has also been studied. However, most current approaches aim to optimize answer completeness but do not provide a generic model for the quality of query plans. In addition, quality assessment has not considered restrictions that are relevant in a federated query processing scenario such as the dynamics of data sources and the restriction to access the data. Moreover, approaches to enable quality-driven query processing in heterogeneous information systems covering various quality dimensions have been proposed for relational databases. Due to the semantics of SPARQL and the specifics of its operators, these approaches cannot be transferred seamlessly to querying federated RDF data sources.

---

[4] The mediator uses query correspondence assertions (QCAs) in order to determine contents, i.e. available relations, of the sources.

3   Problem Statement and Contributions

In federated query processing over RDF data, query plans are determined in three steps: query decomposition, source selection, and query optimization. A query plan P_Q for a SPARQL query Q is a tree where the leaves are requesting a sub-expression of the query at a member of the federation and the inner nodes are SPARQL algebra operators. Furthermore, we denote the universe of all plans for a query Q by $\mathscr{P}_Q$.

Given a query, it is a difficult task to devise optimal query plans which yield complete answers while minimizing processing cost. This is due to the complexity of exploring the space of plans which is an NP-complete problem [13] as well as the difficulty of estimating the cost of those plans [16,20]. Enabling quality-driven federated query processing over RDF data sources also entails additional challenges: *(i)* gathering quality information from various data quality dimensions from the members of the federation, *(ii)* quality estimation of query plans and *(iii)* determining the best query plan according to the quality criteria. These observations lead to our problem statement.

Problem Statement: Given a SPARQL query Q, a federation of RDF data sources $F = \{D_1, \ldots, D_n\}$ and a set of quality descriptions $\mathscr{Q} = \{Q_1, \ldots, Q_n\}$ with $Q_i \in \mathscr{Q}$ a quality description for $D_i \in F$. The quality-driven query plan optimization problem is defined as devising a plan P_Q^* such that

$$P_Q^* = \operatorname*{argmax}_{P_Q \in \mathscr{P}_Q} quality_{\mathscr{Q}}(P_Q)$$

with $quality_{\mathscr{Q}} : \mathscr{P}_Q \rightarrow \mathbb{R}^+$ a quality assessment function for a set of quality description $\mathscr{Q}$ associating every query plan with a quality value.

In other words, we want to find a plan for a given query which maximizes quality according to the quality descriptions of the data sources in the federation. Please note that we do not explicitly encode answer completeness as a constraint in our problem definition since part of the work aims to investigate the trade-off between answer completeness and other quality dimensions of the query plans. Based on the problem statement and according to the challenges associated with it, we formulate the following research questions:

RQ1 Data Source Quality:
  - What quality dimensions of federated RDF data sources can be effectively measured on a fine-grained level?

RQ2 Query Plan Quality:
  - How can we measure the quality of a query plan based on the quality descriptions of the data sources with multiple quality criteria?

RQ3 Query Plan Optimization:
  - What is the impact on time complexity in the federated query optimization problem when considering multiple quality criteria?
  - Which methods are suitable to determine quality maximizing query plans while simultaneously considering execution cost?

Our hypotheses are derived directly from the research questions.

H1 Gathering data quality information from federated RDF data sources and deriving a quality-enhanced source descriptions can be achieved by applying existing data quality metrics and leveraging web query interfaces to RDF data (i.e. SPARQL endpoints and Triple Pattern Fragments).

H2 Existing cost estimation models for query planning can be extended to incorporate multiple quality criteria and determine an aggregated quality value for query plans which considers both data source and query-level quality criteria.

H3 Metaheuristics can be employed to determine (near-)optimal query plans considering various data quality dimensions and therefore, provide query plans with higher quality than existing solutions.

The research to be conducted and the resulting contributions aim to address the presented research problem by investigating the associated hypotheses.

4   Research Methodology and Approach

The methodology adopted in the development of this doctoral work adheres to the following tasks:

1. Investigation of state of the art research relevant to the identified problem. This includes the study of literature about quality assessment and quality-driven query processing in the areas of Databases and Semantic Web.
2. Formalization of the research problem and formulation of research questions and hypotheses.
3. Definition of solutions to address the hypotheses. Identification of novel contributions entailed by the solutions as well as studying formal properties of the proposed solutions.
4. Implementation of the solutions and empirical evaluation of their performance. The performance evaluation is conducted with respect to the state of the art solutions if available. The experiments will be conducted as follows: *(i)* Implementation of state of the art or baselines approaches. *(ii)* Designing an evaluation approach according to the studied research question. Reuse and if necessary adjustment of existing benchmark and evaluation criteria. *(iii)* Execution of experiments based on the benchmarks to obtain data for drawing conclusions about the hypotheses. *(iv)* Analysis of the results.

In order to address the presented research problem, our approach aims to study each of the presented hypotheses. Figure 1 provides an overview of the approach with the corresponding research questions indicated. Hypothesis **H1** will be addressed by developing methods to assess various data quality dimensions of RDF data sources, i.e. retrieving $\mathcal{Q}$ for F. In contrast to existing methods which typically examine a dump of the entire data available at a data source, our methods will be restricted to data access of web querying interfaces for

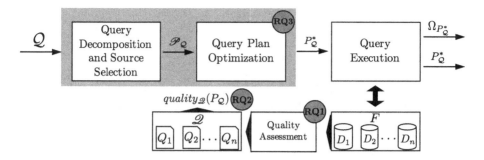

Fig. 1. Our approach: Given a query $\mathcal{Q}$, the quality maximizing query plan $P_{\mathcal{Q}}^* \in \mathscr{P}_{\mathcal{Q}}$ is determined according to the quality description in $\mathscr{D}$. The plan is executed over the federation and the results $\Omega_{P_{\mathcal{Q}}^*}$ and optimized plan $P_{\mathcal{Q}}^*$ are returned.

RDF, namely SPARQL endpoints and Triple Pattern Fragment (TPF) servers. Therefore, we need to select quality dimensions relevant in the realm of query processing and adapt methods to measure these dimensions while considering the access constraints. For instance, the timeliness of the data may be relevant as sources may provide update their data and sources with outdated data may be pruned in the query plan. Furthermore, we aim to investigate which dimensions can be measured on the data source level and which are query-specific.

We want to address the second hypothesis **H2** by determining approaches to estimate the quality of query plans based on the quality assessment of the previous step, i.e., study how to compute $quality_{\mathcal{Q}}(P_{\mathcal{Q}})$. Existing cost estimation methods for query planning (e.g., [16,20]) should be used as a basis and adapted accordingly. Moreover, we aim to investigate how preferences of a user posing a query may be encoded in quality estimation. In experimental studies, the implementations of the approaches will be used to evaluate their feasibility.

Finally, to test our last hypothesis **H3**, we aim to study different meta-heuristics and adapt them to the problem of determining the quality maximizing query plan $P_{\mathcal{Q}}^*$. As previously mentioned, the complexity of determining an optimal plan is NP-complete and optimizing for its quality depending on multiple criteria is likely to disallow using existing heuristics. Implementing these heuristics and conducting an experimental study on their performance with respect to relevant metrics, will allow determining the most suitable method.

5 Evaluation Plan

For the evaluation of the presented approach, we aim to conduct both theoretical and experimental evaluations of the proposed solutions. The goal of the theoretical evaluation will be investigating the complexity of query planning when considering several criteria with respect to the quality of the plans. In the experimental evaluation, the hypotheses will be evaluated by implementing the proposed solutions, conducting a series of experiments and analyzing the results.

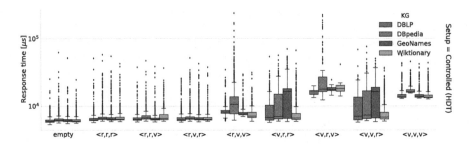

Fig. 2. Preliminary results: Boxplots for the response time of TPF server requesting different triple pattern types.

Query Benchmark and Data Sources: For the experimental evaluation, we require a set of SPARQL queries which can be evaluated over a federation of data sources. Ideally, the data sources provide overlapping or similar data at different quality levels. If necessary such federation will be artificially created. However, our goal is reusing, adapting and extending existing benchmarks (potentially also from relational databases) as far as possible.

Evaluation Metrics: We aim to consider several evaluation metrics including well-established metrics such as answer completeness and execution time to measure the performance of our solution. However, as we are especially interested in the quality of such query plans and the resulting answers, we will need to define a quality metric which allows assessing the quality of query plans considering several data quality metrics on both data source and query-level. Investigating these metrics will, therefore, provide an insight into the potential trade-off between answer completeness, execution time, and the quality of the query plans.

6   Preliminary Results

In previous research [11], we have investigated on hypothesis **H1** and especially the question of determining fine-grained statistics on the quality of RDF data sources. In our work on querying large knowledge graphs over Triple Pattern Fragments (TPFs) [11], we propose the *TPF Profiler* as a resource to retrieve performance statistics of TPF server. For a given TPF server URI and a sample size, the TPF Profiler collects performance measurements when submitting different requests to the server in three steps. First, the TPF Profiler randomly selects a sample of RDF triples from the RDF graph available at the server. Thereafter, a set of triple patterns is generated based on the sampled triples by replacing RDF terms with variables. Finally, the TPF Profiler requests all triple patterns generated in the previous step and measures the response time of the server. The resulting performance data may be analyzed with respect to various factors, such as the number and position of the variable in the triple pattern also referred to as triple pattern type. Figure 2 shows the measured response time from our empirical study for different Knowledge Graphs (KGs) according to the triple pattern type. The results indicate significant differences in response time for different triple pattern types. Hence, the results allow for deriving a triple pattern level quality assessment for the performance dimension which may be used to estimate the overall execution time of query plans.

Summarizing, our preliminary results show that the quality of data sources may vary on query-level, specifically on triple pattern level. Therefore, the results are a first step towards answering our first research question and may be used as a starting point for investigating the remaining hypotheses.

7   Conclusions and Lessons Learned

In this doctoral work, we aim to study the problem of quality-driven query plan optimization problem in the context of federated RDF data sources. We formulate three hypotheses to address the associated research questions and present an evaluation plan to investigate the validity of the hypotheses. Our preliminary results on **H1** provide insights into how query-specific data quality descriptions for data sources on the performance dimension may be assessed and potentially leveraged in query planning. However, it is still an open issue of how our empirical results can be integrated into a strategy for query planning.

Future work addressing **H1** will investigate further query-specific data source description for other quality dimensions as well as adapting existing data quality metrics to be efficiently measured via SPARQL endpoints and TPF servers. Thereafter, we want to address the remaining hypotheses **H2** and **H3**. Integral to this task is providing means to assess the quality of a query plan which takes various quality dimensions into account. Lastly, we need to determine heuristics suitable to explore the space of feasible query plans to find the best query plan.

Acknowledgements. I would like to thank my advisors Dr. Maribel Acosta and Prof. Dr. York Sure-Vetter for their support and valuable feedback.

References

1. Acosta, M., Hartig, O., Sequeda, J.: Federated RDF query processing. In: Sherif Sakr, A.Z. (ed.) Encyclopedia of Big Data Technologies. Springer, Heidelberg (2018). https://doi.org/10.1007/978-3-319-63962-8_228-1
2. Acosta, M., Simperl, E., Flöck, F., Vidal, M.E.: Enhancing answer completeness of SPARQL queries via crowdsourcing. J. Web Semant. **45**, 41–62 (2017)
3. Acosta, M., Vidal, M.-E., Lampo, T., Castillo, J., Ruckhaus, E.: ANAPSID: an adaptive query processing engine for sparql endpoints. In: Aroyo, L., et al. (eds.) ISWC 2011. LNCS, vol. 7031, pp. 18–34. Springer, Heidelberg (2011). https://doi.org/10.1007/978-3-642-25073-6_2
4. Ben Ellefi, M., et al.: RDF dataset profiling - a survey of features, methods, vocabularies and applications. Semant. Web **9**(5), 677–705 (2018)

5. Darari, F., Nutt, W., Pirrò, G., Razniewski, S.: Completeness statements about RDF data sources and their use for query answering. In: Alani, H., et al. (eds.) ISWC 2013. LNCS, vol. 8218, pp. 66–83. Springer, Heidelberg (2013). https://doi.org/10.1007/978-3-642-41335-3_5

6. Endris, K.M., Galkin, M., Lytra, I., Mami, M.N., Vidal, M.-E., Auer, S.: MULDER: querying the linked data web by bridging RDF molecule templates. In: Benslimane, D., Damiani, E., Grosky, W.I., Hameurlain, A., Sheth, A., Wagner, R.R. (eds.) DEXA 2017. LNCS, vol. 10438, pp. 3–18. Springer, Cham (2017). https://doi.org/10.1007/978-3-319-64468-4_1

7. Färber, M., Bartscherer, F., Menne, C., Rettinger, A.: Linked data quality of DBpedia, Freebase, OpenCyc, Wikidata, and YAGO. Semant. Web **9**(1), 77–129 (2017)

8. Görlitz, O., Staab, S.: Splendid: SPARQL endpoint federation exploiting VoID descriptions. In: Proceedings of the Second International Conference on Consuming Linked Data, vol. 782, pp. 13–24. CEUR-WS. org (2011)

9. Harth, A., Hose, K., Karnstedt, M., Polleres, A., Sattler, K.U., Umbrich, J.: Data summaries for on-demand queries over linked data. In: Proceedings of the 19th International Conference on World Wide Web - WWW 2010, p. 411. ACM Press, Raleigh, North Carolina, USA (2010)

10. Hartig, O.: Querying trust in RDF data with tSPARQL. In: Aroyo, L., et al. (eds.) ESWC 2009. LNCS, vol. 5554, pp. 5–20. Springer, Heidelberg (2009). https://doi.org/10.1007/978-3-642-02121-3_5

11. Heling, L., Acosta, M., Maleshkova, M., Sure-Vetter, Y.: Querying large knowledge graphs over triple pattern fragments: an empirical study. In: Vrandečić, D., et al. (eds.) ISWC 2018. LNCS, vol. 11137, pp. 86–102. Springer, Cham (2018). https://doi.org/10.1007/978-3-030-00668-6_6

12. Hui, J., Li, L., Zhang, Z.: Integration of big data: a survey. In: Zhou, Q., Gan, Y., Jing, W., Song, X., Wang, Y., Lu, Z. (eds.) ICPCSEE 2018. CCIS, vol. 901, pp. 101–121. Springer, Singapore (2018). https://doi.org/10.1007/978-981-13-2203-7_9

13. Ibaraki, T., Kameda, T.: On the optimal nesting order for computing N-relational joins. ACM Trans. Database Syst. **9**(3), 482–502 (1984)

14. Lopes, N., Polleres, A., Straccia, U., Zimmermann, A.: AnQL: SPARQLing up annotated RDFS. In: Patel-Schneider, P.F., et al. (eds.) ISWC 2010. LNCS, vol. 6496, pp. 518–533. Springer, Heidelberg (2010). https://doi.org/10.1007/978-3-642-17746-0_33

15. Naumann, F., Leser, U., Freytag, J.C.: Quality-driven integration of heterogenous information systems. In: VLDB 1999, Proceedings of 25th International Conference on Very Large Data Bases, Edinburgh, Scotland, UK, pp. 447–458 (1999)

16. Neumann, T., Moerkotte, G.: Characteristic sets: accurate cardinality estimation for RDF queries with multiple joins. In: 2011 IEEE 27th International Conference on Data Engineering (ICDE), pp. 984–994, April 2011

17. Quilitz, B., Leser, U.: Querying distributed RDF data sources with SPARQL. In: Bechhofer, S., Hauswirth, M., Hoffmann, J., Koubarakis, M. (eds.) ESWC 2008. LNCS, vol. 5021, pp. 524–538. Springer, Heidelberg (2008). https://doi.org/10.1007/978-3-540-68234-9_39

18. Saleem, M., Ngonga Ngomo, A.-C.: HiBISCuS: hypergraph-based source selection for SPARQL endpoint federation. In: Presutti, V., d'Amato, C., Gandon, F., d'Aquin, M., Staab, S., Tordai, A. (eds.) ESWC 2014. LNCS, vol. 8465, pp. 176–191. Springer, Cham (2014). https://doi.org/10.1007/978-3-319-07443-6_13

19. Schwarte, A., Haase, P., Hose, K., Schenkel, R., Schmidt, M.: FedX: optimization techniques for federated query processing on linked data. In: Aroyo, L., et al. (eds.)

ISWC 2011. LNCS, vol. 7031, pp. 601–616. Springer, Heidelberg (2011). https:// doi.org/10.1007/978-3-642-25073-6_38

20. Tsialiamanis, P., Sidirourgos, L., Fundulaki, I., Christophides, V., Boncz, P.: Heuristics-based query optimisation for SPARQL. In: Proceedings of the 15th International Conference on Extending Database Technology - EDBT 2012, p. 324. ACM Press, Berlin, Germany (2012)

21. Wang, R.Y., Strong, D.M.: Beyond accuracy: what data quality means to data consumers. J. Manag. Inf. Syst. **12**(4), 5–33 (1996)

22. Zaveri, A., Rula, A., Maurino, A., Pietrobon, R., Lehmann, J., Auer, S.: Quality assessment for linked data: a survey. Semant. Web **7**(1), 63–93 (2016)

Efficient High-Level Semantic Enrichment of Undocumented Enterprise Data

Markus Schröder[1,2(✉)]

[1] Smart Data & Knowledge Services Department, DFKI GmbH,
Kaiserslautern, Germany
markus.schroeder@dfki.de
[2] Computer Science Department, TU Kaiserslautern, Kaiserslautern, Germany

Abstract. In absence of a data management strategy, undocumented enterprise data piles up and becomes increasingly difficult for companies to use to its full potential. As a solution, we propose the enrichment of such data with meaning, or more precisely, the interlinking of data content with high-level semantic concepts. In contrast to low-level data lifting and mid-level information extraction, we would like to reach a high level of knowledge conceptualization. Currently, this can only be achieved if human experts are integrated into the enrichment process. Since human expertise is costly and limited, our methodology is designed to be as efficient as possible. That includes quantifying enrichment levels as well as assessing efficiency of gathering and exploiting user feedback. This paper proposes research on how semantic enrichment of undocumented enterprise data with humans in the loop can be conducted. We already got promising preliminary results from several projects in which we enriched various enterprise data.

Keywords: Semantic enrichment · Knowledge graph building ·
Enterprise data · Human in the loop

1 Introduction and Motivation

With the accompanying digitalization we are in the midst of the "data everywhere" age. Since the advantages of electronic data processing have long been recognized, companies are increasingly digitizing their processes as well as collecting and processing data in various data pools. However, if necessary data maintenance is lost in hectic everyday work, naturally grown undocumented data piles up. That is why we frequently encounter arbitrarily structured, diverse, heterogeneous and distributed enterprise data sets accumulated over several years.

Therefore, for companies it becomes increasingly difficult to discover and make use of their data. Especially messy data is an obvious obstacle in performing complex data mining analyses which are used to gain new insights from data [35]. This observation also conforms with the statement of data scientists, who

© Springer Nature Switzerland AG 2019
P. Hitzler et al. (Eds.): ESWC 2019 Satellite Events, LNCS 11762, pp. 220–230, 2019.
https://doi.org/10.1007/978-3-030-32327-1_41

regard data preparation as an integral part of their work [10]. Moreover, it hinders employees to efficiently work with the data content in day-to-day business. Here, possible solutions could be workload reducing software tools embedded in the work environment to support employees' daily work [24]. However, such efforts require pre-processed, structured and organized data.

Thus, we propose as a solution the semantic enrichment [6] of such data by meaning. Instead of stopping at a low-level conversion or mid-level information extraction (IE), our plan is to augment data with high-level concepts. While data lifting usually converts the data structure to a knowledge representation and IE further extracts structured data from unstructured one, semantic enrichment in addition precisely annotates data with meaningful concepts obtained by experts. For example, the table with header `|Car-ID|EOP|` can be easily converted to RDF [37] and car configurations hidden in the car's ID can be extracted with rules, however, domain knowledge is needed to reveal that EOP means *End Of Production*. The knowledge to understand the data is hidden in the mindsets of domain experts working daily with their usual data assets. In companies they are usually limited in number and have only restricted time available. Therefore, we plan to integrate their feedback as efficiently as possible into the enrichment process. Only then we can achieve that high-level concepts in the employees' minds are heeded in the leveraging process.

As a concrete example, think of a manufacturing company building products in process pipelines. Its messy dataspace is full of arbitrarily structured data produced by many employees without any consultation: product databases, planning spreadsheets, XML exports, mails and shared drives. This should be semantically enriched to ease the application of data mining tasks across all those data assets. Initially, different information extraction methods are applied to these data pools by a knowledge engineer. Several domain experts are invited to give feedback on extracted results. Iterating between those two procedures, a semantic graph of high-level concepts emerges. Finally, a data analyst is able to use semantic services to exploit gained structured data for various mining tasks.

The remainder of this paper is structured as follows: Sect. 2 lists the state of the art with related work followed by the problem and consequential research questions in Sect. 3. Section 4 outlines the planned research methodology while Sect. 5 sketches a brief evaluation plan. Preliminary results are described in Sect. 6 followed by the conclusion (Sect. 7).

2   State of the Art

This research builds on state of the art and related work from several domains.

Semantic Technologies. The foundation of this PhD is formed by the research area Semantic Web [2]. Commonly, ontologies are used to create a formal, explicit specification of a shared conceptualization [34]. Knowledge bases, usually modelled with the Resource Description Framework (RDF) [37] as sets of facts, interlink resources using URIs and are processed by semantic technologies [15]. If a knowledge base is represented as a graph, we speak of a knowledge graph [26]. In corporations, such semantic networks of domain knowledge are known as *enterprise* knowledge graphs [11,12]. The non-trivial question however is, how to efficiently construct a sophisticated knowledge graph originating from human knowledge, expertise and diverse enterprise data.

Knowledge Graph Construction. Data lifting is a technique that converts well structured data to an RDF representation using mapping definitions (e.g. using R2RML[1] and GRDDL[2], to name prominent ones). While it can convert structured data to RDF, they have several limitations on unstructured or semi-structured data despite some enhancements that were recently made [5]. Usually, they require knowledge engineers who are familiar with the data sources, mapping languages and target ontologies. Current state-of-the-art enterprise knowledge graph construction approaches assume well (semi-)structured data (CSV, relational DB, XML, JSON, etc.) with well-known schemata [22,26,28]. They follow a kind of extract-transform-load (ETL) pipeline which converts data into RDF once the mapping is configured. However, in our scenarios, we can neither assume solely structured data, nor knowledge about schemata, nor existence of suitable ontologies in advance. A deficiency of such approaches is the necessity of comprehensive prior knowledge and rigid processing to perform the construction. We envision an agile workflow which would permit yet unknown parameters (schemata, ontologies) and intermediate feedback loops with users.

Information Extraction on Unstructured Data. We suppose that arbitrarily structured (i.e. not especially well structured) enterprise data is mostly generated by people writing texts such as labels or descriptions. To automatically gain structured information from unstructured and also semi-structured data, various information extraction (IE) methods in the field of NLP have been researched for several years [23]. This includes procedures that find entities in texts (named entity recognition), determine relevant terms from the domain (term extraction) and disambiguate these to knowledge base identifiers (entity linking). They can be used to discover initial suggestions for relevant terms, concepts, instances, or links found in the data. During the dissertation, suitability assessments of several state-of-the-art approaches will be conducted.

However, not all methods are applicable without adaptions, as they make certain assumptions about the input, for example, the text's nature. In companies we often encounter, besides usual documents, short ungrammatical text snippets in their data assets (e.g., file and folder names [3], database schema labels [27] and semi-structured data in general). Particularly, short texts contain no regular grammar, have only few statistical signals and are rather ambiguous [17]. To address text snippets human behaviour could be detected and exploited, because people tend to label elements in their own way but in a repetitive manner. For example, imagine a person always using an underscore (_) to separate tokens,

---

[1] http://www.w3.org/TR/r2rml.
[2] http://www.w3.org/TR/grddl.

while date information formatted as YYYYMMDD is appended at the end. Semantic labelling approaches [27] could annotate such information on a character level: an example would be the annotation in travel_ 20190602 .txt which is linked to the concepts *Date* and *ESWC*. Because usually such labelled data does not exist right from the start the labelling approaches should be unsupervised. If the text additionally shows no clear separation between tokens, approaches like automatic identifier splitting [9] have to be performed up front.

Meta-Data Management on Data Lakes. Aforementioned approaches having particular input assumptions are not sufficient for the huge data diversity in companies. A company's dataspace [14] typically contains not only relational databases and well structured files, but also unstructured (short) texts and weakly semi-structured file formats. There is a new trend to gather raw data in a data lake [20] and integrate it step by step in a pay-as-you-go fashion [18]. Should this fail, the data lake turns more and more into a data swamp: its content becomes difficult to understand and to discover. New research directions tackle this challenge with sophisticated meta-data management [4,13,33]. However, in order to reach a high-level enrichment, we often need to capture and explicitly model the meaning hidden in the data content on a more fine-grained level. This requires to directly descend deeper into its content and annotate meaning on a character level. That way we can more precisely acquire feedback from the user.

Human in the Loop. Regarding involvement of human experts, recent research enables users to semi-automatically populate an ontology by user-defined conceptualisations [7]. They automatically align them with an ontology and let users add new instances or concepts as well as split or merge them. In the context of IE, interactive information extraction [21] allows users to verify and correct extraction results. However, there is still a considerable amount of manual labour to be performed by the user. That is why other research focuses on reducing human annotation effort, for instance on named entity recognition [36] and extraction [8]. Those approaches present users selected sentences containing most likely correctly found entities. We would like to further reduce their effort by showing automatically generated summaries and quickly graspable visualizations. For instance, we could summarize entities by their suggested types. Knowledge acquisition [25] investigates methods to extract expertise from experts. We can apply proven direct methods in order to enrich data with the user's expertise. Promising methods like questionnaire or interview are integrable into the semantic enrichment process.

To the best of our knowledge there is no system yet that deeply integrates experts in the enrichment process like the one we envision.

3   Problem Statement and Contributions

This PhD will be guided by the following main research question:
How can an efficient high-level semantic enrichment of undocumented enterprise data be conducted?

The question focuses specifically on arbitrarily structured data occurring in companies. Such data is rather undocumented and thus difficult to comprehend and to process. In contrast to research with mass data on the web, we focus on semantic enrichment on an enterprise level. Compared with the internet, enterprise data is more limited in quantity while enrichment results are expected by companies to be of high quality. Thus, statistical signals (e.g. based on frequency) will not reveal relevant data points as expected from approaches which use the Internet's mass data. Conversely, enterprises usually have a manageable domain and participants with low variety of possible information. An alternative to statistical signals is human expertise directly suggesting relevant data points. Since experts are costly, we need to make the process efficient. Only with the human component can we reach the intended high semantic level.

Subsequently, the main research question is further divided into subquestions.

RQ 1. *What state-of-the-art approaches can be utilized and how can they be adapted to gain precise results on limited diverse enterprise data?*

By the application of current approaches, we expect an initial mid-level enrichment. However, the special data situation in enterprises will limit the selection of already existing methods. Some supervised approaches can be excluded in advance because they require a considerable amount of labelled data to provide an acceptable outcome (e.g. deep learning). Others have too strong assumptions about the data's nature that do not match with data found in corporations (e.g. short ungrammatical texts). Especially very special data structures (e.g. file trees, spreadsheets, PDFs) require procedures that exploit the unique nature of their contents. Therefore, during this PhD the suitability of several state-of-the-art approaches with regard to concrete data situations will be evaluated. If necessary they will be adapted to the special nature of enterprise data. For instance, unsupervised terminology extraction could be extended with additional metrics reflecting the term's occurrence in the data (e.g. folder hierarchy depths).

Sophisticated algorithms can achieve a considerable enrichment level automatically. However, only with domain experts integrated in this process we will reach the intended high level. That is why we ask the following research question:

RQ 2. *How can we efficiently integrate human experts in the process to achieve our envisioned high level of enrichment?*

In contrast to crowdsourcing, we only have a limited number of experts in the company who can give feedback to enriched results. In addition, employees have only restricted time available for feedback loops. Because of these constraints we need time-saving human-in-the-loop methods that allow to give targeted feedback desirably on a large number of data points. Therefore, the research question also includes the design of efficient graphical user interfaces together with suitable interaction patterns. This involves giving feedback to already organized, thus quickly graspable statements without great effort, for example, using short mouse movements on clustered elements. Every human input, no matter how small, could immediately contribute to the enrichment.

The questions so far emphasized a "high-level" as well as an "efficient" enrichment. We aim to estimate these parameters as well as possible during the process at any time. Assessing the status quo will benefit in choosing the appropriate enrichment algorithms and design of feedback loops. Hence, the next research questions are concerned with such assessments.

RQ 3. *How can we quantify the enrichment level of algorithms?*

The level of enrichment approximates how comprehensive the gained knowledge about enterprise data is. This can vary greatly, depending on current circumstances and field of application. While a high coverage of enterprise data is desired, at the same time, the enrichment results should be as precise as possible. In order to objectively judge the results of algorithms, we will develop semantic enrichment measures. For this, a good starting point provide ontology evaluation metrics [16] like accuracy, completeness, consistency, clarity, etc. However, we have to further adjust them to also reflect data dependent aspects, like for instance file coverage. Our metrics are applied to the algorithms' results to quantify what enrichment level they can reach. This allows to assess and compare state-of-the-art procedures in terms of their suitability in semantic enrichment.

Last, we intent to quantify human effort.

RQ 4. *What are appropriate measures to assess the efficiency of gathering and exploiting user feedback?*

In order to make human in the loop approaches comparable, we will quantify their efficiency in collecting feedback. One dimension is the number of verifications divided by the time the expert needed. This can be combined with the expertise, willingness and available time of domain experts. Moreover, we are interested to quantify how well various feedback types help in the enrichment process. Typical ones include direct methods found in knowledge acquisition [25] like interviews moderated by the knowledge engineer, (auto-generated) questionnaires, user observation, protocol analysis and drawing closed curves. They will be adapted for (digital) enterprise data, for example, a questionnaire directly refers to the data items where feedback is needed.

Summarising, the main contribution is an innovative semi-automatic method to lift enterprise data to a high semantic level by efficiently integrating human in the loop. Suitable procedures will be identified to initially enrich enterprise data. We expect new insights on how to involve experts in the process the best way. The outcome of the PhD will also provide a base for further research in the field of enterprise knowledge graph construction and bootstrapping semantic services (e.g. Semantic Desktop).

4   Research Methodology and Approach

In our research institute, we work closely with industry customers, for whom we develop and apply innovative AI solutions. During the application we usually face different data sources which have to be processed for the actual project's objective. We expect that our developed knowledge services will provide even better results, once we enrich the data with domain knowledge. For such cases, our proposed methodology enables an efficient enrichment in which answers to the stated research questions are provided.

Regarding RQ 1, we would like to mutually compare state-of-the-art approaches and, if necessary, extend them appropriately. By making their enrichment level quantifiable, we verify the usability of individual procedures. Bottom-up, we semantically annotate raw data in order to form a semantic graph originating from the data. Top-down, we heed the conceptualization of the employees by involving them into the process at an early stage. In doing so, we consider two aspects simultaneously: First, information extraction is not solely data-driven, since domain experts directly give feedback to their outcome. Second, the experts' conceptualisation is not modelled in isolation, because concepts are immediately linked to the corresponding data item. By this, we expect to get better results than with existing methods.

Per use case, we will have contact with several domain experts who can be consulted for user studies. In this event, various user interfaces, feedback types and interaction patterns will be designed and tested systematically. We plan to develop graphical interfaces presenting enrichment suggestions in easily comprehensible arrangements. Feedback types will vary from simple questionnaires to costly interviews with a knowledge engineer. Interaction patterns include various mouse gestures (e.g. drag & drop) and keyboard shortcuts. Iteratively, we contribute to the question how to integrate human experts efficiently (RQ 2).

In order to quantify the enrichment level in RQ 3, many dimensions must be considered. First, we will create a classification system to make the current data situation in the enterprise (more) clear. This includes an evaluation of the data variety, availability and quality. In addition, the desired quality of the resulting knowledge graph and its usage by other systems is also taken into account.

5   Evaluation Plan

Our plan is divided into two parts: First, suitability assessments of several state-of-the-art approaches will be conducted. We plan to perform a couple of data-driven evaluations with labelled datasets. This will reveal potential improvements of tested methods on special enterprise data. Various adaptions are planned to be implemented and tested. Proven approaches will be collected in a framework.

Second, our plan is to compare various user interfaces which are designed to gather expert feedback. For that we will conduct several user studies, mainly with university students, but possibly also with domain experts of our different projects. At the same time, we will investigate per use case whether our enrichment results are consistent with the domain experts' conceptual view.

6 Preliminary Results

Regarding the main research question, we already enriched enterprise data in several projects. In the research project PRO-OPT[3], we have gathered first experiences with the construction of a semantic data dictionary in the automotive domain. The insights have been used for a similar industrial project which had the objective to construct a knowledge graph from a given data lake. In another project, we tackled the challenge of enriching several spreadsheets containing manufacturing concepts. Currently, we lift a file tree taken from a shared drive. Regarding the first research question, we tried several unsupervised terminology extraction approaches on tokenized file names, in order to find domain-relevant concepts. However, preliminary findings show that well known approaches like CValue [1] produce insufficient results. Thus, we plan to include certain file system features in the terminology extraction process. Similarly, for our special requirements, we have already enhanced named entity recognition to be tolerant of inflections and for real-time applications [19]. This approach uses language information together with ontologies to also recognize word variations induced by inflection. Our evaluation on Wikipedia shows that we recall considerably more named entities than the baselines.

Regarding integrating human experts (RQ 2), some demos have been published that motivate how domain experts can add or interact with enriched data. It has been shown that spreadsheets enable various kinds of users to easily create semantic data [31,32]. Together with the concept of deep linking [30] they can also semantically annotate semi-structured file contents. For example, via browsing a user obtains a deep link referring to a presentation slide's title and uses the RDF spreadsheet editor to easily make statements about it, like <*this title*, is about, Semantic Web>. We also demonstrated how to intuitively query a semantic graph without knowing about SPARQL [29]. Those approaches are intended to allow users query and enter semantic data in a more familiar way. Yet, these tools are not designed to collect user feedback on the system's enrichment decisions.

7 Conclusion

This paper proposes a PhD topic to investigate an efficient methodology for generating high-level semantic enrichments from undocumented enterprise data. We separated the main research into four partial questions: (1) the utilization of suitable state-of-the-art approaches, (2) the integration of human experts, (3) the quantification of enrichment levels and (4) the efficiency assessment of gathering and exploiting user feedback. Preliminary results show a wide range of potential applications and further research directions. This will impact how enterprise data is transferred into a usable form (again) using semantic technologies. In addition, it will raise awareness of the important involvement of humans during the enrichment process.

---

[3] http://www.pro-opt.org/.

Acknowledgements. Parts of this work have been funded by the German Federal Ministry of Economic Affairs and Energy in the project PRO-OPT (01MD15004D) and by the German Federal Ministry of Food and Agriculture in the project SDSD (2815708615). I thank my doctoral supervisor Prof. Dr. Andreas Dengel and my colleagues Christian Jilek, Dr. Heiko Maus, Dr. Sven Schwarz, Dr. Jörn Hees and Dr. Ansgar Bernardi for their helpful discussions, comments and feedback.

References

1. Ananiadou, S.: A methodology for automatic term recognition. In: The 15th International Conference on Computational Linguistics, COLING 1994, vol. 2, pp. 1034–1038 (1994)
2. Berners-Lee, T., Hendler, J., Lassila, O.: The semantic web. Sci. Am. **284**(5), 34–43 (2001)
3. Bouquet, P., Serafini, L., Zanobini, S., Sceffer, S.: Bootstrapping semantics on the web: meaning elicitation from schemas. In: WWW 2006, pp. 505–512 (2006)
4. Brackenbury, W., et al.: Draining the data swamp: a similarity-based approach. In: Proceedings of the Workshop on Human-In-the-Loop Data Analytics, HILDA 2018. ACM (2018)
5. Chortaras, A., Stamou, G.: D2RML: integrating heterogeneous data and web services into custom RDF graphs. In: Proceedings of the LDOW, vol. 2073. CEUR (2018)
6. Clarke, M., Harley, P.: How smart is your content? Using semantic enrichment to improve your user experience and your bottom line. Sci. Editor **37**(2), 41 (2014)
7. Clarkson, K., Gentile, A.L., Gruhl, D., Ristoski, P., Terdiman, J., Welch, S.: User-centric ontology population. In: Gangemi, A., et al. (eds.) ESWC 2018. LNCS, vol. 10843, pp. 112–127. Springer, Cham (2018). https://doi.org/10.1007/978-3-319-93417-4_8
8. Culotta, A., McCallum, A.: Reducing labeling effort for structured prediction tasks. In: AAAI, vol. 5, pp. 746–751 (2005)
9. Enslen, E., Hill, E., Pollock, L., Vijay-Shanker, K.: Mining source code to automatically split identifiers for software analysis. In: 2009 6th IEEE International Working Conference on Mining Software Repositories, pp. 71–80 (2009)
10. Figure Eight Inc.: Data scientist report 2018 (2018). https://www.figure-eight.com/figure-eight-2018-data-scientist-report/. Accessed 1st Feb 2019
11. Galkin, M., Auer, S., Scerri, S.: Enterprise knowledge graphs : a backbone of linked enterprise data. In: 2016 IEEE/WIC/ACM International Conference on Web Intelligence (2016)
12. Galkin, M., Auer, S., Vidal, M.E., Scerri, S.: Enterprise knowledge graphs: a semantic approach for knowledge management in the next generation of enterprise information systems. In: Proceedings of the 19th International Conference on Enterprise Information Systems (ICEIS), vol. 2, pp. 88–98. SciTePress (2017)
13. Hai, R., Geisler, S., Quix, C.: Constance: an intelligent data lake system. In: Proceedings of the 2016 ACM SIGMOD International Conference on Management of Data. ACM (2016)
14. Halevy, A.Y., Franklin, M.J., Maier, D.: From databases to dataspaces: a new abstraction for information management. ACM Sigmod Rec. **34**, 27–33 (2005)
15. Hitzler, P., Krotzsch, M., Rudolph, S.: Foundations of Semantic Web Technologies. Chapman and Hall/CRC, Boca Raton (2009)

16. Hlomani, H., Stacey, D.: Approaches, methods, metrics, measures, and subjectivity in ontology evaluation: a survey. Semant. Web J. **1**(5), 1–11 (2014)
17. Hua, W., Wang, Z., Wang, H., Zheng, K., Zhou, X.: Short text understanding through lexical-semantic analysis. In: 2015 IEEE 31st International Conference on Data Engineering, pp. 495–506 (2015)
18. Jeffery, S.R., Franklin, M.J., Halevy, A.Y.: Pay-as-you-go user feedback for dataspace systems. In: Proceedings of the 2008 ACM SIGMOD International Conference on Management of Data, pp. 847–860 (2008)
19. Jilek, C., Schröder, M., Novik, R., Schwarz, S., Maus, H., Dengel, A.: Inflection-tolerant ontology-based named entity recognition for real-time applications. In: 2nd Conference on Language, Data and Knowledge, vol. 70. OASIcs (2019, in print)
20. Khine, P.P., Wang, Z.S.: Data lake: a new ideology in big data era. In: ITM Web Conference, vol. 17, p. 03025 (2018)
21. Kristjansson, T., Culotta, A.: Interactive information extraction with constrained conditional random fields. In: AAAI, vol. 4, pp. 412–418 (2004)
22. Li, H., Zhai, J.: Constructing investment open data of Chinese listed companies based on linked data. In: Proceedings of the 17th International Digital Government Research Conference on Digital Government Research, pp. 475–480. ACM (2016)
23. Martinez-Rodriguez, J.L., Hogan, A., Lopez-Arevalo, I.: Information extraction meets the semantic web: a survey. Semant. Web 1–81 (2018). Preprint
24. Maus, H., Schwarz, S., Dengel, A.: Weaving personal knowledge spaces into office applications. In: Fathi, M. (ed.) Integration of Practice-Oriented Knowledge Technology: Trends and Prospectives, pp. 71–82. Springer, Heidelberg (2013). https://doi.org/10.1007/978-3-642-34471-8_6
25. Olson, J.R., Rueter, H.H.: Extracting expertise from experts: methods for knowledge acquisition. Expert Syst. **4**(3), 152–168 (1987)
26. Pan, J.Z., Vetere, G., Gomez-Perez, J.M., Wu, H.: Exploiting Linked Data and Knowledge Graphs in Large Organisations. Springer, Heidelberg (2017). https://doi.org/10.1007/978-3-319-45654-6
27. Pham, M., Alse, S., Knoblock, C.A., Szekely, P.: Semantic labeling: a domain-independent approach. In: Groth, P., et al. (eds.) ISWC 2016. LNCS, vol. 9981, pp. 446–462. Springer, Cham (2016). https://doi.org/10.1007/978-3-319-46523-4_27
28. Rao, S.S., Nayak, A.: LinkED: a novel methodology for publishing linked enterprise data. J. Comput. Inf. Technol. **25**(3), 191–209 (2017)
29. Schröder, M., Hees, J., Bernardi, A., Ewert, D., Klotz, P., Stadtmüller, S.: Simplified SPARQL REST API. In: Gangemi, A., et al. (eds.) ESWC 2018. LNCS, vol. 11155, pp. 40–45. Springer, Cham (2018). https://doi.org/10.1007/978-3-319-98192-5_8
30. Schröder, M., Jilek, C., Dengel, A.: Deep linking desktop resources. In: Gangemi, A., et al. (eds.) ESWC 2018. LNCS, vol. 11155, pp. 202–207. Springer, Cham (2018). https://doi.org/10.1007/978-3-319-98192-5_38
31. Schröder, M., Jilek, C., Hees, J., Hertling, S., Dengel, A.: RDF spreadsheet editor: get (g)rid of your RDF data entry problems. In: ISWC 2017 Posters & Demonstrations and Industry Tracks, vol. 1963. CEUR (2017)
32. Schröder, M., Jilek, C., Hees, J., Hertling, S., Dengel, A.: An easy & collaborative RDF data entry method using the spreadsheet metaphor. arXiv 1804.04175 (2018)
33. Skluzacek, T.J., et al.: Skluma: an extensible metadata extraction pipeline for disorganized data. In: 2018 IEEE 14th International Conference on e-Science, pp. 256–266 (2018)
34. Studer, R., Benjamins, V.R., Fensel, D., et al.: Knowledge engineering: principles and methods. Data Knowl. Eng. **25**(1), 161–198 (1998)

35. Terrizzano, I., Schwarz, P., Roth, M., Colino, J.E.: Data wrangling: the challenging journey from the wild to the lake. In: 7th Biennial Conference on Innovative Data Systems Research (CIDR'15) (2015)
36. Tsuruoka, Y., Tsujii, J., Ananiadou, S.: Accelerating the annotation of sparse named entities by dynamic sentence selection. BMC Bioinf. **9**, S8 (2008)
37. W3C: RDF 1.1 concepts and abstract syntax (2014)

Knowledge-Based Dataless Text Categorization

Rima Türker[1,2(✉)]

[1] FIZ Karlsruhe, Leibniz Institute for Information Infrastructure,
Eggenstein-Leopoldshafen, Germany
`rima.tuerker@fiz-karlsruhe.de`
[2] AIFB, Karlsruhe Institute of Technology (KIT), Karlsruhe, Germany

Abstract. Text categorization is an important task due to the rapid growth of online available text data in various domains such as web search snippets, news documents, etc. Traditional supervised methods require a significant amount of training data and manually labeling such data can be very time-consuming and costly. Moreover, in case the text to be labeled is of a specific domain, then only the expensive domain experts are able to fulfill the manual labeling task. This thesis focuses on the problem of missing labeled data and aims to develop a novel and generic model which does not require any labeled training data to categorize text. Instead, it utilizes the semantic similarity between documents and the predefined categories by leveraging graph embedding techniques.

Keywords: Text categorization · Dataless classification · Network embeddings

1 Introduction

Text categorization plays a fundamental role in many Natural Language Processing applications such as web search, question answering, etc. Traditional text classification approaches require a significant amount of labeled training data and a sophisticated parameter tuning process. Manual labeling of such data can be a rather time-consuming and costly task. Especially, if the text to be labeled is of a specific scientific or technical domain, crowd-sourcing based labeling approaches do not work successfully and only expensive domain experts are able to fulfill the manual labeling task. Alternatively, semi-supervised text classification approaches [10,19] have been proposed to reduce the labeling effort. Yet, due to the diversity of the documents in many applications, generating small training set for semi-supervised approaches still remains an expensive process [6].

To address the lack of labeled data problem, a number of *dataless text classification* methods [1,14] have been proposed. These methods do not require any labelled data to perform text classification. Rather, they rely on the semantic similarity between a given document and a set of predefined categories to determine which category the given document belongs to. In other words, documents

© Springer Nature Switzerland AG 2019
P. Hitzler et al. (Eds.): ESWC 2019 Satellite Events, LNCS 11762, pp. 231–241, 2019.
https://doi.org/10.1007/978-3-030-32327-1_42

and categories are represented in a common semantic space based on the words contained in the documents and category labels, which allows to calculate a meaningful semantic similarity between documents and categories based on their vector representation. However, the most prominent and successful dataless classification approaches are designed for long documents such as news documents, i.e in case of short text most of them fail to classify the text properly as the available context is rather limited.

This thesis aims to address mentioned challenges by developing a **K**nowledge **B**ased **D**ataless **T**ext **C**lassification (KBDTC) approach for documents of arbitrary length without requiring any labeled training data. The method utilizes Knowledge Bases (KBs) as an external source. Moreover, to determine the category of a given text, KBDTC exploits the semantic similarity between the document and the predefined categories by leveraging graph embedding techniques.

The rest of this paper is structured as follows: Sect. 2 discusses related work. The research problems and expected contributions are presented in Sect. 3., while Sect. 4 outlines the research methodology and the approach. Sections 5 and 6 describe the experimental setup for the evaluation as well as discuss the achieved results. Last, Sect. 7, concludes the paper with a discussion of open issues and future work.

2   State of the Art

The aim of this thesis is to develop a Dataless Text Categorizing method which does not require any labeled data for training, instead it utilizes KBs as an external knowledge. Thus, in this section several Dataless Text Classification methods are presented. Since the proposed method (see Sect. 4) has been already applied to short text, the studies related to short text classification are also discussed in the subsequent section.

Dataless Text Classification. In order to address the problem of missing labeled data, [1] introduced a dataless text classification method by representing documents and category labels in a common semantic space. As source, Wikipedia was utilized supported with Explicit Semantic Analysis (ESA) [3] to quantify semantic relatedness between the labels to be assigned and the documents. As a result, it was shown that ESA is able to achieve better classification results than the traditional BOW representations. Further, [14] proposed a dataless hierarchical text classification by dividing the dataless classification task into two steps. In the semantic similarity step, both labels and documents were represented in a common semantic space, which allows to calculate semantic relatedness between documents and labels. In the bootstrapping step, the approach made use of a machine learning based classification procedure with the aim of iteratively improving classification accuracy.

In contrast to these approaches, our goal differs in two main aspects. First, all the mentioned studies were designed for long text such as news articles. However the main purpose of this thesis is categorization of documents of arbitrary length without the necessity of labeled training data. Second, none of the mentioned approaches made use of the entities. Rather, to represent a document, they consider the words contained in the document.

Short Text Classification. To overcome the data sparsity problem of short text, recent works [17,18] proposed deep learning based approaches for short text classification. The results of these approaches have been compared with traditional supervised classification methods, such as SVM, multinomial logistic regression, etc., where the authors showed that in most of the cases their approach achieved superior results. While performing well in practice, the aforementioned approaches are slow both in the training and in the test phases. In addition, their performance highly depends on the size of training data, its distribution, and the chosen hyper parameters. By contrast, our approach does not require any training data nor any parameter tuning.

3   Problem Statement and Contributions

This section presents the research questions that are intended to be answered in this thesis as well as the related hypotheses.

3.1   Problem Statement

In this research we aim to address the following questions:

RQ 1. *How can entities that are associated with hierarchically related categories from a KB be utilized for short text classification without requiring any labeled data as a prerequisite?*

In this thesis, as a first step, we have considered short documents for the categorization task. In short text the available context is rather limited and it is assumed that words tend to be ambiguous, however entities carry much more information [16]. Therefore, we have developed a Knowledge Based Short Text Categorization (KBSTC) method, which considers the semantic similarity between entities (present in a given short text) and a set of predefined categories to derive the category of the text.

Then, the corresponding sub-question is:

RQ 2. *How to capture the semantic relation between entities and categories?*

To calculate the meaningful semantic relatedness, the proper semantic representation of entities and categories in a common vector space is essential. For this reason, we have proposed a new entity and category embedding model which can leverage entities and categories from large KBs, furthermore can embed them into a common vector space.

RQ 3. *Can words along with entities present in a text be utilized to increase the accuracy of KBDTC?*

The subsequent step is to investigate how to incorporate words into KBDTC to enhance the classification accuracy. KBDTC relies on the semantic similarity between documents and categories to determine the category of a given text. In order to exploit words as well as entities, the semantic similarity between words, entities and categories should be captured by a new embedding model. In other words, in this phase of the thesis, the purpose is to develop a joint word, entity and category embedding model, then integrate this model to KBDTC to improve the classification accuracy.

RQ 4. *Can KBDTC be exploited to create labeled data for supervised classification methods?*
Supervised classification methods, especially, deep learning approaches perform very well in short text classification [2,4,5,18]. However, they all require a significant amount of labeled training data. We will investigate how to utilize KBDTC to generate training sets for supervised classification approaches.

RQ 5. *How to generalize KBDTC to perform categorization of arbitrary documents?*
The proposed approach has been assessed in the context of short text classification. The experiments (see Sect. 6) show that KBSTC can categorize short text in an unsupervised way with a high accuracy. As a subsequent step, we plan to generalize the proposed approach for categorization of arbitrary length documents including tweets (short text), search snippets (short text), news data (long text), etc.

RQ 6. *How to generalize KBDTC to be compatible with arbitrary KBs?*
As yet, a general KB, Wikipedia has been utilized for KBSTC task. However, domain specific knowledge is not appropriately covered by general KBs such as Wikipedia. Therefore, in this phase, the goal is to generalize KBDTC to be adaptable to arbitrary KBs from different domains.

The following hypotheses are deducted:

H 1. *"Exploiting a KB can help to conduct text classification without requiring any labelled data"*

H 2. *"Embedding entities and categories into a common vector space enables to calculate meaningful semantic relatedness between them"*

H 3. *"KBDTC can be used to generate training sets for supervised approaches"*

H 4. *"KBDTC can be extended to utilize arbitrary KBs to categorize documents".*

3.2 Contributions

The expected contributions of this research include:

1. A new paradigm for text categorization, based on a KB.
2. A new model for short text categorization so called KBSTC.
3. The development of an entity and category embedding model for calculating the semantic similarity between entities and categories.
4. The improvement of the embedding model by including words into the entity and category embeddings.
5. The development of a generic KBDTC approach, which is compatible with any KBs for categorizing arbitrary text.

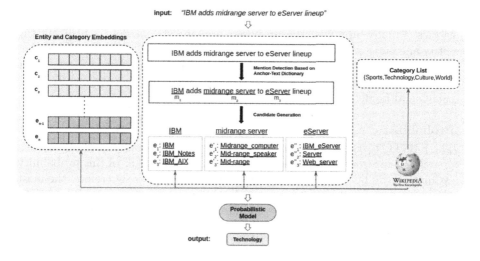

Fig. 1. The work flow of the proposed KBSTC approach (best viewed in color)

4 Research Methodology and Approach

In this research, so far we have developed KBSTC (**RQ 1**) as well as a new entity and category embedding model (**RQ 2**). Therefore, this section provides a formal definition of the KBSTC task, followed by the description of the proposed probabilistic approach for KBSTC. Finally, the plan for tackling the rest of the research questions (**RQ 3, RQ 4, RQ 5, RQ 6**) is presented.

– **RQ 1 and RQ 2**

Definition (KBSTC task). Given an input short text t that contains a set of entities $E_t \subseteq E$ as well as a set of predefined categories $C' \subseteq C$ (from the underlying knowledge base KB), the output of the KBSTC task is the most relevant category $c_i \in C'$ for the given short text t, i.e., we compute the category function $f_{cat}(t) = c_i$, where $c_i \in C'$.

KBSTC Overview. The general workflow of KBSTC is shown in Fig. 1. In the first step, each entity mention present in a given short text t is detected. Next, for each mention, a set of candidate entities are generated based on a prefabricated Anchor-Text Dictionary, which contains all mentions and their corresponding Wikipedia entities. In order to detect entity mentions, first all n-grams from the input text are gathered and then the extracted n-grams matching surface forms of entities (based on the Anchor-Text dictionary) are selected as entity mentions. To construct the Anchor-Text Dictionary, all the anchor texts of hyperlinks in Wikipedia pointing to any Wikipedia articles are extracted, whereby the anchor texts serve as mentions and the links refer to the corresponding entities. Given the short text t as *"IBM adds midrange server to eServer lineup"*, the detected mentions are *"IBM"*, *"midrange server"* and *"eServer"*. Likewise the predefined categories,

$C' = \{Sports, Technology, Culture, World\}$, are mapped to Wikipedia categories. Finally, applying the proposed probabilistic model by utilizing the entity and category embeddings that have been precomputed from Wikipedia, the output of the KBSTC task is the semantically most relevant category for the entities present in t. Thereby, in the given example the category *Technology* should be determined.

Probabilistic Approach

The KBSTC task is formalized as estimating the probability of $P(c|t)$ of each predefined category c and an input short text t. The result of this probability estimation can be considered as a score for each category. Therefore, the most relevant category c for a given text t should maximize the probability $P(c|t)$. Based on Bayes' theorem, the probability $P(c|t)$ can be rewritten as follows:

$$P(c|t) = \frac{P(c,t)}{P(t)} \propto P(c,t). \tag{1}$$

where the denominator $P(t)$ can be ignored as it has no impact on the ranking of the categories. To calculate $P(c|t)$, the proper semantic representation of entities and categories in a common vector space is essential. Hence, in this thesis we have also proposed an entity and category embedding model that embeds entities and categories from Wikipedia into a common vector space. Readers can refer to our research paper [15] for more technical detail of the parameter estimation of Eq. (1) and proposed embedding model.

– **RQ 3**

The next research step is to extend KBSTC towards the additional inclusion of word embeddings into the common entity and category vector space. KBSTC exploits only entities for short text classification, however, words might have a positive impact on the model performance. Since the proposed embedding model is flexible to adopt new type of relations, the inclusion of word embedding is straightforward. In other words, words and word-category relations can be included as an additional type of vertices and edges in already constructed heterogeneous network [15].

– **RQ 4**

As already mentioned supervised methods, especially, deep learning approaches perform very well in short text classification. However, they require million-scale labelled documents [8]. Since KBSTC can classify a given short text without requiring any labelled data, the most confidently classified documents can be collected as a training set for the deep learning phase. Next, the rest of the documents (that could not be properly classified by KBSTC) can be classified with the trained deep learning model.

– **RQ 5 and RQ 6**

Final goal of this thesis is to have a full fledged generic KBDTC approach. The ultimate approach should be capable to categorize a given text (which are of arbitrary length) without requiring any training data and compatible with any KBs.

5   Evaluation Plan

As already mentioned, so far we have developed KBSTC and a new entity and category embedding model. Hence, this section provides a description of the datasets and the baselines for evaluating KBSTC and the embedding model.

5.1   Datasets

The experiments have been conducted on the following two benchmarks (the data distribution of both dataset can be found in [15]):

AG News (AG)[1]**:** This dataset is adopted from [20], which contains both titles and short descriptions (usually one sentence) of news articles. In our experiments, the dataset has two versions, where one contains only titles and the other contains both titles and descriptions. The total number of entities and the average number of entities and words per text in the test datasets are shown in Table 1.

Google Snippets (Snippets)[2]**:** This is a well-known dataset for short text classification, which was introduced in [12] and contains short snippets from Google search results. As shown in Table 1, the test dataset has in total 20,284 entities, an average of 8.9 entities and an average of 17.97 words in each snippet.

Table 1. Statistical analysis of the test datasets

Dataset	#Entities	Avg. #Ent	Avg. #Word
AG News (Title)	24,416	3.21	7.14
AG News (Title+Description)	89,933	11.83	38.65
Google Snippets	20,284	8.90	17.97

As the focus of this work is the KBSTC task, where the goal is to derive the most relevant category from the knowledge base for a given short text, we need to adapt these datasets by aligning the labels/categories with the categories in the used knowledge base. More specifically, each label/category in these datasets is manually mapped to its corresponding Wikipedia category, e.g., the category *Sports* from the AG dataset is mapped to the Wikipedia category *Sports*[3]. Furthermore, as KBSTC does not depend on any training/labeled data, the training datasets of AG and Snippets are only used for the training of the supervised baseline methods. Lastly, to measure the performance of KBSTC, the classification accuracy (the ratio of correctly classified data over all the test data) was used.

---

[1] http://goo.gl/JyCnZq.
[2] http://jwebpro.sourceforge.net/data-web-snippets.tar.gz.
[3] https://en.wikipedia.org/wiki/Category:Sports.

Table 2. The classification accuracy of KBSTC against baselines (%)

Model	AG (title)	AG (title+description)	Snippets
Dataless ESA [14]	53.5	64.1	48.5
Dataless Word2Vec [14]	49.5	52.7	52.4
NB+TF-IDF	86.6	90.2	64.4
SVM+TF-IDF	**87.6**	**91.9**	69.1
LR+TF-IDF	87.1	91.7	63.6
KBSTC+Our Embedding	67.9	80.5	**72.0**

5.2 Baselines

To demonstrate the performance of the KBSTC approach, the following dataless and supervised classification methods have been selected as baselines:

Dataless ESA and Dataless Word2Vec: As described in Sect. 2, the dataless approaches do not require any labeled data or training phase, therefore, they can be considered as the most similar approaches to KBSTC. Two variants of the state-of-the-art dataless approach [14] are considered as baselines, which are based on ESA [3] and Word2Vec [9], respectively.

NB, SVM, LR: Additional baselines include the traditional supervised classifiers, i.e., Naive Bayes (NB), Support Vector Machine (SVM) and Logistic Regression (LR), with the features calculated based on the term frequency and the inverse document frequency (TF-IDF).

6   Intermediate Results

This section provides experimental results as well as a comparison to existing state-of-the-art approaches.

6.1   Evaluation of KBSTC

Table 2 shows the accuracy of the proposed probabilistic KBSTC approach based on our entity and category embedding model in comparison to the baselines on the AG and Snippets datasets.

It is observed that the KBSTC approach considerably outperforms the dataless classification approaches. While Dataless ESA and Dataless Word2Vec have been assessed with longer news articles and achieved promising results in [14], they cannot perform well with short text due to the data sparsity problem.

Remarkably, KBSTC performs better than all the baselines on the Snippets dataset, however, all supervised approaches outperform KBSTC on the AG dataset. The reason here can be attributed to the different characteristics of the two datasets. AG is a larger dataset with more training samples in comparison

Table 3. The classification accuracy of KBSTC with different embedding models (%)

Model	AG (title)	AG (title+description)	Snippets
KBSTC+HCE	67.0	79.6	**72.3**
KBSTC+DeepWalk	57.1	74.2	64.3
KBSTC+RDF2Vec	62.7	77.5	68.2
KBSTC+Our Embedding	**67.9**	**80.5**	72.0

to Snippets. Moreover, the AG dataset provides only 4 different categories in comparison to 8 categories of the Snippets dataset. Those differences might be the reason of the significant decrease in accuracy for the supervised approaches on the Snippets dataset in comparison to the AG dataset. This could be an indicator that the size of the training data and the number of classes make a real impact on the classification accuracy for the supervised approaches. Since KBSTC does not require or use any labeled data, the number of the available training samples has no impact on its accuracy.

Regarding the results of KBSTC, the AG (title+description) dataset yields better accuracy than the Snippets dataset, which in turn, results in better accuracy than the AG (title) dataset. The reason might be found in the nature of the datasets. As shown in Table 1, the average number of entities per text in AG (title+description) is greater than Snippets, followed by AG (title). Often a richer context with more entities can make the categorization more accurate.

Overall, the results in Table 2 have demonstrated that for short text categorization, KBSTC achieves a high accuracy without requiring any labeled data, a time-consuming training phase, or a cumbersome parameter tuning step.

6.2   Evaluation of Entity and Category Embedding

To assess the quality of the proposed entity and category embedding model, we compared it with HCE [7], DeepWalk [11] and RDF2Vec [13] in the context of the KBSTC task.

While the Wikipedia entity and category embeddings generated by HCE can be directly used, DeepWalk has been applied on the network constructed using Wikipedia and RDF2Vec has been applied on the RDF graph of DBpedia to obtain the needed embeddings. Then, these embeddings are integrated into KBSTC to compute the entity-category relatedness. The results of KBSTC with different embedding models are shown in Table 3. The proposed entity and category embedding model outperforms all other embedding models for the KBSTC task on the AG dataset, while HCE performs slightly better than our model on the Snippets dataset.

As HCE is a more specific embedding model that has been designed to learn the representation of entities and their associated categories from Wikipedia, it is not flexible to be adapted to other networks. In contrast, our model can deal with more general networks.

Although DeepWalk and RDF2Vec aim to learn the representation of vertices in general networks and RDF graphs, respectively, they have been either designed for homogeneous networks or treated each type of vertices and edges in a RDF graph equally. The results also indicate that our embedding model enables to capture better semantic representation of vertices by taking into account different types of networks.

7   Conclusions and Lessons Learned

In this thesis, the main goal is to address the labeled data scarcity problem. For this purpose we have proposed a new paradigm for text categorization based on KBs so called KBDTC. Furthermore, a novel KBSTC model which is originated from the proposed paradigm has been presented. The experimental results have proven that it is possible to categorize short text in an unsupervised way with a high accuracy by utilizing a KB. As for future work, we would like to tackle **RQ 3**, **RQ 4**, **RQ 5** and **RQ 6**. In other words, the next research steps includes the extension of KBDTC towards the additional inclusion of words and arbitrary document categorization. Moreover, we intend to utilize KBDTC to generate training set for other supervised classifiers such as deep learning methods.

Acknowledgement. This thesis is supervised by Prof. Harald Sack and Dr. Lei Zhang.

References

1. Chang, M.W., Ratinov, L.A., Roth, D., Srikumar, V.: Importance of semantic representation: dataless classification. In: AAAI (2008)
2. Conneau, A., Schwenk, H., Barrault, L., LeCun, Y.: Very deep convolutional networks for natural language processing. CoRR (2016)
3. Gabrilovich, E., Markovitch, S.: Computing semantic relatedness using Wikipedia-based explicit semantic analysis. In: IJCAI (2007)
4. Kim, Y.: Convolutional neural networks for sentence classification. In: EMNLP (2014)
5. Lee, J.Y., Dernoncourt, F.: Sequential short-text classification with recurrent and convolutional neural networks. In: CoRR (2016)
6. Li, C., Xing, J., Sun, A., Ma, Z.: Effective document labeling with very few seed words: a topic model approach. In: CIKM (2016)
7. Li, Y., Zheng, R., Tian, T., Hu, Z., Iyer, R., Sycara, K.P.: Joint embedding of hierarchical categories and entities for concept categorization and dataless classification. In: COLING (2016)
8. Meng, Y., Shen, J., Zhang, C., Han, J.: Weakly-supervised neural text classification. In: ACM (2018)
9. Mikolov, T., Sutskever, I., Chen, K., Corrado, G.S., Dean, J.: Distributed representations of words and phrases and their compositionality. In: NIPS (2013)
10. Nigam, K., McCallum, A., Thrun, S., Mitchell, T.M.: Text classification from labeled and unlabeled documents using EM. Mach. Learn. **39**, 103–134 (2000)

11. Perozzi, B., Al-Rfou, R., Skiena, S.: Deepwalk: online learning of social representations. In: KDD (2014)
12. Phan, X.H., Nguyen, L.M., Horiguchi, S.: Learning to classify short and sparse text & web with hidden topics from large-scale data collections. In: WWW (2008)
13. Ristoski, P., Paulheim, H.: RDF2Vec: RDF graph embeddings for data mining. In: Groth, P., et al. (eds.) ISWC 2016. LNCS, vol. 9981, pp. 498–514. Springer, Cham (2016). https://doi.org/10.1007/978-3-319-46523-4_30
14. Song, Y., Roth, D.: On dataless hierarchical text classification. In: AAAI (2014)
15. Türker, R., Zhang, L., Koutraki, M., Sack, H.: Knowledge-based short text categorization using entity and category embedding. In: Hitzler, P., et al. (eds.) ESWC 2019. LNCS, vol. 11503, pp. 346–362. Springer, Cham (2019). https://doi.org/10.1007/978-3-030-21348-0_23
16. Wang, C., Song, Y., Li, H., Zhang, M., Han, J.: Text classification with heterogeneous information network kernels. In: AAAI (2016)
17. Wang, J., Wang, Z., Zhang, D., Yan, J.: Combining knowledge with deep convolutional neural networks for short text classification. In: IJCAI (2017)
18. Wang, P., Xu, B., Xu, J., Tian, G., Liu, C.L., Hao, H.: Semantic expansionusing word embedding clustering and convolutional neural network for improving short text classification. Neurocomputing **174**, 806–814 (2016)
19. Xuan, J., Jiang, H., Ren, Z., Yan, J., Luo, Z.: Automatic bug triage using semi-supervised text classification. In: SEKE (2010)
20. Zhang, X., LeCun, Y.: Text understanding from scratch. CoRR (2015)

Methodology for Biomedical Ontology Matching

Jana Vataščinová$^{(\boxtimes)}$ (iD)

University of Economics, nám. W. Churchilla 1938/4, 13067 Prague, Czech Republic
xvatj00@vse.cz

Abstract. This paper introduces a dissertation project in the field of ontology matching. Ontology matching plays an important role in integration of various systems or in connecting data which use different ontologies. One of the domains where different ontologies are used and where large amount of data is being continuously generated is biomedicine. The goal of the dissertation project is to propose a methodology for matching of biomedical ontologies. The existing projects do not address the topic as a whole. The related projects provide a methodology for ontology matching in general or talk about matching of biomedical ontologies (solely receiving a set of mappings). The thesis should define and address this gap. As biomedical ontologies can be quite specific, the need for a methodology for matching of these ontologies arises. To achieve the goal of the dissertation, the analytic steps come first - literature review of the field of matching of biomedical ontologies, use of the current methodologies and evaluation of their efficiency and their limitations, research of characteristics of biomedical ontologies, evaluation of different matching tools, and evaluation of combined results from multiple matching tools. Then, the formulation of the methodology steps will follow. After the formulation of the methodology, it needs to be evaluated. The evaluation should compare results from the matching process which follows the proposed methodology with the result from another methodology. At the end, some results of the analytic steps are drafted and current work to follow is described.

Keywords: Ontology · Ontology matching · Biomedical ontology

1 Motivation

Biomedicine is a domain which plays an important role in our society. Biomedicine is a branch of medical science that applies biological and physiological principles to clinical practice. The branch applies especially to biology and physiology and it can relate to many other categories in health and biological related fields [1]. This domain captures an immense amount of data and new biomedical data is constantly being generated from different studies, experiments, etc. An example of where biomedical data is being used and generated

P. Hitzler et al. (Eds.): ESWC 2019 Satellite Events, LNCS 11762, pp. 242–250, 2019.
https://doi.org/10.1007/978-3-030-32327-1_43

are pharmaceutical companies. Without a good data organization (to which a computer can understand), much of the information can be lost.

Biomedicine is one of the main domains where *ontologies* are used and are of a great importance [2]. Biomedical ontologies are such ontologies which describe part (or whole) of a biomedical domain. The content of many biomedical ontologies overlaps [3]. This points to the need to combine them or to the need of their matching. Ontology matching is the search for identical concepts (connections) in different ontologies. The way a specific part of reality is captured can differ in different designs, therefore, ontologies that belong to the same domain can contain differences. The goal of ontology matching is to determine the similarity of concepts, properties and instances based on their name, structure or logical interpretation [4].

The ontology matching process creates relations between ontologies which can be of a great importance. For example, if an application works with ontology A, it can address data described by ontology B using the correspondences (mappings) between ontology A and ontology B. Biomedical ontologies and their matching can be a challenging task. In biomedicine, concepts can have many synonyms or their meaning can be artificially bordered. Identical concepts can have different names in different ontologies, and the other way around, concepts with corresponding names can have different meanings. The meaning of two concepts from different ontologies can partially correspond, etc.

A practical application can be as follows. There is a pharmaceutical company that has its own laboratories where different studies with drugs are carried out. To describe the data from the studies, the company uses its own ontology. There is a public platform for biomedical data and experiments with their results which uses different ontologies. It is of interest for the company to compare these results with their own results. This can mean comparing the given drug's results in the public experiments and in the internal studies. This would be achieved by query rewriting with the use of ontology alignment.

The question is, *how to carry out the matching process? Which ontology matching algorithm should be applied? Do I need to apply solely one? How to apply the algorithms efficiently?* When pharmaceutical companies start using ontologies, these ontologies can be created by their automatic generation from, for example, Excel sheets. Such ontologies can contain inconsistencies and might not follow best practices. These ontologies are likely to be replaced by new ontologies in the future and therefore, the ontology matching process needs to be repeatable. So, *overall, what strategy should be adopted to match ontologies for biomedicine?*

The goal of the dissertation project is to address why the current methodologies are insufficient and should be extended, and to propose a methodology for biomedical ontology matching.

2   State of the Art

There are many ways how the ontology matching task can be carried out (manual, automatic), many tools have been developed for the subject area (ten tools participated in the Large Biomedical Ontologies track of OAEI 2018 - see further in this Section) and even a general methodology has been proposed. However, we are not aware of any methodologies for biomedical ontology matching specifically. And yet, this area carries a great importance and a great need for data processing.

Considering the topic of matching of biomedical ontologies, there are some main sources to be followed. In the first source, there is a methodology for ontology matching proposed. The other sources are projects which contain matching of biomedical ontologies.

The first resource is the *methodology for ontology matching* by Jérôme Euzenat and Pavel Schvaiko [5]. The methodology consists of eight steps:

1. define the characteristics of the concrete problem to solve,
2. find if available and suitable alignments exist for the given problem,
3. select or build a matcher if necessary,
4. run the matcher,
5. evaluate the obtained alignment,
6. improve it by reiterating the matching process,
7. document and share the satisfying alignment,
8. process the alignment via a generator suitable for the given application task.

These steps are defined in a very general way and do not provide more details for how to execute the steps for a given use case. To complement this methodology, another description of the methodology by Euzenat can be found in [13].

The second main resource are the *OAEI*[1] (Ontology Alignment Evaluation Initiative) campaigns and the reports from their events, such as [6]. OAEI is an international initiative for organizing evaluations of ontology matching systems, which has been active since 2004. It includes biomedical ontology-oriented tracks, which provide a valuable resource for matching of biomedical resources, especially in finding suitable matching systems. The tracks that are of interest are the *Large Biomedical Ontologies* track, then the *Anatomy* track and the *Disease and Phenotype* track [6].

The third main resource is the paper *Tackling the challenges of matching biomedical ontologies* by Faria et al. [7]. The authors describe strategies employed by matching systems to tackle the challenges of matching biomedical ontologies and measures the impact of the challenges themselves on matching performance. The paper addresses the large size of the biomedical ontologies, the biomedical domain and its rich and complex vocabulary, or the different modeling views on the domain which can lead to the mappings to be logically irreconcilable due to conflicting restrictions.

Considering methodologies for matching of biomedical ontologies, there are some articles which introduce different biomedical ontology matching methods which they address as methodologies. However, these methods only provide a way how to obtain a set of mappings, which would correspond to one step of the overall methodology. [8] introduces a method for mapping for life science linked

---

[1] http://oaei.ontologymatching.org/.

data using the mappings from BioPortal[2]. Another method for ontology matching is described in [9], where mappings are obtained from human contributions.

Other resources for the subject area are projects describing specific matching tools [10,11] (these are some of the tools that successfully participated in the OAEI Large Biomedical Ontologies track), technologies or projects [12] (project for biomedical data collecting).

3 Problem Statement and Contributions

The main goal of my dissertation is to propose an efficient methodology for matching of biomedical ontologies. This methodology should include the whole process of ontology matching, starting with identifying ontologies and characterizing needs and ending with the alignments' implementation. The methodology will be based on the already existing methodology for ontology matching (see [5,13]), and it will be specialized for matching of biomedical ontologies (reflecting their needs and characteristics).

The methodology for ontology matching by Euzenat and colleagues [5,13] proposes only a general overview of the ontology matching process. Biomedical ontologies can be very specific and for their efficient matching, a more detailed methodology should be provided. Methodology for biomedical ontology matching should capture the common problems and characteristics for each step of the matching process. In this way, all the important steps should be taken into consideration when carrying out an biomedical ontology matching process.

The main questions that need to be solved are:

- *Why are general methodologies for ontology matching insufficient for biomedical ontology matching?*
- *What are the characteristics of biomedical ontologies and how do they influence the ontology matching process?*
- *Which tools and other techniques are suitable for biomedical ontology matching - how to choose a suitable tool? How to combine them?*

Biomedical ontologies can be quite specific with their representation and biomedical terms can have unique relations and characteristics. These characteristics can play a crucial role in the ontology matching process. For example, they can influence the choice of matching tools that will be used.

The methodology should be a guideline for anyone who uses biomedical ontologies and for whom it is of interest to carry out biomedical ontology matching. An example can be pharmaceutical companies which use their own internal ontologies. By matching these ontologies with public ontologies, they can access relevant public data which can enrich the knowledge the companies have. It can also be common that the internal ontologies were created by automatically generating them from, for example, Excel sheets. Such ontologies are likely to be limited and not following best practices. This can mean that they would need to be replaced by new ontologies and the process of their matching will need to be repeated.

---

[2] https://bioportal.bioontology.org/.

4   Research Methodology and Approach

There are three main premises that the dissertation will be built on:

1. General methodology for ontology matching is not sufficient - there is a need for a specialized methodology for matching of biomedical ontologies.
2. Biomedical ontologies have common characteristics which influence the process of their matching.
3. For biomedical ontology matching, only tools with specific characteristics are suitable.

As the artifact of the dissertation will be a methodology, design research will be used to achieve the goal of the dissertation. Other methods will be used to support achieving the goal. These methods will be:

– literature review of the field of matching of biomedical ontologies,
– use of the current methodologies and evaluation of their efficiency and their limitations,
– research of characteristics of biomedical ontologies,
– evaluation of different matching tools, and evaluation of combined results from multiple matching tools,
– methodology development,
– methodology evaluation.

Regarding the literature review, the goal is to gather all available information about matching of biomedical ontologies, about methodologies for ontology matching in general, and about biomedical ontologies. It is necessary to note all the known challenges and obstacles, as well as the solutions and best practices. This knowledge should then be applied specifically to the matching of biomedical ontologies in cases when it applies to ontology matching in general or to biomedical ontologies.

The use of the current methodologies and their evaluation should result in the analysis of their limitation, which should be further addressed.

In order to obtain characteristics of biomedical ontologies, the first step is to get an overview of all the biomedical ontologies that are available and to select those that are the most 'important' (for example, those that are widely used or those representing more specific domains). For this purpose, the repository of biomedical ontologies BioPortal and Ontology Lookup Service[3] will be used. These ontologies are then to be reviewed with the goal of registering their potential characteristics. In order to receive statistically comparable characteristics, Online Ontology Set Picker[4] (OOSP) tool for obtaining statistics for ontologies may be used. The characteristics obtained are then, again, to be applied in relation to the matching process.

For the part of evaluation of different matching tools, the OAEI campaigns will be used as the main source. Specifically, the tracks which consider biomedical

---

[3] https://www.ebi.ac.uk/ols/index.
[4] https://owl.vse.cz/OOSP/.

ontologies - mainly the Large Biomedical Ontologies track. Other tracks might be the Anatomy track and the Disease and Phenotype track. These tracks provide a summary of results of different ontology matching tools received for given pairs of ontologies. Thus, different ontology matching tools can be compared based on their results. All retrieved results of each tool will be examined with the goal of finding regularity. For example, *does one tool always reliably find mappings of some kind? If one tool finds mappings that none of the other tools found, are those mapping characteristic in some way? Those mapping that a tool returned that are not correct, is there any common characteristic of such mappings - or in other words, in what kind of cases is the tool making mistakes?* In case any common characteristics are found for the tools, these findings can be applied to improve the ontology matching process. Another step to be done is to analyze the mappings in the reference alignment which were not found by any of the tools. Results should then be used for improving the tools so that these matches will be found. Given the characteristics of the purpose of the ontology matching process and of the biomedical ontologies that are to be matched, suitable tools can be chosen or combined.

After gathering all the information from the analysis above, the design of the methodology will follow. Here, the steps of the methodology will be proposed. These steps should be based on the general methodology for ontology matching introduced in the State of the Art Section, where the individual steps should be described in greater detail.

5   Evaluation Plan

The proposed methodology for biomedical ontology matching should be evaluated in the following ways. When carrying out a process of biomedical matching, the process should provide better results when following the biomedical ontology matching methodology compared to when it follows a methodology for ontology matching that is not specifically created for matching of biomedical ontologies. The results can be presented to domain experts for evaluation.

For evaluating the analytic findings that should be used for the methodology forming, the existence of reference alignment is quite desirable due to the large size of the biomedical ontologies. Such an opportunity is provided by the existing challenges reflected by biomedical tracks within OAEI campaigns. These tracks provide reference alignments for evaluating the mappings returned by the tools.

This part should help with the evaluation of the correctness of the obtained alignment. However, the process of matching of biomedical ontologies should not end here. The process of the matching end with the final implementation of the alignment and its final use. The usability and effectiveness of the implemented alignment needs to be evaluated as well with regard to the purpose of the ontology matching process - with regard to the specific use case. For example, it might not be desirable for all the matching processes to consider only those mappings that are logically compatible.

6   Preliminary Results

As the dissertation is still in a very early stage, only some suggestions can be presented so far. These are some basic characteristics of biomedical ontologies (observed without using any tools yet), a connection between the purpose of the ontology matching process and the approach to receiving a set of mappings, and some observations from an (ongoing) analysis of the results of the Large Biomedical track of the OAEI campaigns 2018[5].

6.1   Biomedical Ontologies' Characteristics

As already mentioned, one of the important characteristics of biomedical ontologies is undeniably their large size. In many cases, there can be tens or hundreds of thousand classes solely. This aspect plays an essential role in deciding between manual or automatic ontology matching - considering such size, it is impossible to use manual matching. In case of many mappings found by automatic matching, it might not be possible to even review the proposed mappings. It is, therefore, necessary to choose a reliable tool for automatic ontology matching and to know the risks we might choose to accept.

Another characteristic of biomedical ontologies is the naming of the concepts. In the biomedical ontologies, it is common to use different codes as the concepts' names. Therefore, it is necessary to work with the concepts' labels in the matching task. For example, one of the National Cancer Institute Thesaurus[6] (NCIt) concepts is ncit:C16403 and its label is "Cell Line". In the Semanticscience Integrated Ontology[7] (SIO), the concept with the same label is sio:010054.

In many cases, biomedical ontologies are also represented rather as taxonomies. Looking at the Large Biomedical Ontologies track of the OAEI campaigns, all three of the used ontologies have a taxonomic character (one of them being NCIT). In many cases, they do not define many properties. For example, NCIT defines 145,810 classes and only 97 properties. The hierarchical assignment for biomedical term is often artificial and not clear, thus it can be very different in various ontologies. The ontology matching tools are therefore left with mainly lexical matching.

6.2   OAEI Large Biomedical Track 2018

The Large Biomedical track from the OAEI campaigns poses the tasks of matching three large biomedical ontologies (of hundreds of thousand classes). As seen from the results (those evaluated so far), the mappings were created largely based on the names of the concept containing the same word or synonyms. This corresponds with the fact that the selected ontologies have taxonomy characters with differently constructed hierarchies. These ontologies also have very few properties compared to their size (all having less than 200 properties).

---

[5] http://oaei.ontologymatching.org/2018/.

[6] https://cbiit.cancer.gov/ncip/biomedical-informatics-resources/interoperability-and-semantics/terminology/.

[7] http://sio.semanticscience.org/.

6.3   Purpose of the Matching of Biomedical Ontologies

One of the important aspects that should not be forgotten is the purpose of the process of matching of biomedical ontologies. The purpose should be clear and it should be among the first questions to be decided.

The purpose shall be reflected in the selection of automatic matching tool. For example, *is it desirable to use a tool which excludes mappings with a logical incoherence?* Next, looking back at an example of biomedical ontology use case in Sect. 1, the task of the matching process was query rewriting - seeing the given drug's results in the public experiments and in the internal studies. In this case, the goal is to find the corresponding drug without the need of the two classes from different ontologies to be logically interchangeable.

7   Conclusions

Creating a methodology for biomedical ontology matching is a challenging task. It should be of use to those workplaces where biomedical ontology matching is needed and where it can enable data sharing, data retrieval, etc.

The immediate work to follow inside the analysis of the OAEI Large Biomedical track is to analyze the mappings in the reference alignment which were not found by any of the tools or to analyze the mappings discovered by the tools that were not included in the reference mappings. Both tasks also point to the need to investigate the source of the reference alignment and its reliability. Looking at the mappings discovered by the tools that were not included in the reference mappings so far, most of the mapping included the same word or its synonym, but not in the equivalent meaning. However, some mappings that appear to be correct that were not included in the reference mappings were found as well (having identical name or different names with the same meaning).

Acknowledgement. The research has been partially supported by IGA VSE 33/2019. Additionally, I would like to thank my PhD supervisor Vojtěch Svátek, my PhD adviser Ondřej Zamazal and all the ESWC 2019 reviewers for their valuable comments and feedback.

References

1. Biomedicine. http://www.memidex.com/biomedicine. Accessed 10 Feb 2019
2. Rubin, D.L., Shah, N.H., Noy, N.F.: Biomedical ontologies: a functional perspective. Briefings Bioinf. **9**(1), 75–90 (2008)
3. Gross, A., Hartung, M., Kirsten, T., Rahm, E.: Mapping composition for matching large life science ontologies. In: Proceedings of the Second International Conference on Biomedical Ontology, pp. 109–116, Buffalo, NY (2011)
4. Staab, S., Studer, R.: Handbook on Ontologies, 2nd edn. Springer, Berlin (2009). https://doi.org/10.1007/978-3-540-92673-3
5. Euzenat, J., Schvaiko, P.: Ontology Matching, 2nd edn. Springer, Berlin (2013)

6. Algergawy, A., Cheatham, M., Faria, D., et al.: Results of the ontology alignment evaluation initiative 2018. In: Ontology Matching OM2018, pp. 76–116. CEUR-WS, Cáchy (2018)
7. Faria, D., Pesquita, C., Mott, I., Martins, C., Couto, F.M.: Tackling the challenges of matching biomedical ontologies. J. Biomed. Semant. 9(1), 4 (2018)
8. Zaveri, A., Dumontier, M.: Ontology mapping for life science linked data. In: Proceedings of the First International Workshop on Biomedical Data Integration and Discovery. CEUR-WS, Japan (2016)
9. Sarasua, C., Simperl, E., Noy, N.F.: CROWDMAP: crowdsourcing ontology alignment with microtasks. In: Cudré-Mauroux, P., et al. (eds.) ISWC 2012. LNCS, vol. 7649, pp. 525–541. Springer, Heidelberg (2012). https://doi.org/10.1007/978-3-642-35176-1_33
10. Jiménez-Ruiz, E., Grau, B.C., Zhou, Y., Horrocks, I.: Large-scale interactive ontology matching: algorithms and implementation. In: Proceedings of the 20th European Conference on Artificial Intelligence, pp. 444–449 (2012)
11. Faria, D., Pesquita, C., Santos, E., Palmonari, M., Cruz, I.F., Couto, F.M.: The agreementmakerlight ontology matching system. In: Meersman, R., et al. (eds.) OTM 2013. LNCS, vol. 8185, pp. 527–541. Springer, Heidelberg (2013). https://doi.org/10.1007/978-3-642-41030-7_38
12. PubChem., http://pubchemdocs.ncbi.nlm.nih.gov/rdf. Accessed 10 Feb 2019
13. Euzenat, J., Le Duc, C.: Methodological guidelines for matching ontologies. In: Suárez-Figueroa, M.C., Gómez-Pérez, A., Motta, E., Gangemi, A. (eds.) Ontology Engineering in a Networked World, pp. 257–278. Springer, Heidelberg (2012). https://doi.org/10.1007/978-3-642-24794-1_12

Industry Track

Challenges of Constructing a Railway Knowledge Graph

Stefan Bischof[(⊠)] and Gottfried Schenner

Siemens AG Österreich, Corporate Technology, Vienna, Austria
{bischof.stefan,gottfried.schenner}@siemens.com

1 Introduction

International railway networks are an important means for passenger and freight transport. Railway software systems often must be supported and maintained for decades. Different systems cover different aspects such as train protection, signalling, infrastructure hardware and software. Usage of different standards and regulations, both international (e.g., European Train Control System) and national, for these aspects leads to a large number of incompatible systems.

A wide variety of use cases would profit from a network-wide unified/integrated access to the available different (legacy) tools and databases. Starting with asset management, topological queries, or checking consistency an integrated data access system, i.e., a knowledge graph (KG), could also be used as a basis for ensuring network-wide compliance with (safety) regulations, operational use cases like planning for maintenance or train scheduling. Furthermore the KG could be a precious resource for data analytics use cases.

Applying standard information integration approaches is not feasible because of the complexity of the data sources. This complexity is aggravated by the fact that the (engineering) tools are permanently under development and several versions of one tool are usually in production in parallel. So the integration itself must also be an ongoing process. To avoid big upfront cost we thus aim for an agile process to iteratively integrate the data as needed by new use cases.

Considering the necessary flexibility and the network nature of railway systems we chose a graph based formalism. To ensure long-term support of our solution, we rely on standardised technologies as much as possible. Our approach is to integrate data from different tools in a KG (see Fig. 1) under a common domain model (ontology), ideally based on an existing industry standard. The tool schemata as well as the instance data are transformed to graphs.

Individual tool data models are mapped to the common ontology as far as necessary and feasible. Lightweight ontology mapping is performed by custom SPARQL Update queries. Instance data is represented in terms of the common domain model by physical transformation or virtual integration. Instance linking is implemented by SPARQL Update queries.

With the resulting KG it is possible to access the integrated data using the common data model as well as the data remaining only in the context of specific (legacy) tools. This architecture enables an agile and iterative integration process where we can integrate data as the need arises.

© Springer Nature Switzerland AG 2019
P. Hitzler et al. (Eds.): ESWC 2019 Satellite Events, LNCS 11762, pp. 253–256, 2019.
https://doi.org/10.1007/978-3-030-32327-1_44

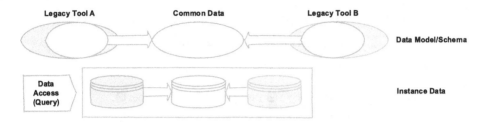

Fig. 1. Integration architecture

2   Challenges

When applying our approach on the railway domain we encountered several challenges. Most of the challenges stem from the characteristics of technical systems. Engineering tools often use data models that are highly specialised. Therefore an ontology derived from these data models reflect the system view of the tool, e.g., a tool for hardware configuration will have a total different view of the infrastructure than a tool used for train scheduling. In an industrial KG the correctness and consistency of instance data is of uttermost importance, as faults in the data could lead to accidents. We identified the following main challenges during the construction of our railway KG.

2.1   Lack of Existing Standard Railway Ontologies

To maximise interoperability and possible long-term support of our common domain model, a railway ontology based on an international standard would be preferable. The existing ontologies, mainly being developed in research projects, are usually not openly available and more importantly not built for reuse.

The best candidate for an internationally standardised railway domain model seems to be the RailML XML Schema specifications. We map the relevant type definitions to an ontology which we then use as common domain model in our architecture. Because of the impedance mismatch between XML and RDF as well as the unsatisfying state of automatic mapping tools, the mapping process is a cumbersome and error-prone task.

2.2   Ontology Alignment

Ontologies derived from technical tools are highly use case specific. In contrast to ontologies for biological systems the number of concepts is usually relatively small but the number of data and object properties is much higher. Automatic ontology alignment is infeasible due to different domains (e.g., hardware, software, communication), different levels of granularity, differences in the modelling approaches, and language (German/English).

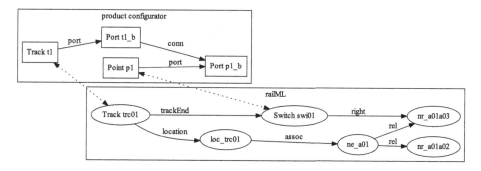

Fig. 2. Example matching of railway switch.

2.3   Complex Instance Matching

Instance matching requires a detailed knowledge of the underlying ontologies. Figure 2 shows the matching of instance data from two different ontologies. The example consists of a railway track that is connected to the right branch of a railway switch. Although there exists a 1-1 mapping (dotted-arrow) between the high level concepts, the determination of the topology of the instances is complex. In the ontology of the legacy tool (in this case a product configurator) the right branch is by convention port "b" of the switch element, whereas in the railML ontology the right branch is defined by linking the switch to the micro topology view of railML. These complex matchings are out of the scope of standard matching tools [3].

2.4   Open and Closed World Reasoning

Technical systems often require to switch between closed and open world reasoning. For example a configurator for interlocking systems will apply closed world reasoning to configure one specific interlocking system. Sometimes partial information of neighbouring interlocking systems is required. These are not completely represented and therefore open world reasoning is applied. The challenge for a KG based system is to apply the right techniques depending on the required reasoning.

2.5   Brownfield Software Development

Brownfield (software) development describes the further development of software in the presence of an existing legacy tool landscape. The challenge is to gradually improve the system while keeping the overall system working. If a KG is introduced into the tool landscape we can not expect that all tools are adapting their knowledge representation accordingly.

The overall management of a railway system involves a lot of different tools. The characteristics of these tools (knowledge representation, programming language, database, data exchange) often reflect the state-of-the-art at the time of their creation. The programming languages range from shell scripts, imperative, object-oriented programming languages to the web-based frameworks currently en vogue. Data exchange between tools is often realised on a tool to tool basis with a proprietary interface definition. Only recently standards like RailML have been defined to facilitate a standardised way of data exchange [1].

When introducing a KG as a first step it is sufficient to extract as much information as possible from the existing data sources and store it similar to a data warehouse approach. This way the consistency of the data can be checked in a unified manner, data analytic tasks are easier and formal reasoning about the properties of the overall system is made possible [2].

The most challenging task, but in our view also the main benefit of a KG, would be to gradually replace legacy tools with tools that operate on the KG, and in this process reduce redundancies in the data. This would also require the tools to reverse the direction of information flow. Instead of extracting information from the tools for the KG the tools should use the KG to persist their data.

3   Conclusions

The use of graph-based formalisms promises great potential when data from several heterogeneous systems of the same domain should be integrated. Currently we are using the system with data provided from product configurators to answer customer queries which were previously either infeasible or at least involved a lot of manual work. Nevertheless we identified several challenges when implementing a flexible integration architecture with graphs. Unfortunately major efforts will be necessary to fully address these challenges.

For the future we hope that graph based data integration architectures can enable us to practically exploit the potential distributed and hidden in our tools and databases. Particularly lifecycle management (ALM, PLM) could benefit from such a KG derived from engineering data. For an upcoming asset management use case we leverage the KG as a data source. Furthermore, by minimising data redundancy we expect to reduce inconsistencies between different tools and aim to streamline engineering processes.

References

1. Bosschaart, M., Quaglietta, E., Janssen, B., Goverde, R.M.: Efficient formalization of railway interlocking data in RailML. Inf. Syst. **49**, 126–141 (2015). https://doi.org/10.1016/j.is.2014.11.007
2. Luteberget, B., Johansen, C., Steffen, M.: Rule-based consistency checking of railway infrastructure designs. In: Ábrahám, E., Huisman, M. (eds.) IFM 2016. LNCS, vol. 9681, pp. 491–507. Springer, Cham (2016). https://doi.org/10.1007/978-3-319-33693-0_31
3. Schenner, G., Bischof, S., Polleres, A., Steyskal, S.: Integrating distributed configurations with RDFS and SPARQL. In: Configuration Workshop, pp. 9–15 (2014). http://ceur-ws.org/Vol-1220/02_confws2014_submission_3.pdf

NOVA: A Knowledge Base for the Node-RED IoT Ecosystem

Arne Bröring[1]($\boxtimes$), Victor Charpenay[2], Darko Anicic[1], and Sebastien Püech[1]

[1] Siemens AG — Corporate Technology, Munich, Germany
arne.broering@siemens.com
[2] Friedrich-Alexander-Universität, Erlangen/Nürnberg, Erlangen, Germany

Abstract. Node-RED is comprised of a large ecosystem of nodes for IoT devices and services that makes it a powerful tool for IoT application development. In order to facilitate the usage of this heterogeneous ecosystem in industrial settings, we present here the NOde-red library eVAluation (NOVA) approach for gathering the relevant metadata in a knowledge base and first analyses of the data.

1 A Knowledge Base for Node-RED

Today, Node-RED's catalog comprises over 3.000 nodes and flows. A *node* implementation can be seen as an adapter of a device or service that makes their functionality available in the Node-RED ecosystem. Using the Node-RED graphical user interface, nodes can then be combined in so-called *flows*. A flow, which can also comprise sub-flows, represents an IoT application [1]. Node-RED's catalog contains nodes for IoT platforms and devices (e.g., Xively or Raspberry Pi), Web services (e.g., Twitter), smart home products (e.g., Philips Hue or Amazon Alexa), industrial automation (e.g., Siemens S7, OPC UA, or ModBus) or analytics and machine learning (e.g., IBM Watson).

The easy usage of the Node-RED UI to mash-up IoT applications in combination with the rich ecosystem makes Node-RED valuable for industrial enterprises and their customers. However, descriptions of nodes and flows are currently not accessible as a structured metadata. This hinders discovery, and does not allow filtering based on the quality rating or licensing information. More importantly metadata, containing explicit links from flows to contained nodes, does not exist at all. All these shortcomings hamper the usage of Node-RED nodes and flows in industrial settings.

In order to address these challenges, we have developed the NOde-red library eVAluation (NOVA) approach[1], which automatically collects large amounts of metadata to feed a knowledge base for further analyses.

At its centre, NOVA comprises a Web crawler that harvests available metadata about nodes and flows, and stores them in a triple store. This is how

---

[1] http://nova.iot-app.siemens.cloud.

P. Hitzler et al. (Eds.): ESWC 2019 Satellite Events, LNCS 11762, pp. 257–261, 2019.
https://doi.org/10.1007/978-3-030-32327-1_45

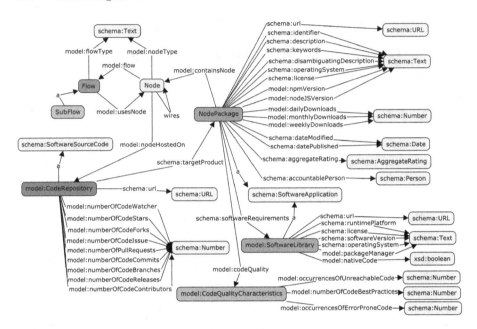

Fig. 1. RDF model of the NOVA knowledge base.

the NOVA knowledge base is created. The process works similarly to DBPedia's extraction manager [3]. Figure 1 shows our RDF model, which is based on schema.org [2]. While typical crawler approaches for the IoT (e.g. [4]) focus on harvesting sensor data from public IoT platforms, we address here the collection of metadata for IoT device adapters and application workflows.

The entry point for our crawler is the Node-RED catalog[2], from which a descriptive Web page for each node package can be found. For example, on the page of the node that connects Particle devices[3], a list of contained nodes can be found, as well as general metadata (e.g., version, rating, keywords, or maintainers). This metadata is stored in the class *NodePackage*. The crawler follows links to listed Web resources: (1) the NPM repository and (2) the GitHub project, and harvests further metadata from these pages.

Using NPM, the crawler downloads the software package and installs it locally. Thereby, all dependent libraries of the node package are downloaded, and their metadata is stored using the *SoftwareLibrary* class. This includes information on license and version, and gives a hint whether the native code is included. This report is relevant for the choice of execution environment. Using GitHub's REST API, the crawler gathers all available metadata regarding the source code (e.g., quality rating and number of commits), and stores this information in the *CodeRepository* class. Additionally, the source code itself is downloaded by the

---

[2] https://flows.nodered.org.
[3] https://flows.nodered.org/node/node-red-contrib-particle.

crawler and an automated analysis is triggered using PMD[4]. This static source code analyzer detects unreachable code, broken best practices, and error prone code. The number of each kind of incident is stored in the *CodeQualityCharacteristics* class.

Finally, all flows are accessed via the Node-RED catalog and their metadata is stored in the *Flow* class. Each flow references multiple nodes that make up its structure. Thereby, a node that is part of a flow specifies, via the *wires* property, to which other nodes its outputs are connected.

2   Data Analyses

The crawling described above runs for several hours and produces currently around 650.000 triples. Using SPARQL, we analyzed the resulting knowledge base. As a starting point, we counted node packages (1.593) and their (directly and transitively) dependent libraries (4,482). In order to make these usable in commercial settings, a license clearing is required. With the installation of the NPM package (Sect. 1), we gathered those license-related data. In the post-processing, we took the SPDX license list as a reference[5] and cleaned the license names by ignoring case, spaces and '-' characters. Thereby, 105 out of overall 128 licenses match an SPDX license. The most used license is MIT (41.528), followed by ISC (7897) and Apache 2.0 (4140). The long tail of licenses (113) have less than 10 occurrences. Now, having the license metadata available enables us to automatically check the license compatibility for a specific node package.

Next, we address a known issue with the Node-RED specification of flows: when a flow refers to some node, reference is not done by node package identifier but simply by name of the node type. Consequently, it can be difficult for the user to find the correct node package, which is required to run a desired flow. This is an even more pressing issue, as the name of the node type can be ambiguous. In the overall 984 flows, we found 20.311 node references to the 5.010 nodes that are available in the 1.593 node packages. From these node references, 8.112 are ambiguous and coming from 90 different node packages. For instance, in a flow[6] implementing smart metering on a Raspberry Pi, the listed "server" node is ambiguous, as it is used in 2 node packages. In order to reuse this flow, a user would have to manually determine the correct node package.

---

[4] https://pmd.github.io/pmd-6.12.0/pmd_rules_ecmascript.html.

[5] https://spdx.org/licenses/.

[6] https://flows.nodered.org/flow/ecd2b4f8af1b218df41258adb019184e.

```
CONSTRUCT {
    ?flowNode schema:sameAs ?node .
} WHERE {
    ?node a model:Node ;
        model:nodeType ?type .
    FILTER NOT EXISTS {
        ?other a model:Node ;
        model:nodeType ?type .
        FILTER (?node != ?other)
    }
    ?flow a model:Flow ;
        model:usesNode ?flowNode .
    ?flowNode model:nodeType ?type
}
```

```
CONSTRUCT {
    ?ambiguous schema:sameAs ?other .
} WHERE {
    ?flow a model:Flow ;
        model:usesNode ?ambiguous , ?unambiguous.
    ?ambiguous model:nodeType ?typeAmbiguous .
    FILTER NOT EXISTS {
        ?ambiguous schema:sameAs ?node .
    }
    ?unambiguous schema:sameAs ?node .
    ?node model:nodeHostedOn ?repo .
    ?other model:nodeType ?typeAmbiguous ;
        model:nodeHostedOn ?repo .
}
```

Listing 1.1. Unambiguous refs. **Listing 1.2.** Refs. from the same repository

We address this issue by disambiguating nodes in flows. Listing 1.1 links nodes packages to node references in flows, if they are unambiguous (i.e. if flows refer to a unique node type value). The query in Listing 1.2 builds upon it and attempts to resolve ambiguity by looking at ambiguous and unambiguous nodes from the same repository (or node package) used in the same flow. Rationale: nodes of the same package tend to be used together. 311 flows could be disambiguated this way (out of 984). In the dataset, 120 nodes with a valid repository URL are ambiguous, 75 of them are used in at least one flow.

3   Conclusions and Future Work

We present the NOVA approach, and showcase e.g. the automated license clearing that can be extended similarly to [5], by checking composite license characteristics for compatibility with the planned usage of a node. Second, we addressed the issue of missing links from flows to contained nodes. In fact, the name of listed nodes can be ambiguous. Using SPARQL, we show a two-fold querying process that addresses this issue and solves ambiguity for many nodes.

The possibilities for future use and research on the created knowledge base are broad. Automated quality checks or indexes can be developed based on different input parameters from the NOVA model. This indicates to the users if a component can be utilized or not. Discovery could be improved too. This can be achieved by semantically annotating nodes and flows with categories, or transforming their keywords into links to well-defined terms. This way, links to a more general knowledge base, such as wikidata, could be built up.

Acknowledgement. This work has been supported through the project SEMIoTICS funded by the European Union H2020 programme under grant agreement No. 780315.

References

1. Giang, N.K., Blackstock, M., Lea, R., Leung, V.C.: Developing IoT applications in the fog: a distributed dataflow approach. In: 2015 5th International Conference on the Internet of Things (IOT), pp. 155–162. IEEE (2015)
2. Guha, R.V., Brickley, D., Macbeth, S.: Schema.org: evolution of structured data on the web. Commun. ACM **59**(2), 44–51 (2016)

3. Lehmann, J., et al.: Dbpedia-a large-scale, multilingual knowledge base extracted from wikipedia. Semant. Web **6**(2), 167–195 (2015)
4. Shemshadi, A., Sheng, Q.Z., Qin, Y.: Thingseek: a crawler and search engine for the internet of things. In: Proceedings of the 39th International ACM SIGIR Conference on Research and Development in Information Retrieval, pp. 1149–1152. ACM (2016)
5. Villata, S., Gandon, F.: Licenses compatibility and composition in the web of data. In: Third International Workshop on Consuming Linked Data (COLD 2012) (2012)

Using Knowledge Graphs to Search
an Enterprise Data Lake

Stefan Schmid[1]([⊠]), Cory Henson[2], and Tuan Tran[3]

[1] Corporate Research, Robert Bosch GmbH, Renningen, Germany
stefan.schmid@de.bosch.com
[2] Corporate Research, Robert Bosch GmbH, Pittsburgh, USA
cory.henson@us.bosch.com
[3] Chassis Systems Control, Robert Bosch GmbH, Abstatt, Germany
anhtuan.tran2@de.bosch.com

Abstract. This paper summarizes our research & development activities in building a semantic data management platform for large enterprise data lakes, with a focus on the automotive domain. We demonstrate the use of ontology models to systematically represent, link, and search large amounts of automotive data. Such search capability is an important enabler for Hadoop-based big data analytics and machine learning. These findings are being transferred to a productive system in order to foster the advanced engineering and AI at Bosch Chassis Systems Control (CC), especially in the automated driving area.

Keywords: Semantic data management · Ontologies · Semantic search · Big data

1 Background

In Bosch Chassis Systems Control (CC), we develop innovative systems and components to ensure the agility, comfort, function and safety of vehicles and driver assistance systems. Our portfolio ranges from classical safety products such as airbag or ESP (Electronic Stability Control) to next-generation automated driving systems, and holistic automotive software architecture. The data generated both in development and service supplying phases have been quickly accumulated in the past few years. To handle such big volume, we resort to building a number of big data storages, connected with an on premise Hadoop cluster to enable efficient computation. These data stores expose a high level of complexity and diversity, including different formats and contents (sensor data, video data, radar/LIDAR data, textual, etc.), different projects (R&D vs. productive projects, different customer platforms and systems, etc.). To handle this complexity and volume, at CC we have developed a holistic architecture for managing our data – the **CC Data Lake**. The data lake architecture is built bottom-up and in an iterative approach: The data lake components are developed (using different development branches) in the context of concrete use cases and projects. In the production branch, teams collaborate with each other to integrate the components into a unified architecture. In this way, we can quickly deliver results for projects with high demand; while at the same time allow the long-term benefit of the uniform data management strategy.

© Springer Nature Switzerland AG 2019
P. Hitzler et al. (Eds.): ESWC 2019 Satellite Events, LNCS 11762, pp. 262–266, 2019.
https://doi.org/10.1007/978-3-030-32327-1_46

To ensure both the integration of data as well as a smooth transition of individual components from development to production, unified semantic models play a vital role and enable reuse of information across individual use cases. Another use of the unified semantic models is to enable semantic search over the data, by inter-connecting different data sources. For example, data from vehicle test drives often contains GPS information, and by linking it with map-based data (e.g. derived from Open Street Map) we can access video data generated during different driving situations (cross roads, highway, tunnel, etc.). Ideally, such situations and their connection with the video content should be well structured to support better data access and analytics. This paper summarizes our approach in using semantic technologies to enable such functionality over our CC Data Lake.

2 Approach

Overall Architecture. Figure 1 shows the overall architecture of our system. The primary goal is to provide a centralized solution to integrate knowledge about our data (i.e. meta-data, context and provenance) from different sources, and to provide unified access. For this purpose, we introduced two additional layers to the data lake. First, the *Semantic Knowledge Layer* enables us to store relevant knowledge about our data assets as well as knowledge extracted from the data in an actionable manner (e.g. to support data (re-)use for analytics and machine learning). Second, the *Data Access Layer* provides applications with uniform access and query of resources in the data lake based on a common REST endpoint and API. The Data Access Engine (DAE) uses the *Data Catalog* knowledge graph to enforce access control of the individual data assets. The DAE supports Kerberos and thus enables easy integration with Enterprise IT systems.

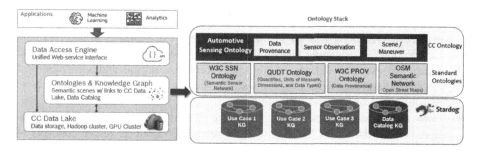

Fig. 1. Left-hand side: An overview of the CC Data Lake with two extensions, the *Data Access Layer* and *Semantic Knowledge Layer*. Right-hand side: The ontologies used to represent and link data across the data lake.

This architecture enables semantic search of data available in the data lake. For instance, if an engineer wants to analyze all test drives with certain characteristics or train a ML model for a given driving context, the *Semantic Knowledge Layer* enables expressive query across all the assets stored in the data lake in order to find the relevant datasets. The *Data Access Layer* gives engineers uniform access to the respective datasets by connecting directly to the data stores (i.e. HBase, Hive tables) in the data lake.

CC Ontologies and Knowledge Graphs. To develop the ontology models we follow an iterative approach, starting with a few core use cases. We aim to develop a foundational ontology to model the common data types in the automotive domain (e.g., observable properties and scenes features), called the Automotive Sensing Ontology (ASO). This foundational ontology is then extended by specific ontologies to cover the requirements of individual projects. Each use case provides a set of requirements, in the form of competency questions, which are developed and discussed together with domain experts. Based on these requirements, we model the use case specific ontologies and develop the processes to construct the respective knowledge graphs, each stored in separate databases on our Stardog [2] cluster. Each knowledge graph relies on both the foundational automotive ontology and the use case specific ontologies. When there is a need to query over several knowledge graphs, a federated SPAQRL query is defined on the *Data Access Layer* and executed by the Data Access Engine (DAE).

Automotive Sensing Ontology (ASO). The Automotive Sensing Ontology is used for annotating and linking sensor observation data in the CC Data Lake. Use of this ontology enables the data to be understood and queried by non-domain experts in support of a wide range of applications and use-cases of interest to CC. The ASO borrows concepts from several standard ontologies and vocabularies (see Fig. 1). In addition, it models the domain of automotive sensing through a set of three distinct modules:

(1) *Scenes & Maneuvers*: defines the concepts to represent the activities that a vehicle may engage in along with its surrounding context. For example, *Maneuvers* may include braking, changing lanes on a highway or stopping at a traffic light.
(2) *Sensor observations*: defines the concepts to represent sensors and observations of the vehicle and its surrounding context; re-using several concepts from the W3C Semantic Sensor Network Ontology [1].
(3) *Data Provenance*: defines the concepts to describe, reference, and trace data stored in the data lake. We follow W3C recommendation to re-use concepts of PROV-O ontology [3].

Table 1 illustrates some of the core concepts.

Table 1. Example classes and properties of *Scenes & Maneuvers* in ASO

Concept	Description	Reference
Classes		
Drive	A drive is the deployment of a vehicle within some particular geospatial region (location/place) and time interval. Sensors hosted on the vehicle may observe properties of the vehicle and/or environment during the deployment	aso:Drive
EgoVehicle	A vehicle is a device that is designed or used to transport people or cargo over land, water, air, or through space	aso:EgoVehicle
Maneuver	A Maneuver is a type of Scene in which a Vehicle engages in some purposeful activity (braking, accelerating)	aso:Maneuver
Scene	A scene is an activity that occurs during a drive, along with the context surrounding the activity. Knowledge (or "detection") of a scene typically results from an analysis of observations that occur during a drive	aso:Scene
Properties		
agent	The direct performer or driver of the action (animate or inanimate) The agent of a drive/maneuver is a EgoVehicle	schema:agent
occursDuringDrive	Relation between a Scene and the Drive during which it occurs (inverse of hasScene)	aso:occursDuringDrive
occursDuringScene	Relation between an Observation and the Scene during which it occurs	aso:occursDuringScene
participant	Relation between a Scene and a FeatureOfInterest; linking the scene to a feature that participated in the scene indirectly	schema:participant

In order to access datasets in the CC Data Lake through semantic search, we use Data Catalog in form of a knowledge graph to allow inferring provenance from semantic data [4]. In this regard, we need a mechanism to reference the datasets in the *Data Catalog*. To accomplish this, each file, table or graph in the data lake is assigned a Global Identifier (GID) that is used as a reference linking data with knowledge in the knowledge graphs.

3   Example Use Case

We have successfully used the above introduced data lake architecture and semantic data management approach in various use cases at CC. For brevity, we introduce here only one representative use case: *context-based maneuver search*. In addition to the general Data Catalog knowledge graph, we also construct a use case specific knowledge graph that captures all the facts about a set of recorded maneuvers. Specifically, for each maneuver we add all the relevant knowledge, including metadata (e.g. time, location, vehicle platform and subsystems), the maneuver type (e.g. braking, lane change), the maneuver context (e.g. highway, bridge, dusk, rain) and relevant features from the sensor data (e.g. vehicle speed, acceleration). This enables our engineers to find all datasets of interest for a specific analysis and perform highly contextualized machine learning trainings.

4   Conclusion

At Bosch, we have used semantic technologies to improve our ability to search for automotive data stored in the CC Data Lake. Our architecture combines the use of semantic technology for metadata management (relying on Stardog) with Hadoop technology. We have developed the Automotive Sensing Ontology for describing and annotating data in the automotive domain. Our next step is to develop our proof-of-concept into a production-grade system.

References

1. Compton, M., et al.: The SSN ontology of the W3C semantic sensor network incubator group. J. Web Semant. **17**, 25–32 (2012)
2. StarDog. http://www.stardog.com. Accessed 13 Mar 2019
3. Lebo, T., et al.: PROV-O: The PROV Ontology. W3C Recommendation (2013). http://www.w3.org/TR/prov-o/. Accessed 12 Mar 2019
4. Compton, M., et al.: Sensor data provenance: SSNO and PROV-O together at last. In: Proceedings of 7th International Workshop on Semantic Sensor Networks (SSN), ISWC, pp. 67–82 (2014)

Best-of-Workshop Papers

LiteMat, an Encoding Scheme with RDFS++ and Multiple Inheritance Support

Olivier Curé[1(✉)], Weiqin Xu[1,2], Hubert Naacke[3], and Philippe Calvez[2]

[1] LIGM (UMR 8049), CNRS, UPEM, 77454 Marne-la-Vallée, France
{olivier.cure,weiqin.xu}@u-pem.fr
[2] ENGIE CRIGEN CSAI Lab, Saint-Denis, France
philippe.calvez1@engie.com
[3] Sorbonne Universités, UPMC Univ Paris 06, 75005 Paris, France
hubert.naacke@lip6.fr

Abstract. In this paper, we extend LiteMat, an RDFS and `owl:sameAs` inference-enabled RDF encoding scheme, which is used in a distributed knowledge graph data management system. Our extensions enable to reach RDFS++ expressiveness by integrating `owl:transitiveProperty` and `owl:inverseOf` properties. Considering the latter, `owl:inverseOf` property, we propose a simple solution that involves a dictionary lookup at query run-time. For the former, we present an efficient approach to encode individuals involved in chain and tree structures of a transitive property. Moreover, our extension also provides an efficient solution to the multiple inheritance problem which sometimes encountered in the concept hierarchy of ontologies. We provide details of a distributed implementation and highlight the efficiency of our encoding and query processing approaches over large synthetic datasets.

1 Introduction

Large scale RDF analytics requires a reliable, distributed knowledge graph data management coupled with an efficient processing of inferences based on expressive ontologies. We consider that with today's distributed computing frameworks and cloud computing infrastructure, it is possible to achieve such a goal when a large portion of the data and knowledge reside in main-memory. In [2] and [6], we have followed this design principle by integrating a semantic-aware encoding of Knowledge Graph (KG) elements, *i.e.*, concepts, properties and individuals, in an RDF store and streaming system that are both based on Apache Spark.

More precisely, LiteMat [2] is an encoding scheme for RDF data that offers a trade-off between materialization (of inferred triples) and query rewriting, in order to obtain complete result sets from queries. It uses an integer interval based encoding for the KG elements that efficiently and effectively captures in a compressed manner cliques and hierarchical structures. In [2], we are applying this encoding to the ρdf [5] fragment of RDFS, *i.e.*, supporting inferences associated to `rdfs:subClassOf`, `rdfs:subPropertyOf`, `rdfs:domain` and

© Springer Nature Switzerland AG 2019
P. Hitzler et al. (Eds.): ESWC 2019 Satellite Events, LNCS 11762, pp. 269–284, 2019.
https://doi.org/10.1007/978-3-030-32327-1_47

`rdfs:range` properties. More recently, $Strider^R$ [6] extended LiteMat to support the `owl:sameAs` property which is quite popular in the Linked Data community. Intuitively, a special encoding was applied to all individuals present in `owl:sameAs` cliques and a representative was selected among them. Like LiteMat, the work presented in [7] models the concept and property subsumption hierarchies with an intelligent integer identification that is used to rewrite SQL queries in the ontology-based data access Quest system. With the latest extension of LiteMat, we go further with a smart identification solution for individuals involved in `owl:sameAs` cliques as well as support for inverse properties and transitive structures taking the form of chains and trees.

Apart from these different contributions, some limitations still exist. One of them is the multiple inheritance problem which appears in some real-world dataset. Essentially encountered in concept hierarchies, it corresponds to the fact that a concept has more than one super concept. Given LiteMat's top-down, single-ancestor directed encoding scheme, providing an efficient solution to the multiple inheritance problem is not that simple. Precisely speaking, the idea of LiteMat is to encode an element by applying the encoding of its direct ancestor as the prefix. This idea leads to a problem where if an element has more than one direct ancestor, it may have multiple possible encodings which breaks the rule that an element can only have one unique identifier in the dictionary. In this work, we propose a solution that fits nicely with LiteMat's encoding approach, i.e., it keeps its binary encoding strategy and limits data structures overload. Moreover, it provides good performance measures on SPARQL query processing.

The contributions presented in this paper permit to extend LiteMat toward RDFS++ expressiveness and to support multiple inheritance in the ontology hierarchies. These extensions concern both an encoding scheme that results in a more compact KG representation and an adapted query processing. We address `owl:inverseOf` properties by applying a simple transformation of the encoded ABox and a property dictionary look-up at query processing-time. Our approach for transitive properties is more involved and is based on (i) an encoding solution of the individuals involved in chains and trees of these properties and (ii) a query processing strategy. Due to a lack of an efficient solution, directed acyclic graphs (DAG) of transitive properties, which are relatively rare in practice, are currently being materialized in the triples store.

The paper is organized as follows: in Sect. 2, we provide an overview of LiteMat's encoding principles. In Sect. 3, we propose a solution to the multiple inheritance problem for the LiteMat encoding scheme. In Sect. 4 we detail our solutions toward supporting `owl:inverseOf` and `owl:transitiveProperty`. In Sect. 5, we present the principles of the query processing in the presence of transitive properties. Section 6 provides an evaluation on synthetic datasets over the memory footprint, encoding duration and query processing dimensions. Finally, Sect. 7 concludes the paper and presents some future work.

2   LiteMat Encoding Approach and Query Processing

In this section, we present LiteMat's encoding scheme using the following ontology concept hierarchy (but this method can also be applied to property hierarchies): $A \sqsubseteq \top$, $B \sqsubseteq \top$, $C \sqsubseteq \top$, $D \sqsubseteq \top$, $A1 \sqsubseteq A$, $C1 \sqsubseteq C$, $F1 \sqsubseteq F$, $E1 \sqsubseteq E$, $E2 \sqsubseteq E$, $F \sqsubseteq B$, $F \sqsubseteq C$, $E \sqsubseteq A1$, $E \sqsubseteq B$ and $E \sqsubseteq C$.

We can see that the last 5 concept subsumptions describe two situations of multiple inheritance, i.e., the concepts E (resp. F) have 3 (resp. 2) super classes.

In Fig. 1(a), we present LiteMat's encoding for this TBox. In a first step, the assignment of an identifier, using a binary representation, for each concept is performed in a top-down recursive manner, i.e., it starts by setting the top concept ($\top$) at 1, and proceeds level-wise on the element hierarchy until all leaves have been processed. Intuitively, for each concept α, we count the number N of direct sub concepts (including α itself), e.g., in our running example $\top$, we have $N = 5$ for $\top$. At this level, $\lceil \log(N) \rceil$ provides the number of bits necessary to represent each sub concept. Then, these sub concepts (excluding α) are prefixed by the binary identifier of α and uniquely get a binary representation of a value $\in [1, N - 1]$. For instance, the concept A is prefixed with '1' ($\top$'s identifier and is assigned the value 1 on 3 bits, i.e., '001', yielding the binary string '1001').

Finally, a normalization step makes sure that all identifiers are encoded on the same binary string length. This is performed as follows: once all concepts have been encoded in the first step, we get the size L of the longest encoding string (i.e., 8 in our running example). Then all concept identifiers with an encoding length lower than L are appended with '0' until their length reaches L. This normalization step is represented with red '0' in Fig. 1(a). The last column of this figure provides the integer identifier corresponding to each concept.

With this encoding scheme, it is clear that multiple inheritance poses a problem since each ontology concept must have a single identifier. For instance, in our running example, we can provide three different identifiers to E: one computed from $A1$, another one from B and a last one from C. In the next section, we propose a solution to this issue.

LiteMat proposes an efficient query processing approach that takes advantage of the semantic-aware encoding. In fact, whenever a query requires to reason over the concept or property hierarchies, the system simply introduces new variables that are filtered on the identifiers of our encoding scheme.

Consider the following Basic Graph Pattern (BGP) of a SPARQL query: {?x rdf:type E}. It would generally be rewritten into {?x rdf:type E} UNION {?x rdf:type E1} UNION {?x rdf:type E2}. Although costly on a query processing point of view, this rewriting also requires to access the ontology to discover sub concepts of E. In LiteMat, the system would identify that E has several sub concepts (only requiring an access to the dictionary), replace E with a new variable (e.g., ?y) and add a FILTER clause that restricts the accepted values of this new variable. This restriction corresponds to an interval of integer values where the lower bound is the identifier of E and the upper bound is easily computing (i.e., using 2 bit shift operations and an addition) from the identifier of E. This computation requires an identifier metadata stating the index on the

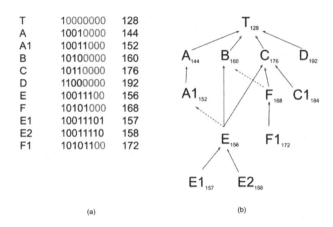

Fig. 1. LiteMat Encoding (a dashed arrow points to a representative, see Sect. 3) (Color figure online)

bit string where the normalization has started. Considering that the identifiers of E, $E1$ and $E2$ are resp. 156, 157 and 158 (to be explained in the next section), our LiteMat rewriting would be: {?x rdf:type ?y. FILTER (?y$\geq$156 && ?y<157)}. This rewriting also applies when sub property relationships are used and the more complex the query, the more efficient our rewriting.

3   Multiple Inheritance Support in LiteMat

3.1   Encoding Scheme

Our support of multiple inheritance is based on the notion of a representative. A representative, denoted C_r, is selected among the super concepts $C_1, .., C_n$ of a concept SC. That is the integer identifier of SC will be computed following Litemat's approach based on the C_r identifier. It is obvious that with this approach SC loses any connection to its non-representative direct and indirect super concepts. Hence it is necessary to keep track of these super concepts. In the following, the remaining super classes of SC, i.e., $\{C_1,..,C_n\}\setminus C_r$ are considered as non-representative of SC.

Let consider that the representative of the concept E is $A1$. Hence, the non-representatives of E are the concepts B and C. In Fig. 1(b) (where each concept has its identifier in subscript), a representative is pointed by a dashed arrow and we can observe that the identifiers of concepts E, $E1$ and $E2$ (resp. 156, 157 and 158) are computed from $A1$'s identifier (i.e., 152).

To support an efficient query processing, we require a key/value data structure, denoted nonRep. Intuitively, each non representative of the ontology is an entry in that data structure and the value associated to a key corresponds to a set containing all the sub concepts involved in a multiple inheritance with the key concept as one of its super concept. In our running example, nonRep(B) = {E} and nonRep(C) = {E,F}.

3.2   Query Processing and Optimization

The query processing presented in Sect. 2 is extended to produce complete and correct result sets for ontologies involving multiple inheritance. The extension coincides to the addition of disjunction in the generated FILTER clause of the rewritten SPARQL queries. Like in the original rewriting approach of Sect. 2, the disjuncts correspond to interval descriptions for a given query variable. An interval is computed using the nonRep data structure. Note that queries involving representatives do not necessarily involve this form of query processing. Due to space limitation, we present this processing and a simple optimization through the following example.

We consider the following BGP of a simple query, denoted Q, which involves a multiple inheritance: {?x rdf:type C}. The query rewriting denoted Q' corresponds to: {?x rdf:type ?y. filter((?y $\geq$ 176 && ?y < 192) || (?y $\geq$ 156 && ?y < 160) || (?y $\geq$ 168 && ?y < 176)) where the first disjunct corresponds to the standard interval defined in Sect. 2 and last two are computed using the nonRep data structures. That is, we search whether C is involved in a multiple inheritance by checking its presence as a key in nonRep. If it is the case, it will return a set of concepts and for each of these concepts a disjunct is added to the FILTER clause over that variable. In our running example, nonRep(C) returns a set with concepts E and F, resp. the identifiers 156 and 168. These values correspond to the lower bounds of the intervals and upper bounds are compute as stated in LiteMat.

Based on the intervals present in this FILTER clause, a simple optimization can be performed. It has the possible effect of reducing the number of disjuncts in a query rewriting. The optimized queries are Q'' : {?x 0 ?y. filter((?y $\geq$ 168 && ?y < 192) || (?y $\geq$ 156 && ?y < 160)), i.e., it contains one less disjunct.

4   RDFS++ Extensions for LiteMat

4.1   Support for `owl:inverseOf`

Concerning `owl:inverseOf` properties, we propose the following simple approach. For each URI property and its inverse, denoted $\langle p, p^- \rangle$, we retain in our ABox, only one of the two URIs which is therefore denoted as the property representative, i.e., p_r. For each pair $\langle p, p^- \rangle$ in the ABox, a representative, p_r, is selected based on the largest number of occurrences over the pair $\langle p, p^- \rangle$.

In the LiteMat property dictionary associated to the locate function [1], i.e., URI to identifier key-value structure, both property URIs are associated to the same integer identifier: both p_r and p^- are associated to a unique pid value as computed in [2]. In the extract property dictionary, i.e., id to URI key-value structure, only the representative property is stored since answers to queries requiring an extract operation on the property are expressed with p_r.

During the ABox encoding, all triples already expressed with p_r are normally encoded using the individuals and properties dictionaries. Concerning all triples expressed with p_r^-, e.g., $i1$ p_r^- $i2$, they are transformed as follows: the subject and object of the original triples respectively become the object and subject of a new triple and the property is switched to the representative.

Example: Let *parentOf* `owl:inverseOf` *childOf* be a TBox axiom and *parentOf* is selected as the representative in this property pair. Table 1 displays an original ABox and its resulting transformation.

Table 1. TBox encoding facts

Original ABox	Transformed ABox
dominique parentOf jean	dominique parentOf jean
dominique parentOf pierre	dominique parentOf pierre
marie childOf pierre	**pierre parentOf marie**

A similar transformation is applied to graph patterns of a SPARQL query whenever the inverse of a representative is identified in a BGP. That is the query `SELECT ?x ?y WHERE {?x childOf ?y}` would be transformed into `SELECT ?y ?x WHERE {?y parentOf ?x}`. This would return an answer with 3 tuples including the pair ⟨pierre, marie⟩.

4.2   Support for `owl:transitiveProperty`

Let consider a function $trans(G, p) = G'$, with G an RDF graph, p a transitive property and G' a subgraph of G solely composed of triples with the p property. Intuitively, G' is composed of, not necessarily connected, chains, trees or DAGs of individuals (see Fig. 2 for examples of the first two structures).

In this section, we propose two encoding schemes, one for the chain and another one for tree structures that are following the logical approach of LiteMat. That is, it provides semantic-aware identifiers to ABox individuals encountered in these structures. We leave the issue of encoding the DAG transitive structures to a future work and will consider that in the current state of the LiteMat data management system, the transitive closure of these structures is materialized.

The characteristics that we are aiming for in this encoding schemes are: (i) **compactness** since no materialization is required for the chain and tree structures, (ii) **determinism** since the identifier of each individual in a chain or tree is computed deterministically and (iii) **scalability** since all encoding tasks are performed in a distributed manner on a distributed engine, namely Apache Spark and its GraphX graph computing component.

In both the chain and tree encoding, our processing starts with the computation of $trans(G, p)$ for all transitive properties of the associated ontology, resulting in a set of subgraphs. Then, the system computes the connected components for each of these subgraphs. Intuitively, the connected components operation groups vertices into connected subgraphs. This can easily be performed in a scalable manner with Spark's GraphX component. Such a resulting connected component is assigned a distinct identifier corresponding to the lowest node identifier of the connected component. The encoding of individuals in these graphs is made of a quadruple of integer values which correspond to: fid which is 0 if the transitive structure is a chain or 1 if it is a tree, pid the identifier of the transitive property, $ccid$ the connected component identifier and lid a local node identifier.

The chain and tree structures are distinguished by the computation of their local identifiers. Figure 2 presents in each node the label of the individuals (*i.e.*, URIs) and its identifier. In the case of a chain structure, it is sufficient to assign integer values that define a total order over the set of lid of a given triple $\langle fid, pid, ccid \rangle$. With such an approach, the computation of all descendants (respectively ancestors) of a given individuals $\langle fid, pid, ccid, lid_i \rangle$ will amount to retrieve individuals identified by $\langle fid, pid, ccid, lid_x \rangle$ for all $lid_i < lid_x$ (respectively, $lid_i > lid_x$).

The encoding of tree structures is more involved. For instance, in Fig. 2(b), individuals E, F and G do not belong in the transitive closure of B or D. In this case, the incremental, naive assignment of local identifier is not sufficient to efficiently detect that a node is not in the transitive closure of another node in this graph. We adopt a local node identifier approach that is inspired by our LiteMat binary approach. Intuitively, the encoding algorithm is recursively assigning binary identifiers in a top-down manner from the root of the tree. The root node starts with a single bit set to 1. Then we identify all directly linked individuals for a node. The size of this set of individuals justifies the length of the binary encoding for each of these individuals. For instance, in Fig. 2(b), A has three directly connected individuals (namely B, C and D) so two bits are necessary to encode them. The temporary local identifier at each level starts with counter set to 1 and is incremented by 1, and each of these individuals is prefixed with the identifier of their local root. Thus the identifier of B in Fig. 2(b) is 101 (with the left most bit inherited from A and 01 computed at this level). This computation is performed recursively until all nodes are assigned a value. A final step consists in normalizing the temporary identifier: all identifiers have to be encoding with the same binary length. In our example, F and G are the identifiers with the longest binary encoding (*i.e.*, 6 bits) so all nodes of the tree are right-completed with bits set at 0 to reach the same length. The identifiers for each node in Fig. 2(b) are displayed in each box, the gray 0 of an identifier are the results of the normalization while the local fragment is in black.

Given this local identifier strategy, we can easily find whether a given node is in the transitive closure of another node of that same graph. This operation is based on checking whether the subtraction of two identifiers is contained in a given interval. Let consider the connected component graph of a transitive property. Due to the normalization step, all identifiers of this connected component are encoded using n bits. Moreover, we introduce a function, *localLength*, that returns the non-normalized binary encoding length of a node. For instance, in Fig. 2(b), *localLength* of A, C and G are respectively 1, 3 and 6. For two nodes of this graph, α and β, β is in the transitive closure of α if $\beta - \alpha$ is included in $[0, 2^{n-localLength(\alpha)}]$.

Using this approach, we can efficiently compute that G is in the transitive closure of A, B and E but not of B, D and F.

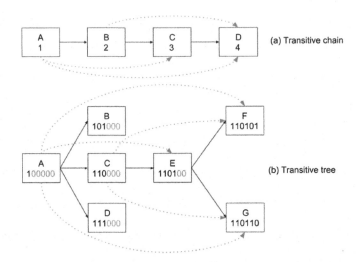

Fig. 2. A chain and a tree of a transitive property. Dotted red arrows correspond to the transitive closure. In each node, a label and its local identifier (lid) (Color figure online)

Since our `owl:sameAs` encoding scheme, *i.e.*, a tuple $\langle cliqueId, localId \rangle$, does not rely on a local identification total order, it is possible to compose `owl:sameAs` identifiers with transitive ones. This means that individuals involved in a chain or tree transitive structure can be involved in a `owl:sameAs` clique by reusing their identifiers in the sameAs encoding scheme. In such a case, the *localId* corresponds to the whole transitive identifier.

5 Query Processing in the Presence of Transitive Properties

We present a sketch of query processing with a BGP involving a transitive property. We consider a BGP containing a single triple pattern asking for all subjects (respectively objects) related, via a transitive property, to an object (respectively subject). A similar approach can be applied for more complex BGPs.

5.1 Query Encoding

As with most RDF triples, the query needs to be translated to an identifier-based form which requires look-ups to several LiteMat dictionaries. Using the property dictionary, we obtain the identifier of the property and we will also get the information that this property is transitive. Then, we search for the identifier of the object (respectively subject). In a full materialization case, this identifier corresponds to a single identifier while in the case of LiteMat, it corresponds to a 4-tuple identifier, *i.e.*, $\langle$fid, pid, ccid, lid$\rangle$.

5.2 Variable Assignments

While the full materialization approach requires a complete scan over all triples plus an extraction from the individuals dictionary, the same query can be answered much more efficiently with LiteMat. Intuitively, due to LiteMat's semantic-aware encoding, we can rely solely on some simple computation to directly search for answers in the dictionary. In fact, we will search for all individual dictionary entries where the key is of the form $\langle fid, pid, ccid, X \rangle$ where one of the following computations is performed:

- if fid corresponds to a chain, *i.e.*, $fid = 0$, then the system retrieves all values lower then lid.
- if fid is a tree, *i.e.*, $fid = 1$, then the system retrieves all values comprised between $]lid, ((lid \gg lid$ encoding length$) + 1) \ll lid$ encoding length$)[$

6 Evaluation

6.1 Multiple Inheritance Evaluation

Our multiple inheritance experimentation consists in evaluating the performance of the database construction and query processing phases. In the database construction phase, we evaluate the duration and memory consumption dimensions. In the query processing phase, we compare LiteMat with FullMat using a set of SPARQL queries. Our implementation can be accessed at this github link[1]. We will explain these two phases in detail within the following section.

Experimental Setting. The experimentation was ran on a MacBook pro with a 2.9 GHz Intel Core i5 and 8 GB LPDDR3 RAM. The scripts use Apache Spark 2.4.3 running with Scala of version 2.11.8.

Datasets and Query Workload. The purpose of this evaluation is to compare the performance of LiteMat approach with that of a full materialization (denoted FullMat) approach in the context of TBox multiple inheritance. In this evaluation, we test some simple BGPs which enables us to use some auto-generated ontologies containing only a hierarchy of concepts as datasets. Each ontology is associated with an ABox that involves only some facts in form of $\{X$ *rdf:type* $Y\}$ where X is an instance and Y is a concept.

---

[1] https://github.com/xwq610728213/multipleInheritanceEvaluation.

In order to construct our multiple inheritance datasets, we first generate a hierarchy in form of a tree where each node is a concept. Once we add a certain concept to the bottom of the tree, there will be a chance of 30% that this concept is involved in a multiple inheritance. If so, we will choose a certain number of concepts from higher levels as its super concepts and register the corresponding triples. After the ontology construction, we will pick 50% of the concepts and create triples like {X rdf:type Y} in the ABox.

Table 2. Details of testing data sets

DataSet	Maximum depth	Maximum branches	Maximum inheritance	TboxSize (KB)	AboxSize (KB)
Dataset 1	5	4	4	25	8
Dataset 2	6	6	3	476	176
Dataset 3	6	5	3	90	34
Dataset 4	7	3	3	22	8
Dataset 5	7	5	4	514	169
Dataset 6	8	3	3	51	18

Table 2 shows details of each dataset. Maximum Depth gives the depth of the deepest concept in the hierarchy. Maximum Branches indicates how many branches a node can possess in maximum. While generating sub concepts of a certain concept, we will choose a random number between 0 and Maximum Branches as the number of its sub concepts. Once a concept is chosen to be part of a multiple inheritance, Maximum Inheritance limits the number of its direct super concepts. For example, Dataset 1 is a DAG structure with a maximum depth of 5, each node has [0, 4] branches and a multiple inheritance concept has [2, 4] super concepts. More details can be found with the link[2].

Database Construction Performance. In this section, we compare LiteMat encoding with a FullMat encoding in two aspects, database construction time and memory consumption.

Figure 3 shows the comparison of database construction time between LiteMat and FullMat within each data set. The database construction time includes encoding elements, constructing dictionary and other necessary data structures, e.g., triple store for FullMat and nonRep list for LiteMat. Obviously, LiteMat constructs database much faster than FullMat in all tests because Full-Mat needs to deduct all the possible statements, i.e., direct and indirect ones, during database construction, which takes some time, while LiteMat encodes elements only by direct connections.

---

[2] https://github.com/xwq610728213/MultiInheritanceGenerator.

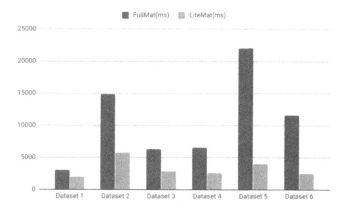

Fig. 3. Database construction time of LiteMat vs a full materialization

The comparison of memory consumption is given in Fig. 4. We can not directly compare the RAM consumption during runtime, thus we store the in-memory data structures, *e.g.*, dictionary, triple store and nonRep structure, into files and directly compare the size of these files. Because the size of these files is proportional to the RAM consumption, we consider the comparison in size of these files reflects the relation of RAM consumption between two approaches. As we can conclude from the figure, although the dictionary of LiteMat is a little bit larger than that of FullMat, considering the nonRep list of Litemat is much smaller than the triple store of FullMat, our LiteMat approach takes much less total space than FullMat.

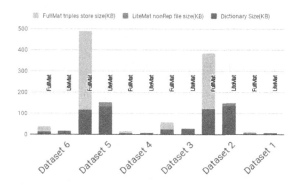

Fig. 4. Memory space required by LiteMat vs a full materialization

Query Performance. As for query evaluation, we only test the query pattern in form of $\{?x\ rdf{:}type\ C\}$, which is a frequently appearing triple pattern in the query concerning concept hierarchy. This query pattern demands all the instances belonging to a concept C or its sub-concepts. We randomly retrieve 15 concepts as C from the ontology and generate 15 queries for each datasets, and compare the query processing time between LiteMat and FullMat.

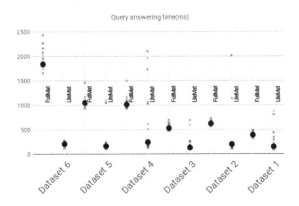

Fig. 5. Query answering time distribution of LiteMat vs full materialization

Figure 5 shows the results. Each cross in the figure represents the answering time of a query with different approaches. The big black point indicates the median of the 15 queries answering times. As we can see from the figure, the median of query answering time with LiteMat is always smaller than that of FullMat, thus we can say our LiteMat approach performs better in the most of queries. However, there exists some queries with which LiteMat takes more time than FullMat. One reason is that in order to answer these queries, LiteMat needs to search nonRep data structure many times, because some values of a nonRep structure appear as the key (or the super concept of the key) in other nonRep structure recursively.

6.2 Transitive Property Evaluation

Experimental Setting. The evaluation was conducted on a cluster composed of three Dell PowerEdge R410 running a Debian GNU/Linux distribution with a 3.16.0-4-amd64 kernel version. Each machine has 64 GB of DDR3 RAM, a 900 GB 7200 rpm SATA disk and two Intel Xeon E5645 processors. Each processor is constituted of 12 cores running at 2.40 GHz and allowing to run two threads in parallel (hyper threading). The machines are connected via a 1 GB/s Ethernet network adapter. We used Spark version 2.3.2 and implemented all experiments in Scala version 2.11.6. More details on the scripts can be found here[3]. The Spark configuration of our evaluation runs our prototype on a subset of the cluster corresponding to 36 cores and 24 GB of RAM per machine.

---

[3] https://github.com/xwq610728213/LitematPlusPlus.

Datasets and Query Workload. In this evaluation, we are aiming to test and stress our approaches with different sizes of transitive chains and trees. We thus resort to a synthetic benchmark solution, namely the Lehigh University Bench-Mark (LUBM)[3], a well-established benchmark on the university domain that contains a transitive property, named `lubm:subOrganisationOf`. Since both the `rdfs:domain` and `rdfs:range` of this property are the Organization concept, we can use it to create long chain and tree structures.

Table 3 presents the datasets that we are using throughout this experimentation. Intuitively, the name of each dataset describes the number of universities, *e.g.*, 5K or 10K for respectively 5.000 and 10.000 universities, a letter, *i.e.*, either 'c' or 't' which respectively stand for chain and tree structures and a number that corresponds to the maximum depth of the structure. Note that the 5K_c20 and 10_c20 correspond to large shallow trees which are supposed to mitigate the advantages provided by LiteMat. In total, 10 datasets are evaluated, 4 chains and 6 trees.

In this section, we are providing a preliminary evaluation of our query processing solution. Due to space limitation, we are only considering answering a single triple pattern that retrieves either all the ancestors or descendants of a group in the transitive closure of the `lubm:subOrganisationOf` property. These two queries have been executed over the some of the 10K datasets and respectively correspond to SELECT ?X WHERE {?x lubm:subOrganisationOf C} to compute ancestors and SELECT ?X WHERE {C lubm:subOrganisationOf ?x} to retrieve descendants where C is an individual involved in the queried dataset, *e.g.*, <http://www.Department10.University1000.edu/ResearchGroup1>.

This limited evaluation already provides some valuable insight on the potential of LiteMat query processing with transitive properties.

Table 3. Characteristics of evaluated datasets

Dataset name	Depth sizes [min,max]	#Branches [min,max]	#Triples	Size (MB)	#Triples materialized	Increase due to materialization
5K_c20	[10, 20]	1	1.689.907	318,4	23.579.485	x 14
5K_c100	[20, 100]	1	6.752.637	1.280	230.004.339	x 34.1
5K_t5	[10, 20]	[1, 5]	5.062.616	957.9	39.362.874	x 7.8
5K_t10	[20, 100]	[5, 10]	12.624.667	2.400	109.223.271	x 8.7
5K_t20	[2, 5]	[10, 20]	5.898.803	1.120	14.064.044	x 2.4
10K_c20	[10, 20]	1	3.376.055	636,8	48.712.856	x 14.4
10K_c100	[20, 100]	1	13.522.653	2.560	461.042.361	x 34.1
10K_t5	[10, 20]	[1, 5]	10.119.755	1.920	71.304.115	x 7.0
10K_t10	[20, 100]	[5, 10]	25.260.771	4.800	216.690.752	x 8.6
10K_t20	[2, 5]	[10, 20]	11.804.988	2.240	28.155.826	x 2.4

Compression and Encoding Performance. In this section, we are mainly interested in two performance dimensions: the memory space reduction provided by LiteMat compared to a full materialization and the duration of LiteMat's encoding against the full materialization computation.

Figure 6 presents comparisons of the memory space required by the LiteMat approach against a full materialization. In the latter approach, both the set of materialized triples as well as the dictionaries are required to answer inference-enabled SPARQL queries while in the case of LiteMat, only the dictionaries are necessary. The figure emphasizes that, for any datasets, both dictionaries are about the same size, with the ones of FullMat being a little bit more compact for trees due to the overhead LiteMat identifiers, *i.e.*, a long value for the materialization against a 4-tuple of long values and an integer for LiteMat.

Obviously, for long chains and large trees, the amount of materialized triples can be quite important, *i.e.*, for 5K_c100 and 10K_c100, the set of materialized triples of 34 times larger than to their original triple sets. Figure 3 and the LiteMat approaches correspond to only 10% of their sizes. Considering 5K_c20 and 10K_c20, LiteMat's approach is still around 70% of total materialized approach.

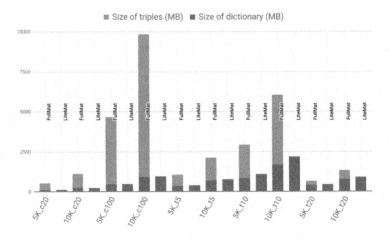

Fig. 6. Memory space required by LiteMat vs a full materialization

Figure 7 provides some details on the duration of the different computation steps involved in both the full materialization and LiteMat approaches. The common steps of these two approaches are the loading of the dataset and the computation of the connected components. We can see that the time taken by the former is quite negligible compared to the other tasks. Unsurprisingly, the computation of the connected components takes a lot of time on all experimentation. The LiteMat encoding and full materialization share a common naïve encoding of individuals step (which is included in both times). Overall, we note that for chains of a transitive property, the difference between both approaches is not significant, *i.e.*, LiteMat is only between 2 and 3% faster than the full materialization. This is not true for structures taking the form of a tree. In that case, LiteMat's encoding is 45 to 50% faster when the depths of structure is relative large for transitive properties, *i.e.*, [10, 20] and [20, 100]. We consider that this is mainly due to the recursive parsing of the tree to compute the transitive closure. The duration difference between the two approaches is less important, *i.e.*, around 11%, when the tree structure depths lies in the [2, 5] range.

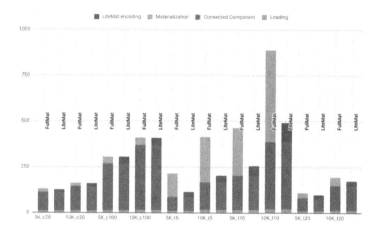

Fig. 7. Durations (in seconds) for the full materialization and LiteMat approaches

Query Processing. Our preliminary evaluation of the query processing consists of a cold retrieval of all descendants of a give individual and the average of five hot queries that retrieve all descendants (*i.e.*, hot1) and ancestors (*i.e.*, hot2). Figure 8 provides measures conducted on the largest datasets of our experimentation, *e.g.*, 10K_c100 and 10K_t20 of respectively 9.8 GB and 6 GB for the materialized approaches. In order to provide a complete overview of the approaches, In this figure, all measures (loading time, cold, hot1 and hot2) emphasize shorter execution times for LiteMat. Considering the loading times, LiteMat is between 6 to 10 times faster than the complete materialization. This is mainly due to the fact that LiteMat solely relies on the dictionaries and not on the triples set. This aspect impacts the cold runs where LiteMat is between 2 and 8 times faster then the full materialization. Finally, for hot runs, LiteMat is 2 to 3 times faster than a complete materialization.

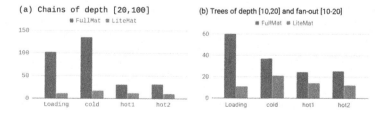

Fig. 8. Query processing on chains and trees with full materialization and liteMat (times in seconds)

7 Conclusion

In this paper we have extended the expressiveness of LiteMat to reach the level of RDFS++ with multiple inheritance. This has been achieved by pushing the original logical approach of LiteMat that consists in assigning meaningful identifiers to elements of the TBox and the ABox. The evaluation of transitive structures taking the forms of chains and trees is quite convincing is terms of memory space economized, speed of encoding and efficiency of query processing. Nevertheless, there is room for improvement in directions such as a more efficient support of graph transitive structures and the fact that certain individuals can be contained in structures of different transitive properties. The optimization of query processing, considering both RDFS++ and multiple inheritance aspects, is another direction for future work. On the implementation side, we are considering using indexed Spark abstractions and are considering algorithms such those presented in [4] to compute connected components.

References

1. Curé, O., Blin, G.: RDF Database Systems: Triples Storage and SPARQL Query Processing. Morgan Kaufmann (2015)
2. Curé, O., Naacke, H., Randriamalala, T., Amann, B.: LiteMat: a scalable, cost-efficient inference encoding scheme for large RDF graphs. In: 2015 IEEE International Conference on Big Data, Santa Clara, CA, USA, pp. 1823–1830 (2015)
3. Guo, Y., Pan, Z., Heflin, J.: LUBM: a benchmark for OWl knowledge base systems. J. Web Sem. **3**(2–3), 158–182 (2005)
4. Kiveris, R., Lattanzi, S., Mirrokni, V., Rastogi, V., Vassilvitskii, S.: Connected components in MapReduce and beyond. In: Proceedings of the ACM Symposium on Cloud Computing, SOCC 2014, pp. 18:1–18:13. ACM, New York (2014)
5. Muñoz, S., Pérez, J., Gutierrez, C.: Simple and efficient minimal RDFs. Web Semant. **7**(3), 220–234 (2009)
6. Ren, X., Curé, O., Naacke, H., Lhez, J., Ke, L.: Strider^r: massive and distributed RDF graph stream reasoning. In: 2017 IEEE International Conference on Big Data, BigData 2017, Boston, MA, USA, 11–14 December 2017, pp. 3358–3367 (2017)
7. Rodríguez-Muro, M., Calvanese, D.: High performance query answering over DL-Lite ontologies. In: Proceedings of the International Conference on Principles of Knowledge Representation and Reasoning, KR 2012, pp. 308–318. AAAI Press (2012)

Building Knowledge Graphs from Survey Data: A Use Case in the Social Sciences (Extended Version)

Lars Heling[1]([✉]), Felix Bensmann[2], Benjamin Zapilko[2], Maribel Acosta[1], and York Sure-Vetter[1]

[1] Institute AIFB, Karlsruhe Institute of Technology (KIT), Karlsruhe, Germany
{lars.heling,maribel.acosta,york.sure-vetter}@kit.edu
[2] GESIS - Leibniz Institute for the Social Sciences, Cologne, Germany
{felix.bensmann,benjamin.zapilko}@gesis.org

Abstract. Many research endeavors in the social sciences rely on high-quality empirical data. Survey data is often used as a foundation to investigate social behavior. The GESIS Panel is a probability-based mixed-mode panel survey in Germany providing high-quality survey and statistical data about e.g. political opinions, well-being, and other contemporary societal topics. In general, the integration and analysis of relevant data is a time-consuming process for researchers. This is due to the fact that search, discovery, and retrieval of the survey data requires accessing various data sources providing different information in different file formats. In this paper, we present our architecture for building a Knowledge Graph of the GESIS Panel data. We present the relevant heterogeneous data sources and demonstrate how we semantically lift and interlink the data in a shared RDF model. At the core of our architecture is a Knowledge Graph representing all aspects of the surveys. It is generated in a modular fashion and, therefore, our solution can be transferred to the existing infrastructure of other survey data publishers.

Keywords: Knowledge Graph · Survey data · RDF · DDI

1 Introduction and Motivation

Linked Open Data (LOD) initiatives have led to an increasing amount of data being published using the Resource Description Framework (RDF) on the web. At the core of LOD is the concept of linking resources within or across RDF graphs such that the resulting dataspace can be understood as a Knowledge Graph (KG) [8]. This allows data publishers to independently administer and publish their own data and improving its value and visibility by linking it to data of other publishers offering similar or additional information on the resources. In this paper, we present a use case of such a KG in the domain of the social sciences at GESIS - Leibniz Institute for the Social Sciences. Our work is motivated by the circumstance that data related to the GESIS Panel[1] such as study-level

---

[1] https://www.gesis.org/en/gesis-panel/gesis-panel-home/.

© Springer Nature Switzerland AG 2019
P. Hitzler et al. (Eds.): ESWC 2019 Satellite Events, LNCS 11762, pp. 285–299, 2019.
https://doi.org/10.1007/978-3-030-32327-1_48

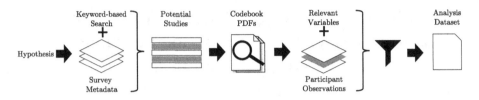

Fig. 1. Motivation: current process to retrieve survey data based on a hypothesis.

metadata, questionnaire descriptions, and participant observation data is administered and published in different datasets varying in format and representation. As a result, the current process for researchers aiming to use the rich collection of surveys available at GESIS requires manually consulting different information sources to search for, discover, and access relevant data which is a costly task in terms of time.

Motivating Scenario. Consider the current process to discover and retrieve the data from the GESIS Panel outlined in Fig. 1. A researcher aims to study a research question and formulates a hypothesis accordingly. She aims to investigate the hypothesis by leveraging the data provided by the GESIS Panel. Typically, the researcher first starts to discover the available survey datasets by a keyword-based search in the Data Catalog (DBK)[2], which is the online portal to search and retrieve survey-related data. The search results are a list of surveys which match the keyword on the survey-level metadata, e.g. in the abstract summarizing the survey. Based on this list, the researcher can retrieve the codebook PDFs for all surveys from the portal. In the codebooks, the variables assessed in the surveys and the corresponding questions are detailed, and the researcher may search for all relevant variables (c.f. Fig. 2). For panel surveys, such as the GESIS Panel, which cover a large variety of topics and measure them in a frequent manner, the keyword-based search typically leads to a large number of results. Therefore, it is often necessary to consult a large number of PDF codebooks to find the relevant variables. To obtain the final analysis dataset, the researcher needs to access the CSV documents with the recorded participant answers (or observations) for the variables. In some cases, a download directly from the DBK is not available due to data protection laws and, therefore, researchers are required to physically visit the Secure Data Center Safe Room at GESIS to access and work with the data on site. After retrieving the final dataset, the researcher may use statistical analysis tools to investigate the hypothesis. This tedious process from a hypothesis to gaining first insights into the actual data impedes the research process for social researchers.

Consequently, the goal of building a KG for the survey data is improving this process for researchers by facilitating the discovery and retrieval of relevant data. Semantic Web technologies as a foundation allow for publishing and linking data of independent sources, providing a holistic picture of the GESIS Panel in the form of a KG. Summarizing, the contributions of this work are the following:

---

[2] https://dbk.gesis.org/dbksearch/.

C1 Description and analysis of a real-world scenario from the social sciences domain with corresponding requirements,

C2 Outline of our solution to handle data organization requirements by applying Semantic Web technologies to create a Knowledge Graph, and

C3 Presentation of encountered challenges, lessons learned, and an indication of future extensions.

In addition, to showcase the presented architecture, we provide a demo[3] to provide access to parts of the KG. The remainder of this paper is structured as follows. In Sect. 2, we provide the preliminaries by introducing the GESIS Panel and relevant vocabularies, i.e., the DDI and the DDI-RDF Discovery Vocabulary. In Sect. 3, we present the architecture of our approach and describe the original data sources and the semantic lifting process to create the KG. In Sect. 4, we revisit our motivating scenario and outline the challenges encountered and lessons learned. In Sect. 5 we introduce relevant related work. Finally, we summarize our work in Sect. 6 and indicate future directions.

2 Preliminaries

In the following, we introduce the GESIS Panel, the Data Documentation Initiative (DDI) and the corresponding DDI-RDF Discovery Vocabulary, which is the core RDF vocabulary for representing survey data in this work.

2.1 GESIS Panel

The GESIS Panel (see footnote 1) is a probability-based mixed-mode panel survey in Germany which is open to the research community [3]. The goal is obtaining high-quality survey data by employing a cross-sectional or longitudinal survey design. Probability-based indicates a participant selection optimized to accurately estimating the target population, which are German-speaking persons between age 18 and 70 who live in private households in Germany. Mixed-mode refers to the two modes of the data collection process, namely via web-based surveys or via traditional paper-and-pencil surveys sent to the participants. The data collection started in August 2013 and is performed periodically in *waves* on a bimonthly basis with a new questionnaire in each period, producing a continuously growing dataset. The participants are asked to answer a questionnaire which is designed to take about 20 min during a two-month time frame. The data is published in three editions: standard edition, extended edition and campus file, each covering different subsets of the recorded data. Standard edition and campus file can be retrieved online, while the extended edition may only be accessed within the aforementioned Safe Room. The data collected in the GESIS Panel may serve as a basis for analyses in the social sciences and it has been used in several studies, for example, to examine the political opinions of the German population [5,7]. An example of a variable to measure the political interest of

---

[3] https://km.aifb.kit.edu/sites/gesispanel-demo/.

Variable name	bbzc001a	
Variable label	Politisches Interesse	
	Political interest	
Question type	Single Choice	
Intro text	Zu Beginn möchten wir Ihnen gerne einige Fragen zum Thema Politik stellen.	
	At the beginning, we would like to ask some questions concerning politics.	
Question text	Wie stark interessieren Sie sich für Politik?	
	How interested are you in politics?	
Value labels		
	1	Sehr stark
		Very strong
	2	Stark
		Strong
	3	Mittel
		Moderately
	4	Wenig
		Little
	5	Überhaupt nicht
		Not at all
	-22	Not in panel
	-33	Unit nonresponse
	-77	Not reached
	-88	Missing by filter
	-99	Item nonresponse
	-111	Ambiguous answer

Position within wave	Online	Offline
Question Order	1	1
Page ID/Page	2362	1

Fig. 2. Excerpt from the codebook PDF of the GESIS Panel providing the description for a variable ta assess *political interest.*

the population is presented in Fig. 2. It shows an excerpt of the codebook PDF for the GESIS Panel describing a variable to measure *political interest* on a scale from 1 to 5. The description includes a unique identifier, the variable label, the question type, an introductory text, the question text, and the labels for the possible answers including their notation.

2.2   DDI and DDI-RDF Discovery Vocabulary

The Data Documentation Initiative (DDI)[4] is an internationally acknowledged standard to facilitate data management by documenting metadata of datasets in the area of social, behavioral and economic sciences [10]. Therefore, the standard aims to improve data quality and ensure the long-term preservation of the information. The initiative is driven by an alliance of data producers, archivists and users to jointly collaborate on the standard [10]. The DDI-RDF Discovery Vocabulary[5] (disco) aims at transferring the DDI standard to the Linked Data community. It is based on a subset of DDI allowing for describing survey data in the social sciences which facilitates the discovery of this data and related metadata [1,2]. It reuses terms of existing vocabularies such as the Dublin Core Metadata Initiative[6] (dcterms) or the RDF Data Cube Vocabulary[7](qb). At the core of the vocabulary is the Study class which represents the generation process

---

[4] https://www.ddialliance.org.
[5] http://rdf-vocabulary.ddialliance.org/discovery.html.
[6] http://dublincore.org.
[7] https://www.w3.org/TR/vocab-data-cube/.

of a dataset. A set of studies is compiled in a `StudyGroup` in case the surveys are conducted in a continuous or periodic process. For example, each wave of the GESIS Panel can be modeled as a `Study` and they are combined into one `StudyGroup`. The content of the physical dataset holding the actual original survey data is represented in a `LogicalDataSet` for which licensing information and access policies may be attached using the `dcterms` vocabulary. The content of a dataset is described by `Variables`. Variables represent different aspects which are measured as part of a `Study` and, thus, are typically the columns in a tabular representation of the survey records. The data of a survey is commonly collected using a `Questionnaire` which consists of a set of `Questions` to measure the variables. Variables are associated with a `Representation` which is typically the set of answers for the associated question and the corresponding notation used in the dataset. The `Representation` is linked as the `responseDomain` to a question. Furthermore, the target population of a `Study` may be described using the classes `Universe` and `AnalysisUnit`. For instance, the target population of the GESIS Panel is a representative sample of the German population and, thus, the analysis unit is persons. The development of an RDF vocabulary along with the already existing DDI standard is motivated by various use cases which mostly support the discoverability of the data [1,12]. For instance, free text keyword-based search may be enabled and once studies and relevant data has been found, related studies and additional data may be discovered exploiting the links across the datasets.

3   Building a Knowledge Graph for the GESIS Panel

The goal of building a Knowledge Graph (KG) for the GESIS Panel by semantically lifting the original data sources to a shared RDF data model is improving the discovery, search, and retrieval of survey data for social scientists. In the following, we provide an overview of the architecture and, thereafter, describe the original data sources as well as the semantic lifting process in more detail.

3.1   Architecture

Figure 3 provides an overview of our architecture and the main components. From a data processing perspective, the integration process is visualized in a bottom-up manner. At the bottom are the original data sources providing different parts of data comprised by the GESIS Panel: (*i*) the access right management data associated with the datasets, (*ii*) the survey metadata providing general information about surveys and corresponding waves, (*iii*) the codebooks with information on how the variables in a survey are to be interpreted, and (*iv*) the participant observations (unit-records) which encode the respondents' answers to the questionnaires. The data sources vary in format and schema. Therefore, each data source requires a custom *semantic lifting process* to transfer the original data to the shared RDF data model. Since the data sources are heterogeneous in nature and their maintenance is deeply rooted in and grown

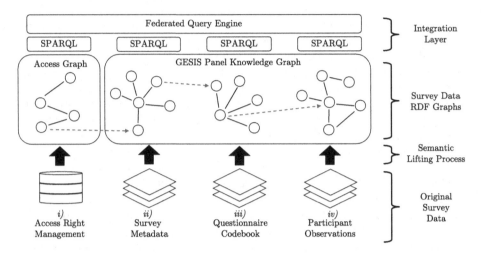

Fig. 3. Architecture of the infrastructure for building the GESIS Panel KG.

together with the organization of GESIS, the lifting processes need to be invoked individually, whenever updates on a specific dataset are to be made. Each semantic lifting process takes an original dataset as input and returns an RDF graph. By defining conventions for naming resources (URIs) of common instances across the different data sources, they are interlinked across the RDF graphs. As a result, each graph stands for itself but combined together they provide a holistic KG of the GESIS Panel. In our implementation, each graph is provided via an individual SPARQL endpoint as this allows for the original data providers to independently manage and publish their data. Furthermore, survey metadata and codebook data may be offered via public endpoints to allow researchers to discover available data while parts of the participant observations may only be accessed within the Safe Room to comply to data security and privacy regulations of GESIS. Finally, at the top is the integration layer consisting of SPARQL endpoints which may be accessed by a federated engine to query the KG. The integration layer may be directly queried by users or, alternatively, accessed by an application such as a GUI. In our specific case, the non-sensitive data may be merged and provided by a single endpoint for performance improvement when querying the data. Here, we present the generic architecture as this may not be applicable in every organization. According to this bottom-up architecture and existing processes at GESIS, changes in individual data sources are propagated from the original data to the KG via a dedicated semantic lifting process.

3.2 GESIS Panel Knowledge Graph

We provide a simplified example extract of the GESIS Panel KG in Fig. 4 to illustrate the RDF graphs from the different data sources and how they are interlinked. Thereafter, we detail the semantic lifting process. Starting at the top,

Fig. 4a shows user `User1` and a `RightStatement` to indicate the user's permissions to access the extended edition of GESIS Panel data. This `RightStatement` is linked to the metadata for the survey `WaveA` as shown in Fig. 4b. The figure shows a subset of the original metadata that includes the `LogicalDataSet` providing the data, title, subjects, variables of the wave, as well as the time period in which the wave was conducted. In the example, the variable *Gender* is shown for the wave. The variable is linked to the questionnaire codebook subgraph shown in Fig. 4c which provides details for the variable such as the question text and corresponding answers as well as their notation. Moreover, each variable has a corresponding property which is used in the participant observation subgraph. Figure 4d shows the recorded data for a participant represented using the RDF Data Cube Vocabulary[8]. Each observation is a blank node linked to the participant's identifier and the recorded variable values using the corresponding properties. In the example, the participant is *male* according to the notation provided in the questionnaire codebook.

3.3   Original Data Sources

In the following, we describe the original data available at GESIS and detail how the data is semantically lifted to the shared RDF data model of our KG. The semantic enrichment process includes mapping concepts and instances to RDF as well as minor semantic refinement by interlinking them.

Access Right Management. Considering the access policies, there are three different editions of the GESIS Panel: campus file, standard edition, and extended edition. In each edition, a different subset of survey data and variables are available. Accordingly, the access rights need to be defined on this level. The Dublin Core vocabulary (`dcterms`), which is reused in the `disco` vocabulary, allows for defining such access right statements on the level `LogicalDataSets` and the data is associated with the corresponding access rights according to the edition. Furthermore, a user model is employed to define users and link them to the access right statements. Currently, this process is implemented in a manual fashion, however, we aim to integrate the access right management for our KG to existing solutions, such as the Lightweight Directory Access Protocol (LDAP).

Survey Metadata. The Data Catalog (DBK) (see footnote 2) is the online portal provided by GESIS to search and retrieve survey data including the GESIS Panel. The DBK operates on metadata describing surveys as a whole but not on the level of individual variables. Important aspects in the metadata are, for instance, citation data, version information, date of collection, or methodology. The survey-level metadata may also be retrieved from an internal database as XML documents following the DDI standard, where the data is continuously updated in an automatic fashion. As the GESIS Panel is considered as a single evergrowing survey, it is represented in a single large DDI file comprising the information of all associated waves. However, each time a wave is added, a new

---

[8] https://www.w3.org/TR/vocab-data-cube/.

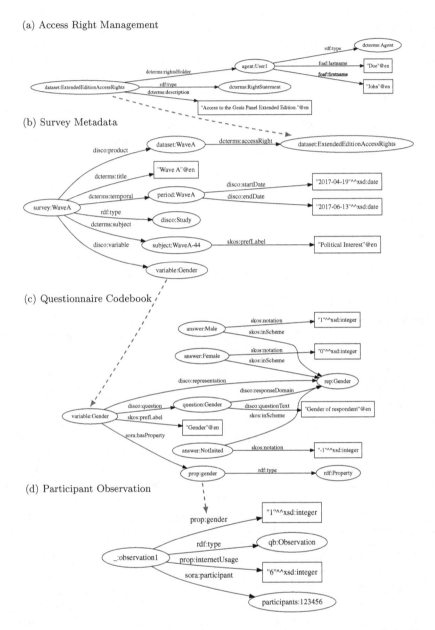

Fig. 4. Knowledge Graph Extract: The figures visualize the subgraphs of the Knowledge Graph to provide an overview of the shared RDF data model and the interlinking between the data sources. The dashed arrows indicate these relationships between shared resources. (The prefixes for **dcterms**, **disco**, **foaf**, **rdf**, **skos** and **qb** are used as in **prefix.cc**. The **sora** prefix is used for our vocabulary[9]. The other prefixes adhere to the scheme **http://.../gesis/resource/<prefix>/**.)

version is created for researchers to keep track of data provenance. We choose to represent the survey on the level of waves as individual `Studys` to allow for a consistent and retraceable mapping to the corresponding concepts of the `disco` vocabulary.

Questionnaire Codebook. The detailed information on the variables and the corresponding questionnaires for each wave are provided in *codebooks*. For researchers, the codebooks are accessible as PDF files in the DBK portal. Internally, these PDFs are generated from CSV files containing all the necessary information in a tabular format. The data for the example extract is shown in Table 1. Variables are uniquely identified by a `varname` which is based on the identifier of the corresponding wave (i.e., `waveID`) and a number (omitted for visualization purposes). Variables are represented in the rows and depending on the type of question and set of answers, several rows represent a single variable. This type of tabular representation requires two major aspects to be considered in the semantic lifting process: (*i*) information related to variables such as corresponding answers and their notation may be stored in a redundant fashion, and (*ii*) semantically identical variables are assessed in various waves but differently identified in each wave, which requires means of linking them. In order to address the first aspect, the URI for the representation of a variable is derived from the URI of the variable itself, e.g. `variable:Gender → rep:Gender`. The URIs for answers are based on hashing the German and English answer text in combination with the notation of the answer. Incorporating several aspects of an answer for the URI generation is required to unequivocally identify answers. For instance, the notation needs to be incorporated as it may differ for the same answer text depending on the used scale (e.g., 1–5 vs. 1–10). Consequently, answer URIs are unique and reoccurring answers are identified by existing URIs to avoid redundancies and facilitate linking between questions. The second aspect is addressed by defining properties as part of our own vocabulary[9], prefixed with `sora`, to link the reoccurring variables. For instance, `sora:betweenCorrespondence` links a variable to a similar variable in another survey. The vocabulary also provides terms to associate variables with additional information from the original CSV files, such as introductory texts for the questions.

Participant Observations. The last data source provides the participant observations, i.e., the answer provided by the participants to the questions of each survey. The observations are provided in a tabular form with each row corresponding to a participant and the columns to the measured value for the variables. The column names for the variables are the `varname` identifiers from the codebooks. The data is distributed over several CSV files which allows for restricting the access according to the aforementioned editions. The first columns provide basic metadata, such as the unique personal identifier (`PID`) of the participants and the version of the data. In the semantic lifting process, for each row, a data cube `Observation` is modelled as a blank node and it is linked to the respective participant URI which is derived from the `PID`. This representation

---

[9] https://w3id.org/sora/resource/vocabulary.

Table 1. Questionnaire codebook: simplified example extract of the codebook for a variable assessing a participant's gender measured in two surveys.

varname	labelEn	questionText	code	valueLabel	waveID	betweenCorrespondence	...
gender	Gender	Gender of the respondent	−1	Not inited	WaveA	genderB	...
gender	Gender	Gender of the respondent	0	Female	WaveA	genderB	...
gender	Gender	Gender of the respondent	1	Male	WaveA	genderB	...
...	...	...	...	...	...	...	...
genderB	Gender	Gender of the respondent	−1	Not inited	WaveB		...
genderB	Gender	Gender of the respondent	0	Female	WaveB		...
genderB	Gender	Gender of the respondent	1	Male	WaveB		...
...	...	...	...	...	...	...	...

allows for linking the observations for the same participant across several studies. The answers are added to the observation using the corresponding property. Since the identifiers `varname` from the codebooks and the column names in the observation files coincide, the URIs for the properties can be created independently of the codebooks. For example, column *gender* → `prop:gender`.

3.4   Semantic Lifting Process

The semantic lifting process aims to map the presented original data sources to the shared RDF data model. It is specifically tailored to the requirements present at GESIS, however, may be adapted to other institutions as well. A key requirement for the semantic lifting process was a lightweight solution applicable to all data sources to facilitate maintenance and adoption within the organization. An overview of the semantic lifting process is shown in Fig. 5.

According to the requirements, we investigated existing mapping languages and integration tools, coming to the conclusion that due to discrepancies in the structure of some original data sources and the target DDI-RDF data model, there is no single out-of-the-box solution for our use-case. Especially, the original data requires various data pre-processing steps before it can be mapped to the data model. For instance, the GESIS Panel is considered a single (evergrowing) study according to the DDI Standard, but each wave is considered as a distinct study in our RDF data model. Therefore, to obtain the information on the level of waves from the original DDI XML file, we need to apply complex regular expressions on the textual study description. For example, the topics of the different waves are listed in the free-text section in the abstract of the study which requires extracting these topics from the abstract and associate them with the corresponding waves. As a result, applying an existing generic mapping

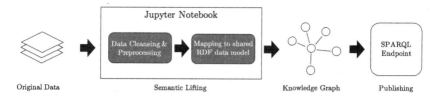

Fig. 5. Overview of the semantic lifting process.

language, such as RML[10], which is able to handle all original data formats, would still require an additional separate data cleansing and preprocessing step. In order to obtain a solution including both data cleansing and preprocessing as well as the mapping to the shared RDF data model, we decided to implement the semantic lifting process in one Jupyter notebook[11] per data source. The data cleansing and preprocessing is implemented using the built-in Python `xml` library and `pandas`[12]. The mapping to RDF is implemented using the `RDFLib`[13] library and the resulting RDF graph is loaded into the SPARQL endpoint. Whenever the original data changes, the input files are updated and the notebooks are executed to generate the RDF data. This process encompasses data cleaning, semantic lifting, and refinement in a single notebook facilitating its maintenance.

In the future, we aim to investigate a more robust solution for the semantic lifting process, such as existing data integration tools (e.g., Karma[14]) or other mapping languages to support declarative mapping processes. Furthermore, for the participant observation, we aim to investigate solutions which do not require materializing the data in RDF but allow for querying the data as a virtual Knowledge Graph as suggested by Chaves-Fraga et al. [4].

4   Challenges and Lessons Learned

In the following, we revisit the motivating scenario and show how the discovery and retrieval of survey data are enhanced with our current solution. Thereafter, we discuss the challenges we encountered during the construction of the Knowledge Graph and the lessons learned.

Motivating Scenario Revisited. In Sect. 1, we outlined the current process for a researcher to follow in order to search, discover, and retrieve survey data of the GESIS Panel. The process starts with a keyword-based search on the metadata of the studies to retrieve the codebooks as PDFs for the relevant ones. Thereafter, relevant variables may be searched in the codebooks and finally,

---

[10] http://rml.io/index.html.
[11] https://jupyter.org/.
[12] https://pandas.pydata.org.
[13] https://github.com/RDFLib.
[14] https://usc-isi-i2.github.io/karma/.

the participant observations can be accessed and filter according to the relevant variables. As our example shows, the current process requires consulting various data sources in different formats and representations entailing a time-consuming process for users. Especially for complex analyses, which may require the co-occurrence of several variables within the same wave, this process becomes very tedious. This shortcoming is addressed by our approach as the KG may be queried via a single interface accessing the data represented in the shared RDF model. As a result, federated SPARQL queries may be processed over the different data sources which improve both the discovery of relevant data as well as its retrieval. Moreover, a more fine-grained search leveraging the information of the questionnaires is supported as this information is represented in our KG.

Let us consider the following example: "Find the questions and surveys where the variable label or the question text contains the term *politic* from the Extended Edition of the GESIS Panel of surveys conducted in 2014". In the current process, this would require searching all surveys conducted in 2014 and examining every corresponding codebook PDF manually for the term *politic*. In contrast, the required information can be retrieved from our KG using a single SPARQL query executed by a federated query engine. The query is shown in Listing 1.1. In lines 2 and 3, the information for the survey are retrieved and filtered in line 5 to include only surveys from 2014. In line 7, all associated variables are selected and the corresponding label and question texts are selected in lines 8 and 9. Finally, the results are filtered in line 11 according to the keyword *politic*. This example illustrates how the KG facilitates the search for relevant survey data as it provides the ability for researchers to process complex queries over all data sources simultaneously and search for various combinations of variables and filter the results according to the metadata of the studies.

Challenges. There are several challenges that needed to be addressed building the KG for the GESIS Panel. They mostly originate from the organizational structure encountered at GESIS as well as the specificities of survey data such as data security and privacy requirements. The relevant GESIS Panel data is distributed across independently administered datasets with varying formats and schema, hindering the integration of the data into a single repository. We address this issue by defining semantic lifting processes for each data source to create RDF graphs according to the shared RDF data model. By defining conventions for naming common resources across the data sources (i.e., URI generation), the resulting graphs are interlinked and can be understood as single KG. For example, the variables which are detailed in the codebook are also listed in the study-level metadata and by using their **varname** in the URI generation, they are linked in the resulting graphs. As the data sources may be updated independently, the corresponding semantic lifting process can be executed whenever one of the original data changes to generate the updated graph. Accordingly, whenever a new version of a graph is created, the data is published via the corresponding SPARQL endpoint such that a federated query engine and other applications may access the most recent data. Furthermore, the presented semi-automatic and curated semantic lifting process to generate the RDF graphs were

Listing 1.1. SPARQL query exemplifying a search to retrieve questions and corresponding waves related concerning politics.

```
 0  SELECT ?question ?wave WHERE {
 1      # Retrieve accessible waves
 2      ?wave disco:product [ dcterms:accessRights dataset:ExtendedEditionAccessRights ] .
 3      ?wave dcterms:temporal [disco:endDate ?end ; disco:startDate ?start ] .
 4      # Filter according to the time period
 5      FILTER (?start >="2014−01−01"^^xsd:date && ?end <"2015−01−01"^^xsd:date)
 6      # Retrieve variable label and question text
 7      ?wave disco:variable ?variable .
 8      ?variable skos:prefLabel ?varLabel .
 9      ?variable disco:question [ disco:questionText ?question ].
10      # Filter according to the keyword
11      FILTER (regex(?varLabel, "politic") || regex(?question, "politic"))  }
```

chosen to assure the provisioning of high-quality data. Finally, considering the data security challenges, the main requirement was a fine-grained physical data access control. The presented modular architecture fulfills these requirements, as sensitive data may be provided by endpoints only accessible in the physical network of the Safe Room at GESIS.

Lessons Learned. Finally, we want to discuss the lessons learned during the development of the architecture to create the GESIS Panel KG. The major lesson learned was embracing the existing infrastructures and processes at the GESIS and develop an architecture which adapts to these existing structures. This allows for a sustainable solution which can be implemented by the organizations and will be maintained in the future. Furthermore, using a federated approach to provide the data from the original data sources allowed for addressing the data access requirements by restricting access not only at a logical level but also at a physical level, which is an important aspect when working with sensitive private data. Moreover, our project showed that the `disco` vocabulary provides the necessary terms and concepts for building the shared RDF data model in our use case and it covers almost all relevant aspects of our KG. Defining a few additional terms to cover all aspects specific to the data publisher is inevitable.

5   Related Work

The application of Semantic Web technologies and publishing data according to the Linked Data principles have been studied in the area of social sciences. The motivation of most research endeavors is improving the discovery and use of survey and statistical data by publishing metadata and facilitating integration.

Similar to our work, Gottron et al. [6] address the problem of survey and statistical data being scattered across various files and data sources. They propose the use of open semantic models to facilitate the searching, merging and aggregating such distributed data. They present the Semantic Digital Library of Linked Data, a framework tailored to the social sciences. The authors mainly focus on integrating and merging data from two data sources, survey and statistical data, on an aggregation level using the Data Cube vocabulary (see footnote 8). In contrast to our work, they do not include search capabilities in their prototype but mostly focus on visualization and lightweight calculations over the integrated data.

Zapilko et al. [11] present a solution to provide a linked thesaurus for the social sciences (TheSoz), which is essential for indexing documents and research information in the social sciences, such as survey descriptions. The original thesaurus is administered in a database and the authors present their approach transforming the thesaurus to Linked Data using the Simple Knowledge Organization System (SKOS)[15] vocabulary. The presented thesaurus allows for connecting heterogeneous datasets which may be linked to our KG to further improve the discovery of survey data by leveraging annotations using TheSoz.

Similarly, Schaible et al. [9] aim to interlink study descriptions to the Linked Open Data Cloud. They also transform DDI XML documents providing the study-level descriptions to RDF in order to link the resulting dataset to resources from the Integrated Name Authority File (GND) and DBpedia. For the linking task, they use Silk[16] to discover and generate `owl:sameAs` links between a source dataset and target datasets. In contrast to our work, the authors focus on the study-level metadata and do not provide a holistic approach spanning all relevant data sources and the associated intricacies, such as privacy requirements. Furthermore, their primary goal was linking resources from the description to other resources in the LOD Cloud. As a result, their approach may be applied as a subsequent refinement step after the KG is created and may be extended to the semantic data about variables and questionnaires produced with our solution.

6   Conclusions and Future Directions

In this work, we presented our solution to build a Knowledge Graph (KG) for survey data to facilitate search, discovery, and retrieval of survey data. This is achieved by semantically lifting data from heterogeneous data sources to a shared RDF data model based on the DDI-RDF Discovery Vocabulary and providing the resulting graphs via SPARQL endpoints to enable the integration using federated SPARQL query processing while adhering to data security and privacy requirements. The presented solution overcomes various challenges and requirements common to organizations publishing survey data and, therefore, may be applied in other organizations as well. The described architecture is used in the *SoRa* project[17] which aims to link survey data with geospatial information.

In the future, we aim at extending our current approach by including an additional refinement step to further enhance the information in the KG. For example, similar to [9], NLP may be applied to extract information from the

---

[15] https://www.w3.org/2004/02/skos/.

[16] http://silkframework.org/.

[17] www.sora-projekt.de (note: German only).

questions text and survey descriptions to associate them with specific topics or link them to named entities. In addition, we want to extend the KG to include further surveys conducted by GESIS which will enable researchers to discover more relevant surveys. Furthermore, as part of the *SoRa* project we will apply our solution at other survey data providers, namely the German Socio-Economic Panel[18]. Ultimately, future work may focus on enabling querying KGs of survey data across different organizations.

Acknowledgments. This work was carried out with the support of the German Research Foundation (DFG) within the project "SoRa - Sozial-Raumwissenschaftliche Forschungsdateninfrastruktur" (see footnote 17).

References

1. Bosch, T., Cyganiak, R., Gregory, A., Wackerow, J.: DDI-RDF discovery vocabulary: a metadata vocabulary for documenting research and survey data. In: LDOW (2013)
2. Bosch, T., Wackerow, J., Cyganiak, R., Zapilko, B.: Leveraging the DDI model for linked statistical data in the social, behavioural, and economic sciences, p. 10 (2012)
3. Bosnjak, M., et al.: Establishing an open probability-based mixed-mode panel of the general population in Germany: the GESIS Ppanel. Social Science Computer Review **36**(1), 103–115 (2018)
4. Chaves-Fraga, D., Priyatna, F., Santana-Pérez, I., Corcho, Ó.: Virtual statistics knowledge graph generation from CSV files. In: Emerging Topics in Semantic Technologies - ISWC 2018 Satellite Events (best papers from 13 of the Workshops Co-located with the ISWC 2018 Conference), pp. 235–244 (2018). https://doi.org/10.3233/978-1-61499-894-5-235
5. Gherghina, S., Geissel, B.: Citizens' conceptions of democracy and political participation in Germany. In: Workshops of European Consortium for Political Research, p. 25 (2015)
6. Gottron, T., Hachenberg, C., Harth, A., Zapilko, B.: Towards a semantic data library for the social sciences, p. 13 (2011)
7. Mayer, S.J., Schultze, M.: The effects of political involvement and cross-pressures on multiple party identifications in multi-party systems - evidence from Germany. J. Elections Public Opin. Parties **29**, 1–17 (2018)
8. Paulheim, H.: Knowledge graph refinement: a survey of approaches and evaluation methods. Semant. Web **8**(3), 489–508 (2017)
9. Schaible, J., Zapilko, B., Bosch, T., Zenk-Möltgen, W.: Linking study descriptions to the linked open data cloud. IASSIST Q. **38**(4), 38 (2015)
10. Vardigan, M., Heus, P., Thomas, W.: Data documentation initiative: toward a standard for the social sciences. Int. J. Digit. Curation **3**(1), 107–113 (2008)
11. Zapilko, B., Schaible, J., Mayr, P., Mathiak, B.: TheSoz: a SKOS representation of the thesaurus for the social sciences, p. 7 (2012)
12. Zapilko, B., Schaible, J., Wandhöfer, T., Mutschke, P.: Applying linked data technologies in the social sciences. KI -Künstliche Intelligenz **30**(2), 159–162 (2016)

---

[18] https://www.diw.de/en/soep.

Author Index

Printed in the United States
By Bookmasters